The humanitarian world passes no judgement on the quality of normality; crises happen, the norm slips and the good humanitarian steps in with temporary action to return society to 'normality'. But the received wisdom, the history, the model, is now stretched beyond credulity. The real world of crisis and crisis response is far more diverse, messy, shot with tensions and contradictions. *The New Humanitarians in International Practice* describes and explores the real humanitarian world in all its uncomfortable diversity from politicized donors to profit-seeking companies, taking in the fighting humanitarians and evangelists on the way. It explores the regional and local humanitarian groups contrasting them with the romantic image of the international, patriotically neutered agency of the TV adverts.

Peter Walker, Chatham University, USA

This important book is a superb blend of scholarship on and real-world experience with contemporary humanitarian action. Sezgin and Dijkzeul have brought together an exceptional group of contributors – both scholars and practitioners – to examine the implications of an array of emerging new players of an increasingly fragmented humanitarian system. The book's eight 'new' humanitarianisms offer a bold, critical perspective on the aims and activities of a variety of new humanitarian actors and their impact on humanitarian principles and practices. An excellent and much needed look at what is happening to the humanitarian system – it should be required reading for scholars and policymakers of humanitarian action!

James P. Muldoon Jr., Vice Chair, The Mosaic Institute, Canada

The New Humanitarians in International Practice

As humanitarian needs continue to grow rapidly, humanitarian action has become more contested, with new actors entering the field to address unmet needs, but also challenging long-held principles and precepts.

This volume provides detailed empirical comparisons between emerging and traditional humanitarian actors. It sheds light on why and how the emerging actors engage in humanitarian crises and how their humanitarian activities are perceived in their transnational organisational environment. It develops and applies a conceptual framework that fosters research on humanitarian actors and the humanitarian principles. In particular, it simultaneously refers to theories of organisational sociology and international relations to identify both the structural and the situational factors that influence the motivations, aims and activities of these actors, and their different levels of commitment to the traditional humanitarian principles. It thus elucidates the role of humanitarian principles in promoting coherence and coordination in the crowded and diverse world of humanitarian action, and discusses whether alternative principles and parallel humanitarian systems are in the making.

This volume will be of great interest to postgraduate students and scholars in humanitarian studies, globalisation and transnationalism research, organisational sociology, international relations, development studies, and migration and diaspora studies, as well as policymakers and practitioners engaged in humanitarian action, development cooperation and migration issues.

Zeynep Sezgin is Lise-Meitner Fellow of the Austrian Science Fund (FWF) and leads the research project 'Legitimacy of Faith-Based Humanitarian Organisations in Austria, Germany and Pakistan' at the Department of Development Studies at the University of Vienna, Austria.

Dennis Dijkzeul is Professor of Conflict and Organisation Research at the Social Science School and the Institute for International Law of Peace and Armed Conflict (IFHV) at Ruhr University Bochum, Germany.

Routledge Humanitarian Studies Series
Series editors: Alex de Waal and Dorothea Hilhorst
Editorial Board: Mihir Bhatt, Dennis Dijkzeul, Wendy Fenton, Kirsten Johnson, Julia Streets, Peter Walker

The Routledge Humanitarian Studies series in collaboration with the International Humanitarian Studies Association (IHSA) takes a comprehensive approach to the growing field of expertise that is humanitarian studies. This field is concerned with humanitarian crises caused by natural disaster, conflict or political instability and deals with the study of how humanitarian crises evolve, how they affect people and their institutions and societies, and the responses they trigger.
We invite book proposals that address, amongst other topics, questions of aid delivery, institutional aspects of service provision, the dynamics of rebel wars, state building after war, the international architecture of peacekeeping, the ways in which ordinary people continue to make a living throughout crises, and the effect of crises on gender relations.

This interdisciplinary series draws on and is relevant to a range of disciplines, including development studies, international relations, international law, anthropology, peace and conflict studies, public health and migration studies.

Disaster, Conflict and Society in Crises
Everyday politics of crisis response
Edited by Dorothea Hilhorst

Human Security and Natural Disasters
Edited by Christopher Hobson, Paul Bacon and Robin Cameron

Human Security and Japan's Triple Disaster
Responding to the 2011 earthquake, tsunami and Fukushima nuclear crisis
Edited by Paul Bacon and Christopher Hobson

The Paradoxes of Aid Work
Passionate professionals
Silke Roth

Disaster Research
Multidisciplinary and international perspectives
Edited by Morten Thanning Vendelø, Olivier Rubin, Rasmus Dahlberg

The New Humanitarians in International Practice
Emerging actors and contested principles
Edited by Zeynep Sezgin and Dennis Dijkzeul

Natural Hazards, Risk and Vulnerability
Floods and slum life in Indonesia
Roanne van Voorst

The New Humanitarians in International Practice

Emerging Actors and Contested Principles

Edited by Zeynep Sezgin and Dennis Dijkzeul

Routledge
Taylor & Francis Group

LONDON AND NEW YORK

First published 2016
by Routledge

2 Park Square, Milton Park, Abingdon, Oxfordshire OX14 4RN
711 Third Avenue, New York, NY 10017

Routledge is an imprint of the Taylor & Francis Group, an informa business

First issued in paperback 2017

British Library Cataloguing-in-Publication Data
A catalogue record for this book is available from the British Library

Library of Congress Cataloging-in-Publication Data
Names: Sezgin, Zeynep, 1978- editor. | Dijkzeul, Dennis, editor.
Title: The new humanitarians in international practice : emerging actors and contested principles / edited by Zeynep Sezgin and Dennis Dijkzeul.
Description: New York, NY : Routledge, 2016. | Includes bibliographical references and index.
Identifiers: LCCN 2015021335| ISBN 9781138829718 (hardback) | ISBN 9781315737621 (ebook)
Subjects: LCSH: Humanitarian assistance. | International relief.
Classification: LCC JZ4973.5 .N48 2016 | DDC 363.34/526–dc23
LC record available at http://lccn.loc.gov/2015021335

ISBN: 978-1-138-82971-8 (hbk)
ISBN: 978-0-8153-9424-2 (pbk)

Typeset in Baskerville
by GreenGate Publishing Services, Tonbridge, Kent

Contents

Illustrations

Tables

Figures

Contributors

Gilles Carbonnier is Professor of International and Development Economics at the Graduate Institute of International and Development Studies. He is Editor-in-Chief of *International Development Policy*, President of Geneva's Centre for Education and Research in Humanitarian Action, and Vice-President of the European Association of Development Research and Training Institutes. His research focuses on the political economy of humanitarian crises and responses, international development cooperation as well as on the energy–development nexus and the governance of extractive resources. He is author of a forthcoming book on 'humanitarian economics'.

Samuel Carpenter is a Humanitarian Policy Adviser in the International Division at the British Red Cross. Prior to this, he worked with the Humanitarian Futures Programme at King's College London and the Secure Livelihoods Research Consortium at the Overseas Development Institute. He has operational humanitarian experience working with an international NGO in South Sudan and has undertaken research, evaluations and advisory missions in Bangladesh, Haiti, Kenya, Nepal, Nigeria and Senegal.

Dennis Dijkzeul is Professor of Conflict and Organization Research at the Social Science School and Research Coordinator of the Institute of International Law of Peace and Armed Conflict at Ruhr University Bochum. His main research interests concern humanitarian studies, new humanitarian actors, the management of international governmental and non-governmental organisations, and local participation in humanitarian crises.

Wolf-Dieter Eberwein recently retired as Professor of Political Science/ International Relations of the Institut de Science Politique de Grenoble, where he was also in charge of the MA Program International Organisation. From 2008 to 2012, he was President of VOICE, the Voluntary Organisations in Cooperation in Emergencies, which includes 86 humanitarian organisations from Europe. He was also the director of the research group of International Politics at the Wissenschaftszentrum

Berlin. He is a specialist of the politics of humanitarian aid, as well as of armed conflicts and security policy.

Lillian Fan is a humanitarian professional with more than 10 years of experience working on refugees, disaster, conflict and complex emergencies, including in Aceh after the 2004 tsunami and 2005 peace agreement, in Myanmar with ASEAN following Cyclone Nargis, and in Haiti following the 2010 earthquake. Currently, she leads the Humanitarian Policy Group's growing engagement on humanitarian action in Asia. Her work focuses on promoting principled humanitarian response to emerging and new humanitarian actors, such as regional intergovernmental organisations, developing country governments, local organisations, religious networks and the private sector.

Elena Fiddian-Qasmiyeh is Lecturer in Geography at University College London. Her recent publications include *South–South Educational Migration, Development and Humanitarianism* (Routledge, 2015), *The Ideal Refugees: Gender, Islam and the Sahrawi Politics of Survival* (Syracuse University Press, 2014) and *The Oxford Handbook of Refugee and Forced Migration Studies* (Oxford University Press, 2014).

Dorothea Hilhorst is professor of Humanitarian Aid and Reconstruction at Wageningen University. Her research concerns the ways in which people seek access to livelihoods and services in the midst of crises, how institutions form and reform in crises and how aid interventions affect conditions and societies experiencing humanitarian crises. She coordinates research programmes in Angola, DRC, Afghanistan, Ethiopia, Sudan, Mozambique and Uganda. She is general secretary of the International Humanitarian Studies Association. Her publications focus on the everyday practices of humanitarian aid, disaster risk reduction, climate change adaptation, reconstruction and peace-building. Her most recent publication is *Disaster, Conflict and Society: Everyday Politics of Crisis and Crisis Response* (Routledge, 2013).

Cindy Horst is Research Director and Research Professor in Migration and Refugee Studies at the Peace Research Institute Oslo (PRIO). Her research focuses on mobility in conflict; diaspora; humanitarianism; refugee protection; and (transnational) civic engagement. Her most recent publications include 'Migrants as Agents of Development: Diaspora Engagement Discourse and Practice in Europe' (*Ethnicities*, 2015), with Giulia Sinatti, and 'The Depoliticization of Diasporas from the Horn of Africa: From Refugees to Transnational Aid Workers' (*African Studies*, 2013).

Jutta Joachim is Associate Professor in the Institute of Political Science. She is author of *Agenda Setting, the UN, and NGOs: Gender Violence and Reproductive Rights* (Georgetown University Press) and co-editor of *International Organizations and Implementation: Enforcers, Managers,*

Authorities and *Transnational Activism in the UN and the EU: A Comparative Study* (both Routledge). Her articles have appeared in *International Studies Quarterly, German Journal for International Relations, Security Dialogue, Millennium, Cambridge Review of International Affairs, Comparative European Politics* and *Journal of European Public Policy.*

Marie Juul Petersen is a researcher at the Danish Institute for Human Rights. Her research interests include Islam, development, human rights, international organisations and civil society, and she has published extensively on these topics, including several journal articles and book chapters, as well as the monograph *For Humanity or for the Umma? Aid and Islam in Transnational Muslim NGOs* (Hurst, forthcoming).

Randolph Kent is Director of the Planning from the Futures project, based at King's College. This post and his previous post with the Humanitarian Futures Programme followed his career with the UN as Resident and Humanitarian Coordinator for Somalia (1999–2002), Humanitarian Coordinator in Kosovo (1999), Humanitarian Coordinator in Rwanda (1994–1995), Chief of the IASC's Inter-Agency Support Unit (1992–1994), Chief of the UN Emergency Unit in Sudan (1989–1991) and Chief of Emergency Prevention and Preparedness in Ethiopia (1987–1989).

Piedra Lightfoot specialises in conflict and peace-building at the Graduate Institute of International and Development Studies. Her research focuses on the private sector role in development and humanitarianism, innovation in humanitarian assistance, and mediation in armed conflict. She has consulted for the World Bank Group and interned with the Centre for Strategic and International Studies, the UN World Food Programme and the Centre for Humanitarian Dialogue.

Stephen Lubkemann is Associate Professor of Anthropology and International Affairs at George Washington University. His work focuses primarily on social and political change in nations that have experienced protracted conflict and violence; on migrants, refugees, and diasporas; on international development and humanitarian action; and on cultural heritage and maritime archaeology. He has conducted fieldwork with migrants and refugees in Mozambique, South Africa, Angola, and Liberia, and among diasporas in Portugal and the US.

Ryan O'Neill is a PhD Candidate in the Faculty of Environmental Studies at York University. His research examines the politics of genocide in the Great Lakes Region and Sudan. He presently lives in Goma, Democratic Republic of the Congo, where he is carrying out research on NGO–UN relations in the context of counterinsurgency war and the role of South Africa in both the Congo Wars and the recent UN Force Intervention Brigade.

Alpaslan Özerdem is Co-Director of Centre for Trust, Peace and Social Relations at Coventry University. He specialises in the politics of post-conflict reconstruction, reintegration of ex-combatants and peace-building. He is the co-author of *Peace in Turkey 2023: The Question of Human Security and Conflict Transformation* (Lexington Books, 2013) and co-editor of *Human Security in Turkey: Challenges for the 21st Century* (Routledge, 2013).

Julia Pacitto is a postgraduate research student at the Refugee Studies Centre (RSC), University of Oxford. Her research focuses on the politics and embodied experiences of refugee journeys to Europe. Between 2012 and 2013, she worked as a research assistant at the RSC, examining South–South humanitarianism in contexts of forced displacement.

Robtel Neajai Pailey is a Liberian academic and activist. Her writing and research have appeared in publications such as the *Sea Breeze Journal of Contemporary Liberian Writings*, *Humanitas*, *Liberian Studies Journal*, *New York Times*, *International Herald Tribune*, *Newsweek–Daily Beast*, *the Guardian*, *New African Magazine*, *Africa Today* and *Red Pepper Magazine*. She completed a doctorate in Development Studies at SOAS, University of London, as a Mo Ibrahim Foundation PhD Scholar.

Eline Pereboom is a humanitarian adviser, currently working for Cordaid in Iraq. After finishing her studies in International Development and Conflict, she specialised in disaster management and preparedness. She has been working for Oxfam Novib and SHO (Dutch appeal alliance), where she focused on humanitarian programme and strategy development, as well as coordination between NGOs during crises. Additionally, she has been involved in the preparations of the Dutch Humanitarian Summit, held in February 2015 in The Hague. In 2014, she published the report 'Dutch Humanitarian Aid: Now and in the Future' with Dorothea Hilhorst.

Bob Reinalda is Senior Researcher at Radboud University Nijmegen. He has published the *Routledge History of International Organizations: From 1815 to the Present Day* (2009) and has edited the *Ashgate Research Companion to Non-State Actors* (2011) as well as the *Routledge Handbook of International Organization* (2013). He is an Editor of IO BIO, the *Biographical Dictionary of Secretaries-General of International Organizations*: www.ru.nl/fm/iobio.

Kristina Roepstorff is a lecturer at the Institute of Asian and African Studies at Humboldt University Berlin and Occasional Lecturer on the Joint European Master's Degree in International Humanitarian Action (NOHA) at University College Dublin. As a scholar, practitioner and policy adviser she has expertise in the field of conflict transformation, peace-building and humanitarian action with a primary focus on South and Southeast Asia.

Andrea Schneiker is professor of political science at the University of Siegen. She received a PhD in political science from the University in Münster in 2008 for her research on the self- and co-regulation of private military and security companies. She has published in *Millennium: Journal of International Studies, Comparative European Politics, Security Dialogue, Cambridge Review of International Affairs* (all co-authored with Jutta Joachim), *Disasters* and *VOLUNTAS: International Journal of Voluntary and Nonprofit Organizations*.

Zeynep Sezgin is Lise-Meitner Fellow of the Austrian Science Fund (FWF) and conducts postdoctoral research on the 'Legitimacy of faith-based humanitarian organisations in Austria, Germany and Pakistan' at the Department of Development Studies, University of Vienna. Her research interests are transnational migration, migration and development, and the so-called 'new' humanitarian actors, including cross-border migrant organisations and faith-based NGOs. Her recent publications are 'Turkish Migrant Organisations after the 2011 Van Earthquake: Member Interests vs. Humanitarian Principles' (*Oxford Development Studies*), 'Islamic Migrant Organisations: Little-Studied Actors in Humanitarian Action' (co-authored with K. Rosenow-Williams, *International Migration Review*) and 'Migrant Organisations in Humanitarian Action' (co-authored with D. Dijkzeul, *Journal of International Migration and Integration*).

Tony Vaux worked for Oxfam from 1972 to 2000. As a Field Director for India in the 1970s and early 1980s he promoted local development and responded to disasters. From 1984, he was Oxfam's global Emergencies Coordinator. In the 1990s, he focused on Eastern Europe and the former Soviet Union, becoming Regional Manager in 1994. With Oxfam support he published a memoir, *The Selfish Altruist*, in 2001. He became a regular consultant for DFID, specialising in conflict analysis. Following the Gujarat earthquake in 2001, he conducted an evaluation of the response by international agencies for the Disasters Emergency Committee (DEC). He led a similar DEC Evaluation following the Indian Ocean Tsunami of 2004 and has subsequently undertaken humanitarian evaluations for a wide range of organisations.

Acknowledgements

The aim of this edited volume is to better understand the growing diversity of humanitarian action. This diversity needs to be understood at three levels simultaneously: those of the individual organisation, the international humanitarian system and 'on the ground' against the global backdrop of growing humanitarian needs. After all, even if each and every organisation did a good job in the locations where it works, the cumulative effect of its actions may nevertheless be suboptimal, because other humanitarian organisations often work in very different ways and try to reach different goals. For example, the new actors may diverge from the traditional humanitarian principles. Hence, while each chapter in this volume examines a 'new' or non-traditional actor and its organisational norms, the book as a whole attempts to capture the fragmentation of the international humanitarian system and its effects on both humanitarian action and crises.

We would like to thank the contributors to this volume. Without their enthusiasm and insights this book would not have been possible. In the process, we have learned much, for example about Islamic humanitarianism. While we would have liked to have covered more actors, actions and interactions, this was simply not possible in a single volume. However, we hope our work will inspire other authors to investigate those 'new' actors that we could not describe and analyse here.

Our special thanks goes to Ryan O'Neill for helping us to flesh out the meaning of the word 'new' as it pertains to humanitarian principles and actors, as well as for helping us with language editing. We also would like to thank the Routledge Humanitarian Studies Series for accepting this edited volume, and the editors of the series, Helen Bell and Khanam Virjee, for supporting our book. We are also grateful to Michael Barnett and Peter Walker, who shared with us their book proposal on alternative humanitarian actors. Although, in the end, they decided not to carry out their project, it was an inspiration to us. Finally, we would like to thank our partners and children for their patience while we were finishing this volume. It goes without saying that all mistakes are our responsibility.

Zeynep Sezgin, Vienna
Dennis Dijkzeul, Bochum

Abbreviations

AADMER	ASEAN Agreement on Disaster Management and Emergency Response
ACDM	ASEAN Committee on Disaster Management
ADFL	Allied Democratic Forces for the Liberation of the Congo/Zaire
ADPC	Asian Disaster Preparedness Center
AFRICOM	US Africa Command
ALNAP	Active Learning Network for Accountability and Performance
AMISOM	African Union Mission in Somalia
ASEAN	Association of Southeast Asian Nations
AU	African Union
BHP	business–humanitarian partnership
BRICS	Brazil, Russia, India, China and South Africa
CCL	Coalition of Concerned Liberians
CERF	UN Central Emergency Response Fund
CEWARN	Conflict Early Warning and Response Mechanism
CHS	Core Humanitarian Standard
CNDP	National Congress for the Defence of the People
CSO	civil-society organisation
DAC	Development Assistance Committee
DANIDA	Danish International Development Agency
DARPA	Defence Advanced Research Projects Agency
DCDC	Development Concepts Doctrine Centre
DEC	Disasters Emergency Committee
DFID	UK Department for International Development
DFS	Department of Field Support
DHA	UN Department of Humanitarian Affairs
DO	diaspora organisation
DPKO	UN Department of Peacekeeping Operations
DRC	Democratic Republic of the Congo
DSF	German–Syrian Forum
DSV	German–Syrian Association for the Promotion of Freedom and Human Rights

ECHO	European Union's Humanitarian Aid and Civil Protection department
ECOWAS	Economic Community of West African States
EPLF	Eritrean People's Liberation Front
ERA	Eritrean Relief Association
ERD	Emergency Relief Desk
EWB	Engineers Without Borders
FAO	Food and Agriculture Organization
FBO	faith-based organisation
FIB	Force Intervention Brigade
GHA	Global Humanitarian Assistance
HEARTT	Health Education and Relief through Training
HFA	Hyogo Framework for Action
HRW	Human Rights Watch
IADB	Inter-American Development Bank
IASC	Inter-Agency Standing Committee
ICHAD	Islamic Conference Humanitarian Affairs Department
ICRC	International Committee of the Red Cross
ICVA	International Council of Voluntary Agencies
IdEA	International Diaspora Engagement Alliance
IFRC	International Federation of the Red Cross
IGADD	East African Inter-Governmental Authority on Drought and Development
IGMG	Islamic Community Millî Görüş
IHL	International Humanitarian Law
IHSA	International Humanitarian Studies Association
INGO	international non-governmental organisation
IOM	International Organization for Migration
IRIN	Integrated Regional Information Networks
IS	Islamic State
ISAF	International Security Assistance Force
ITF	International Transportworkers Federation
JHCO	Jordan Hashemite Charity Organization
LECBS	Liberian Emergency Capacity Building Support
LRRD	linking relief, rehabilitation and development
LSA	Liberian Studies Association
M23	March 23rd Movement
MEA	Ministry of External Affairs
MINTs	Mexico, Indonesia, Nigeria, Turkey
MONUSCO	United Nations Organization Stabilization Mission in the Democratic Republic of the Congo
MSF	Médecins Sans Frontières
NAM	Non-Aligned Movement
NDMA	National Disaster Management Authorities
NPA	Norwegian People's Aid

NRA	National Resistance Army
NRC	Norwegian Refugee Council
OAU	Organization of African Unity
OCHA	UN Office for the Coordination of Humanitarian Affairs
OECD	Organisation for Economic Co-operation and Development
OIC	Organisation of Islamic Cooperation
PIF	Pacific Island Forum
PMSCs	private military and security companies
PPPs	public–private partnerships
RCD	Rally for Congolese Democracy
RSS	Rashtriya Swayamsevak Sangh
SAARC	South Asian Association for Regional Cooperation
SADC	Southern African Development Community
SADKN	South Asian Disaster Knowledge Network
SARC	Syrian Arab Red Crescent
SCF	Save the Children Fund
SCHR	Steering Committee for Humanitarian Response
SCPR	Syrian Center for Policy Research
SEWA	Self-Employed Women's Association
SPLA	Sudan People's Liberation Army
SSRA	Sudan Relief and Rehabilitation Association
TLA	Textile Labour Association
TOKTEN	Transfer of Knowledge Through Expatriate Nationals
TPLF	Tigray People's Liberation Front
ULO-UK	Union of Liberian Organisations in the UK
UMCOR	United Methodist Committee on Relief
UNDRO	UN Disaster and Relief Organization
UNHCR	United Nations High Commissioner for Refugees
UNIBOA	United Bassa Organizations in the Americas
UNICEF	United Nations Children's Fund
UNRRA	United Nations Relief and Rehabilitation Administration
VOICE	Voluntary Organisations in Cooperation in Emergencies
WEF	World Economic Forum
WFP	World Food Programme
WHO	World Health Organization

Introduction

New Humanitarians Getting Old?

Zeynep Sezgin and Dennis Dijkzeul

Introduction

Humanitarian action takes place in contexts working against its success, such as armed conflicts, natural disasters and often international neglect. Yet alleviating suffering and saving lives remain absolutely necessary. In 2013, humanitarian crises affected about 148.4 million people worldwide (OCHA 2014: 5) and, 'the cost of helping them has increased significantly over the last decade' (OCHA 2013: 2). In the coming decades, the number and intensity of humanitarian crises will grow fast, in particular due to population growth, climate change, environmental deterioration, economic inequality and the conflicts these generate. Although the number and diversity of actors addressing these crises has been increasing in particular since the end of the Cold War,[1] rapidly growing needs are perilously outstripping the resources and capacities to fulfil them. The humanitarian system is coming under great strain (Barnett and Walker forthcoming).

When most people hear the word 'humanitarian', a series of slogans and attention-grabbing logos come to mind, generally those of the well-financed NGOs headquartered in Europe and North America, such as Care and Caritas. They may also recall the Red Cross or Red Crescent organisations as well as the white land cruisers and branded tarps of the larger UN agencies, such as the United Nations High Commissioner for Refugees (UNHCR) and the World Food Programme (WFP). Some might even know a few large donors represented in the Development Assistance Committee (DAC) of the Organisation for Economic Co-operation and Development (OECD).[2] In this volume, we refer to these actors as 'traditional' or simply as 'old' humanitarians. Together, these well-established actors 'constitute the multibillion dollar visible face of humanitarianism. They dominate international debates, coordination bodies, advocacy campaigns, funding appeals and media attention, and thus dictate the principles of humanitarian action.' They are quintessentially a 'Northern/Western humanitarian movement, rooted in various traditions of charity and philanthropy and in the civilizing impulses of the Enlightenment, as well as their subsequent manifestations in the expanses of what we now call the global south' (Donini 2010: 220).

In the shadow of this group, however, rapidly evolving types of humanitarian actors, often referred to as 'non-traditional', 'new' or 'emergent' humanitarians, play a variety of roles. They provide aid, protect and carry out advocacy. Some of them also play more political, economic or security roles. Although these actors may have access, legitimacy and capacities in crisis zones, they are not seen as equals and are placed outside of the humanitarian system by the traditional humanitarian actors, who consider themselves to be the standard bearers (Labbé 2012). Nevertheless, the 'new' actors are changing the humanitarian system.

Currently, this system is fragmenting, with many actors following their own approaches, which, from a systemic perspective, fosters ineffectiveness. The humanitarian system, in short, is smaller than its parts. The 2016 World Humanitarian Summit in Istanbul, in response, aims to facilitate the participation of the new actors in the international humanitarian system, in the hope that this will contribute to greater effectiveness. But who are the new humanitarians and what is so 'new' about them?

The term 'new humanitarians' fuses together two common understandings of the word 'new': *contemporary* – the fact that the actors contained in this work are some of the most recent entrants to humanitarian action, and *originality* – their apparent reworking of the humanitarian practices and the principles of humanity, impartiality, neutrality and independence. These two meanings do not necessarily coincide, with the newest actors in any given humanitarian context often times being mere 'briefcase NGOs' who emerge only in order to absorb excess funding and/or skim off the top. While originality, by contrast, often springs forth not from new actors entering the field but from a reappraisal of past successes and failures. In other words, old actors learning new tricks. New, however, does not automatically mean improved. Some 'new' actors may actually succeed in improving their work, but others may fail. Their degree of success is always an empirical question. Combining both meanings of 'new', this volume studies the interests and principles of the new humanitarian actors, their influence on humanitarian crises and implications for the traditional humanitarian actors.

This introductory chapter consists of six parts, of which this is the first. The next two parts provide a common terminology, focusing especially on the terms 'humanitarianism' and 'humanitarian action', while also explaining the four core 'humanitarian principles' that underlie these definitions. Fourth, we discuss the challenges to these principles. Fifth, we apply theories from organisational sociology and international relations perspectives to understand and describe the aims, activities and roles of the new humanitarians and whether and how they diverge or converge with the traditional humanitarian actors and the core principles. Finally, we present an overview of the different chapters in this volume.

The 'New' Humanitarianisms

Since the end of the Cold War, humanitarian crises and by the same token traditional humanitarian actors have attracted growing social and scientific interest. However, the same cannot be said yet of the 'new' humanitarian actors. Humanitarian assistance provided by these actors is not currently quantified and remains invisible in statistics despite its importance for saving lives and protecting livelihoods (GHA 2009). Various studies mention the relevance of these actors in humanitarian crises, but provide insufficient systematic analysis of their aims and activities. Hence, it is often not clear, why and how they engage in humanitarian action? Which factors (such as organisational characteristics and internal or external expectations) influence their aims, activities and roles in humanitarian crises? Whether and how do they diverge from the traditional humanitarian actors? Do they interpret the core principles in new ways, or are new principles emerging? In order to address these questions, this volume draws attention to eight 'new' humanitarianisms, which partly overlap and regularly evolve together.[3]

First, although most of the official humanitarian assistance still comes from OECD-DAC member countries, *'new' donors*, such as the Arab Gulf States, China, India and Turkey have entered the humanitarian arena over the last two decades (ibid.). Some of these state donors are operating outside the DAC and independently of the Good Humanitarian Donorship Initiative. A prevalent trend of non-DAC donor governments is to channel funds through host countries rather than through humanitarian organisations, providing most support to neighbouring countries. Increasingly, humanitarian funding is also provided by different types of non-governmental donors, such as the Bill & Melinda Gates Foundation, but this is rarely systematically reported by the established financial tracking mechanisms.

The second type of humanitarianism concerns the *multi-mandate organisations*. Humanitarian action helps to relieve the suffering, but does not address the root causes of humanitarian crises. Hence, many humanitarian organisations have taken on development, conflict resolution, human rights and rehabilitation tasks in the hope of transforming humanitarian crises. Several development organisations have also taken on humanitarian tasks. As a result, the internal coherence of the humanitarian system has increasingly been tested, as tensions arise between strict single-mandate humanitarian actors, in particular the International Committee of the Red Cross (ICRC) and Médecins Sans Frontières (MSF), and the multi-mandate organisations. Although the well-established multi-mandate organisations are mainly funded by the DAC donor countries and have a long history of combining development cooperation and humanitarian action, their more recent expansion into peace-building and human-rights advocacy has pushed them further afield from the humanitarian norm, hence we also refer to them in this volume as new humanitarian actors.

The third type of humanitarianism is *armed humanitarianism*. The level of civil–military cooperation has been increasing and new institutional structures have been established between political, military and humanitarian actors in various countries, such as Kosovo, Afghanistan and Iraq, as well as by insurgents and other armed movements. This has led to a blurring of the lines between humanitarian, political and armed actors, and reinforced the politicisation and militarisation of humanitarian action. It has also caused a conflict of ideas and motives, particularly regarding why aid should be given: should it be provided on the basis of need alone? Can assistance given in support of military or rebel objectives ever be humanitarian? Nonetheless, national and multilateral militaries do possess some capacities (e.g. search and rescue, demining, logistics, evacuation and surge capacity) that traditional humanitarian actors lack, but need on occasion.

Fourth, we pay attention to *for-profit humanitarianism*. Subcontracting in war zones is often carried out by a motley crew of sometimes shady NGOs, private military and security companies (PMSCs), as well as private construction, engineering and/or oil companies with close links to donor governments, such as Bechtel and Halliburton (Singer 2007). These organisations may disregard or use – if not abuse – humanitarian principles and arguments to make a profit or to win hearts and minds for their paymasters.

Fifth, we focus on *diaspora humanitarianism*. Remittances have become a decentralised but large system of money transfer, often putting official development assistance (ODA) to shame (Savage and Harvey 2007). Similarly, diaspora organisations (DOs) provide humanitarian and development assistance in their members' countries of origin and in third countries based on their members' national, ethnic, religious and/or ideological affiliations (Sezgin and Dijkzeul 2013; Rosenow-Williams and Sezgin 2014; Sezgin 2014).

Sixth, we discuss *faith-based humanitarianism*. Faith-based organisations have always provided aid to the needy. Yet, in recent years, the number, size and impact of especially Islamic organisations, many of which have a migrant background, have rapidly grown. Today, faith-based organisations (FBOs) constitute a prominent part of the humanitarian community. Interreligious dialogue organisations, faith-based philanthropic foundations, Islamic aid organisations based in the Persian Gulf or in the West and faith-based migrant organisations are now often at the forefront of humanitarian action.

This volume also focuses on two humanitarianisms that are by their very nature not global in their scope: *local* and *regional humanitarianisms*. In most humanitarian crises local communities, displaying a wide variety of formal and non-formal institutions, provide the lion's share of aid. They usually save most lives before the well-known Western organisations appear on the scene and often immediately begin with the arduous task of rebuilding. Moreover, the diversity and roles of regional organisations have been growing, but remain underappreciated.

These 'new' humanitarians often operate differently from traditional humanitarian actors and do not necessarily abide by the core humanitarian principles. Where and when they do, their interpretation often varies from that of traditional organisations. This calls into question the added value of both traditional and new humanitarian actors, as well as their mechanisms to prevent fragmentation of the overall humanitarian system (McGoldrick 2011).

Humanitarian Action and the Principles

A comprehensive and generally accepted legal definition of 'humanitarian action' has never been formulated. The four Geneva Conventions and the additional protocols, which constitute the core of international humanitarian law, do not even provide a full definition of the word 'humanitarian'.[4]

Yet, there are two ways to delineate humanitarian action. First, we can define it in terms of the types of activities carried out – mainly assistance and (physical) protection – as well as by those activities traditional humanitarians generally do not perform, development cooperation and the maintenance of law and order. It normally includes food, water, shelter, medicine and occasionally clothing. Nowadays, cash transfers are partially supplementing or replacing these traditional aid commodities. In addition, protection, in line with international humanitarian law, should also be provided, though there is little agreement over were this begins and ends. Together humanitarian assistance and protection constitute humanitarian action.

Second, we can define humanitarian action in terms of the principles by which it is guided.[5] Developed by the ICRC as an ethical and pragmatic framework to guide the behaviour of humanitarian organisations and to facilitate humanitarian engagement in crisis zones, the four core humanitarian principles are *humanity* (to prevent and alleviate human suffering wherever it may be found), *impartiality* (to make no discrimination as to nationality, race, religious beliefs, class or political opinions, and to give priority to the most urgent cases of distress), *neutrality* (not to take sides in hostilities or engage in political, racial, religious or ideological controversies in the crisis zones, to provide aid without favouring any side in a conflict or in a dispute) and *independence* (to maintain autonomy from donors and to be free from any economic, political, or military interests at stake) (ICRC 1986). These principles favour a deontological or duty-based ethic centred on the intentions of humanitarian actors that always have to assist people in need. ICRC and MSF are the main proponents of this ethic. By contrast, a consequentialist ethic focuses more on the outcomes of action than on the purity of its intentions, and does not necessarily follow the principles. One central question in this volume is which ethic the emergent actors follow, wholly or partly.

Officially, the principles have been widely adopted by traditional humanitarian organisations. The United Nations System supports them.[6] They are also the foundation of the 1994 Code of Conduct for the International Red Cross and Red Crescent Movement and NGOs in Disaster Relief. In addition, the Sphere Standards attempt to specify and codify the practical obligations that flow from these core principles.

The core principles, however, do not provide a blueprint for carrying out humanitarian action. Rather, they serve as a mindset through which humanitarian organisations hope to establish and maintain access to people in need and ensure the safety of humanitarian personnel and beneficiaries. They are considered central to establishing credibility as humanitarian actors and gaining acceptance from local populations, warring factions and other actors in crisis zones. In other words, they help to build trust. In addition, compliance with them fosters humanitarian coordination. Yet, as the next part shows, various factors challenge these principles and affect humanitarian outcomes.

Challenges to the Humanitarian Principles

The humanitarian principles were first developed, though not codified, as a deal between military commanders, the governments that controlled them and humanitarian actors on the battlefields of Europe in the nineteenth century (Leader 2000). These principles – and much of international humanitarian law – are 'based on the assumption that states behave in a civilised manner, that non-state actors are only marginally relevant, and that states can be trusted to provide security, allowing humanitarians to focus on relief' (Salomons 2015: 33). Moreover, international humanitarian law assumes 'highly specific conditions: armed conflict waged by established states, among clearly identifiable uniformed combatants acting under a clear chain of command, in a political setting where war [is] a temporary aberration from an otherwise stable and well-regulated society, subject to the rule of law' (ibid.: 36). In this context, an established state is a Weberian state that controls or monopolises monetary matters and physical coercion.

International humanitarian law is thus directed at the states that control their military forces. This state-centric approach, however, is less appropriate in most current crises, where state institutions have been weakened, are sometimes unwilling or unable to take care of their population and where humanitarians have no choice but to interact with various non-state actors, including warring factions, ethnic militia, armed gangs, transnational criminal syndicates, (drugged) child soldiers, local self-defence groups and local leaders, as well as with the national army and international peacekeepers. In fact, most people in need live in states that are either weak or have failed.

Second, upholding the principles is gravely complicated by the fact that humanitarian action takes place in a context where the norms of social interaction are challenged by 'war, flight, hunger and disease' (Harrel-Bond 1986: 104). In recent civil wars, varying from former Yugoslavia to

Mali, warlords and politicians have ruthlessly pursued their own political, economic and military agendas via humanitarian action. This instrumentalisation complicates humanitarian action severely and in extreme cases renders it counterproductive. For instance, helping refugees can facilitate ethnic cleansing or aid resources may contribute to the political economy of war. As a consequence, humanitarian action can worsen the suffering it intends to alleviate (Terry 2002). This has led to a continuous debate on the obligations and responsibilities of humanitarian actors.

Third, disagreements have always existed on the exact interpretation and implementation of each humanitarian principle. Officially, over 520 agencies have signed the Red Cross and NGO Code of Conduct. Neutrality is debated more widely than the other principles: is it morally justified to remain neutral and not to take a position when confronting mass atrocities, such as the Holocaust, the Biafran War and the Rwandan Genocide (ibid.)? In addition, it is often not clear how well individual organisations actually understand these principles. And if they do, to what extent they are able to implement them (Slim 1997).

Fourth, the rapidly growing number and size of non-traditional humanitarian actors with different priorities and approaches constitute an additional set of challenges for the humanitarian principles (Macrae 2002). The humanitarian agenda has been extended to include more activities such as advocacy, peace-building, post-conflict recovery, human rights and development without any clear consensus of how these activities change the meaning or reality of each principle (Labbé 2012).

Finally, over the past two decades, the prevalence and intensity of natural disasters and armed conflicts have increased (HSRP 2011). The number of chronic crises, such as Somalia, Afghanistan, Colombia and the DRC, has also grown. For humanitarian actors this means that they have to stay in these crises areas for long periods of time. As a consequence, it has become more likely that they also become seen as part of the conflict. The principles work best when organisations can come in, save lives and leave, because then they are only active for a relatively short period of time.

In sum, as the number and types of humanitarian crises have multiplied, so too have the number and types of actors going by the name 'humanitarian'. As a result, the role of the humanitarian principles in promoting coherence and coordination in the crowded and diverse world of humanitarian actors remains unclear. Are parallel humanitarian systems in the making? Where and how do the actors converge or diverge? And which theories can be used to study these developments?

Theoretical Framework

This part develops the theoretical framework of this volume in two rounds. In the first one, we briefly discuss the three traditional institutionalist schools, in particular how they overlap and where they differ. In the second

Table 1.1 Processes of change and persistence

Theory	Rational Choice Institutionalism	Sociological Institutionalism	Historical Institutionalism	Institutional Multiplicity	Constructivism
Convergence	Actors purposely create institutions to reduce transaction costs and/or avoid sanctions	Normative (standards), regulative (coercion) and cognitive (anticipation) pillars lead to 'isomorphism' in organisational field	Path dependency after a critical juncture leads to lock-in effects	Convergence not likely due to low degree of institutionalisation in the international system as well as in crisis countries	Discursive action, such as socialisation, professionalisation, learning and persuasion influence actors' world views and acceptance of norms and principles
Persistence	Actors purposely maintain institutions to reduce uncertainty and/or avoid sanctions, but lack of information leads to collective action dilemmas	Reduce uncertainty, taken-for-granted ideas, institutionalised scripts in an organisational field	Reduced uncertainty due to lock in effects	Actors lack power to effect change with other actors, but gain economic benefits in current situation	Socialisation, professionalisation, learning and persuasion lead to stable identities and taken-for-granted ideas
Divergence	Inefficiencies cause collective action dilemmas; activities to address dilemmas do not lead to coherence	Without legal sanctions/ enforcement, new actors with new ideas and values disrupt isomorphic processes	Gradual feedback, inefficiencies, incrementalism or new critical junctures foster change	Diversity of actors leads to co-existence of different institutions and institution shopping	Discursive action, in particular bricolage, leads to co-existing or conflicting world views and norms

Source: the authors.

round, we analyse two ways in which these schools have evolved further, namely institutional multiplicity and constructivism (see Table I.1). Each of these theories attempts to explain the overlap, convergence or divergence of multiple actors, institutions and, ultimately normative systems. In this way, the actual degree of compliance with the humanitarian principles, as well as the degree of fragmentation of the humanitarian system, can be understood in more detail.

First Round: The Three Institutionalist Schools

The three main institutional schools are rational choice (economic), sociological and historical institutionalism (Hall and Taylor 1996).[7] As their names indicate, they have different disciplinary backgrounds, and despite their similar interests in how and why institutions, including organisations, originate, persist and evolve (Vijge 2013), they originally developed quite separately (Hall and Taylor 1996: 5). They 'developed in reaction to the behavioural perspectives that were influential during the 1960s and 1970s and ... seek to elucidate the role that institutions play in the determination of social and political outcomes' (ibid.: 5).[8] Theorists from each camp thus tend towards structuralism, beginning from the view that the environment determines organisational activities and change. All three see institutions as relatively durable patterns of behaviour 'and observe that institutions affect action by structuring expectations about what others will do, even if they model the sources of these expectations slightly differently' (ibid.: 23).

Rational Choice Institutionalism

Rational choice (economic) institutionalists assume that self-interested actors with exogenously given preferences/utilities strategically pursue their self-interests. Institutions persist because they reduce uncertainty and help to reduce transaction costs of collective action. In this conception of institutionalism actors comply with rules and norms, if they perceive the costs (material and non-material) of non-compliance as higher than those of compliance (Hurd 1999). Absent social costs of this nature, there needs to be some kind of external sanctions in place in order to enforce compliance (Sending 2002).

The underlying logic of action is rational choice, or what March and Olsen (1989) call the 'logic of consequences' (actions which are the product of rational calculation based on the actors' interests and preferences). Rationalists, in other words, see people making decisions using a strategic logic of consequences, instead of following the deontological ethic, if necessary, acting against appropriate or exemplary behaviour to maximise their individual interests. Generally, these interests are considered rather stable. As a consequence, 'rational institutionalism tends to view the creation of institutions and the occurrence of (incremental) institutional changes as highly purposive, being established or embarked upon by actors who think this will maximise their interests' (Vijge 2013: 159). In this respect,

> rational choice institutionalism is rather functionalistic, putting much emphasis on the functions that institutions fulfil and the efficiencies they display. [It] can, however, also explain inefficiencies in institutional structures by referring to deficiencies in these structures. An example is the case of a collective action dilemma. This is a situation in which, due to insufficient information to make a judgment about the optimal outcome of their actions, actors think they act in order to maximise the attainment of their preferences, but end up producing an outcome that neither represents actors' individual preference, nor a collectively optimal outcome.
>
> (Ibid.: 159–160)

While rational choice theorists argue that institutions are purposeful human constructions designed to solve collective action problems', sociological institutionalists stress the embeddedness of institutions 'within temporal and cultural contexts' (Lowndes 2010: 66).[9]

Sociological Institutionalism

Sociological institutionalism focuses on (shared) norms, rules and knowledge to explain organisational behaviour. It does not see organisations as rational actors that function as mechanical instruments to achieve certain goals. Instead, organisations 'are adaptive, organic systems that over time become infused with value "beyond the technical requirements of the task at hand" as they ... adapt to their environment and thereby become institutionalized' (Ohanyan 2015: 91).

Sociological institutionalists focus on how institutions (as rules and practices of conduct and routines within social, cultural, political and economic fields) limit, condition and/or direct social agency, performance and change. These institutions become 'relatively stable, recurring patterns of behaviour' (Goodin 1996: 22). Sociological institutionalists hold that institutionalisation constrains organisational rationality. Institutions structure the thinking and preferences of actors, reacting to and producing what is referred to as 'bounded rationality'.

For institutional sociologists, actors are socially embedded in an organisational environment constituted by normative (morally governed), regulative (legally sanctioned) and cognitive pillars (cultural frames of reference that are taken for granted) (Scott 2001). Each organisational environment develops its own distinctive institutions, which, in turn, influence the structure and activities of actors in the forms of coercion (regulatory orders, government regulations), standards (internalised and shared ideals and ideas) or anticipation (expectations and attitudes of other players in the field), resulting in substantial *isomorphism* (Meyer and Rowan 1991). 'Compliance occurs in many circumstances because other types of behaviour are inconceivable; routines are followed because they are taken for granted as "the way we do these things"' (Scott 2001: 57). Organisations also employ institutionalised scripts for action because those that 'incorporate societally legitimated rationalised elements in their formal structures maximize their legitimacy and increase their resources and survival capacities' (Meyer and Rowan 1991: 53). This helps, for instance, to explain why the humanitarian field has experienced an increase in donor-driven standardisation in planning, reporting and accountability in the past two decades (Rauh 2011).

The main logic in sociological institutionalism is the 'logic of appropriateness' (Finnemore and Sikkink 1998; March and Olsen 1989, 2004), in which actors are driven by rules of appropriate or exemplary behaviour. To act appropriately is to proceed according to the institutionalised practices of collectivity, based on mutual and often tacit understandings of what is true, reasonable, natural, right and good. Institutions are in this sense the prime supplier of and partly constitutive for the very frames of understanding through which individuals come to interpret and understand the world.[10]

As stated, the core humanitarian principles constitute the basis for the deontological ethic of traditional humanitarian action, providing a moral code of appropriate or exemplary behaviour for humanitarians. This ethic is a form of the 'logic of appropriateness', which thus has overtones of morality. Yet this logic can also underlie atrocities of action, such as ethnic cleansing and blood feuds. The fact that an action is defined as appropriate by an individual or a collectivity does not mean that it is efficient or morally acceptable (ibid.). Building on the logic of appropriateness, several scholars in this volume apply the concept of *isomorphism* to explain the *convergent* change within the humanitarian organisational field(s).

Historical Institutionalism

Historical institutionalists stress path dependence, critical junctures and unintended consequences, and often critically combine approaches from the other two schools. In line with the logic of consequences, they show that institutions determine choices, but they also indicate that institutions determine worldviews and interpretations, which corresponds with the logic of appropriateness. Yet, historical institutionalism can also deviate from the logic of consequences when it emphasises that path dependency can cause unintended consequences, for

> once an organisation has chosen a path (a way of solving a problem) it tends to stick to this path both formally (relying on its rules) and

informally (relying on its practice). Path dependency thus refers to the dynamics of self-reinforcing or positive feedback processes …

(Reinalda 2013: 16)

Historical institutionalists identify critical junctures as rare events, often outside shocks, that strongly influence institution building, as for example has happened after major wars with the creation of the League of Nations and the UN. 'The outcomes at a critical juncture trigger feedback mechanisms that reinforce the recurrence of a particular path into the future' (ibid.).

Although historical institutionalists see 'institutions as relatively persistent, it can account for … change through gradual adaptation, causing every greater change down the path by means of positive feedback' (Vijge 2013: 158).[11] Negative feedback can also produce normative change, when, for instance, top administrators squash low or mid-level initiatives, leading staff-members to mockingly 'stick to the letter of the law', precisely in order to expose the irrationality of certain norms. Such actions often lead to a further hardening of attitudes or outright conflict (though this may itself lead to long-run change). Interestingly, path dependency can thus be a useful concept explaining either the occurrence of incremental change and inefficiencies that ultimately lead to greater divergence or explaining the convergence or persistence of institutional structures, when initial, path-dependent changes become *locked in*, so that subsequent change becomes less likely. In both respects, historical institutionalism does not posit that critical junctures and subsequent path-dependent developments necessarily mean virtuous progress, instead they can also lead to inefficient, unintended or even vicious outcomes (ibid.; Lowndes 2010: 295).

The three institutional schools initially focused mainly on politics and organisations at the national level or within international relations theory on interstate relations, but rarely on humanitarian crises. Over the years they have increasingly been combined and updated to provide richer explanations of more aspects of political and social life (Hall and Taylor 1996: 23–24; Ohanyan 2015).

Second Round: The Socially Constructed Humanitarian System

In this round, we describe two theories that build in different ways on the aforementioned schools in order to further enable the study of convergence or divergence from the humanitarian principles and actors.

Institutional Multiplicity

Combining rational choice and sociological institutionalism, institutional multiplicity focuses on local, national, international and transnational normative frameworks, which both overlap and clash and which may lead to *divergent* change within a given field, in this case humanitarian action. It explains change in situations defined by low levels of institutionalisation – for instance, the interstate system or weak states, while also explaining why institutionalisation in such situations remains sporadic. At the same time, the goal is also to show how a plurality, or even excess of norms at lower order spatial scales may contribute to institutional conflict or failure at higher levels, for instance the state.

As humanitarian actors (and crises) regularly cross borders, they are embedded in *transnational* organisational fields with different institutional logics and governance systems and have to justify themselves simultaneously to diverse groups of actors with complex and sometimes contradictory expectations, including the governments in the countries of their headquarters, governments in humanitarian crisis zones, donors, humanitarian organisations (local and international) and the beneficiaries of their activities.

Sometimes organisations may not be able to follow their preferred course of action because the expectations of other actors from diverging traditions hamper cooperation. New humanitarians, for example, are limited by the seemingly 'conservative' demands placed upon them by more traditional actors, which have greater material and symbolic power by the existing regulation and valuation of skills, competencies and organising strategies, and, ultimately, by their inexperience in dealing with this multiplicity. That is, new humanitarians are constrained by their 'newness' to the humanitarian field, a relatively open and diverse field which requires significant experience to navigate.

In this vein, multiple institutions, such as traditional leaders, warlords, governmental bodies, NGOs and UN organisations, operate and sometimes compete with each other in crisis zones. According to DiJohn (2008: 33),

> Institutional multiplicity is a situation in which different sets of rules of the game, often contradictory, coexist in the same territory, putting citizens and economic agents in complex, often unsolvable, situations, but at the same time offering them the possibility of switching strategically from one institutional universe to the other.

(See also van der Haar and Heijke 2013: 99.) The term *institutional multiplicity* has mainly been used in ethnographic studies (e.g. Hilhorst 2013), in particular in situations of protracted conflict. Van der Haar and Heijke (2013: 99) state that

> The attractiveness of the concept of institutional multiplicity is its lack of normative and prescriptive connotation. It does not, a priori, privilege or dismiss any type of governance arrangement. It does not juxtapose institutions in binary terms, as state versus non-state, or 'formal' versus 'informal'.

In terms of this volume, we could add 'traditional' versus 'non-traditional' humanitarian actors. Van der Haar and Heijke continue (ibid.):

> In this way, [the concept of institutional multiplicity] opens up the space to consider the structure, workings and impact of any source of authority and regulation, without predefined notions of what type of institutions should fulfil what functions or what principles should be expected to govern its operation. Researching institutional multiplicity, then, means to investigate empirically the make-up, reach, effectiveness and legitimation efforts of different institutional offers or claims to governance, in a field in which a multiplicity of such claims operate. It implies examining the way these different sets of institutions interact and influence one another, and the way this shapes social life.

The interaction of institutional forms spans a range of organisational reactions 'that may occur alongside each other: contradiction, confrontation and friction, as well as accommodation, mutual adjustment and negotiation' (ibid.: 100). In the context of institutional multiplicity, actors become more likely to pursue their interests strategically. They can, for example, go institution shopping, choosing which norms and institutions will govern their actions. In other words, choosing their own path dependencies more or less consciously. Institutional multiplicity often entails concerns about legitimacy 'and moral arguments around the values and virtues of the different sets of institutions' (ibid.). In our volume, this comes back in debates about the relevance of different interpretations of or alternatives to the humanitarian principles.

Constructivism

In international relations, the *constructivist approach* concentrates on identifying and explaining profound changes in the actors or practices of world politics. It focuses on 'actors under construction'. Constructivists claim that people act in a specific way and not another, 'due to the presence of certain "social constructs": ideas, beliefs, norms, identities, or some other interpretative filter through which people perceive the world. According to them we inhabit a "world of our making" ... and action is structured by the meanings that particular groups of people develop to interpret and organise their identities, interests, relationships and environment' (Parsons 2010: 80). Just like sociological institutionalism, constructivism focuses on interpretation, but pays more attention to contention and instability.[12]

Constructivists mean by 'social construction' of the international (humanitarian) system that its creation takes place through a process of interaction between actors (individuals, states, non-state organisations) and the structures of their broader environment. According to them, this process is shaped by the actors' identities and practices as well as by (changing) normative institutional structures. Individuals, non-state actors and states craft institutions, in particular norms, 'which confine behaviour, while defining identities, and set the context for future interactions' (Bloodgood 2015: 131). Constructivists also seek to demonstrate how new norms can be created by breaking down older ones, or denaturalising them through criticism.

Constructivists thus see people making decisions using a social logic, based on social norms and the expectations of others. According to the constructivist approach, the term 'comply with' can be misleading as norms become internalised through processes of *socialisation, professionalisation,*[13] *learning, persuasion* or *bricolage.* Socialisation suggests 'a diffused, decentralised, collective and consensual process in which a group of people work their way to certain norms or ideas' (Parsons 2010: 95). Professionalisation is a specific form of socialisation through education and associations that promote joint standards of behaviour and quality in a specific occupational group to establish a cognitive base and legitimation for their occupational autonomy (DiMaggio and Powell 1991). Learning, in its formal (classroom) and informal (on-the-job) varieties, concerns the obtainment of both the cognitive base and practical skills for action in a specific area of activity. It generally implies considerable investment in terms of financial resources and time to become fully effective, but for those who have 'learned', it carries a high degree of legitimacy (Parsons 2010: 95–96). Persuasion arguments

> rely on explicit advocates, who clearly believe in their new ideas or norms at a time before the ideas in question are embedded in broader action ... The more social construction operates by persuasion, the more we should see a world of conscious advocates jockeying to persuade other key actors to adopt their agenda.
>
> (Ibid.)

Bricolage 'tends to develop ideas and norms and practices to suit rather discrete problems and goals, and we end up with a complex landscape of overlapping realms of action. ... This is a world of incoherence, not consensual, collective identities' (ibid.).

Being internalised and constitutive for an actor's identity, norms attain a motivationally efficacious power in explaining action in the sense that there is what Hurd (1999: 387) refers to as an 'internal sense of moral obligation' that explains action. Yet, the mechanisms described above provide different degrees and ways in which norms can be internalised and/or become constitutive for an actor's identity. Using these mechanisms helps the authors in this volume to distinguish different ways in which different actors active in humanitarian crises propose either more respect for the humanitarian principles or advocate alternative norms.

Several authors in this volume use constructivism to see whether and how the new and traditional actors in the humanitarian field are changing.

They discuss whether the 'new' humanitarian actors are mainly influenced by their organisational environment, or if they also construct and change it.

Outline of this Volume

We analyse the above-mentioned eight humanitarianisms in eight parts and examine how these actors emerge, carry out or influence humanitarian action, accept, reject or modify the humanitarian principles and contribute to the politics of humanitarian crises.

As a background to the other chapters in this volume, in Part I Eberwein and Reinalda describe the history of humanitarian law and organisations, providing an understanding of the emergence and transformation of the humanitarian principles, actors and the humanitarian organisational field(s).

In Part II, Roepstorff draws attention to India's growing role as a humanitarian donor. In line with constructivist theory, she finds that India's humanitarian engagement is not just influenced by the existing humanitarian system – India subscribes to the humanitarian principles in general but also deviates from DAC donor approaches.

Similarly, Özerdem studies in Chapter 3 the rise of Turkey as a humanitarian donor. In the case of Somalia, he describes how Turkey has linked its soft-power tools of transportation links, trade and education with its foreign policy, putting a strong emphasis on responding to humanitarian crises. The chapter shows how Turkey works with populations directly and keeps a close proximity to them, offering an alternative to traditional actors' remote aid provision.

Part III focuses on multi-mandate organisations and developmental humanitarianism. In their chapter, Hilhorst and Pereboom study the activities of multi-mandate organisations, distinguish different crisis scenarios and assess in which cases multi-mandate organisations may have a comparative advantage over their traditional counterparts. They see humanitarian aid provision as an arena where the conditions, organisations and practices are emergent properties co-determined by a multiplicity of actors.

Part IV looks at armed humanitarianism. In Chapter 5 O'Neill describes how the Force Intervention Brigade (FIB), a 'new' part of the United Nations Organization Stabilization Mission in the Democratic Republic of the Congo (MONUSCO), uses force to neutralise armed groups and restore state authority. He also discusses how NGOs successfully challenged certain aspects of the mission, such as the explicit use of humanitarian action for the purpose of counterinsurgency, but the FIB's adverse effects on the humanitarian principles and operations have remained largely taboo. Only MSF has taken up this issue, but this has not been well received by other humanitarians.

In his next chapter, O'Neill describes the changing patterns of interaction between humanitarian NGOs and insurgents. African insurgents have come to recognise humanitarian organisations not only as sources of finance or food, but also as political actors in their own right, capable of conferring quasi-diplomatic recognition upon their 'partners.' These insurgents have mimicked the humanitarian principles and practice, which has made humanitarian advocacy in the DRC an increasingly political game.

Through various examples of both military and private-sector engagement in the response to crises, as well as their development of innovative approaches, Carpenter and Kent examine in Chapter 7 both the opportunities to meet increasing humanitarian needs and the challenges this creates for staff safety, security and respecting the humanitarian principles.

Part V examines for-profit humanitarianism. Carbonnier and Lightfoot notice the recent surge in business–humanitarian partnerships (BHPs) in Chapter 8. They argue that establishing the legitimacy of BHPs through close alignment with ethical and effectiveness principles is essential for their long-term success *and* the integrity and reputation of humanitarian agencies. Building on institutional theories of global legitimacy, the authors discuss three sources of legitimacy for BHPs. In particular, they focus on the United Nations Children's Fund (UNICEF) and the International Movement of the Red Cross and Red Crescent to assess how their BHP legitimation strategies have evolved.

In Chapter 9, Joachim and Schneiker claim that PMSCs increasingly enter the humanitarian arena to offer support services for humanitarian NGOs or provide humanitarian services themselves. Comparing selected PMSCs and NGOs, they show that their participation in security governance reflects isomorphism. PMSCs not only present themselves as serving those in need, but also pretend to base their activities on altruistic motivations. As a result, it becomes difficult to distinguish between PMSCs and traditional humanitarian actors, forcing the latter to explore new ways and strategies to present themselves as different, unique humanitarian actors.

Part VI examines diaspora humanitarianism. In Chapter 10, Horst, Lubkemann and Pailey argue that Liberian and Somali diasporas not only provide an additional stream of aid, but do so in ways that strongly differ from that of international and local actors. They caution, however, that while necessary, these alternative flows of aid risk creating parallel structures that replicate recognised flaws in the current humanitarian system.

In Chapter 11, Sezgin examines how two DOs in Germany – the Islamic Community Millî Görüş and the German–Syrian Association for the Promotion of Freedom and Human Rights (DSV) – have responded to the Syrian conflict and refugee crisis. She applies neo-institutionalism, associational theory and transnationalism to examine how they understand the traditional humanitarian principles and why they reject some of them. Finally, she explores their alternative principles and the implications for the humanitarian field.

Part VII looks at faith-based humanitarianism. In Chapter 12, Juul Petersen asks what the emergence and increasing integration of international Muslim

NGOs imply for mainstream humanitarian action. Describing the different reactions to these Muslim NGOs, she argues that this integration does not lead to radical changes in the humanitarian organisational field, rather it seems to change these organisations. Based on the study of Islamic Relief and Muslim aid, Juul Petersen explores how these processes of isomorphism take place, discussing the resulting conflicts and challenges.

By exploring faith-based humanitarianism through the lens of emerging debates surrounding South–South humanitarianism, Fiddian-Qasmiyeh and Pacitto simultaneously affirm in Chapter 13 the value of what they refer to as 'writing the "Other" into humanitarian discourse' and redress the biases inherent to much humanitarian theory. Drawing on examples of Southern faith-based actors' responses to recent and ongoing processes of displacement, including case studies of Myanmar and Syria, the authors re-engage with popular debates around religion/secularism, politics and humanitarianism.

In Part VIII on local and regional organisations, Fan traces the histori-cal evolution of humanitarian engagement by regional organisations. She focuses on two case studies, the Association of Southeast Asian Nations (ASEAN) and the Organisation of Islamic Cooperation (OIC), to examine more closely their particular approaches. Finally, she considers the broader implications of these developments, both for humanitarian crises and for the future of the humanitarian sector as a whole.

In Chapter 15, Vaux compares the approach to humanitarian action by Western agencies with the Ghandian self-sufficiency approach taken by the Self-Employed Women's Association (SEWA), a union of poor working women in India. He shows that during the 2001 Gujarat earthquake and the Communal Violence of 2002, the activities of Western agencies were driven by 'supply' factors such as availability of funding and Western public sym-pathy. By contrast SEWA is driven strongly by 'demand' factors, notably the interests of its members. Vaux argues that although SEWA does not actively use the humanitarian principles, its activities are largely consistent with them.

Finally, in the conclusion, Dijkzeul, O'Neill and Sezgin review the contri-butions to this volume and draw conclusions for the humanitarian system as a whole. They ask:

1   Are the old and new humanitarian actors converging or diverging?
2   Are new, parallel, competitive or complementary humanitarian systems developing?

Notes

1 When the blanket of superpower rivalry lifted, sovereignty became less sacro-sanct and it became easier to intervene. Furthermore, crisis zones became more visible in the media and donor funding grew.

2 The OECD-DAC is the club of advanced industrialised countries who provide the bulk of overseas development assistance and humanitarian aid.

3 We considered including celebrity humanitarianism, but celebrities are generally more involved in advocacy and public relations than in carrying out humanitarian activities on the ground.

4 Nevertheless, from the first Additional Protocol, art. 23 ff., as well as from the International Court of Justice's verdict on *Nicaragua v. US* (1986) concerning intervention, some aspects of such a definition can be deduced. Yet, international law is a law of consent and the 'sovereign' states have never been willing to reach a full agreement on the meaning of 'humanitarian'.

5 Norms, understood as intersubjective, widely shared beliefs about appropriate behaviour, shape the activities, identity and interests of actors (Finnemore and Sikkink 1998). Principles are norms that are considered fundamental to action in a specific area. They usually provide legitimacy to such action (Alpa 1994).

6 General Assembly Resolution 46/182 of 1991 endorsed the principles of humanity, neutrality and impartiality; Resolution 58/114 of 2004 included the principle of independence (Lieser and Dijkzeul 2013).

7 Since Hall and Taylor have published their paper, other authors have identified more institutionalisms. In contrast with the three schools, these institutionalisms 'denote particular clusters of academic activity and the elaboration of institutionalist insights in different contexts, rather than representing distinct ontological [or epistemological] positions in their own right' (Lowndes 2010: 66).

8 Behaviouralists believed social norms, political institutions and economic structures to be little more than epiphenomena of individual interests. Hence, institutionalists set out to explore the manifold ways in which social interaction shapes individual behaviour (DiMaggio and Powell 1991: 2).

9 Principal-agent theory is an important type of rationalist institutional theory. In the principal-agent relationship, which is a contractual one, the principal delegates, but does not surrender authority to the agent (Reinalda 2013: 17). However, as the authors in this volume stress the initiatives of the 'new' humanitarian actors as individual organisations, they do not use principal-agent theory.

10 'The core notion is that life is organised by sets of shared meanings and practices that come to be taken as given. Political actors act and organize themselves in accordance with rules and practices that are socially constructed, publicly known, anticipated and accepted. Actions of individuals and collectivities occur within these shared meanings and practices, which can be called identities and institutions ... Institutions and identities constitute and legitimize political actors and provide them with consistent behavioural rules, conceptions of reality, standards of assessments, affective ties, and endowments' (March and Olsen 1989: 41).

11 Negative feedback can lead to the persistence of older forms of behaviour, as newly initiated changes are not received positively and these initiatives peter out.

12 The constructivist approach has built on organisational sociology. In international relations it criticised neo-realism and neoliberalism – that were actually strongly influenced by rationalist approaches – which had failed to predict the geopolitical changes of the Cold War and its aftermath.

13 Professionalisation also plays an important role in sociological institutionalism (DiMaggio and Powell 1991).

References

Alpa, G. (1994) 'General Principles of Law', *Annual Survey of International & Comparative Law*, 1(2):1–37.

Barnett, M. and Walker, P. (forthcoming) 'Can Humanitarianism Face the Future?' *Foreign Affairs*.

Bloodgood, E.A. (2015) 'Being an NGO in the OECD', in: B. DeMars and D. Dijkzeul (eds) *The NGO Challenge for International Relations Theory*, Abingdon: Routledge, 130–158.

DiJohn, J. (2008) 'Conceptualising the Causes and Consequences of Failed States: A Critical Review of the Literature', Crisis States Research Center, *Working Paper No. 25*, DESTIN, London: London School of Economics and Political Science.

DiMaggio, P.J. and Powell, W.W. (1991) 'The Iron Cage Revisited: Institutional Isomorphism and Collective Rationality in Organization Fields', in: W.W. Powell and P.J. DiMaggio (eds) *The New Institutionalism in Organizational Analysis*, Chicago and London: University of Chicago Press, 63–82.

Donini, A. (2010) 'The Far Side: The Meta Functions of Humanitarianism in a Globalised World', *Disasters*, 34(2):220–237.

Finnemore, M. and Sikkink, K. (1998) 'International Norm Dynamics and Political Change', *International Organization*, 52(4):887–917.

GHA (2009) *GHA Report 2009*, Wells: Global Humanitarian Assistance.

Goodin, R. (ed.) (1996) *The Theory of Institutional Design*, Cambridge: Cambridge University Press.

Hall, P.A. and Taylor, C.R. (1996) 'Political Science and the Three New Instituionalisms', *MPIFG Discussion Paper*, 96/6, Cologne: Max Planck Institut für Gesellschaftsforschung.

Harrel-Bond, B.E. (1986) *Imposing Aid: Emergency Assistance to Refugees*, Oxford: Oxford University Press.

Hilhorst, D. (ed.) (2013) *Disasters, Conflict and Society in Crises: Everyday Politics of Crisis Response*, London and New York: Routledge, 97–113.

HSRP (2011) *Human Security Report 2009/2010: The Causes of Peace and the Shrinking Costs of War*, New York: Oxford University Press.

Hurd, I. (1999) 'Legitimacy and Authority in International Politics', *International Organization*, 53(2):379–408.

ICRC (1986) The Fundamental Principles of the International Red Cross and Red Crescent Movement (www.icrc.org/eng/resources/documents/red-cross-crescent-movement/fundamental-principles-movement-1986-10-31.htm) accessed 23 March 2015.

Labbé, J. (2012) Rethinking Humanitarianism: Adapting to 21st Century Challenges (http://reliefweb.int/sites/reliefweb.int/files/resources/ipi_pub_rethinking_humanitarianism.pdf) accessed 23 March 2015.

Leader, N. (2000) 'The Politics of Principle: The Principles of Humanitarian Action in Practice', *HPG Report 2*, London: ODI.

Lieser, J. and Dijkzeul, D. (eds) (2013) *Handbuch Humanitäre Hilfe*, Heidelberg: Springer Verlag.

Lowndes, V. (2010) 'The Institutional Approach', in: D. Marsh and G. Stoker *Theory and Methods in Political Science*, Basingstoke: Palgrave Macmillan, 60–79.

Macrae, J. (ed.) (2002) *The New Humanitarianisms: A Review of Trends in Global Humanitarian Action*, London: ODI.

March, J.G. and Olsen, J.P. (1989) *Rediscovering Institutions*, New York: Free Press.

March, J.G. and Olsen, J.P. (2004) The Logic of Appropriateness (www.sv.uio.no/arena/english/research/publications/arena-publications/workingpapers/working-papers2004/wp04_9.pdf) accessed 25 March 2015.

McGoldrick, C. (2011) 'The Future of Humanitarian Action: An ICRC Perspective', *International Review of the Red Cross*, 93(884):965–991.

Meyer, J.W. and Rowan, B. (1991) 'Institutionalized Isomorphism and Collective Rationality', in: W.W. Powell and P.J. DiMaggio (eds) *The New Institutionalism in Organizational Analysis*, Chicago: University of Chicago Press, 41–62.

OCHA (2013) *World Humanitarian Data and Trends 2013*, New York: OCHA.

OCHA (2014) OCHA Factsheet: Global Challenges and the Changing Humanitarian Landscape: Projections to 2025, OCHA, in mimeo.

Ohanyan, A. (2015) 'Network Institutionalism: A New Synthesis for NGO Studies', in: B. DeMars and D. Dijkzeul (eds) *The NGO Challenge for International Relations Theory*, Abingdon: Routledge, 82–104.

Parsons, C. (2010) 'Constructivism and Interpretive Theory', in: D. Marsh and G. Stoker (eds) *Theory and Methods in Political Science*, Basingstoke: Palgrave Macmillan, 80–98.

Rauh, K. (2011) 'NGOs, Foreign Donors, and Organizational Processes: Passive NGO Recipients or Strategic Actors?' *McGill Sociological Review*, 1:29–45.

Reinalda, B. (2013) 'International Organization as a Field of Research', in: B. Reinalda (ed.) *Routledge Handbook of International Organization*, Abingdon: Routledge, 1–23.

Rosenow-Williams, K. and Sezgin, Z. (2014) 'Islamic Migrant Organizations: Little-Studied Actors in Humanitarian Action', *International Migration Review*, 48(2):324–353.

Salomons, D. (2015) 'The Perils of Dunantism: The Need for a Rights-Based Approach to Humanitarianism', in: A. Zwitter, C.K. Lamont, H.J. Heintze and J. Herman (eds) *Humanitarian Action: Global, Regional and Domestic Legal Responses*, Cambridge: Cambridge University Press, 33–53.

Savage, K. and Harvey, P. (eds) (2007) *Remittances during Crises: Implications for Humanitarian Response*, HPG Paper 25, London: ODI.

Scott, R.W. (2001) *Institutions and Organizations: Ideas, Interests, and Identities*, Los Angeles: SAGE.

Sending, O.J. (2002) 'Constitution, Choice and Change: Problems with the "Logic of Appropriateness" and its Use in Constructivist Theory', *European Journal of International Relations*, 8(4):443–470.

Sezgin, Z. (2014) 'Turkish Migrant Organizations after the 2011 Van Earthquake: Member Interests Versus Humanitarian Principles', *Oxford Development Studies*, 42(1):19–37.

Sezgin, Z. and Dijkzeul, D. (2013) 'Migrant Organizations in Humanitarian Action', *Journal of International Migration and Integration*, 15(2):159–177.

Singer, P.W. (2007) *Corporate Warriors: The Rise of the Privatized Military Industry*, New York: Cornell University Press.

Slim, H. (1997) 'Relief Agencies and Moral Standing in War: Principles of Humanity, Neutrality, Impartiality and Solidarity', *Development in Practice*, 4:342–352.

Terry, F. (2002) *Condemned to Repeat? The Paradox of Humanitarian Action*, Ithaca: Cornell University Press.

van der Haar, G. and Heijke, M. (2013) 'Conflict, Governance and Institutional Multiplicity: Parallel Governance in Kosovo and Chiapas, Mexico', in: D. Hilhorst (ed.) *Disasters, Conflict and Society in Crises: Everyday Politics of Crisis Response,* Abingdon: Routledge, 97–113.

Vijge, M.J. (2013) 'The Promise of New Institutionalism: Explaining the Absence of a World or United Nations Environment Organisation', *International Environmental Agreements,* 13:153–176.

Part I

History

Old and New Humanitarian Actors

1 A Brief History of Humanitarian Actors and Principles

Wolf-Dieter Eberwein and Bob Reinalda

Introduction

This chapter provides a brief history of humanitarian actors and principles, covering two complementary groups: humanitarian organisations in a wider (focused on improving people's lives) and a more restrictive-sense (focused on saving lives, with a recognised status in international humanitarian law). It also analyses the rise of two branches of what is now called international humanitarian law: *ius in bello* or Hague Law, which regulates the conduct of armed conflicts and so-called Geneva Law that protects those who are not, or no longer, taking part in hostilities: civilian populations and prisoners of war.

The normative institutionalisation of humanitarian action by non-governmental organisations (NGOs), governments and in particular international governmental organisations (IGOs) associated with the UN has been a long process, which began with the first Geneva Convention of 1864 (Eberwein 2011). The main organisational institutionalisation process started at about the same time and intensified after the end of the Cold War.

The Rise of Private Actors with Public Aims

The appearance of private actors with public aims, such as NGOs, in Western Europe from the mid-eighteenth century on was related to the emergence of the middle classes and the growth in education and resources which enabled people to take part in the activities of such organisations, as well as to advances in communication (roads, trains, shipping, postal services, the telegraph, the press, etc.) (Seary 1996: 17).

This citizens' engagement took place against the wider backdrop of the Enlightenment. Political theorists argued that democratic institutions would allow citizens to accept the curtailment of their various rights by the state and provide them with procedures to correct their government if necessary. This model for legitimate government was founded on the idea of a social contract. While citizens accept the power of the government, they are also guaranteed certain inalienable rights and liberties, according to

Jean-Jacques Rousseau. The notion of 'popular sovereignty' then regards the will and consent of the people as the source of all political power and of a state's legitimacy. This was clearly expressed in the 1787 Constitution of the United States, while the first declarations of the rights of the citizens followed during the French Revolution of 1789 and in the American Bill of Rights of 1791. However, the mere proclamation of such rights did not yet make them effective. The way to transform these new ideas into political reality was through political struggles by the citizens, first in Europe and Northern America and after the Second World War also elsewhere. During the nineteenth and twentieth centuries this struggle included the restriction of state power through the greater accountability of the executive to the parliamentary representation of the people, the separation of powers between legislature, executive and judiciary in a *trias politica* and the acquisition of more power by the people through a gradual extension of the popular vote. The emergence and evolution of humanitarian actors and principles can be seen as part of this effort to modernise and democratise the state and the relations between states.

NGOs have been closely associated with democratisation processes within states and the international system of states. Partly this consisted of the formulation as well as the elaboration and specification of human rights, which allowed the emancipation of civil society (Davies 2013). Small groups of citizens took up ideas related to ethical, economic, social and political problems, predicated on the assumption that they could contribute to the solution of problems at the national and international levels by appealing to the (governments of) states. Some of these groups are social movements, characterised by public campaigns, action repertoires and collective self-representation (Tilly 2004: 3–4). Others are advocacy organisations, such as Amnesty International, appealing to the public and even more to governments, to respect human rights and refrain from human-rights violations. Still other associations deliver services related to disasters and development and environmental issues. A final group consists of people involved in the creation and dissemination of knowledge: epistemic communities.

Both governments and NGOs are faced with societal changes, forcing them to adapt internally and externally. Issues come and go; new problems are identified as they show up, very often as a result of the increase in scientific knowledge. Most non-profit NGOs could be characterised as humanitarian. Humanitarian organisations in a wider sense are those active in the domain of social welfare, such as development in general, the environment, peace and human rights. Humanitarian organisations in a more restrictive sense are those NGOs that provide emergency relief in case of war and natural or technical disasters. There is a basic distinction between the two: the wider group wants to improve the existence of individuals, or groups of individuals, while the more restrictive group wants to save lives. There is another relevant distinction, because unlike the wider group humanitarian organisations in the more narrow sense have a recognised status in international humanitarian law, which is a particular set of legal provisions prescribing and proscribing the behaviour of both governments and humanitarian organisations, as will be elaborated below.

The Rise of International Peace Movements and the Idea of Arbitration

The wars that revolutionary and later Napoleonic France fought from 1791 until 1815 popularised the ideas of a nation in arms, glorifying the figure of the soldier, but there was also awareness of the destructiveness and waste of war. The Spanish painter Francisco de Goya documented the cruelties of both the Napoleonic army of occupation and the Spanish people's guerrilla resistance in the paintings and etchings he made during the wars in Spain, and saw his etchings about 'The Disasters of War' disseminated widely across Europe thanks to new printing techniques. In this vein, Quakers, who regard waging war as incompatible with Christianity, were among the first to establish peace societies in the UK (the British Peace Society of 1819) and the US, where 36 Quaker and other societies merged into the American Peace Society in 1828. The latter aimed at settling international controversies by an appeal to reason and by arbitration between states. In this it followed James Jay, who was the American negotiator in concluding a treaty between the UK and the US in 1794 to settle disagreements between the two states. Jay regarded arbitration as a means to prevent conflicts, rather than as a way to end hostilities. While old ethical critiques of warfare found new arguments in Goya's etchings, arbitration emerged as a means to avoid the cruelties of war and was discussed at the first international peace congress in 1843 in London (Reinalda 2009: 44–45).

Free trade advocates also reflected on peace and peaceful means such as arbitration. They regarded trade as a more effective way of exerting influence in the world than the bullying of other states and argued that it could make war obsolete. During the 1840s free trade advocates gained support from businessmen who would profit from free trade and became allied to the Quaker-influenced peace groups. However, a closer look at the peace movement in the Anglo-Saxon world reveals that it was split between religion-inspired pacifists who wished to oppose all wars and peace advocates who gave primacy to free trade. Factors such as Protestantism and the rise of liberal politics and a free-enterprise economy provided a favourable setting for the promotion of peace societies in the US and the UK, which spread to the Continent, in particular Western Europe, with Central and Eastern Europe being less in favour of liberal and democratic aspirations.

The idea of arbitration attracted new diplomatic attention as a result of the *Alabama* dispute between the US and the UK, in which the US demanded compensation because the UK had violated neutrality by opening its ports to belligerent ships during the American Civil War (the

Alabama was on the side of the Southern US states and operated from Liverpool). Negotiations resulted in the Treaty of Washington (1871) and in an arbitration procedure in Geneva the following year. That both parties accepted the outcome and the UK paid within the time stipulated enhanced the idea of arbitration and its practicability, both in public opinion and in parliamentary debates on international arbitration. Interstate arbitration became prevalent, in particular in tribunals in which either the US or the UK participated, while the Universal Postal Union of 1874 was the first IGO with a provision for (compulsory) arbitration in its constitution. Shortly after the *Alabama* issue citizens founded two private institutes of international law. The Institute of International Law (1873) aimed to encourage the general progress of international law and developed into an epistemic community of experts on international arbitration to which governments increasingly began to pay attention. The International Law Association, founded in the same year by lawyers committed to the peace movement, focused more on public opinion. In practice the two organisations proved to be complementary to each other in promoting arbitration. Another organisation in favour of arbitration was the Inter-Parliamentary Union of 1889, which created a network of parliamentarians who discussed the question of how to make their respective governments conclude permanent arbitration treaties and include arbitration clauses in commercial treaties. A division of labour evolved between these parliamentarians and the Universal Peace Congress, a collection of peace groups that organised annual international conferences.

The activities of the various international peace movements reached a high point in the so-called Hague system, which resulted from the 1899 Peace Conference in The Hague. The Convention on the Pacific Settlement of International Disputes promoted arbitration and was followed by the establishment of the Permanent Court of Arbitration in 1900. Although these were the results of intergovernmental negotiation, the peace movements had done much of the preparatory work. Essential is the universal character of the Hague system; although its first members were mainly European states, the Latin American states decided to join the system *en bloc* in 1901. Other manifestations of universal peace efforts were the creation of the Nobel Peace Prize in 1901, paid out of the industrialist Alfred Nobel's bequest, and the opening of the Peace Palace in The Hague in 1913, donated by the American industrialist Andrew Carnegie.

Geneva Law: Humanising War

As humanitarians in the wider sense the peace movements proved a constant factor in the nineteenth century, which should be kept in mind when discussing humanitarianism and international law. The conference in Paris that settled the outcome of the Crimean War of 1854–56 between Russia and Turkey was important for several reasons. It was the first enlargement of the Concert of Europe system beyond Europe in the strictest sense, because it admitted Turkey to the then-existing community of nations. It also marked the beginning of rule-making on navigation in times of war and the relations between belligerents and neutrals, when it issued the Declaration Respecting Maritime Law. This prohibited privateering and the capture of enemy goods on neutral ships, with the former requiring blockades to be effective. These rules were made more precise and were codified in later treaties, among them the Treaty of Washington of 1871 mentioned above and the sixth convention of the second Hague Peace Conference in 1907. The 1856 Paris Declaration marked the beginning of the branch of international law that regulates the conduct of armed conflicts, also called *ius in bello*. The law of 'war proper', as it was called at the time, defines the rights and duties of belligerents regarding the methods of warfare. Since the Hague Peace Conferences and their various conventions this has also been called 'Hague Law', to be distinguished from 'Geneva Law' (discussed below), the two branches of what is now called international humanitarian law.

A new element in the Crimean War was concern for the welfare of the wounded. Whereas the peace movements wanted to abolish war, the humanitarian movement was hoping that as long as wars were not abolished the fighting at least could be humanised. The beginning of humanitarian action can be associated with Florence Nightingale, who had gained experience in hospital administration. She had offered her help to the British secretary of war after she read about the unhealthy conditions at the front and in the military hospital in Scutari. She was sent to Scutari with a group of nurses, to support the British army by attacking the unhygienic conditions through proper organisation, ensuring sufficient medical supplies and thereby trying to reduce the death rate of the wounded soldiers. Following her work British military medical services were overhauled and expanded in such a way that they could adequately care for the military wounded without civilian assistance. This British attitude to taking care of the wounded on the battlefield became a state obligation as a result of a private initiative (Finnemore 1996: 79).

The Swiss banker Henri Dunant started the development of humanitarian action, humanitarianism in the narrow sense, but went much further than Nightingale by proposing a universal strategy. Having seen the wounded and dying soldiers on the battlefield of Solferino in the war between French and Austrian troops in 1859, he proposed the creation of national organisations to accompany the military to the theatre of war so that civilians could take care of the wounded, so-called *comités de secours*. His friend Gustave Moynier, who from personal experience knew about diplomacy, tried to persuade a number of European governments to agree to such an international convention. In the meantime Dunant had in early 1863 visited the international statistical congress in Berlin to gain insight into the available comparative health and death statistics and to raise political support for the proposed *comités de secours*. At the conference in Geneva in October 1863 representatives from 16 nations approved the foundation of private national societies, staffed by volunteers and funded by private donations, that were to seek recognition from national governments and could act as neutrals in armed conflict. Results were not achieved easily, as the British argued that the armies were already taking care of the wounded themselves; the French distrusted the competence and integrity of the volunteers; and the Prussians had a different tradition, of Knights Hospitallers. The designer of the Swiss flag, General Guillaume-Henri Dufour, managed to keep the debate going and recommended using the Swiss flag reversed – a red cross on a white background – as a symbol of neutrality for the medical units. Consensus was finally reached, which resulted in the establishment of the ICRC, the International Committee of the Red Cross, in 1863. Thanks to the initiative of the Swiss government a diplomatic multilateral conference was convened in 1864, which signed the Convention for the Amelioration of the Condition of the Wounded in Armies in the Field and recognised the Red Cross emblem.

This Geneva Convention was a first and major step in institutionalising humanitarian action. Revised versions of the first Geneva Convention followed in the nineteenth and twentieth centuries. Brazil, Mexico and Turkey were absent in Geneva, but supported the project. The US Sanitary Commission sent an observer, given its interest in rules on the battlefield during the ongoing US civil war and its 1863 Instructions for United States Armies in the Field, also called the Lieber Code after its author Francis Lieber.

Implementing the new humanitarian principles proved difficult. The ICRC promoted the progress of national Red Cross societies, but came up against governments and military commanders who sought to nationalise and militarise the charitable contributions of the national societies. Those became subsidiaries of the army medical services in case of war, but were neutral in status and thus protected from having to fight. As the 'red cross' was – incorrectly – interpreted as a Christian symbol in the Islamic world, the Ottoman society opted for a red crescent instead, which the ICRC accepted. Once the ICRC realised that it could not provide support to prisoners of war (Forsythe 2005: 24; Forsythe and Rieffer-Flanagan 2007: 8–11), it began to consider revising the original Geneva Convention, which was found to be an arduous task. When the ICRC began to report on prisoners of war it was based not on Geneva Law, but on the Hague Law of 1907 (Forsythe 2005: 31). However, at the 1899 Hague conference a second Geneva Convention had been adopted, which extended the principles of war on land to maritime warfare. During the intergovernmental conference in 1906 a more detailed and more precise text of the 1864 convention was drafted, replacing the original. This marks a further development of the Geneva Law, intended to protect the victims and injured of armed forces in war, as part of international humanitarian law, through the initiative of civil-society representatives, primarily Dunant and Moynier.

The Impact of the First World War: Multiple Humanitarian Actors

The ICRC became involved in the First World War without strategic planning or a large staff and, partly due to this lack of organisational capacity, focused on the Western rather than the Eastern front. Apart from helping wounded soldiers, the Red Cross also aided prisoners of war and civilians. It visited prison camps in order to improve conditions and set up offices to assist in tracing prisoners of war. These activities enhanced the organisation's reputation and in 1917 it was awarded the Nobel Peace Prize for its work. The war had shown that the national societies needed to cooperate more closely and in 1919 Henry Davidson of the American Red Cross, which had been very active during the war, succeeded in establishing the League of Red Cross Societies as an international NGO. However, while this objective was achieved, the attempt to gain power over the ICRC, whose status was protected by international law, failed. The first goal of the new institution was to help the inhabitants of countries that had suffered during the war.

Article 25 of the Covenant of the newly founded League of Nations encouraged the establishment and cooperation of 'duly authorised voluntary national Red Cross organisations having as purposes the improvement of health, the prevention of disease and the mitigation of suffering throughout the world'. At the same time this new IGO itself also became involved in the humanitarian field. When the situation of the many prisoners taken by the Russian armies and the disorganised state of Russia after the revolutionary events became a problem that went beyond the scope of the national Red Cross societies and the ICRC, they appealed to the Council of the League of Nations. The Council appointed Fridtjof Nansen, the famous Norwegian Arctic explorer and scientist, to set up relief plans for prisoners of war and to expedite their repatriation from both Germany and Siberia. Nansen contacted governments but also encouraged the work of NGOs and coordinated all activities. When in 1921 the League set up its Refugee Organisation, Gustave Ador of the ICRC was asked to become its High Commissioner. After he declined, Nansen accepted the position (Walters 1952: 99–100, 187) and was almost simultaneously appointed High Commissioner of the ICRC-convened Geneva Conference to deal with the severe famine in Russia. This led to the well-known controversy between Nansen and Herbert Hoover, who had organised relief work in Belgium and Central Europe during the First World War, on how to provide help to civilian populations. Hoover emphasised the neutral status of the Red Cross and insisted on working independently of the Soviet political authorities to deliver help, whereas Nansen was willing to give the aid to the Soviet authorities and leave it to them to distribute it according to their (political) criteria. This was the first major clash within humanitarian organisations, as well as between them and government authorities, on the demarcation of public and private humanitarian action. It revealed the unavoidable humanitarian dilemma when neutral humanitarian actors are faced with politics (Cabanes 2014).

During this period other private organisations were created to provide relief to the victims of war as well as other disasters, prominent among them the Save the Children Fund (SCF). Set up in May 1919 by Eglantyne Jebb, it arose out of opposition from British citizens to the continued Allied blockade of Germany after the armistice and aimed to provide direct relief to those suffering. Jebb insisted that relief should go to all children, including German ones, which was a controversial and courageous stand (Barnett 2011: 83). Money was raised quickly and the campaign became a permanent organisation, which dealt with emergency after emergency, starting with the Russian famine of 1921. The International Transportworkers Federation (ITF), led by Edo Fimmen who was aware of the international political situation, organised a boycott in 1920 of munitions transports to Poland for military intervention in Soviet Russia by former Allied powers and then through trade unions began arranging food relief for starving Russians between 1921 and 1923. International relief, whether warfare-related or not, had become the work of multiple actors. When an earthquake and a tsunami hit Japan in 1923, the Red Cross Movement (the ICRC and League combined) collected large sums of money to support the relief operation for survivors, but it was not the only humanitarian organisation to help and both the UK and the US assisted promptly by sending warships with food and other necessary supplies.

The ICRC continued its extension of international humanitarian law. The third Geneva Convention, adopted in 1929, prescribed that belligerent states must treat prisoners of war humanely at all times and entrusted the ICRC with the specific task of forwarding information on prisoners of war to their relatives. The Hague Law was not amended at this time, the 1925 Geneva Poison Gas Protocol, banning the use of poison gas and bacteriological weapons, being the exception. The ICRC in turn expanded and systemised its actions in internal wars, among others during the Spanish Civil War (1936–39). It also became active in Africa during the Italo-Abyssinian War (1935–36). Action during civil wars was not part of the Geneva Conventions at the time and it was not until 1977 that the second Additional Protocol to the four Geneva Conventions of 1949 (see below) would integrate internal armed conflicts in international humanitarian law.

Developments after the Second World War

As with the First World War, the ICRC entered the Second World War without strategic planning or a large staff. However, the main contributions of the ICRC and the national societies during the war (detention visits, delivery of relief and registration of persons) once again meant that the ICRC was awarded the Nobel Peace Prize, in 1944. But there were important criticisms: the ICRC's silence on the German concentration camps and the fate of the prisoners of war held by Japan and the Soviet Union. The UN Charter of 1945 did not explicitly mention the role of the ICRC, but in practice, in cases of conflict, the UN has called upon the ICRC for its good offices. Several UN agencies have engaged the International League (renamed International Federation in 1991) and national societies as partners in solving humanitarian problems.

The experience of the Second World War, with the atrocities committed against civilian populations such as the bombings of cities like London and Dresden, called for a revision of the Geneva Conventions. The idea was not new, as including this dimension in a revised Geneva Convention had already been suggested at the 1934 Tokyo international conference of the Red Cross Movement. Then, however, the proposal had been aborted, but it was once again discussed after 1945. The process of revising the existing Geneva Conventions was completed in 1949 with the four Geneva Conventions. The first Convention regulates war on land, the second war at sea and the third prisoners of war. The fourth deals with the protection of civilians in times of war, comprising various prohibitions with regard to citizens in occupied territories, such as deportation, the taking of hostages, torture and collective punishments. At the same time, and this is often overlooked, existing international humanitarian law theoretically and logically contradicts the proscription of war making in the UN Charter. The adoption of the four Conventions coincided with the division of the Allied powers into two blocs as manifested in the Cold War, for example in the coup in Prague, the blockade of Berlin, the civil wars in Greece and China, the war in Indochina and the nuclear arms race.

The ICRC and the Red Cross societies had up to that point dominated the field of humanitarian action in war. But new actors began to establish themselves in the domain of emergency relief. Among these were Oxfam and CARE. Oxfam was founded in the UK in 1942 as the Oxford Committee for Famine Relief, which, against the will of the British government, delivered humanitarian aid to the Greek population during the Second World War and the civil war in Greece. After the end of the Second World War Oxfam became active in other parts of Europe too, also arguing that Germans were equally deserving of relief, thus emphasising the principle of aid based on needs (Barnett 2011: 117–18). Later Oxfam developed into an international NGO with the objective of combating the causes of famine. CARE was set up by a number of American NGOs in 1945 to provide relief to the survivors of the war and it sent millions of lifesaving aid packages, first to the nations in Europe and later to Asia. Due to its shift in purpose its name was changed from 'Cooperative for American Remittances to Europe' to 'Cooperative for Assistance and Relief Everywhere' when it used American food surpluses to feed the hungry in the developing world during the 1950s and 1960s and it gradually developed long-term programmes for large-scale problems such as health care and famines.

Compared to the League of Nations, the UN system proved an active player in the field of humanitarian work in general. This began even before the UN was established, with the United Nations Relief and Rehabilitation Administration (UNRRA) set up by the Allied powers in 1943 to assist civilians from Allied nations and displaced persons in states liberated by their troops. But with the end of the war the refugee issue became prominent, even though that was seen as a temporary and local problem. It resulted in a permanent organisation operating worldwide, the UN High Commissioner for Refugees (UNHCR). The need to reconstruct post-war economies in general and solve problems related to food supplies, provision of capital and the protection of children specifically, led to the establishment of IGOs such as the Food and Agriculture Organization (FAO), the International Bank for Reconstruction and Development, the International Monetary Fund, the UN Children's Fund (UNICEF, originally set up on a temporary basis) and the World Health Organization (WHO). These organisations have acted as humanitarian actors in both the wider sense of humanitarian action (development and social welfare) and the narrow sense (providing emergency relief). Parallel to the creation of a wide array of IGOs, new NGOs were founded. IGOs have often worked in cooperation with NGOs, which did not keep the latter from developing into international actors in their own right in the fields of relief and development.

Growth and Diversification of NGOs

The institutionalisation process in the humanitarian domain in general, in terms of the participation of non-governmental actors in various policy domains and the regulatory activities of states, finally unfolded with full speed after the Second World War. The number of NGOs grew systematically and they became increasingly diversified. The *Yearbook of International Organisations* (2005/2006, volume IB: 2966) counted 832 international NGOs in 1951, 1,718 in 1964 and 2,795 in 1972, followed by no fewer than 13,768 in 1985. In the 1960s a first new group of NGOs, focusing on the problems of development and underdevelopment, augmented the existing ones. Somewhat later, in the 1970s, another group joined them: environmental organisations such as Greenpeace and the World Wildlife Fund. Around the same time various emergency relief organisations were created and development organisations expanded their missions by becoming active during conflicts or natural disasters. A general explanation could be that the complexity of problems was magnified by the ever-increasing interdependence in the world, partly due to discoveries and the identification of problems by scholars and practitioners, but also because NGOs became the advocates of issues that had not yet made it onto the political agenda. This is related to the growing importance of civil society. Civil-society organisations (CSOs) can be discerned in three functional forms: advocacy organisations, such as human-rights organisations, service delivery organisations, such as development or emergency relief organisations, and epistemic communities, producing and disseminating knowledge. In reality, most organisations do not limit themselves to only one of these three roles.

The World Culture Project by Boli and Thomas (1999) analysed the creation and dissolution of international NGOs, starting in 1875 and ending in 1975. The time series shows that before both the First and the Second World Wars the formation of international NGOs came close to zero, after periods of systematic growth. The approaching wars reduced the general international climate of cooperation which favours the creation of such actors and this deteriorated further the nearer the dangers of war came. After each of the wars the foundation of new international NGOs started again, reaching unprecedented heights after 1945. What the data also reveal is the continuing numbers of NGOs that are dissolved (Bloodgood 2011: 29–30). Longevity is not a general characteristic of NGOs.

A second element in the creation of NGOs is regionalism. Compared to universal NGOs, until the end of the Second World War only a very small number of regional NGOs existed, with a high point of 10 in 1935. Between 1965 and 1975 the creation of regional NGOs caught up with that of global ones, reaching 3,440 in 1985. The decolonisation process in the international system and the increase in independent sovereign states partly explain these trends, as the number of regional problems that are best dealt with at that rather than the global level is growing. Overall, democratisation also favoured increasing emancipation of CSOs outside Europe and North America.

The data with regard to the types of NGO analysed by the Johns Hopkins project (Anheier *et al.* 2001) show that around 40 per cent can be identified as social welfare or general humanitarian organisations. Emergency relief is not mentioned as such, which probably means that in terms of numbers it is of little significance. But obviously there are national differences. Comparing the global figures with those for the US, we see that of all US international NGOs 29 per cent are active in the emergency relief sector, while 21 per cent are involved in general development and assistance (Werker and Ahmed 2008: 80). The overall proportion of development and social welfare NGOs is much higher, as there are additional groupings that could also be subsumed under this category. The figures provide some rough estimates for NGOs globally and nationally.

The increasing differentiation among NGOs over time is in part the result of their growth. The oldest sectors, as discussed before, are the domains of conflict and peace as well as human rights, followed by development and environment. The example of the evolution of the environment sector as a function of the growth in knowledge is instructive, given its relationship to the growth in knowledge of environmental issues and threats (Jacobsen 2000). Around 1870 we find the first environment-related organisations, primarily concerned with the protection of animals and with affection as the basic motive. When knowledge increased, in terms of the exploitation of nature, organisations were created that focused on the issue of resources, relevant for instance in forestry. A new way of looking at nature and the environment started in the early 1970s, when the Club of Rome published its *Limits to Growth* (Meadows *et al.* 1972), which uses a systemic and integrated approach. Today nobody would contest that nature and human behaviour interact and that no simple causal pattern can provide a satisfactory explanation for environmental deterioration.

The narrowly defined humanitarian group of NGOs is not only a latecomer in the NGO world but is also a privileged sector, because international humanitarian law guarantees its activities. Furthermore, a mutual dependency exists between governments and IGOs on the one hand and NGOs on the other.

> Extrapolating from Development Initiatives estimates, it can be said that between two-thirds and three-quarters of all recorded humanitarian assistance is provided through the UN system, ICRC and a cartel of five consortia of transnational NGOs: World Vision, CARE, Oxfam, Save the Children and MSF [Médecins Sans Frontières].
>
> (Donini 2012: 187)

This indicates a growing concentration process in the emergency relief sector, with fewer actors providing an increasingly large share of the service delivery.

Three conditions have determined the growing institutionalisation of the sector:

1   the behaviour of states, which continuously improved international humanitarian law;
2   the institutionalisation of national and international governmental agencies in the emergency relief sector; and
3   the emergence and self-regulation of NGOs in this domain, both in terms of professional criteria and normative principles.

It is difficult to say who influenced whom: either the states induced NGO creation or the emergence of NGOs as new actors affected the relevance of humanitarian aid. In general terms democratic states certainly favoured the emancipation of civil society and its organisations for the pursuit of public goods. But it is also evident that the French MSF played an important role in the development of an ever-growing number of humanitarian actors. The fact is that the institutionalisation of the so-called international humanitarian system predominantly took place in the Western industrialised countries and established democracies. Governments in the rest of the world became players in this domain only recently, which is why they are referred to as 'new' donors. In Asia, Africa and Latin America, NGOs were created and became increasingly active, mainly in natural disasters but also during military conflicts. This is why one could argue that both the new actors (NGOs in particular) and the new donors are now integrating into the existing humanitarian system.

As a consequence, the assumption that the principles of humanitarian action are only Western and thus their universal character is questionable is wrong. The humanitarian principles are enshrined in international humanitarian law and imply the obligation of *all* states to help to save populations whose lives are in danger. The principles of humanitarian action that the Red Cross/Red Crescent Movement has formulated – humanity, impartiality, independence and neutrality – are derived from international humanitarian law. However, not all humanitarian NGOs subscribe to these principles in practice.

Principles of Humanitarian Action

The post-war experience was also relevant in the elaboration of the so-called principles of humanitarian action and the modification of the humanitarian principles that were laid down in international humanitarian law. The Red Cross/Red Crescent Movement had already begun to formulate and elaborate its principles after the First World War. Between 1955 and 1965 these principles were discussed more systematically. In his short volume *Les Principes de la Croix-Rouge,* Jean Pictet (1955) had expanded upon the seven principles of the movement. The discussion resulted in the proclamation of the Fundamental Principles of the Red Cross by the twentieth international conference of the Red Cross Movement in Vienna in 1965 and included governments as signatories to the Geneva Conventions.

The fundamental principles of humanitarian action are humanity, impartiality, neutrality and independence, as well as voluntary service, unity and universality. The first four are known as core humanitarian principles, relevant in the specification of emergency relief for all actors in this domain (the three additional ones relate to the Red Cross/Red Crescent organisations' specific roles and are irrelevant for the NGOs in general). Common Article 3 of the four Geneva Conventions, however, only refers to the principle of impartiality, which 'humanitarian actors such as the ICRC' have to respect. A number of organisations challenge the principle of neutrality by arguing that one cannot be neutral in a political, or an armed, conflict as it is not possible not to take sides. This also applies to the principle of impartiality, which implies that one should take care of every person whose life is endangered.

In 1994, the Red Cross/Red Crescent Movement published its Code of Conduct about the principles of humanitarian action, to which more than 520 organisations have now subscribed. Even though several others have been issued since then, the Red Cross/Red Crescent Code is regarded as the standard. Both the international humanitarian law conventions and the code(s) of conduct emphasise the complementary role of states and NGOs. Today the body of international humanitarian law includes

72 treaties, which are supplemented by several non-binding UN General Assembly Resolutions and by the European Consensus on Humanitarian Aid of December 2007 – also a non-binding document although adhered to by all EU member states. These various agreements are so impressive that David Rieff (2002) argued that there have never been better laws yet worse practices than in the twentieth century.

In terms of institutionalisation there have also been noticeable advances regarding the growing budgets for emergency relief. In 2012 the overall figure was about US$18 billion. The largest donors are the EU, with both EU and member-state contributions, the US and the UK.

In particular the UN-based humanitarian organisations, including its coordination system, have seen several cycles of reform. Because of its poor performance, the UN Disaster and Relief Organization (UNDRO) was replaced by the Department of Humanitarian Affairs (DHA), and complemented with the Inter-Agency Standing Committee (IASC) and the annual Consolidated Appeals process, based on UN General Assembly Resolution 46/182 of 1992. IASC includes representatives of the relevant humanitarian UN agencies, the International Organization for Migration, the ICRC and the International Federation, and two NGOs delegated by the international non-governmental organisation (INGO) network the International Council of Voluntary Agencies (ICVA). One of the purposes of UN resolution 46/182 was to establish a coordinating role in humanitarian emergencies for the UN Department of Humanitarian Affairs. In 1998 the DHA was superseded by the OCHA, the Office for the Coordination of Humanitarian Affairs, with an Emergency Relief Coordinator, who is simultaneously Under-Secretary-General of the UN, as its head. The cycle of UN reforms continued with the publication of the *Humanitarian Response Review* in 2005, establishing the so-called cluster system (bringing together international humanitarian actors in specific sectoral areas, such as refugee camps, water and sanitation, emergency shelter and early recovery). A humanitarian coordinator (nominated by OCHA) and humanitarian country teams accompanied this reform. In addition a UN Central Emergency Response Fund (CERF) of 500 million US dollars was created, which replaced the original Emergency Relief Fund of 50 million US dollars. The new fund makes it possible for the Emergency Relief Coordinator to quickly provide aid in emergencies, without the need to wait for voluntary contributions from the UN member states. The UN reforms are still going on. Equally, in 1992 the EU's Commission established its Humanitarian Aid and Civil Protection department (ECHO), which was made permanent after the first five years of its trial phase. In 2004 ECHO became the Directorate-General for Humanitarian Aid, integrating Civil Protection in 2010.

The NGOs in the field recognised the need to become organised in networks very early on. Examples include VOICE (Voluntary Organisations in Cooperation in Emergencies), created in Brussels in 1992, at the same time as ECHO, focusing on the EU and ICVA, which originally concentrated on development but then developed into a network for humanitarian aid with a global outlook and focus on the UN system. However, the real momentum for the institutional development of networks began after the Rwandan genocide of 1994. The first major evaluation of this failure to act by the international community was launched by the Danish agency for humanitarian aid DANIDA (Danish International Development Agency), which led to the SPHERE Project and ALNAP (Active Learning Network for Accountability and Performance). The SPHERE Project, set up in 1997, was a voluntary initiative to formulate minimum standards for humanitarian operations, while ALNAP became the reference forum for issues of evaluation and accountability, later also addressing other issues such as innovation. Finally, in 2009, the International Humanitarian Studies Association (IHSA) and its two-yearly World Conferences on Humanitarian Studies were created as the forum for discussing relevant issues in humanitarian crises.

As this short overview shows, the organisational institutionalisation process actually intensified relatively late (i.e. at the end of the Cold War, 1989–90). At the time the hope was that the anticipated process of democratisation would first of all reduce interstate armed conflict and secondly and simultaneously increase the respect for international humanitarian law. This hope was dashed, even though the number of interstate armed conflicts decreased to almost zero after the end of the Cold War. Yet the number of intra-state or non-international armed conflicts, which had started to increase in the 1980s, began to slowly decline only after 1994.

The two 1977 Additional Protocols to the Geneva Conventions on international and non-international armed conflict turned out to be based on wishful thinking. What happened instead was that humanitarian aid was increasingly politicised. The involvement of the military in humanitarian activities, which blurred the borders between what governments tried to do and what NGOs were supposed to do, became even more pronounced after 9/11, the 2001 terrorist attack on the US, and the ensuing fight against terrorism with the US at the forefront, when once again attempts to integrate emergency relief into security or stabilisation policies could be seen.

A closer look at the development of humanitarian NGOs reveals that until the Biafra war of secession (1967–70) the ICRC had a more or less uncontested monopoly on emergency relief action in interstate armed conflicts, with other international actors playing lesser roles. The frustration of a number of humanitarian workers during this civil war over the fact that they had been able to work in a foreign state only with the consent of its government, particularly formulated by Bernard Kouchner as a delegate of the ICRC, led to what one could call the beginning of the global humanitarian movement, with the creation of *sans frontièrisme* in France and the founding of MSF, Doctors without Borders, in 1971. The growth in government resources for emergency relief (i.e. humanitarian aid) from around US$700 million in the early 1980s attracted an increasing number of new actors, some expanding their missions from development to emergency relief, others being new creations. The Balkan Wars in the former Yugoslavia (1991–95) accelerated the expansion of this sector, although quite a few actors did not survive after the end of this conflict.

Given the different backgrounds of the growing number of humanitarian NGOs, with many attracted by the resources made available by national governments and IGOs, it is obvious that finding a consensus on standards and principles would be difficult. Yet they became conscious of the fact that they needed some standards and/or principles, in order to demonstrate that they were capable of self-regulation without any political interference. The most recent initiative is the outcome of discussions on professionalisation in general and certification in particular. This project is pursued by the Joint Initiative Standards with the strong support of the Steering Committee for Humanitarian Response (SCHR) and is related to certification. The SCHR includes the eight largest humanitarian NGOs and the ICRC, which given its legal status as guardian of international humanitarian law is not an NGO. Whether this initiative will be successful is another matter, as there are quite a number of sceptical NGOs that do not believe that practical solutions can be found to implement its objective. But it does show the intention of humanitarian organisations to demonstrate their efforts at professionalism.

The states, it seems, have also been concerned with principles and standards. One central issue is civil-military cooperation and the definition of specific roles. During the war in Kosovo the military had increased its involvement in humanitarian action already and the 'war on terror' from 2001 changed the relationship between humanitarians and the military dramatically. In Afghanistan this involvement culminated in the inclusion of humanitarian aid as an instrument in the counterinsurgency strategy of the nations, foremost by the US. However, this was contrary to the 2003 UN General Assembly Resolution on the use of the Military Civil Defence Assets and the so-called Oslo Guidelines (released in 1994 and updated in 2006 and 2007) on the division of labour between the military, specifically civil protection, and the humanitarian organisations. Both exclude a humanitarian role for military or civil defence units. The EU, which fully supports the UN General Assembly resolution and the Oslo Guidelines, made the issue clear in its 2007 European Consensus on Humanitarian Aid. The four basic principles of humanitarian action are explicitly postulated as the basis of the European Humanitarian Policy, with diversity listed as another constitutive policy principle. In other words, like most humanitarian NGOs and – naturally – the ICRC, the EU rejects the notion of the soldier as a humanitarian.

Yet when it comes to assessing the degree to which humanitarian law and the principles of humanitarian action have been implemented, and actually respected, the results are deceptive. Neither the states nor the parties to armed conflicts take the obligations imposed by international humanitarian law seriously if they regard them as contrary to their objectives, while at least some NGOs do not honour the principles in actions they have committed themselves to. There is a widespread lack of respect for international humanitarian law: humanitarian access is often impeded and humanitarian workers and recipients are all too often exposed to violence.

Conclusion

This short review documents the institutionalisation process in the humanitarian domain, both in its wider and its more restricted provision of public goods. Generally speaking the democratisation of societies and with it the emergence of new ideas led to the creation of non-governmental actors, which shows the importance of civil engagement. Institutionalisation in the humanitarian field started early, with the formulation of specific norms for international wars. For a long time the domain remained limited to the ICRC, but from the second half of the nineteenth century onwards the normative frame of reference has become larger and larger. This normative institutionalisation process continued until shortly after the collapse of the Soviet Union.

The core elements of the organisational institutionalisation are humanitarian policies of (predominantly) Western states which provide the necessary resources for emergency relief, non-governmental actors, instigated by MSF, which established themselves alongside the Red Cross/Red Crescent Movement, UN reform and finally the professionalisation and self-regulation of non-governmental actors, a direction the ICRC had taken earlier. Today the normative institutionalisation process can be considered to be robust, in the sense that its full implementation would ensure successful humanitarian action. Yet, this does not mean that the humanitarian system does not need to be improved further. Rather, the system needs to adapt to the new challenges its actors are facing: resurgence of the non-intervention principle and the hard-core notion of state sovereignty promoted by newly emerging donors such as China and Arab countries, instrumentalisation and politicisation of humanitarian aid, civil protection and military interference in emergency situations, threatening, if not ignoring, the fundamental principles of humanitarian action, and lastly the potential gap between limited resources on the one hand, and an increasing number of natural disasters on the other.

Which direction the system, or its actors, will take is unclear. Within the humanitarian NGO community there is no consensus on the proper role for humanitarian action. There are issues such as the extent to which it should include peace-making activities or human-rights strategies, and should one cooperate fully with the military or dissociate oneself from the armed forces? Some NGOs, journalists and government representatives even accuse the NGO community of a Western, if not imperialist, approach, although they forget that the overwhelming majority of aid comes from the rich Northern countries and that saving lives is not typically an exclusive Western strategy. Therefore how the international humanitarian system will evolve in the future is hard to assess, also because we do not know what the new donors, such as Brazil, China and the Arab Gulf states, as well as new actors, such as migrant and Islamic organisations, will do.

References

Anheier, H. Glasius, M. and Kaldor, M. (eds) (2001) *Global Civil Society*, Oxford: Oxford University Press.

Barnett, M. (2011) *Empire of Humanity: A History of Humanitarianism*, Ithaca, NY: Cornell University Press.

Bloodgood, E. (2011) 'The *Yearbook of International Organizations* and Quantitative Non-State Actor Research', in: B. Reinalda (ed.) *The Ashgate Research Companion to Non-State Actors*, Farnham: Ashgate, 19–33.

Boli, J. and Thomas, G.M. (eds) (1999) *Constructing World Culture: International Nongovernmental Organizations since 1875*, Stanford, CA: Stanford University Press.

Cabanes, B. (2014) *The Great War and the Origins of Humanitarianism 1918–1924*, Cambridge: Cambridge University Press.

Davies, T. (2013) *NGOs: A New History of Transnational Civil Society*, London: Hurst & Company.

Donini, A. (2012) 'Humanitarianism, Perceptions, Power', in: C. Abu-Sada (ed.) *In the Eyes of Others: How People in Crisis Perceive Humanitarian Aid*, New York: MSF-USA, 183–192.

Eberwein, W.-D. (2011) 'Politics and the World of Humanitarian Aid', in: B. Reinalda (ed.) *The Ashgate Research Companion to Non-State Actors*, Farnham: Ashgate, 363–375.

Finnemore, M. (1996) *National Interests in International Society*, Ithaca, NY: Cornell University Press.

Forsythe, D.P. (2005) *The Humanitarians: The International Committee of the Red Cross*, Cambridge: Cambridge University Press.

Forsythe, D.P. and Rieffer-Flanagan, B.A.J. (2007) *The International Committee of the Red Cross: A Neutral Humanitarian Actor*, Abingdon: Routledge.

Jacobsen, S. (2000) 'Transnational Environmental Groups, Media, Science, and Public Sentiment(s) in Domestic Policy-Making on Climate Change', in: R.A. Higgott, G.R.D. Underhill and A. Bieler (eds) *Non-State Actors and Authority in the Global System*, Abingdon: Routledge, 274–289.

Meadows, D.H., Meadows, D.L., Randers, J. and Behrens III, W.W. (1972) *Limits to Growth*, New York: New American Library.

Pictet, J. (1955) *Les Principes de la Croix-Rouge*, Geneva: ICRC.

Reinalda, B. (2009) *Routledge History of International Organizations: From 1815 to the Present Day*, Abingdon: Routledge.

Rieff, D. (2002) *A Bed for the Night: Humanitarianism in Crisis*, New York: Simon & Schuster.

Seary, B. (1996) 'The Early History from the Congress of Vienna to the San Francisco Conference', in: P. Willetts (ed.) *'The Conscience of the World': The Influence of Non-Governmental Organizations in the UN System*, London: Hurst & Company, 15–30.

Tilly, C. (2004) *Social Movements, 1768–2004*, Boulder, CO: Paradigm Publishers.

Walters, F.P. (1952) *A History of the League of Nations*, Westport: Greenwood Press.

Werker, E. and Ahmed, F.Z. (2008) 'What Do Nongovernmental Organizations Do?', *Journal of Economic Perspectives*, 22(2):73–92.

Part II
New Donor Humanitarianism

2 India as Humanitarian Actor

Convergences and Divergences with DAC Donor Principles and Practices

Kristina Roepstorff

Introduction

For decades, the discourse and practice of foreign aid has been dominated by a small group of industrialised states that have come together in the Organisation for Economic Co-operation and Development (OECD) Development Assistance Committee (DAC). These states have established a set of principles, norms and best practices for delivering Official Development Assistance (ODA). Within the DAC aid regime, ODA entails both long-term development cooperation and short-term humanitarian action, channelled either bilaterally or multilaterally. The aim of such humanitarian action is to 'save lives, alleviate suffering and maintain and protect human dignity during and in the aftermath of emergencies' (OECD no date a). Accordingly, humanitarian action includes disaster prevention and preparedness, reconstruction, relief coordination, protection and support services, emergency food aid and other emergency relief activities. At the heart of DAC humanitarian action are the well-established and widely recognised principles of humanity, impartiality, neutrality and independence.

Recent years have seen a growing importance of and interest in so-called 'emerging donors' or 'new donors' who, to a large extent, operate outside the framework of the DAC. However, the labelling of these donors as 'new' or 'emerging' is problematic in several ways; using the term 'emerging' places these donors within the broader debate on 'emerging powers' and 'emerging economies', which comes with its own sets of underlying assumptions and controversy (Cohen 2001: 31; Mawdsley 2012: 4).[1] Furthermore, the label 'new donor' is also problematic in its implication that these donors have only recently engaged in providing foreign aid. This view is reinforced by the fact that many of these donors have been, and as in the case of India, continue to be, principal recipients of foreign aid.

Although the relatively recent interest by scholars and policymakers suggests otherwise, many of these non-DAC donors like China, Brazil, or India actually have a long-standing record of providing aid (Manning 2006: 384; Mawdsley 2012: 77; Smith 2011). Hence, the assumption of aid being exclusively provided by the 'developed global North' to the 'developing global South' gives a distorted picture of actual aid flows. DAC and non-DAC aid have coexisted since at least the mid-twentieth century, with a major increase by non-DAC donors over the last decade (Manning 2006). Smith (2011: 7) finds that humanitarian action from non-DAC donors increased from US$34.7 million in 2000 to US$622.5 million in 2010. Yet, the comprehensive AidData database does not capture information on aid flows for any non-DAC donors except for Kuwait, Saudi Arabia and Taiwan (Sinha and Hubbard 2012). While this lack of data on non-DAC donors renders it difficult to accurately assess their contribution to foreign aid in general and humanitarian action in particular, a growing number of historical studies suggest that non-DAC donors have engaged in overseas development and humanitarian aid for quite some time (Celik 2014).

The alternative term 'post-colonial donor', proposed in reference to India (Six 2009), has the advantage of 'disrupting Orientalist binaries which set up the "North" as giver and the "South" as receiver'. Though this label may be useful in the case of India, it excludes other important actors operating outside the DAC framework, such as China and Russia. It also raises the question of whether former colonies like Canada or the US should be included into this category (Mawdsley 2012: 5). As with many labels in the social sciences, none of the terms that have been evoked in order to take into account the diversification of international humanitarian donorship seem entirely suitable. This chapter is mainly concerned with the degree of convergence or divergence between the Indian principles and practices of humanitarian action and those of the DAC donors. Therefore, the use of the term 'non-DAC donors' seems the most fitting for the aims of this chapter.[2]

Having embarked on the path of economic growth, a number of non-DAC countries have not only repositioned themselves vis-à-vis the 'global North', but also have increased their engagement in the foreign aid arena (Smith 2011). The growing engagement of non-DAC donors in the international aid regime was, however, not met with unmitigated enthusiasm by the DAC members. Instead, it invoked concern surrounding how they would 'change the face of international cooperation' (Manning 2006: 1) and how their growing importance in the international aid architecture would lead to an undermining of the norms and principles that have been so painstakingly achieved (Dreher *et al.* 2011; Severino and Ray 2009). To say that a general uneasiness about their motives and norms exists seems to be an understatement. As Woods (2008: 1207) notes, non-DAC donors are accused of 'introducing and pushing "toxic ideas" that would harm both poor countries and established donors'. Their 'rogue aid' (Naim 2007) has been perceived as posing a serious threat to the existing multilateral aid regime. Questions have also been raised regarding the extent to which the DAC-established aid framework may need to be modified (Kim and Lightfoot 2011; Paulo and Reisen 2010). Despite these reservations, little systematic research has been conducted on non-DAC donors, their motives, or the norms that guide their engagement in the provision of foreign aid.

The field of humanitarian action has received particularly little attention. Whereas humanitarian assistance does not constitute the lion's share of foreign aid, humanitarian expenditure by both DAC and non-DAC donors have risen notably over the last two decades (GHA 2013). Though most official humanitarian action still comes from traditional DAC donors, the last decade in particular has seen an increase in non-DAC donor engagement in the humanitarian arena. A recent study by the Centre for Policy Research found that India's foreign aid has increased fourfold from 2003 to 2014 with most aid being provided to neighbouring countries (CPR 2013). Since 2005, India contributed US$56.5 million in humanitarian aid, not including unreported aid to Bhutan and Nepal, and became the fifth largest bilateral donor to Afghanistan. As humanitarian action is, however, not listed separately but subsumed under technical and economic cooperation, no detailed figures are available from India's annual reports. Thus, apart from insufficient data, the fact that the non-DAC donor definition of what constitutes foreign aid does not correspond to the DAC definition also helps explain the general misconception of aid flows (Smith 2011: 4).

In light of India's increasing contribution to international humanitarian action in both its immediate neighbourhood and beyond, this chapter explores the degree of isomorphism between the humanitarian principles and practices of India and DAC donors. It follows a constructivist approach that examines how actors emerge and find their organisational niche while not only being influenced by their organisational environment but also accepting, rejecting, or modifying existing humanitarian principles and practices, thereby ultimately contributing to the politics of humanitarian crises. The analysis draws upon secondary data, relevant official documents and statements as well as specific examples of India's humanitarian action. This chapter's contribution is thus twofold: first, it provides particular knowledge on the principles and practices guiding India's approach to humanitarian action; second, it contributes to the more general discussion of how the humanitarian action of non-DAC donors may change and (re) construct international aid regimes.

India's Foreign Policy and Humanitarian Action

When governments engage in humanitarian action, it is part of their foreign policy agenda. Foreign aid is essentially a foreign policy tool and therefore subject to the 'same strategic calculations ... made in other [policy] areas' (Mawdsley 2012: 27). India's humanitarian engagement thus has to be placed within the broader context of its foreign policy. When analysing the principles and preferences of Indian foreign policy, two important factors stand out: first, the region's historical experiences, above all with regards to colonialism. Malone writes that 'how Indians conceive of their country, its origins, its development through history, and its past relations with others is a vital component of how they imagine, construct, and aspire to develop India's contemporary international relations' (2011: 19). The second important factor is how domestic concerns feed into India's foreign policy strategy. This is especially relevant in relation to its immediate neighbours, who are also – as will be discussed later – the principal recipients of India's foreign aid.

India's Foreign Policy in a Nutshell: Historical Legacies and Current Strategic Interests

India's foreign policy since independence in 1947 can be divided into three main phases: Nehruvian idealism in the 1950s and 1960s; a realist turn in the 1970s and 1980s; and a pragmatic shift in the 1990s. India's foreign policy in the aftermath of independence, the first phase, has to be seen in the light of its colonial experience, the struggle for independence and the bloody partition of the subcontinent. Primarily associated with India's first Prime Minister Jawaharlal Nehru, the first decades after independence became dominated by a policy of strategic autonomy and non-interventionism and a siding with other 'Third World' countries against the 'imperialist forces of the West' (Malone 2011: 49). During the 1950s and 1960s, within the context of the Cold War, India followed a policy of international independence and non-alignment, which Nehru described as 'the natural consequence of an independent nation functioning according to its own rights' (cited in Malone 2011: 252).

Conflicts with neighbouring China (1962 and 1965) and Pakistan (1971) and a leadership change at the domestic level prompted a realist turn in Indian foreign policy (Ogden 2011: 10). Indira Gandhi's *Realpolitik* at home and abroad, an alignment with the Soviet Union and interventions in East Pakistan and Sri Lanka dominated India's foreign policy during this second phase between the 1970s and 1980s. Tellingly, in a speech in 1970, Indira Gandhi stated that the problems of developing countries needed to be faced 'not merely by idealism, not merely by sentimentalism, but by very clear thinking and hard-headed analysis' (cited in Malone 2011: 50).

The end of the Cold War and the accompanying transition from a planned to a free market economy resulted in the third major shift in India's foreign policy. A more pragmatic course was adopted, with India shedding its 'non-aligned and anti-Western ideologies' (Malone 2011: 52). This allowed normalising relationships with neighbouring countries as well as a greater commitment to international institutions in line with the country's growing power and aspirations. In addition to better relations with China, this shift manifested itself in India's 1992 Look East Policy, which aimed at improving relations with Asia and ASEAN. In 1996, the so-called Gujral-Doctrine dominated India's foreign policy (Murthy 1999). The doctrine, named after the then Prime Minister I.K. Gujral, underlined the importance of maintaining friendly relations with neighbouring countries and reinforced the principle of non-interference in their internal affairs (Gujral 1998). In line with the Nehruvian foreign policy tradition of non-interventionism, the Gujral Doctrine constituted a break with India's interventionist foreign policy of the years before.

Today, India's foreign policy displays both realist and idealist features, standing in continuous tension with each other (Stuenkel 2013: 347). Whereas traits of Nehruvian idealism are still discernible, Indian foreign policy is increasingly characterised by a growing pragmatism, and this is also reflected in its foreign aid. Calculating the 'strategic benefit' of such aid, India is principally concerned with the promotion of its economic interests, its graduation to the high table of international relations and enhancing its security within the immediate neighbourhood and beyond (Mawdsley 2012: 70). At the same time, anti-imperialism, anti-colonialism and a sense of solidarity with other former colonised countries, reflected for instance in South–South cooperation,[3] still form the ideological basis of India's foreign aid.

Providing Humanitarian Action: India's Foreign Policy Rationale

Considering the domestic challenges of mass poverty and vulnerability to disasters that India continues to face, the question arises of why India has increased its contribution to international humanitarian action. As with all donors, the motives for providing aid stem from both a genuine desire to alleviate suffering and from economic and political interests (Dreher *et al.* 2011: 1951; Manning 2006; Meier and Murthy 2011). Indeed, humanitarianism and the idea of giving to the needy lies at the heart of Indian cultural values – as reflected in the term *dāna* which stands for the religious practice of non-reciprocal giving in Hinduism, Jainism and Buddhism (Bornstein 2012; Heim 2004; Meier and Murthy 2011: 7) and the Islamic concepts of *zakat* and *sadaqa*, which take the form of charitable giving (Khan 2012; Krafess 2005).

Politically, India uses humanitarian action as a soft-power instrument to foster friendly relations with other countries. Soon after independence, India sought to establish friendly relations with neighbours like Nepal and Bhutan by providing substantial aid. In doing so, it was looking to secure regional allies and create buffer states in light of the conflict with Pakistan and rivalry with China. Moreover, as Chanana (2009: 11) notes, a 'new consciousness of aid as an instrument of foreign policy' has inspired India's rising expenditure in the field of foreign aid, in order to foster its economic interests and to gain access to new markets and energy supplies both in its neighbourhood and beyond. For instance, India's relations with African countries are strongly driven by its search for energy supplies and economic interests (Mawdsley and McCann 2011; Taylor 2012: 780), as is its increasing engagement with Central Asian countries (Shivakumar *et al.* 2014).

By staging itself as a responsible donor and maintaining friendly relations with other countries, India seeks to advance its global power ambition and gain support for its bid to a permanent seat on the UN Security Council (Mawdsley 2012: 73; Rowlands 2012: 636). India's ready provision of relief aid to other countries in the immediate aftermath of the 2004 Indian Ocean tsunami and its rejection of incoming assistance demonstrated its pre-eminence within South Asia and its aspiration to become a power of global significance (Price 2005: 17). India wants to change its image from a needy recipient of aid to a strong, independent nation. When in 2003, the Government, under the leadership of the conservative Bharatiya Janata Party (BJP), launched the India Development Initiative, a large part of the budget for development cooperation was spent on the 'India Shining' campaign that celebrated India's economic success in order to attract foreign investors (Price 2004).

India's Shift from Recipient to Donor

When India gained independence from British colonial rule, it faced serious development challenges. Despite the government's reluctance to become so, the country was soon one of the world's major aid recipients (Mawdsley 2012: 71; Price 2005: 3). However, India also established itself as an important provider of aid, especially in its immediate neighbourhood. Although data is still scarce, a new wave of historical research is likely to provide insight in the near future.

In the 1950s, India signed the Colombo Plan, a framework for bilateral cooperation between countries in South and Southeast Asia, comprising South–South cooperation and technical assistance for economic and social development (Colombo Plan no date). It also provided substantial aid to neighbouring Nepal in 1951 and to Bhutan in the 1960s (Mawdsley 2012: 71; Price 2005: 7). By 1964, India had founded the Indian Technical and Economic Cooperation Programme (ITEC), through which the country's bilateral aid was to be channelled.

Various political interests and ideological factors therefore informed India's aid programmes. The ideological facets of India's post-independence aid policy are closely tied to Nehru's policy of non-alignment and the formation of the Non-Alignment Movement (NAM) in the 1950s. Though foreign aid was never central to the NAM, some principles echo in today's non-DAC aid discourse (Mawdsley 2012: 63). With its anti-colonial leanings, the NAM promoted assistance between newly independent developing states and South–South cooperation while upholding the respect for sovereignty and territorial integrity. These principles continue to be at the core of Indian and other non-DAC aid programmes (Harmer and Cotterrell 2005: 5). Indeed, India seems particularly keen to cooperate with other countries of the 'global South', as illustrated by the India–Brazil–South Africa (IBSA) initiative (Rowlands 2012: 643).

While on a global scale Indian foreign aid has been minor until recently, two events signified a remarkable shift in India's position within the international aid regime, also demonstrating how India constructed itself as a donor. After a decade of economic liberalisation and growth, the BJP-led government in 2003 announced that all but its six largest donors were to cease their aid flows into India. Other donors were to channel future aid through either NGOs or multilateral agencies (Price 2005: 3). While this was justified by a need to cut administration costs, it was also a clear demonstration of India's aspirations to change its image from recipient to generous donor. This new attitude is captured in the 2003/04 budget speech of the then finance minister, Jaswant Singh (cited in Price 2004: 4):

> A stage has come in our development where we should now, firstly, review our dependence on external donors. Second, extend support to the national efforts of other developing countries. And, thirdly, re-examine the line of credit route of international assistance to others ... [w]hile being grateful to all our development partners of the past, I wish to announce that the Government of India would now prefer to provide relief to certain bilateral partners, with smaller assistance packages, so that their resources can be transferred to specified non-governmental organisations (NGOs) in greater need of official development assistance.

To underscore its new aid policy, India paid off outstanding debts to 14 bilateral donors, announced debt relief to seven African countries and launched a new aid programme, the aforementioned Indian Development Initiative (Mawdsley 2012: 74). The new foreign aid policy was, however, abolished just one year later by the Congress-led government (Price 2005: 3). Nevertheless, India has pursued changing its status from recipient of aid to a donor of international standing ever since. This general shift in India's aid policy was prominently reflected (and heavily criticised) in its rejection of incoming humanitarian action after the 2004 Indian Ocean tsunami. Instead, it was among the first countries to provide emergency aid to other affected countries like Sri Lanka, Indonesia and the Maldives (Rowlands 2012: 636; Price 2005: 15). This highlighted India's shift from recipient to donor and received vast international (media) attention.

As stated earlier, India's foreign aid has increased fourfold from 2003 to 2014 (CPR 2013). According to the Ministry of External Affairs (MEA) Outcome Budget Report 2013–14, nearly 47 per cent of the ministry's overall budget pertains to technical and economic cooperation with other countries (Ministry of Finance 2014: 12). Most aid goes to South Asia (76 per cent), but the share going to Africa and Latin America (3 and 4 per cent respectively) is growing rapidly from a very small base. Though not listed separately, the substantial provision of humanitarian action to a number of countries shows that its scope and expenditures are increasing too. In South Asia, the largest recipients are Pakistan, Afghanistan, Sri Lanka and Bangladesh. India was the largest government donor to the 2010 Pakistan floods and an important donor during the 2005 Pakistan earthquake (GHA 2013). Increasingly, India also provides humanitarian action beyond its immediate neighbourhood and was among the first countries to provide humanitarian action in the aftermath of the 2010 Haiti earthquake. In 2011, it pledged US$8 million for humanitarian action to countries in the Horn of Africa (MEA 2011). Furthermore, it provided humanitarian action to the people of Palestine and Lebanon (2006), Kyrgyzstan (2005), Mongolia (2008), North Korea (2009), Libya and Yemen (2012) (MEA 2012). In 2013, India, 'being deeply conscious of the humanitarian dimension of the conflict' supplied food items to Syria through the World Food Programme (WFP) and pledged US$2.5 million towards humanitarian action at the 2nd International Pledging Conference for Syria in 2014.[4] Recently, India has provided assistance to cyclone-affected areas of the Philippines, Bangladesh and Fiji (Ministry of Finance 2014: 16).

At the same time, about 40 per cent of the Indian population continue to live on less than US$1.25 a day. In 2008, India was the eighth-largest ODA recipient (US$2.1 billion) and fourth overall from 1995–2009 (IRIN 2011). Despite economic growth since economic reforms were introduced in the 1990s, India continues to struggle with mass poverty and socio-economic problems. This makes it difficult for India to sell increasing expenditure on foreign aid at home (Price 2005: 18). The impact of the economic slowdown on India's engagement in humanitarian action remains unclear. However, with the BJP in power once again in 2014, it is likely that India will claim its place even more assertively as a strong and independent nation in its international relations, including through foreign aid instruments (BJP 2014: 39–40; Mullen 2014).

At the same time, India itself is vulnerable to disasters. Between 2002 and 2011, China and India have accounted for 78 per cent of people affected by natural disasters. Receiving little international assistance, both countries have taken an increasingly strong role in responding to disasters within their own borders (GHA 2013). To increase disaster preparedness, address vulnerabilities and mitigate the impact of disaster, the Indian government passed the Disaster Management Act in 2005. This also foresaw the establishment of the National Disaster Management Authority (NDMA) and State Disaster Management Authorities (SDMAs). These bodies aim to implement a 'holistic and integrated approach to Disaster Management'. They are now part of India's institutional structure of humanitarian action. India also increasingly shares its experience in disaster risk assessment, risk prevention, mitigation and preparedness and disaster response, relief, recovery and reconstruction regionally and internationally. In response to the 2004 Indian Ocean tsunami, member states of the South Asian Association for Regional Cooperation (SAARC) established the SAARC Disaster Management Centre (SDMC) in New Delhi. Through this and the South Asian Disaster Knowledge Network (SADKN), which was launched by the SDMC, India shares knowledge with other SAARC members on various dimensions of disaster management.[5] At the global level, the NDMA has participated in joint trainings; for instance, in the 2010 Tunisia chemical mock-exercise, it sent trainers to Singapore and cooperated and exchanged knowledge with Switzerland and the United States. In 2011, the NDMA dispatched its National Disaster Response Force (NDRF) for the first time ever in response to the 2011 Japan tsunami (Bhalla no date).

Institutional Structure of India's Humanitarian Action

Though India's institutional structures in the field of foreign aid are highly fragmented, the MEA remains the key agency in India's provision of aid. Within the MEA, a number of geographically and functionally specialised divisions make and implement decisions on humanitarian action. However, due to high levels of fragmentation and lack of cooperation, the budget for humanitarian action is divided between different ministries and aid instruments (Meier and Murthy 2011: 9–11). In line with the broader aim of strengthening the Indian Foreign Service (IFS), India in 2012 took a first step in establishing a long-announced foreign aid agency. The newly established Development Partnership Administration (DPA) remains, however, a department of the MEA. Its objective is to manage India's aid projects. It is divided into three divisions: DPA I deals with project appraisal and lines of credit; DPA II deals with capacity building schemes, disaster relief and the Indian Technical and Economic Cooperation Programme (ITEC); and DPA III deals with project implementation. The ITEC is a government-funded programme, which is also administered by the MEA. As stated on its website, 'it is a demand-driven development scheme which aims at bilateral cooperation and partnership for mutual benefit'. ITEC invites countries to 'share in the Indian development experience' and consists of six components: training (civilian and defence) in India of nominees from ITEC partner countries; projects and project-related activities such as feasibility studies and consultancy services; deputation of Indian experts abroad; study tours; gifting/donation of equipment; and aid for disaster relief.[6] However, both the MEA and the DPA continue to suffer from a lack of staff, resources and strategy (Roepstorff 2013). Unlike China, India still has no formal policy document, and the establishment of the DPA in 2012 merely presents a new institutional arrangement rather than constituting a real shift in India's aid policy (Campbell and Suri 2013).

Another key actor, India's armed forces actively engage in the implementation of humanitarian action (Meier and Murthy 2011: 13). Being the third-largest contributor to UN peacekeeping and having long-term experience in dealing with disasters domestically, India's armed forces were, for instance, charged with providing humanitarian relief during the 1993–94 UN Operation in Somalia (Price 2005: 14). Yet, strained relations with neighbouring countries prevent India's armed forces from acting in a long-term capacity in the immediate neighbourhood and limit its aid activities in the region (Harmer and Cotterrell 2005: 13). For instance, aid from India was rejected by Bangladesh in the aftermath of the 1988 flooding (Price 2005: 14).

Apart from the armed forces, the country's National Disaster Management Authority is likely to increasingly dispatch the National Disaster Response Force (NDRF) internationally after its first successful deployment to Japan in 2011 (Bhalla no date). Similarly, the National Crisis Management Committee (NCMC), an inter-ministerial coordination committee, has also reacted to crises abroad. Though the private sector is likely to increasingly engage in external assistance, as with the tsunami relief effort, Indian NGOs play a marginal role so far in humanitarian action abroad (Meier and Murthy 2011: 14; Price 2005: 5). However, as indicated by Tony Vaux in this volume, numerous Indian organisations play a vital role in disaster mitigation and relief at the national and local levels.

A Divergence or Convergence of Principles and Practice of Humanitarian Action

Rowlands (2012: 633) asserts that global and regional powers, with their differing economic, political and military strengths and their specific geopolitical agendas, are less likely to simply accept or adhere to traditional DAC norms. Instead, they may challenge the 'Western-dominated system'. This assertion supports the constructivist argument in this volume and India is no exception to this. A regional power in South Asia, India has become an increasingly important actor in the international playing field of foreign aid and has leverage in shaping the discourse and influencing the practices of humanitarian action. This is especially important as India operates outside the DAC and the Good Humanitarian Donorship Initiative. Thereby, India's significance as a non-DAC donor has more to do with its ability to challenge the 'mainstream' than with the actual size of its aid programmes (Mawdsley 2012: 74). In comparison with other non-DAC donors, India's contribution in foreign aid lags behind countries like Saudi Arabia, Kuwait, the United Arab Emirates, South Korea or China (GHA 2013: fig. 2.7). Though figures in humanitarian action are less consistent and more fluctuating, India is not the most significant of the non-DAC donors here either (Smith 2011). Nonetheless, India – a country that has taken a lead role in speaking on behalf of developing countries since its independence – actively shapes international humanitarian action (Chanana 2009: 12) with the potential of constructing and changing the politics of humanitarian crises.

In 2007, India promoted the creation of the Development Cooperation Forum (DCF) under the United Nations' Economic and Social Council. The DCF differs from the DAC in that it is composed of both donors and recipients of aid, 'seeking to identify mutually acceptable principles and priorities' (Chanana 2009: 12). At the regional level, India, as a member of SAARC, signed a disaster cooperation agreement with neighbouring countries at the 17th Annual Summit in 2012. This agreement obliges member states to take legislative and administrative measures, including the development of standard operating procedures, to implement its provisions. As the agreement is based on the key principles of sovereignty and territorial integrity, assistance will only be provided upon request by the affected state (Cipullo 2012). This echoes the NAM principles at the core of India's aid policy.

Principles Guiding India's Humanitarian Action

India – like other non-DAC donors – has been accused of being guided by mere self-interest in humanitarian engagement and of eroding the merit-based DAC system of aid provision (Naim 2007; Manning 2006). This understanding of the rationale behind India's engagement in humanitarian and development assistance finds resonance in India itself. In 2012, a group of prominent Indian analysts and policymakers, supported by senior officials in the Indian government, attempted to formally identify the basic principles that should guide India's foreign and strategic policy. Their report, *Nonalignment 2.0* (Khilnani *et al.* 2013: 34) discusses India's strategic opportunities, stating:

> India is operating in a context where rapidly growing economies like China have become substantial bilateral donors. Such new donor states have also got the ability to invest immense resources in the creation of new institutions. The entrance of new donor states, and donor competition between them and the old donor states, is a feature of the new global economic landscape. While India is now bulking up and systematising its aid program, more attention and resources will be needed to be given to this. This aid could potentially open strategic opportunities and spaces.

However, determining this as a specificity of non-DAC donor approach to aid seems difficult to uphold when 'the reality of established donors often falls short of their rhetoric and therefore DAC norms' too (Kim and Lightfoot 2011: 715). Just like other countries, India thus has to 'reconcile the tension between geopolitical strategy and humanitarian benevolence, and their tolerance of gaps between rhetoric and action' (Rowlands 2012: 637). In a comparison of the allocation behaviour of new and old donors, Dreher *et al.* (2011) find that allegations of aid being driven by mere self-interest seem to be exaggerated for both groups of donors. There is also a genuine desire to alleviate suffering and an aspiration to be perceived as a moral and responsible international actor.

Although there exists no official Indian policy on foreign aid in general or humanitarian action in particular, the priorities and principles that guide engagement in the humanitarian field can be derived from statements, official documents and practice. Their analysis shows that while India subscribes to the international humanitarian principles of universality, impartiality and neutrality, it is also guided by other principles that present major divergences with DAC norms (Meier and Murthy 2011: 7–8). Price (2005: 3) identified three central ideas underlying India's attitude towards aid: first, aid is given for political and economic purposes and can be an effective means for improving bilateral relations; second, giving the wrong kind of aid can be counterproductive; and third, conditional aid can be degrading for the recipient. These ideas feed into India's principles and practice of humanitarian action. Apart from its colonial past and Nehruvian legacy, these ideas stem from the country's own experiences as an aid recipient and its desire to free itself from outside interference. Thus, in the spirit of the NAM and the Five Principles of Peaceful Coexistence (Panchsheel),[7] India strongly adheres to the principles of non-interference and respect for the sovereignty of other states (Meier and Murthy 2011: 7; Paulo and Reisen 2010: 549). Undoubtedly, respect for the sovereignty of the affected state is a fundamental principle that guides India's approach to foreign aid and lies at the heart of controversies between India and DAC donors.

Until recently, countries in need of outside assistance had little choice other than complying with DAC donor policies (Dreher *et al.* 2011: 1951, cit. Gilpin 2001). With a diversification in humanitarian donorship, recipient countries are now increasingly in a position to decide whom they accept assistance from (Paulo and Reisen 2010: 535). Objecting to the politicisation of aid and emphasising the principle of non-interference, India rejects aid conditionality (Price 2005; Rowlands 2012: 636). Thus, India has resisted pressure from the DAC to sign the Paris Declaration for aid effectiveness and attaches far less conditionality to its aid, seeking to give beneficiaries a greater voice in the process and not using aid as a means to demand regime change or interfere domestically (Chanana 2009: 12). This, of course, provides a welcome alternative to countries suspicious of the hidden or open political agendas of 'Western' donors. Whereas India and other non-DAC donors have been accused of undermining the 'governance and democratisation agenda of DAC donors' (Dreher *et al.* 2011: 1951), its policy also provides a niche for Indian humanitarian action. Due to its objection to the politicisation of aid, India was one of the first countries the military regime in Myanmar granted access to when Cyclone Nargis hit the country's delta region.

Another related controversy concerns transparency and accountability. Operating outside the OECD framework, non-DAC donors are not subject to the same reporting obligations as DAC donors. However, transparency is an essential principle of DAC aid. While a number of non-DAC donors make their aid information accessible and report voluntarily, India's level of reporting to various established databases is low (Smith 2011: fig. 24). Paulo and Reisen (2010: 550) note, 'while India does share the transparency features of Western democracies, its development policy is not exactly transparent'. This applies equally to its humanitarian action, which is not listed separately but seen as part of its development assistance. Moreover, India has been criticised for not monitoring how its aid is spent, as there are no control or reporting mechanisms in place (Meier and Murthy 2011: 34). India's deficient monitoring mechanism may be explained by the country's fragmented aid architecture and the fact that it emphasises non-interference and provides aid with 'no strings attached'.

Divergent Labels and Practices: Who and What

While the term 'donor' is generally accepted within the DAC-system, many non-DAC actors refuse to use this term as for them, it reflects the hierarchical structure of traditional aid from donors to recipients. Thus, like Brazil, India prefers to refer to itself as a 'partner' rather than 'donor' (Meier and Murthy 2011: 8). This is also reflected in the name of the country's newly established aid agency, the Development *Partnership* Administration.

Different understandings of what counts as humanitarian action and how it is to be distinguished from development cooperation are a 'potential source of misunderstanding' between different humanitarian actors (Binder and Meier 2011: 1138). While India now shares the DAC's conceptual distinction between short-term relief aid and development assistance, it emphasises the need to link immediate relief to long-term development and has played an important role in the drafting of the General Assembly Resolution 64/251 from 2010 on linking relief, rehabilitation and development (LRRD) (Meier and Murthy 2011: 6ff.). As a result, both in its rhetoric and in its budget categories, India does not clearly differentiate between development and humanitarian action.

Moreover, the government of India uses the terms 'humanitarian assistance' or 'disaster relief' only in reference to activities that address human suffering caused by natural disasters. This definition is narrower than the DAC definition; it excludes the protection of civilian populations affected by armed conflicts (Meier and Murthy 2011: 6). A closer look at India's actual engagement in humanitarian action shows, however, that it has also provided aid to conflict-affected countries. In Sri Lanka, for instance, India provided aid to conflict-affected areas in 1987 and, more recently, to internally displaced persons (Ministry of Finance 2014: 15). Similarly, the Outcome Budget 2013–14 (ibid.) shows that India has been active in other conflict-affected regions: the same paragraph that states that India has responded to humanitarian challenges from natural disasters also includes the fact that 'relief supply and medicines have been supplied to war-affected Libya and Syria'. And at the Geneva II Conference on Syria in January 2014, India's then External Affairs Minister, Salman Khurshid,[8] declared India's commitment to humanitarian action to conflict-affected Syria. In sum, India's assistance to a number of conflict-affected countries shows that the alleged narrow understanding of humanitarian assistance does not hold true. However, when engaging in conflict contexts, India preferably contributes to humanitarian action through multilateral channels, arguably to prevent straining bilateral relations and 'to bypass politically sensitive relationship barriers and channel their aid through more neutral mechanisms' (Smith 2011: 14). For instance, by channelling its funds through multilateral institutions, India was able to provide aid to Pakistan despite the long-standing conflict between the two countries (Meier and Murthy 2011: 17).

It needs to be noted, however, that India as an aid recipient has a strong preference for multilateral assistance and, like other non-DAC donors, it primarily uses bilateral aid channels in its provision of aid (Price 2005: 13). This may indicate a prioritisation of national over global interests (Mawdsley 2012: 31). A statement by India's National Security Advisor Menon during the 3rd International Studies Convention in New Delhi on 11 December 2013 supports this view. In his speech, Menon contended, 'we seem to use multilateralism for our values and bilateralism for our interests'.[9] Indeed, India has strong relationships with the UN system and its multilateral contributions have risen significantly over the last two decades (Price 2005: 13), contributing substantially to the WFP[10] and the UN Central Emergency Response Fund (CERF). In 2010, India was the largest government donor to the Pakistan Emergency Response Fund (ERF) and the eleventh largest donor to multilateral humanitarian financing mechanisms, just behind Germany, channelling 56 per cent of its aid that way (Smith 2011: 14). The following statement in *Nonalignment 2.0* (Khilnani *et al.* 2013: 34) provides further insight on India's stance towards bilateral and multilateral aid channels respectively:

> India's engagement with the U.N. will continue to be at several levels, and will also pose new questions for our policies. There is, for instance, often a trade-off between investment in bilateral engagements and the commitment of resources to multilateral institutions. On the one hand, bilateral aid is usually more flexible; and the donor is also more clearly identifiable and visible to the recipient. On the other hand, multilateral institutions like the U.N. are often less flexible, and donor identity is not highlighted: but participation in their program budgets can enable India to shape the global agenda. While there are real trade-offs, particularly in terms of beneficial use of resources, India's best option is to engage at different levels, and to use different levers.

In its provision of bilateral aid, India has been criticised by DAC donors for providing government-to-government aid rather than channelling it directly to the affected population. This approach, which reflects India's emphasis on respecting sovereignty and objections to the politicisation of aid, constitutes a major divergence from the DAC member preference to provide aid more directly (Meier and Murthy 2011: 8). Where a government is highly corrupt or itself accused of causing suffering, giving aid directly to the government may not reach the population in need.

India has further been openly critical of the 'supply-driven' aid of DAC donors (Meier and Murthy 2011: 8). In what India has labelled a 'demand-driven' approach to aid, assistance should be provided according to the requirements and needs identified by the affected government. In general, due to their own experience as recipients of aid, non-DAC donors are presumed to be more familiar with recipient needs and able to provide better-targeted aid than their DAC counterparts. In their comparative study of 16 'new donors', Dreher *et al.* (2011) could not verify this assumption. However, their study did not include India. Further empirical research on the correspondence between recipient needs and India's provision of aid is required in order to make an informed assessment. Yet, the fact that India shares a preference for in-kind aid with other non-DAC donors is well documented; food and medicine are favoured items (Binder and Meier 2011: 1139; Manning 2006: 379). This stands in contrast to the trend of DAC donors to favour cash transfers over in-kind aid, as the latter has been criticised for having negative effects on the local economy as well as being inappropriate in many cases (Harvey 2007; Oxfam International 2005).

Conclusions

Fearing the undermining of the traditional norms of good donorship, DAC donors have expressed their concerns over humanitarian action led by non-DAC donors. As an increasingly important actor with a lead role on behalf of developing countries, India has the potential to change and (re)construct the international humanitarian aid regime. As constructivist theory suggests, India is thereby not merely influenced by the existing organisational environment but contributes to the politics of humanitarian crises by actively challenging, accepting, rejecting and modifying established DAC principles and practices of humanitarian action. Its isomorphism to DAC donors is only partial. While it subscribes to the humanitarian principles in general, some major divergences to DAC donor approaches to humanitarian action can be detected, with the issue of non-interference likely to remain at the core of controversy between India and the DAC donors.

Along with other non-DAC actors like Brazil, India challenges the hierarchical structures of current international aid regimes discursively by using terms like 'partner' rather than 'recipient' or 'donor'. With an emphasis on national and local needs, it also refers to its aid as 'demand-driven' as opposed to the alleged 'supply-driven' aid of other donors. More crucially, apart from different labelling and categorisation practices, a major divergence between India and the DAC donors exists in India's categorical rejection of interference with the domestic affairs of other states. Shaped by India's own experience as a recipient of foreign aid, the specific role of the NAM, a Nehruvian foreign policy tradition, the principles of non-interference in internal affairs and respect for sovereignty remain at the core of India's foreign policy norms and of its engagement in the humanitarian field. This position results in a divergence in both norms and practice as reflected, for instance, in the emphasis on aid unconditionality and the rejection of what India sees as the politicisation of aid; a consequential preference of direct government-to-government aid; a lack of reporting and monitoring mechanisms that is only partly due to a poor institutional structure; and a continued preference of bilateral and in-kind aid.

Somewhat paradoxically, while India challenges the traditional framework of humanitarian action in many ways, it is increasingly taking part in multilateral aid operations, especially in politically sensitive contexts in order to bypass conflicts with beneficiary governments and to project itself as an important and responsible global actor. This may well result in a continuing integration of India within the international aid regime and a gradual convergence of principles and practice. Acknowledging humanitarian action as a soft-power instrument to further its geopolitical interests and great power ambitions, India has both a keen interest in integrating into the international humanitarian system and setting its own standards in accordance with its own foreign policy ideals and practices.

Whereas India's influence must not be underestimated, the extent to which it will actually be able to (re)construct and change international aid discourse and regimes remains to be seen. Still, the fact remains that as India's contribution to and institutionalisation of humanitarian action is increasing both in numbers and scope, the country's role in international humanitarian action can no longer be ignored.

Notes

1 The term 're-emerging' is also used to emphasise the fact that the country is in the process of restoring its historical position in the international hierarchy and distribution of power. See for instance the statement of India's National Security Advisor, Shivshankar Menon, at the Munich Security Conference (quoted in Dikshit 2013).

2 This category is problematic for negatively defining what these countries are not, and for using the DAC as the ultimate reference point, thereby replicating its hegemony and suggesting a uniformity within the DAC, an institution that has 28 member states with diverging interests and opinions (Mawdsley 2012: 4).

3 South–South cooperation is a vague term applied to any form of interaction between developing countries (Mawdsley 2012: 63). As stated in the Paris Declaration, 'South–South co-operation on development aims to observe the principle of non-interference in internal affairs, equality among developing partners and respect for their independence, national sovereignty, cultural diversity and identity and local content. It plays an important role in international development co-operation and is a valuable complement to North–South co-operation' (OECD no date b).

4 See the statement of the Minister of State for External Affairs: www.mea.gov.in/Speeches-Statements.htm?dtl/21138/Address+by+Minister+of+State+for+External+Affairs+Shri+E+Ahamed+at+Highlevel+International+Humanitarian+Pledging+Conference+for+Syria; and the statement by the External Affairs Minister: www.mea.gov.in/Speeches-Statements.htm?dtl/22765/External+Affairs+Ministers+Statement+at+the+International+Conference+on+Syria+GenevaII (accessed 20 February 2014).

5 In 2006, the SDMC was established in New Delhi with the mandate to serve the Member Countries of SAARC by providing policy advice and facilitating

capacity development for effective disaster risk reduction and management at the regional level. See: http://saarc-sdmc.nic.in/index.asp and www.saarc-sadkn.org/about.aspx (accessed 30 May 2014).

6 Website of the Ministry of External Affairs: http://itec.mea.gov.in/?1320?000 (accessed 25 January 2014).

7 As set out in the Agreement on Trade and Intercourse between China and India in 1954 and which were subsequently incorporated into the Ten Principles of International Peace and Cooperation at the Bandung Conference in 1955.

8 See the statement of the External Affairs Minister: www.mea.gov.in/Speeches-Statements.htm?dtl/22765/External+Affairs+Ministers+Statement+at+the+Inte rnational+Conference+on+Syria+GenevaII (accessed 20 February 2014).

9 See the statement of the National Security Advisor: www.mea.gov.in/Speeches-Statements.htm?dtl/22632/Address+by+National+Security+Advisor+Shiv+Shan kar+Menon+on+Strategic+Culture+and+IR+Studies+in+India+at+the+3rd+Inte rnational+Studies+Convention+held+at+JNU+Convention+Centre+New+Delhi (accessed 20 February 2014).

10 In 2005, India became the 15th largest donor to WFP.

References

Bhalla, A. (no date) India Sends out Disaster Warriors (www.ndma.gov.in/images/mainstreaming/epaper.pdf) accessed 30 May 2014.

Binder, A. and Meier, C. (2011) 'Opportunity Knocks: Why Non-Western Donors Enter Humanitarianism and How to Make the Best of It', *International Review of the Red Cross*, 93(884):1135–1149.

BJP (2014) Election Manifesto 2014 (http://bjpelectionmanifesto.com/pdf/manifesto2014.pdf) accessed 5 June 2014.

Bornstein, E. (2012) *Disquieting Gifts: Humanitarianism in New Delhi*, Stanford: Stanford University Press.

Campbell, I. and Suri, S. (2013) India's Development Cooperation: Post-2015 and Beyond (www.saferworld.org.uk/news-and-views/comment/113-indias-development-cooperation-post-2015-and-beyond) accessed 30 January 2014.

Celik, S. (2014) 'Between History of Humanitarianism and Humanitarianization of History: A Discussion on Ottoman Help for the Victims of the Great Irish Famine, 1845–1852', *WerkstattGeschichte*, Autumn 2014, forthcoming.

Chanana, D. (2009) 'India as an Emerging Donor', *Economic and Political Weekly*, 44(12):11–14.

Cipullo, L. (2012) New SAARC Treaty Aims to Strengthen Disaster Cooperation in South Asia (www.ifrc.org/en/what-we-do/idrl/latest-news/disaster-law-newsletter-february-2012/saarc-agreement-aims-to-strengthen-disaster-cooperation-in-south-asia) accessed 6 June 2014.

Colombo Plan (no date) History (www.colombo-plan.org/index.php/about-cps/history) accessed 10 February 2014.

CPR (2013) IDCR Report: The State of India's Development Cooperation (http://cprindia.org/idcr_report_state_of_indian_development_cooperation.pdf) accessed 5 June 2014.

Dikshit, S. (2013) We Would Rather Be Called Re-Emerging Powers (www.thehindu.com/news/national/we-would-rather-be-called-reemerging-powers-says-nsa/article4373075.ece) accessed 28 January 2014.

Dreher, A., Nunnenkamp, P. and Thiele, R. (2011) 'Are "New" Donors Different? Comparing the Allocation of Bilateral Aid Between non-DAC and DAC Donor Countries', *World Development*, 39(11):1950–1968.

GHA (2013) Global Humanitarian Assistance Report 2013 (www. globalhumanitarianassistance.org/wp-content/uploads/2013/07/GHA-Report-2013l.pdf) accessed 8 June 2014.

Gilpin, R. (2001) *Global Political Economy: Understanding the International Economic Order*, Princeton, NJ: Princeton University Press.

Gujral, I.K. (1998) *A Foreign Policy for India*, New Delhi: Ministry of External Affairs, External Publicity Division.

Harmer, A. and Cotterrell, L. (2005) 'Diversity in Donorship: The Changing Landscape of Official Humanitarian Aid', *HPG Research Report*, London: ODI.

Harvey, A. (2007) 'Cash-Based Responses in Emergencies', *HPG Briefing Paper 25*, London: ODI.

Heim, M. (2004) *Theories of the Gift in South Asia: Hindu, Buddhist, and Jain Reflections on Dana*, Abingdon: Routledge.

IRIN (2011) In-depth: The Rise of the 'New' Donors (www.irinnews.org/ indepthmain.aspx?indepthid=91&reportid=94008) accessed 30 May 2014.

Khan, A.A. (2012) 'Religious Obligation or Altruistic Giving? Muslims and Charitable Donations', in M. Barnett and J. Gross Stein (eds), *Sacred Aid: Faith and Humanitarianism*, New York: Oxford University Press, 90–115.

Khilnani, S., Kumar, R., Mehta, P.B., Menon, P., Nilekani, N., Raghavan, S., Saran, S. and Varadarajan, S. (2013) *Nonalignment 2.0: A Foreign and Strategic Policy for India in the Twenty First Century*, New Delhi: Penguin (Kindle Edition).

Kim, S. and Lightfoot, S. (2011) 'Does "DAC-Ability" Really Matter? The Emergence of Non-DAC Donors: Introduction to Policy Arena', *Journal of International Development*, 23:711–721.

Krafess, J. (2005) 'The Influence of the Muslim Religion in Humanitarian Aid', *International Review of the Red Cross*, 87(858):327–342

Malone, D. (2011) *Does the Elephant Dance? Contemporary Indian Foreign Policy*, Oxford: Oxford University Press.

Manning, R. (2006) 'Will "Emerging Donors" Change the Face of International Co-operation?', *Development Policy Review*, 24(4):371–385.

Mawdsley, E. (2012) *From Recipients to Donors. Emerging Powers and the Changing Development Landscape*, London: Zed Books.

Mawdsley, E. and McCann, G. (eds) (2011) *India in Africa: Changing Geographies of Power*, Cape Town: Pambazuka Press.

MEA (2011) India to Provide Humanitarian Assistance to Horn of Africa Nations (www.mea.gov.in/press-releases.htm?dtl/472/India+to+provide+humanitarian+ assistance+to+Horn+of+Africa+nations) accessed 20 February 2014.

MEA (2012) India's Humanitarian Food Assistance to Republic of Yemen (www. mea.gov.in/press-releases.htm?dtl/20092/Indias+Humanitarian+Food+Assistan ce+to+Republic+of+Yemen) accessed 20 February 2014.

Meier, C. and Murthy, C.S.R. (2011) *India's Growing Involvement in Humanitarian Assistance*, GPPi Research Paper No. 13, Berlin: GPPi.

Ministry of Finance (2014) Outcome Budget, Ministry of Finance, Government of India (http://finmin.nic.in/reports/OutcomeBudget2013_14.pdf) accessed 2 August 2015.

Mullen, R. (2014) 5 Predictions for India's Development Cooperation under New Government. (http://asiafoundation.org/in-asia/2014/05/28/5-predictions-for-indias-development-cooperation-under-new-government) accessed 30 May 2014.

Murthy, P. (1999) 'The Gujral Doctrine and Beyond', *Strategic Analysis*, 23(4):639–652.

Naim, M. (2007) 'Rogue Aid', *Foreign Policy*, 159:95–96.

OECD (no date a) Glossary (www.oecd.org/site/dacsmpd11/glossary.htm) accessed 23 February 2014.

OECD (no date b) Paris Declaration on Aid Effectiveness (www.oecd.org/dac/effectiveness/parisdeclarationandaccraagendaforaction.htm#Documents) accessed 30 May 2014.

Ogden, C. (2011) 'International "Aspirations" of a Rising Power', in D. Scott (ed.) *Handbook of India's International Relations*, London: Routledge.

Oxfam International (2005) Food Aid or Hidden Dumping? (www.oxfam.org/sites/www.oxfam.org/files/bp71_food_aid.pdf) accessed 6 June 2014.

Paulo, S. and Reisen, H. (2010) 'Eastern Donors and Western Soft Law: Towards a DAC Donor Peer Review of China and India?', *Development Policy Review*, 28(5):535–552.

Price, G. (2004) 'India's Aid Dynamics: From Recipient to Donor?', *Asia Programme Working Paper*, London: Chatham House.

Price, G. (2005) 'Diversity in Donorship: The Changing Landscape of Official Humanitarian Aid. India's Official Aid Programme', *HPG Background Paper*, London: ODI.

Roepstorff, K. (2013) *Demokratieförderung in Myanmar: Indien als Partner für die deutsche und europäische Außenpolitik?*, SWP-Aktuell 2013/A 04.

Rowlands, D. (2012) 'Individual BRICS or a Collective Bloc? Convergence and Divergence amongst "Emerging Donor" Nations', *Cambridge Review of International Affairs*, 25(4):629–649.

Severino, J.M. and Ray, O. (2009) 'The End of ODA: Death and Rebirth of a Global Public Policy', *Working Paper Number 167*, Washington D.C.: Centre for Global Development.

Shivakumar, H., Taraporevala, P., Prasad, K.K. and Mullen, R.D. (2014) India – Central Asia Relations: Moving towards Broader Development Partnerships (http://idcr.cprindia.org/blog/india-central-asia-backgrounder) accessed 30 May 2014.

Sinha, P. and Hubbard, M. (2012) The Non DAC Donor's Data Availability Index (www.birmingham.ac.uk/Documents/college-social-sciences/government-society/idd/research/aid-data/chapter1.pdf) accessed 20 May 2014.

Six, C. (2009) 'The Rise of Postcolonial States as Donors: A Challenge to the Development Paradigm?', *Third World Quarterly*, 30(6):1103–1121.

Smith, K. (2011) Non-DAC Donors and Humanitarian Aid – Shifting Structures, Changing Trends (www.globalhumanitarianassistance.org/wp-content/uploads/2011/07/NDDs-humanitarian-aid.pdf) accessed 28 January 2014.

Stuenkel, O. (2013) 'Rising Powers and the Future of Democracy Promotion: The Case of Brazil and India', *Third World Quarterly*, 34(2):339–355.

Taylor, I. (2012) 'India's Rise in Africa', *International Affairs*, 88(4):779–798.

Woods, N. (2008) 'Whose Aid? Whose Influence? China, Emerging Donors and the Silent Revolution in Development Assistance,' *International Affairs*, 84(6):1205–1221.

3 Turkey as a Rising Power

An Emerging Global Humanitarian Actor

Alpaslan Özerdem

Introduction

Since the end of the Cold War, Turkey has been trying to regain its former influence in a wide spectrum of places from Central Asia to the Balkans and Middle East. This policy has become particularly apparent over the last five years, as Turkey has increasingly engaged in international relations. This development is probably not surprising because it occupies a critical geo-political position between Europe, the Middle East and the Caucasus. It has a burgeoning economy (sixteenth largest in the world), a relatively strong democracy and vibrant civil society, and membership of a wide range of organisations from NATO and the Organisation for Economic Co-operation and Development (OECD) to the Islamic Conference, G20 and candidacy to the EU. Turkey has at times played an important peace broker role in regional conflicts and it is a leading country for peacekeeping operations around the world. Moreover, Turkey has become an important actor in international humanitarian and development efforts as a generous donor for disaster response and peace-building efforts, especially in Africa. In 2010, with its official development assistance (ODA) of nearly US$1 billion, Turkey's ODA/GNI ratio was 0.13 per cent. This was already similar to a number of DAC members such as Greece, Italy and Korea. In 2011, while ODA fell in 16 DAC countries, Turkey's net ODA increased by over 38 per cent. In Somalia, Turkey has become the largest donor among non-OECD-DAC countries.[1]

In the early 1990s Turkey started to play an active role in peacekeeping and peace-building operations, especially in its immediate regional context, such as the Balkans. Starting with the humanitarian crisis in Bosnia-Herzegovina in the mid-1990s and then particularly in Kosovo in the aftermath of the 1999 NATO military intervention, not only humanitarian operations but wider state building and post-conflict reconstruction efforts in the Balkans received substantial engagement from Turkish actors (Turkish Foreign Ministry 2014a). This was mainly through the deployment of the Turkish army in the UN- or NATO-led peacekeeping operations and aid efforts by the Turkish Red Crescent. Similarly, after the 2002 Bonn Agreement that set the scene for international peace-building efforts in

Afghanistan, Turkey worked with the international community in key areas such as security sector reform. It led the NATO-led International Security Assistance Force (ISAF) a number of times (Kaya 2013).

The critical turning point for increasing Turkish aid efforts and engagement came with the 2002 general elections, which was a major shift in Turkish politics. It brought the AK Party (Justice and Development Party) to power, and consequently paved the way for a Turkish foreign policy that was prepared to tackle some of the most intractable conflicts in the Middle East. Under the leadership of the then Prime Minister Recep Tayyip Erdoğan, Turkey's profile as a mediator and trustworthy partner in responding to emergencies and humanitarian crises rose quickly. The Turkish government at the time could talk to the Assad regime in Syria and the Hezbullah in Lebanon, as well as having strong economic, political and diplomatic relationships with Israel. With the 'zero problem with neighbours' doctrine of Ahmet Davutoğlu, who became Foreign Minister in 2004 and recently Prime Minister, a new era in Turkish foreign policy started. While the country was making significant progress with its EU membership negotiations, it was also talking to Syria, Jordan and Lebanon to create a free economic area in the Middle East and explore the possibility of moving to a visa-free movement system for citizens (Today's Zaman 2011). In the second part of the decade, these countries were even holding joint cabinet meetings in order to harmonise their relationships in a number of key economic and governance areas. During this period Turkey also struck many deals with the oil- and gas-rich countries of Central Asia, the Caucasus and the Middle East to act as an 'energy bridge' linking to markets in Europe (Gavin 2012; Larrabee 2007). In 2010, in cooperation with Brazil, Turkey managed to convince Iran to sign a nuclear fuel swap deal, which was a major breakthrough that was, however, rejected by international powers for being weak (BBC 2010).

Such a change in Turkish foreign policy with much wider and more active engagement in international affairs has come as a surprise to many. It is often coined as 'neo-Ottomanism' – a term that describes the country's ambitions to expand and revitalise its political influence in large territories once controlled by the Ottoman Empire. With the neo-Ottomanism argument, Turkey, a long time loyal ally of the West in international affairs from the 1950s to the late 1990s, was considered to be a rising power trying to put its own stamp on international affairs by pursuing its own foreign policy priorities. The reference to the Ottoman Empire was to indicate that Turkey, with its increasing economic power and geopolitical advantages, would no longer be the sidekick of Western interests in the Middle East or elsewhere (Taşpınar 2008). Rather it would like to sit with the major powers at the same table when critical decisions are being made for global peace and security. Turkey pursued an active campaign to be elected as a non-permanent member of the UN Security Council and served from 2009 to 2010. However, it lost its bid for the same membership for the 2015–2016 period (Turkish Foreign Ministry 2014b).

In addition to its key strengths – an expanding economy, strong military, geopolitical position, and a relatively well-educated young population – the influence of Turkey's soft power has also been used to strengthen the 'neo-Ottomanism' argument. Attracting nearly 40 million tourists every year, most of whom are from neighbouring countries and Europe, and with the increasing popularity of Turkish soap operas in countries from Albania to Afghanistan, Turkey has painted a picture of a soft power that has to be recognised as a new player in international affairs (Öner 2013).

Within the 'neo-Ottomanism' argument and Turkey's increasing engagement in peace and conflict issues across the world, particularly in the Middle East, one of the key theses has been the claim over Erdoğan's attempt to become the leader of the Islamic world. As the AK Party is an Islamist-rooted party, it has often been argued that the Islamic position was one of the main drivers of the country's new foreign policy and its approach to the Middle East and the wider Islamic world. Erdoğan's clash with the Israeli Prime Minister Shimon Peres at a Davos meeting in January 2009 is a case in point. This was dubbed the 'one-minute' crisis as Erdoğan reacted to Peres's defence of Israel's actions in Gaza, accusing the debate's moderator of not allowing him to speak and storming off saying that he would not return to Davos again. It suddenly made him one of the most popular and respected politicians in the Middle East, especially with the Palestinians (BBC 2009). After the 'one-minute' crisis, Turkish–Israeli relationships have worsened gradually due to various diplomatic crises. They hit rock bottom with the Blue Marmara flotilla crisis, when a Turkish humanitarian aid ship was intercepted by Israeli forces while trying to break the Israeli blockade of Gaza, killing nine Turkish nationals (Booth 2010). With the so-called 'Arab Spring' removing many authoritarian regimes in countries from Egypt and Tunisia to Libya, Erdoğan positioned himself as the politician of people in the streets. He claimed to stand for human rights, democracy and rule of law, increasing his popularity further in the Middle East and North Africa. Turkey was then considered as a possible model country for emerging regimes in the region (Tol 2012). Until the Gezi protests of 2013, Erdoğan was the rising star of international politics and was respected across the world. However, the heavy-handed response of the security forces to the protests and accusations over Erdoğan's increasingly authoritarian and uncompromising rule have diminished his international standing considerably (Letsch 2014).

It is in this bigger picture of international politics and Turkey's increasing engagement globally that Africa has emerged as a new arena for the country in humanitarian aid and peace-building operations, as well as an arena for increasing trade links and diplomatic missions. Within this overall context, this chapter investigates Turkey's aid engagement in Africa with particular reference to Somalia, questioning what drives Turkey's interest in becoming an active humanitarian actor and whether it brings anything unique and different in responding to such challenges. To what extent do, for instance, the Islamic position and regional aspirations of the Erdoğan government play a role in Turkey's humanitarian policies and activities? By undertaking this exploration, the chapter considers what other emerging and traditional actors could learn from Turkey's experiences. In a more general perspective, what possible trajectories of relationships between rising powers and traditional actors could be expected in the arenas of humanitarian and peace-building operations in the short to medium term?

To answer these questions, field research in Mogadishu, the capital of Somalia, was conducted in June 2014. Informants included a number of Turkish aid actors in Somalia such as TIKA (Turkish Cooperation and Coordination Agency), Turkish Red Crescent, Turkish Religious Directorate Foundation, Istanbul Greater Municipality, NGOs such as the Humanitarian Aid Foundation (IHH) and Yardım Eli, as well as the Turkish Embassy and a number of Somali aid agencies, such as Zam Zam. This field research also gave the opportunity to consult Somali recipients of Turkish assistance and understand how they perceived such engagement and why it mattered to them.

Turkey in Somalia

Back in 2009 Turkey had 12 embassies in the entire continent of Africa. Today there are 35 and more to be opened soon. Similarly while there were 10 African Embassies in Ankara five years ago there are now 28. Turkey hosted the Turkey–Africa Cooperation Summit in Istanbul in August 2008, and subsequently the African Union declared Turkey a 'Strategic Partner'. In May 2010, Istanbul was the venue for the 4th UN Conference on the Least Developed Countries (LDCs) (Turkish Foreign Ministry 2014c). With Turkey's influence the conference incorporated recommendations on the private sector, education and youth, which form some of the main characteristics of Turkey's bilateral approach to aid. Compared to a number of other actors, such as Western European powers, the US and China, Turkey is relatively new in African politics and trade circles. However, it has already expanded its area of influence in the continent by linking its soft power tools of transportation links, trade and education closely with its foreign policy. In its most generalised and simplified terms, the process undertaken by Turkey is as follows: once an African country is identified as a strategic foreign policy priority and the Turkish Foreign Ministry establishes its diplomatic presence there, it is very likely that Turkish Airlines will soon launch a flight route to that country. This is followed by increasing economic links formed by a wide range of globally active Turkish companies. Meanwhile, the Foreign Ministry probably sign an agreement to ease the existing visa regime between Turkey and that country to increase the level of interaction in the realms of commerce, academia and culture. A number of Turkish schools linked to the Gülen movement, one of the most established religious brotherhoods in Turkey, in the country concerned are also likely to play an active role in consolidating diplomatic and trade relations (Balcı 2014). These private schools are highly sought after by local communities, as they provide top level education. Finally, the Turkish government may provide scholarship opportunities to graduates of these schools to take an additional university degree in Turkey.

In a wide range of African countries this foreign policy strategy has proved to be successful, with fast growing partnerships in the economic and political spheres. Some of these measures may be fairly traditional means for bilateral relations for other countries too, but what Turkey does differently from many other countries is that it joins up its efforts in the realms of diplomacy, economics, trade, culture and education with humanitarian aid and peace-building. In Somalia for example, Turkey has become one of the most active actors in humanitarian aid and peace-building. According to the International Crisis Group this is to a large extent because Turkey 'is seen as a country to emulate, rather than an external power to be feared' (ICG 2012).

Somalia became an interest for Turkey for a number of reasons, such as geopolitical interests, sociocultural and religious ties, and Turkey's wider business interests in Africa, as well as Turkey's newly gained confidence and enthusiasm in tackling global challenges.

In August 2011, Erdoğan, accompanied by a large entourage of 200 people, including his family, ministers, aid organisation representatives, business people and celebrities, travelled to Somalia. He was the first non-African leader to visit Somalia over the last two decades. The visit brought Somalia back to the attention of a number of other donors, as it received huge coverage by the international media (BBC 2011). It was followed by the reopening of the Turkish Embassy in November 2011. A former medical doctor and member of the Doctors Worldwide, Cemalettin Kani Torun, was appointed Turkey's ambassador to Somalia (Turkish Foreign Ministry 2011). For Turkey's internal politics, such high-profile international media coverage meant strong public support to the Somalia aid campaign and in return, popularity for the governing party. There have also been a number of Somalia peace talk initiatives organised by Turkey acting as an independent third party respected by almost all conflicting sides in Somalia. For example, Turkey co-hosted two international conferences on Somalia in May 2010 and 2012 (Istanbul I and Istanbul II). The latter included a Somali civil-society gathering and was attended by all organised Somali political groupings, business leaders and even delegates from self-declared independent regions like Somaliland (Akpınar 2012).

Turkish aid organisations such as Turkish Red Crescent (Kızılay) and the Turkish bilateral development agency TIKA are highly active in a wide range of infrastructure, welfare and service sector programmes in Somalia. These include clearing mountains of rubbish, providing clean water, building hospitals and running Mogadishu's permanent settlement for displaced Somalis, whom according to Kilian Kelinschmidt, the UN's Deputy

Humanitarian Coordinator in Somalia, 'are the only displaced people in all of Somalia who don't need to worry how they'll eat or sleep or worry that they'll be raped during the day' (cited in Harte 2012). In 2011, the Turkish government donated US$49 million to Somalia, but its successful mobilisation of private donations resulted in another sum of US$365 million (Harte 2012). In 2012, over 1,200 Somali students received full scholarships to study in Turkey, worth a total of nearly US$70 million. Turkish Airlines provides the only international gateway for Mogadishu. Until very recently the Turkish Embassy was the only foreign representation in the capital. Jamal Mohamed Barrow, Deputy Foreign Minister of Somalia explained:

> People were to die but because of his [Prime Minister Erdoğan] visit it opened a gate for others to come and support Somalia. It was a political, moral, economic support at that time. Because, the international NGOs always wait that people start to die. They take photos and send it as the problem in Somalia. At that time, Somalia hadn't reached that situation because of the visit of the Prime Minister. It raised hope really.
> (Center for Strategic Research 2013)

Furthermore, the Somali ambassador to Turkey describes Turkey as 'a saviour sent by God to Somalia', while Erdoğan was voted as 'Man of the Somali People' by the Somali cabinet (ibid.).

There are a number of reasons for Turkey's positive reputation as an aid actor among the Somali population. First of all, the historic visit by Erdoğan in August 2011 played a very important role in winning the hearts and minds of the local people. From the way he came with his family and interacted with Somalis in the camps for internally displaced people to the decision not to use AMISOM (African Union Mission in Somalia) for his protection, he made a huge impact, especially in terms of building trust and confidence. According to Tovrov (2012), while most nations in the world were either unable or unwilling to provide more than the occasional aid package, Turkey focused its attention on Somalia. For Somalis his visit showed that he cared for them and he was different than other political leaders. 'He was in Mogadishu for us but not for his political goals', pointed out a Somali aid worker.[2] A number of Somali government representatives explained that the reason they decided to give up their jobs and comfortable lives in the US and return to Mogadishu to work for the government was because of Erdoğan's visit, because he 'embarrassed' them by risking his own and his family's life to help Somalis.[3] Such anecdotal views underline the significance of Erdoğan's visit, which took place at a time when most Somalis were thinking that they had been forgotten by the international community. As a number of Somali interviewees pointed out, it was a visit by the Prime Minister of a Muslim country. This seems to have been a critical factor in their decision to lend their trust to a new aid actor arriving in their country, while the majority of the population saw the international presence in a highly sceptical way.

Second, Turkey might not be the biggest donor in Somalia, but it has much more presence in the streets of Mogadishu than many other actors. Even when other agencies were running their programmes through remote management from Nairobi due to security challenges in Somalia, Turkey ran its own programmes and continued its presence in the country. There is a major contrast that while most foreign organisations in Mogadishu are concentrated in the AMISOM base, Turkish officials and aid workers live and work in the city. According to Matt Baugh, the UK's ambassador to Somalia, 'the Turkish have shown what it is possible to do operationally … They've brought a really strong political force to bear. They're intimately involved – a real force.' This is largely due to the way Turkey has established a high level of trust within government, various armed groups and war-torn communities. According to Kleinschmidt, the UN's deputy humanitarian co-ordinator in Somalia, its Islamic background is also a factor in the way that 'Turkish aid is setting a lot of pace' (cited in Harding 2012). During the field research in Mogadishu, it was strikingly visible in the way Turkish aid actors were liked by the population. For example, at the road blocks by the Somali security forces, it was enough for the author to be identified as Turkish to pass through without being subject to any searches. Almost every time security personnel made an effort to show their appreciation for Turks being in Somalia in different ways – the phrase they often used for this was 'we like our Turkish brothers'.

Third, the Turkish assistance in the country and particularly in Mogadishu has so far focused on tangible areas that really matter in the day-to-day lives of Somalis. For example, with the accumulation of waste during the civil war over the last couple of decades, many streets of Mogadishu were simply inaccessible. Rotting rubbish was posing a huge health risk to people. The Turkish Red Crescent, in cooperation with the Istanbul Greater Municipality for the material assistance of trucks and other equipment, has undertaken the task of clearing the rubbish. More than 750,000 tonnes of accumulated waste have been collected and cleared, and Turkish assistance still provides this service in the city. The Turkish aid agencies have already built and operate a number of schools, hospitals and orphanages. Yardım Eli is currently building one of the largest women and children's hospitals in the Horn of Africa in Mogadishu. The Turkish Health Ministry has just opened the region's largest hospital and it will be operated by Turkish assistance for the next five years. IHH runs an orphanage with a capacity of 400 beds and a school for 1,200 students. They run an agriculture school that provides a monthly training programme for 30 students each intake, with 300 alumni over the last one and half years. TIKA has been investing in the reconstruction of roads and brought street lighting to the main roads of Mogadishu. The Somalis interviewed during the field research praised this project, as they would now stay out and run their daily routines until 9–10 pm whereas before they had to stop their activities after dark. In short, it seems that Turkey has seen the challenges beyond the 2011 humanitarian crisis. TIKA's

Chairman, Dr Serdar Çam, recalls his first visit to Mogadishu as a member of the Erdoğan's entourage in August 2011: 'Somalia was in a strong situation in the past on agriculture, animal breeding and fishing. However, they need systems to discipline and manage those' and hence TIKA aimed to transfer the know-how and experiences of Turkey on this and other matters (World Bulletin 2011).

Fourthly, one of the key means of support for the Turkish aid presence in Somalia has been the Turkish airlines connection between Istanbul and Mogadishu. This transportation link has played a significant role in gaining the trust and backing of the Somali population. Before this international route with connections to a major city with trade and transportation connections to the rest of the world was established, the population had to travel to Kenya and faced many logistical difficulties and delays. In other words, in the eyes of Somalis the Turkish presence in their country had not only filled a major vacuum in humanitarian aid, but has also provided them with opportunities of trade and travel for education and health needs (Harding 2012). As mentioned, the Turkish embassy was the only one in central Mogadishu. The usual location for others is the AMISOM protected area near the airport. Although having an international flight route or a foreign embassy in any other context might not be significant, for Somalia these factors really matter. It is important to recognise the way Somalia has been isolated from the rest of the world and how this has impacted on the trust and confidence of people in their future (Hammond and Vaughan-Lee 2012). For war-torn societies to be mobilised for peace-building efforts, they would first need to see tangible improvements as peace dividends, and it could be argued that for Somalis the Turkish presence with its airways and embassy presence is in a way a sign of normalisation of life.

Fifthly, Turkish aid providers have entered in a context where other international aid actors seem to have a tainted image in the eyes of local populations. As a new actor Turkey had the advantage of getting involved in a country with which it had no significant historical baggage, such as the colonial rule by the UK in Somaliland or military interventions undertaken by the US. In terms of the provision of humanitarian aid, actors such as the UN and EU have been working in Somalia for decades, and it seems that some of these organisations have damaged their reputation badly. A number of Somali interviewees have repeatedly pointed out how the UN-led programmes in their country, for example, have no real impact in their lives (Hammond and Vaughan-Lee 2012). The author came across many rumours for the way the UN had been spending the aid money for Somalia for the comfort of its staff by building swimming pools and carrying its personnel back and forth between Nairobi and Mogadishu. It was clear that there was a total breakdown of trust for the UN's presence. Seeing that Turkish organisations could deliver large-scale relief aid and reconstruction programmes with a very modest personnel presence has further strengthened Somali's beliefs about the waste of funds by the international community (Ali 2013).

Finally, in relation to the tainted reputation of the international community in Somalia and the lack of trust that the Somali population seems to have for the motivations and benefits of other international aid actors in the country, the Turkish presence has managed to be perceived as independent and neutral. Their involvement in tangible aid programmes has built an overall image and perception that the Turks are in Somalia for helping Somalis, but not for geopolitical interests or exploitation of the recently discovered off-shore oil and gas resources, which seem to be considered as the main drivers for a number of Western powers. This has meant that Turkish aid has been provided without any significant coordination with other international actors. According to Turkish aid agencies, being seen to be working with other international actors would have hugely damaged their image of neutrality in the country. For some Turkish agencies with strong Islamic roots, the reason for not coordinating or cooperating with Western actors might also have been ideological and this was clearly pointed at in a number of interviews with those organisations. However, at a more prudential and tactical level, although cooperation could have meant more funding opportunities and expansion of their programmes Turkish actors seem to have made a deliberate effort to avoid misalignment with other international actors. In fact, it is important to note that Turkish aid agencies have kept their distance from other Muslim aid actors, mainly from the Gulf countries too. Therefore, as will be explored further in the last part of this chapter, the lack of interest from Turkish agencies in coordination with other aid actors should not necessarily be seen from the binary of Muslim versus Western perspectives. It is important to recognise that the special socio-political aid context of Somalia brought about a certain set of parameters that played a significant role in determining both the way that Turkish aid was perceived and the behaviour of Turkish aid actors.

Overall, the analysis of the Turkish aid experience in Somalia shows that Turkey is no longer a shy actor within international relations. It is steadily increasing its presence in the aid sector. In keeping with the growing Turkish proclivity for developing its relations with African countries in commerce, trade, education and culture, there are likely to be other cases similar to Somalia. However, if this is a likely scenario for Turkey in Africa, what should be the main cornerstones of its approach to humanitarian crises so that it can avoid mistakes made by other external actors? Also, considering that Turkey claims its increasing interest and influence in Africa have nothing to do with the exploitation of the rich natural resources, as might be the case for other external actors, and on the contrary is all about working with African countries as equal partners, how could and should its approach differ? And how can it develop its own trademark approach in assisting those countries in the enormous challenge of building peace?

Turkey's Islamic Position and Regional Aspirations

For Turkey's increasing engagement in humanitarian assistance and peace-building operations globally, but particularly in Muslim countries, one of the arguments that is often put forward is about the AK Party's Islamic roots. Furthermore, whether such an active role in peace and conflict environments, such as Somalia, has a strong connection with Erdoğan's personal political objectives is also questioned. First of all, it is important to separate the official assistance provided by the Turkish government through TIKA and aid funding that originates from private donations and gets channelled primarily through humanitarian aid NGOs.

TIKA was founded in 1992, initially to provide development assistance to the newly independent Central Asian countries such as Azerbaijan, Kazakhstan, Kyrgyzstan, Tajikistan and Uzbekistan after the collapse of the Union of Soviet Socialist Republics (USSR). The linguistic and cultural ties with these countries, coupled with the drivers of Eurasianist politics in Turkey, meant that development assistance was considered to be a primary tool that could reduce the influence of Russia and compete with the increasing regional interest of Iran in countries with significant geo-political importance due to their rich oil and gas resources. As pointed out by TIKA (2014a), it 'became an implementing intermediary of Turkish foreign policy, particularly in the countries with whom we have shared values, as well as in many other areas and countries'. TIKA's assistance to the Turkic Republics was mainly through reconstruction and development programmes in the areas of health, education, infrastructure, agriculture, cultural heritage conservation and tourism.

It was only after 2000 that TIKA started to work outside the Central Asia context in line with the changes in the Turkish foreign policy from 2002 onwards, as explained earlier. The organisation today operates in over 110 different countries throughout the world from the Caucasus, Middle East and Balkans to the Pacific, South America and Africa. TIKA is still the implementing intermediary of Turkish foreign policy but probably this is not that different from what is the case for other bilateral aid organisations. However, what makes TIKA a very interesting case is that its assistance has increased from a budget of US$85 million in 2002 to US$1.3 billion in 2011 (TIKA 2014b). It should also be noted that as well as running development programmes in Muslim countries, TIKA is active in many other countries. Some of its recent aid programmes have been in Cameroon, Chad, Ethiopia, Georgia, Niger, Serbia, Sri Lanka and Ukraine as well as Afghanistan, Bosnia-Herzegovina, Gaza and Somalia. Therefore, at least with official Turkish development aid in mind, it would be hard to argue that there is a particular Islamic agenda. In fact, to do this would ignore the recent Turkish foreign policy trajectories. As explained in the first part of this chapter, Turkey is bidding to become a global player. Focusing on an Islamic agenda in its aid policies would narrow down its options drastically.

On the contrary, although it might have Islamic roots, the AK Party has overall been very pragmatic in responding to a wide range of domestic and international political matters. Therefore, reducing the reasons of why and how the AK Party government has been using its development aid as a foreign policy tool to the point of a narrow Islamic agenda would risk ignoring many other significant factors in this complex picture. According to Davutoğlu, Turkey's involvement in Somalia should be seen as a result of Turkey's new 'humanitarian diplomacy' which is 'something more than humanitarian aid. Yet any diplomacy that does not touch human beings, that does not have a humanitarian essence and does not speak to human conscience will not last for long' (cited in Akpınar 2012: 736). In other words, Davutoğlu's thesis is based on finding a right balance between 'conscience and power' and he attempts to conceptualise this beyond the binary of realism-idealism and argues that it has to be more than the hard-power versus soft-power dichotomy (Akpınar 2013: 736). Akpınar (2013) underscores the main characteristic of the Turkish humanitarian diplomacy being 'multi-track', involving a number of state and civil-society actors and operating in the realms of diplomacy, humanitarian and economic capabilities of Turkey in a human-oriented perspective.

It is important to point out that the public in Turkey seems to enjoy the strong leadership profile presented by Erdoğan in global peace and conflict matters. From a neo-Ottomanism perspective this could be explained as the public's longing for Turkey's Ottoman past during which the Empire ruled large geographies, and for a long time was one of the 'superpowers' of the world. With the founding of the Turkish Republic in 1923 from the ruins of the Ottoman Empire, and since then, being a low-middle income country with no significant presence in international affairs, what the AK Party and Erdoğan have managed to bring to the public during the last decade is regained confidence. This has been a much-needed remedy for the wounds of the Turkish public, whose pride has been badly bruised by the never-ending EU membership negotiations. Running an active foreign policy and reaching out to populations across the world, Muslim or not, has been a great catalyst to increase the political popularity of Erdoğan and the AK Party domestically.

Meanwhile, when it comes to aid funding through private donations, two main characteristics should be noted. First, there has been an increasing trend for the public to provide donations in response to humanitarian crises in recent years. For the refugee influx from Syria to Turkey, and in recent humanitarian aid campaigns for Somalia and the Rohingya Muslims in Myanmar, the Turkish public has donated generously. This has been partly because Turkey today is a relatively richer country than a decade ago. Also, with the increasingly active engagement of Turkish foreign policy in different parts of the world, there is now more awareness around global challenges in Turkey than before. The Turkish public has donated for major humanitarian crises before, such as the 2004 Tsunami disaster in Southeast Asia, but it would not be an exaggeration to claim that the aid campaign for Somalia has made humanitarianism a household issue. People from all walks of life have responded generously to the campaign. Such an outpouring of interest for a country like Somalia with which Turkey did not have any significant historical or cultural connections was a major turning point. It is also important to bear in mind that since the Marmara earthquake of August 1999, there has been an increasing trend for the involvement of Turkish NGOs in the provision of humanitarian aid and reconstruction in Turkey and beyond (Deniz 2011; Turkish Foreign Ministry 2014d). Second, Muslim brotherhoods in Turkey, which are very active in the socio-political and cultural life in the country, tend to take the lead in running aid campaigns, especially for those crises in Muslim countries. They are active in collecting donations and most of them are linked with a number of Turkish NGOs with strong Islamic roots and vision. For example, in the case of Somalia most active Turkish NGOs could be categorised in this group. Although they use their own private donations for aid programmes, their strong affiliation with the AK Party over Islamic values seems to have helped them to become more active in the international arena. In many aid contexts including Somalia, there tends to be a strong cooperation between state aid actors such as TIKA and Islam-affiliated Turkish NGOs. This seems to give a certain Islamic nature to the Turkish aid response and presence. Hence, there have been some questions over the Islamic agenda of Turkey's aid policies.

Turkey's engagement in Somalia was considered political opportunism by some, while others argued that shared Islam and geopolitical interests should not be neglected either (ICG 2012). Analysts from a realist perspective would likely consider Turkey's engagement in Somalia more in terms of legitimising its own strategic interests in the region. Considering that TIKA openly accepts being an intermediary of Turkish foreign policy, the influence of geopolitical interests over aid programmes cannot be ignored. On a wider level, Turkey has been investing heavily to become an active actor in Africa. There are a number of reasons for this. As is the case for other rising powers such as India, China and Brazil, Turkey recognises that Africa is a continent where it could have new opportunities of trade, investment and political influence. From the natural resource needs of these rising powers, to their desire for new economic opportunities, to the possibility of exerting influence on African aid recipient countries at times where international support is needed (such as voting for the UN Security Council non-permanent membership or selecting a city for hosting the Olympics), there are many reasons to build stronger links. This is perhaps not that surprising considering that traditional aid donors from the West have been doing this for decades. In other words, statements that raise Turkey's geopolitical interests in the Horn of Africa for the protection of sea transportation routes or investment and trade opportunities for its private sector should be considered together with the geopolitical interests of other key actors. These would include the US security agenda vis-a-vis al-Shabaab and jihadist terrorism in the region, and the UK's interest in exploiting off-shore oil and gas reserves. Rising powers like Turkey engage in Africa similar to the traditional aid actors. To some extent this engagement might be for altruistic reasons, but geopolitics and economic interests are significant drivers too. However, rising powers put much less emphasis on governance and human rights. While the traditional development agenda from the West tends to have a strong conditionality, rising powers seem to be much less interested in this. Hence, for many African leaders, working with the rising powers has become an attractive alternative. Not having any colonial past with African countries is also a major advantage for rising powers, which can establish relationships on the basis of forming more equal partnerships.

During our interviews with Turkish aid actors in Somalia all respondents were asked to describe Turkey's role in the country. All of them underlined the driver of humanitarianism for their actions, based on helping populations who have religious, historical and cultural ties with Turkey. Yet, their responses also had a much stronger liberal perspective, as they considered Turkey's response as an altruistic responsibility, making references to 'interdependence' between states and nations. They insisted that this was not because of imperialistic purposes and that Turkey did not have a hidden agenda for the exploitation of natural resources in Somalia. They entered into the humanitarian context because there was a large scale crisis over hunger and displacement, and nobody seemed to be helping Somalis. One of the interviewees accepted that 'Naturally we might have some Islamic concerns, but our aim has always been humanitarian.'[4] According to the Turkish Ambassador, the dire conditions of Somalia brought Turkey to the humanitarian cause. After Prime Minister Erdoğan's visit, the collection of private donations amounting US$365 million has allowed implementation of a wide range of programmes. However, he also stated that Somalia has now become the most important aspect of Turkey's 'Africa Opening' policy. Turkey has done more than deliver humanitarian aid. He pointed out that the Turkish Embassy has been trying to attract Turkish investment to the country and create 'win-win' scenarios for both sides. Moreover, he also alluded to the fact that the geopolitical importance of Somalia is such that it should not come as a surprise for Turkey to want to be active in the region. Almost all other interviewees also stated that Somalis have in fact understood and fully appreciated Turkey's position as an aid actor and economic partner in their country and such societal acceptance is the main driver and guarantor of their programmes. An interesting point vis-a-vis Erdoğan's particular vision for Somalia was made by one of the Turkish aid workers interviewed. Erdoğan, he said, tries to create a new Turkey that is confident and proud. Through running large scale humanitarian programmes in Somalia, the interviewee claimed that 'Turkey has become aware of its own power'. He continued by pointing out that Erdoğan is a pragmatic leader and 'his vision in Somalia has shown what Turkey could achieve with its own resources'. In other words, what Erdoğan is trying to do in Somalia, he said, is to strengthen Turkey's presence as a rising power, which 'has scared the traditional powers, and this has now turned into a conflict'.[5]

This point on the future of relationships between traditional actors and Turkey as a rising power is hugely important. The Turkish experience in Somalia over the last three years seems to have surprised both sides. It is clear that such a positive performance by Turkey as a humanitarian actor was not really expected by the traditional aid actors in the country. Probably they had expected Turkey's involvement to be brief and come to a conclusion soon after Erdoğan's visit. It is clear that the way the Turkish presence has so much been owned and supported by the Somalis was initially hard to comprehend by traditional actors. However, they now realise that the way that the Turkish assistance has been delivered has played a significant role in this. In fact, this difference between Turkey and traditional aid donors in Somalia can also provide a number of opportunities of cooperation. As pointed out by Tovrov (2012), the US has been unable to deliver aid to parts of Somalia because of the proximity of al-Shabaab. Turkey can bypass the bureaucratic red tape associated with Western governments and inject funding directly into specific projects such as those in education and health.

In other words, as explained earlier, the way Turkish aid workers are based in Somalia and do their work directly within Somali communities, while traditional donors lock themselves up at the airport or stay in Nairobi and run their programmes through remote management, has been a key difference with serious ramifications in the way that the two sets of actors have been perceived by local populations. It was also surprising for traditional donors that Turkey has shown a high tolerance to attacks against their aid workers and diplomatic personnel in the country. In comparison to other nationals Turks are subject to such attacks much less, but there have been a number of them in recent months. In particular, al-Shabaab has bombed (2013) and fired rockets (2014) at the Turkish embassy. Nevertheless, the Turkish presence has shown a high degree of resilience and Turkish organisations have evidenced a higher tolerance to risk, working directly with local people in highly insecure areas, and have absorbed casualties without exiting entirely. The resilience towards risks and absorbing casualties have also been the characteristics of Turkish aid presence in other contexts such as Afghanistan, Bosnia and Kosovo, and therefore, this was not particularly surprising for Turkish actors themselves. However, the way that the Turkish humanitarian assistance and wider presence have been received so wholeheartedly by Somalis has been a surprise even for them. The Turkish presence in Somalia is a totally unique and unusual phenomenon in which the local population appreciates a particular donor country and its aid presence very much.

Conclusions

Turkey is a new actor within the spheres of humanitarian aid, peace-building and post-conflict reconstruction, and as a rising power it has already shown a strong indication that it will be playing an even more active role, particularly in Africa. Its aid budget, both official and though private donations, has risen significantly and it now has more funding than ever to respond to challenges across the world. However, as has been seen in the case of Somalia, the uniqueness of what Turkey could offer is not necessarily in the size of its funding. In fact, in comparison to traditional donor countries and organisations, the scale of its funding is quite modest. However, the way it has been delivered in contexts like Somalia has provided alternatives and perhaps a more effective means of assisting war-torn societies. Working with populations directly and keeping a close proximity to them, and bearing the challenges and difficulties of such environments alongside local people, has played a significant role in gaining their trust, confidence and respect. This in return, has allowed the Turkish aid presence to deliver their programmes more effectively and efficiently. Therefore, Turkish aid in Somalia has underlined the importance of building constructive and enabling relationships with local populations. The basics of being able to work with communities and making efforts towards this goal rather than just opting for easier alternatives of remote management of aid provision clearly need to be debated further. The Turkish presence in Somalia has shown that this is possible.

The question of whether or not Turkey as a donor could repeat its successful humanitarian presence in Somalia elsewhere would need to factor in the specific conditions of the overall Somali context. The need to be in the right place at the right time should be borne in mind, as the Turkish aid presence has filled a major gap left by other aid actors. Having said that, it is also important to note the way assistance has been delivered. There are a number of lessons that traditional aid donors could learn from the Turkish experience for both Somalia and other aid contexts. It is understandable that the Turkish aid agencies have been reluctant to coordinate their activities with other international organisations. The fragility of overall aid context in Somalia and its highly politicised nature leaves little room for manoeuvring or attempting to test how such coordination would impact the continuation of Turkish aid programmes. Almost all Turkish aid representatives have underlined the sensitivities with this issue and the risk of their reputation being tainted because of such cooperation. However, they have also been aware of the challenges of Turkish aid presence in Somalia because it has now become clear that if that presence is to continue it will need to actively engage with wider socio-economic and political challenges, and address more complex issues within the peace-building framework.

Whether Turkey's geopolitical interests or Erdoğan's religious and/or political motives have played a role in the Somalia engagement has been an important aspect of the debate around Turkey as a rising power in humanitarian crises. It is hard to conclude one way or another, but there are a number of indicators that such politics of humanitarian aid have been in action and they have been a contributing factor for explaining why Turkey has been an active donor in Africa. The demands of Turkish foreign policy seem to respond to using relief and development aid as tools to some extent, but it would go too far to claim that such involvement has been purely for religious or political interests and humanitarianism has been no factor at all. In support of this view, Tank (2013) points out, 'Turkey's interest in Africa is part of the AKP's multi-dimensional foreign policy agenda and its efforts to develop Turkey's identity as a global peace mediator'. However, 'focusing only on state interests risks undervaluing the importance of the normative agenda in Turkey's humanitarian out-reach to Somalia' (ibid.). In other words, for Turkish aid agencies in the field, the goals also seem to be altruistic. Through their commitment and actions of living and working with Somalis over the last three years, they seem to have proven this.

It is also important to remember that Turkey's cohesive response in Somalia has already placed Turkey in a unique position in responding to a complex set of peace and development-related challenges. However, this could only be sustained and transformed as part of a long-term strat-egy for peace-building in Africa and elsewhere. For Somalia, for example, according to Aynte (2012), 'Turkey has notable advantages in mediation ... notwithstanding its shared Islamic values and its lack of local proxies or other incentives to meddle in the internal politics'. Turkey needs to come up with effective strategies, and the way Turkish aid agencies have shown their ability to listen to war-torn societies and work with them directly should be the main cornerstone of such strategies that would enable local populations to build their own peace. It seems that Turkey has a unique opportunity to come up with viable alternatives to what Western-centric conflict responses often fail to achieve.

Notes

1 The OECD Development Assistance Committee (DAC) includes the largest bilat-eral providers of development cooperation with 24 member countries. One of the main criteria of joining DAC is to provide an accepted volume of aid (e.g. ODA/GNI ratio over 0.20 per cent or ODA volume above US$100 million). See www.oecd.org/newsroom/developmentaidtodevelopingcountriesfallsbecause ofglobalrecession.htm; www.oecd.org/dac/stats/donorcharts.htm; www.aid effectiveness.org/busanhlf4/en/countries/europe-and-the-cis/717.html.
2 Interview was conducted on 6 June 2014.
3 Focus group interview with Somali advisers to the government.
4 Interview was conducted on 7 June 2014.
5 Interview was conducted on 10 June 2014.

References

Akpınar, P. (2012) 'Turkey's Peacebuilding in Somalia: The Limits of Humanitarian Diplomacy', *Turkish Studies*, 14(4):735–757.

Ali, A. (2013) Turkish Aid in Somalia: The Irresistible Appeal of Boots on the Ground (www.theguardian.com/global-development-professionals-network/2013/sep/30/turkey-aid-somalia-aid-effectiveness) accessed 18 August 2014.

Aynte, A. (2012) Turkey in Somalia: An Emerging Donor? (http://studies.aljazeera.net) accessed 10 August 2014.

Balcı, B. (2014) The Gülen Movement and Turkish Soft Power (http://carnegieendowment.org/2014/02/04/gülen-movement-and-turkish-soft-power) accessed 10 September 2014.

BBC (2009) Turkish PM Storms Off in Gaza Row (http://news.bbc.co.uk/1/hi/business/davos/7859417.stm) accessed 1 September 2014.

BBC (2010) Iran Signs Nuclear Fuel-Swap Deal with Turkey (http://news.bbc.co.uk/1/hi/world/middle_east/8685846.stm) accessed 15 August 2014.

BBC (2011) Somalia Famine: Turkish PM Erdogan Visits Mogadishu (www.bbc.co.uk/news/world-africa-14588960) accessed 15 August 2014.

Booth, R. (2010) Israeli Attack on Gaza Flotilla Sparks International Outrage (www.theguardian.com/world/2010/may/31/israeli-attacks-gaza-flotilla-activists) accessed 4 September 2014.

Center for Strategic Research (2013) Interview with Mr Jamal Mohamed Barrow, Deputy Foreign Minister of Somalia 2013 (http://sam.gov.tr/interview-with-mr-jamal-mohamed-barrow-deputy-foreign-minister-of-somalia) accessed 5 September 2014.

Deniz, D. (2011) Top Development Aid Agencies in Turkey: A Primer (www.devex.com/news/top-development-aid-agencies-in-turkey-a-primer-73930) accessed 12 September 2014.

Gavin, J. (2012) Policy in Turkey Drives Trade with Middle East (www.meed.com/supplements/2012/turkey-and-the-middle-east/policy-in-turkey-drives-trade-with-middle-east/3143297.article) accessed 15 August 2014.

Hammond, L. and Vaughan-Lee, H. (2012) Humanitarian Space in Somalia: A Scarce Commodity (www.odi.org/sites/odi.org.uk/files/odi-assets/publications-opinion-files/7646.pdf) accessed 12 August 2014.

Harding, A. (2012) Turkey – Somalia Aid Pioneers? (www.bbc.co.uk/news/world-africa-17124899) accessed 2 February 2015.

Harte, J. (2012) Turkey Shocks Africa (www.worldpolicy.org/journal/winter2012/turkey-shocks-africa) accessed 10 June 2014.

ICG (2012) Assessing Turkey's Role in Somalia (www.crisisgroup.org/~/media/Files/africa/horn-of-africa/somalia/b092-assessing-turkeys-role-in-somalia.pdf) accessed 9 August 2014.

Kaya, K. (2013) Turkey's Role in Afghanistan and Afghan Stabilization (http://usacac.army.mil/CAC2/MilitaryReview/Archives/English/MilitaryReview_20130831_art007.pdf) accessed 10 September 2014.

Larrabee, S. (2007) Turkey Rediscovers the Middle East (www.foreignaffairs.com/articles/62649/f-stephen-larrabee/turkey-rediscovers-the-middle-east) accessed 20 September 2014.

Letsch, C. (2014) A Year after the Protests, Gezi Park Nurtures the Seeds of a New Turkey (www.theguardian.com/world/2014/may/29/gezi-park-year-after-protests-seeds-new-turkey) accessed 10 July 2014.

Öner, S. (2013) Soft Power in Turkish Foreign Policy: New Instruments and Challenges (www.gce.unisg.ch/~/media/internet/content/dateien/instituteundcenters/gce/euxeinos/oener_euxeinos%2010_2013.pdf) accessed 11 September 2014.

Tank, P. (2013) Turkey's New Humanitarian Approach in Somalia (www.peacebuilding.no/Themes/Emerging-powers/Publications/Turkey-s-new-humanitarian-approach-in-Somalia) accessed 18 February 2015.

Taşpınar, Ö (2008) Turkey's Middle East Policies: Between Neo-Ottomanism and Kemalism (http://carnegieendowment.org/2008/10/07/turkey-s-middle-east-policies-between-neo-ottomanism-and-kemalism) accessed 17 July 2014.

TIKA (2014a) About Us (www.tika.gov.tr/en/about-us/1) accessed 10 August 2014.

TIKA (2014b) Online (www.tika.gov.tr) accessed 11 August 2014.

Today's Zaman (2011) Turkey, Syria, Jordan, Lebanon to Sign Banking Cooperation Deal (www.todayszaman.com/news-239473-turkey-syria-jordan-lebanon-to-sign-banking-cooperation-deal.html) accessed 14 September 2014.

Tol, G. (2012) The 'Turkish Model' in the Middle East (www.mei.edu/content/'turkish-model'-middle-east-0) accessed 19 August 2014.

Tovrov, D. (2012) 'Why Turkey is Coming to Somalia's Aid?', *International Business Times*, 8 March 2012.

Turkish Foreign Ministry (2011) No: 248, 1 November 2011, Press Release Regarding the Re-opening of the Turkish Embassy in Mogadishu (www.mfa.gov.tr/no_-248_-1-november-2011_-press-release-regarding-the-re-opening-of-the-turkish-embassy-in-mogadishu.en.mfa) accessed 19 July 2014.

Turkish Foreign Ministry (2014a) The United Nations Organisation and Turkey (www.mfa.gov.tr/the-united-nations-organisation-and-turkey.en.mfa) accessed 15 September 2014.

Turkish Foreign Ministry (2014b) Turkey: Candidate for the United Nations Security Council for the Term 2015–2016 (www.turkey4unsc.org/index.php) accessed 10 July 2014.

Turkish Foreign Ministry (2014c) Foreign Minister Mevlüt Çavuşoğlu Attended the African Union Summit (www.mfa.gov.tr/default.en.mfa) accessed 10 July 2014.

Turkish Foreign Ministry (2014d) Humanitarian Assistance by Turkey (www.mfa.gov.tr/humanitarian-assistance-by-turkey.en.mfa) accessed 9 August 2014.

World Bulletin (2011) Turkish Development Agency to Open Office in Somalia (www.worldbulletin.net/?aType=haber&ArticleID=77308,August2011) accessed 12 June 2014.

Part III

Developmental Humanitarianism

4 Multi-Mandate Organisations in Humanitarian Aid

Dorothea Hilhorst and Eline Pereboom

Introduction

One common distinction within the humanitarian sector concerns the difference between single- and multi-mandate humanitarian organisations. The difference comes up in a large variety of issues, including discussions on principles, the role of the national government and national agencies in crisis response, and the linkage between relief and development.

Single-mandate organisations would be organisations that have a strict focus on life-saving humanitarian assistance. The term multi-mandate organisations is usually applied to international NGOs that have a humanitarian mandate in addition to other mandates, such as reconstruction, development or peace-building.

In its usage in humanitarian debate, the concept 'multi-mandate' is limited in two ways. First, the term should include national organisations, but is usually reserved for international organisations. This is typical for humanitarian studies, where national organisations are perceived as partners of these international organisations. Unfortunately, as this chapter analyses issues and trends in humanitarian discussion, it risks reproducing this Western-centric way of thinking about humanitarianism. Second, the term 'multi-mandate' is also rarely used to denote the system of the UN, even though many of the discussions associated with the mandate question are also applicable to the UN.

Multi-mandate organisations are the rule in humanitarian aid, even though 'pure' humanitarian agencies are the exception. The International Committee of the Red Cross (ICRC) and Médecins Sans Frontières (MSF) are usually considered single-mandate, while the others are all seen as multi-mandate. A number of these agencies have multiple mandates, yet focus on working in humanitarian crisis areas. While they specifically address crisis, they have a broad mandate that can include emergency aid, reconstruction and development. A prominent international example is the International Rescue Committee. Most multi-mandate organisations, on the other hand, also work in areas that are not affected by immediate crises, such as Oxfam, which works on a wide range of issues in all developing countries.

This chapter reviews a number of issues that are associated with the question of mandates. Following this first introductory section, the second section provides some methodological notes. Section three raises the interesting question of why humanitarian narratives usually present multi-mandate organisations as deviant from the norm, whereas they actually represent the rule. Section four elaborates on different types of humanitarian crisis. A major premise of the chapter is that the way multi-mandate issues play out in a particular crisis and become contested depends primarily on the type of crisis. For most of these issues, it makes a difference whether the crisis concerns an open, violent conflict, a refugee situation, a fragile post-conflict setting or a natural disaster. Section five deals with the issue of the ways in which multi-mandate agencies relate to the humanitarian principles of humanity, impartiality, neutrality and independence. Section six is about the relation between mandates and the ways in which agencies work with national governments and local partners. Section seven takes up the discussion of linking relief, rehabilitation and development (LRRD). Section eight forms the discussion and conclusion.

Methodology

This chapter is partly based on eight workshops with multi-mandate organisations that we held in the Netherlands in the summer of 2014. The participating organisations were Cordaid, Oxfamnovib, Healthnet/TPO, ICCO & Kerk in Actie, Save the Children, Stichting Vluchteling, Warchild and ZOA. We also held four additional interviews with representatives of Médecins Sans Frontières Netherlands, the Netherlands Red Cross, Care Netherlands and the Ministry of Foreign Affairs. The participation in the workshops varied from six to 60 persons. These workshops were organized in preparation of the Dutch humanitarian summit, which was held on 12 February 2015, as a prelude to the 2016 World Humanitarian Summit in Istanbul. The agenda in the workshops was open and gave space to the participants to freely identify questions they considered relevant and timely for their organisation (see Hilhorst and Pereboom 2014).

Multi-mandate Organisations Challenge Ideal-Typical Humanitarian Action

An interesting question is why multi-mandate organisations, despite representing the vast majority of agencies active in any type of crisis, continue to draw policy and academic attention as if they deviate from the norm in humanitarian action. We argue that this is because these organisations challenge the ideal-typical notions associated with humanitarian aid.

Humanitarian crises are populated by a large range of actors that all affect the organisation and outcome of (life-saving) service delivery. Theoretically, service delivery in crisis situations can be characterised as an arena where actors negotiate the outcomes of aid (Hilhorst and Jansen 2010). Social negotiation encompasses any kind of strategy, including coercive violence, written statements, formal interactions, schemes deployed in the shadows of the official process and the banalities of everyday gossiping. The realities and outcomes of aid depend on how actors along and around the aid chain – donor representatives, headquarters, field staff, aid recipients and surrounding actors – interpret the context, the needs, their own role and each other. The idea of an arena is founded in an actor-oriented approach that starts from the assumption that social actors reflect upon their experiences and what happens around them and use their knowledge and capabilities to interpret and respond to their environment (Long 1992, 2001). 'Aid, in this perspective, is the outcome of the messy interaction of social actors struggling, negotiating and at times guessing to further their interests' (Bakewell 2000: 108–9).

In an arena approach, the kinds of actions or actors considered to be humanitarian are not predetermined nor are the principles that qualify as humanitarian established in advance; instead we ask how the conditions of service delivery in crisis situations are shaped in practice. In the humanitarian arena, aid gets shaped through the interactions between these multiple actors. Service delivery during crises is in reality not only delivered by humanitarian agencies but encompasses many more actors. These include UN agencies, multiple-mandate NGOs, suppliers from the international and local private sector, and military contingents providing aid in inaccessible areas or protecting its delivery by civilian actors.

Nonetheless, humanitarian action is driven by an image that stands in strong contrast with the empirical realities of the humanitarian arena, namely the ideal-typical image associated with the service delivery of international humanitarian organisations in temporary conflict situations, according to principles of impartiality, neutrality and independence. This image is epitomised by the concept of humanitarian space. Humanitarian space is defined as 'an environment where humanitarians can work without hindrance and follow the humanitarian principles of neutrality, impartiality and humanity' (Spearin 2001: 22). Like any type of space, humanitarian space has physical and metaphorical dimensions. It refers to physical environments: refugee camps, humanitarian corridors during ceasefires or safe havens where peacekeepers and humanitarians provide physical protection and basic services. It also refers to the room for manoeuvre of humanitarians to work without fear of attack in dangerous situations and alongside other actors. This notion of humanitarian space is rooted in the work of Henri Dunant who founded the ICRC in 1862. He believed that the organisation, in order to gain access to war victims, would have to remain *neutral* and maintain *independence* from sponsoring governments (Dunant 1986; Thürer 2007).

It has been amply demonstrated that the effectiveness of humanitarian spaces is very limited in practice. Many safe havens and refugee camps become militarised, and the abuse of humanitarian aid often makes a mockery of the traditional principles (Keen 1994; Le Billon 2000; Rieff 2002). Also, even among the humanitarian agencies, as stated in the introduction to this chapter, 'pure' humanitarian agencies that have a single mandate to work according to these humanitarian principles are only a fraction of this multitude of actors. Nonetheless, the notion of humanitarian space as the site of principled aid remains widely accepted as the expression and aspiration of humanitarian assistance. The Red Cross/Red Crescent movement, the UN bodies, the NGO Code of Conduct and the Good Humanitarian Donorship Initiative all adopt similar wording to embrace the traditional humanitarian principles of impartiality, neutrality and independence. Research in 12 humanitarian crisis situations has shown that actors and aid recipients worldwide acknowledge and appreciate its universal character (Donini *et al.* 2008).

A major paradox of humanitarian aid is therefore that the ideal-typical representation of aid, the single-mandate principled humanitarian organisation, only corresponds to a handful of agencies among thousands, and that the organisation and principles these few agencies stand for nonetheless continue to dominate humanitarian policy, academia and debate.

One important reason why this ideal-type continues to be so dominant is because the imagery of the humanitarian space provides the language in which access and service delivery to people in need can be negotiated. Many humanitarians and surrounding actors sincerely believe in its power to protect and assist victims of violence or disaster and thus maintain the ideal to uphold the standards embedded in the concept. Hugo Slim observes about this aspirational dimension:

> The main purpose of selling humanitarian norms is to ensure that their successful promotion will mean that many others live. If those who hold economic, social, political and military power in a war can be persuaded to 'buy' the humanitarian norms and principles of International Humanitarian Law (IHL) then civilians are more likely be protected than killed.
>
> (Slim 2003: 3)

This also means that the core notions of humanitarian aid are also meaningful to multi-mandate organisations. Most of these organisations feel compelled to define their work in crisis-affected areas with reference to the humanitarian principles. Many agencies have organised their humanitarian work separately from their development work. This means that they have a humanitarian division, which foregrounds its humanitarian identity, while other divisions take up more political, developmental, or rights-based working principles. Agencies may also alter their representation to the context. This means that they foreground their humanitarian nature in acute crisis situations, whereas they show their other faces in contexts with more space to address other concerns of reconstruction or development. This juggling with identities is not an easy or self-evident endeavour, and underlies many of the problems and dilemmas of aid.

The Type of Crises Matters for Issues of Multi-Mandate Organisations

When we asked the Dutch multi-mandate organisations during the workshops about their approaches, dilemmas and issues with humanitarian aid, the usual answer was, 'that depends on what crisis we are talking about'. Humanitarian budgets are being used for several ends. These vary from acute crisis to many years – sometimes decades – of support for the care and maintenance of refugees, for providing all kinds of aid to fragile states, for institutionalising support to disaster prevention, risk reduction and preparedness. General discussions about multi-mandate organisations are often hindered by the fact that proponents have different humanitarian scenarios in mind. Hence, before addressing the issues regarding multi-mandate organisations thematically, this section introduces a number of these scenarios and the roles played in these scenarios by single- and multi-mandate organisations.

Open Conflicts

History chapters about modern humanitarian aid regularly begin with the battlefield of Solferino in 1859 where Henry Dunant witnessed a heavy and bloody battle, inspiring him to organise medical care, and then promoting the development of IHL and the formation of the ICRC. Ironically, humanitarian aid is least effective in accessing and assisting affected people in these iconic situations of open, violent conflict. Areas are often inaccessible and it can be too dangerous for people in need to reach the assistance. When it is too dangerous for aid workers, aid will be withdrawn. Needs in these situations are always vastly larger than aid can accommodate for and coverage is often a major issue.

The problem of access in these kinds of situations is not new. There are, however, some recent developments and debates. Since 2001, initiated by the 'war on terror', we have been faced with international conflicts in which the so-called international community is either seen as a 'neutral outsider' or as a 'warring party' depending on the speaker's political point of view. In some conflicts, this has led to distrust of humanitarian organisations and the UN as they were associated with the Western domination of the international response. The credibility of aid has been severely affected in some countries.

Although most humanitarian organisations have the ambition to provide services in conflict areas, high-intensity conflicts are more in the domain of intervention of single-mandate organisations than multi-mandate organisations. In such situations, ICRC typically plays a large role and MSF is usually at the forefront of aid delivery. This does not mean that multi-mandate organisations are not around or have no role to play. Scenarios of open, violent conflicts are often local and periodic. In many cases, some parts of the country are subjected to heavy fighting while in other parts of the country aid is being delivered for reconstruction or development. Proportionality may be an issue. In a recent report Doctors without Borders asks for awareness for these situations. With the title 'Where Is Everyone?' (MSF 2014a), the report states that in the worst conflicts few organisations provide aid while the humanitarian system responds inertly and inadequately to the logistical complexities. While this is ascribed partly to contextual issues, the report raises questions about the efficiency and independent decisiveness of aid. One of the examples is the situation in Goma in Eastern Congo, where an intensification of violence of rebel group M-23 led to the evacuation of aid organisations just when people needed aid more than ever.

Fragile Setting

A number of countries have an official peace agreement and an internationally accepted government, while conflict continues at a low level or flares up regularly. Governments in these countries are often not willing or able to realise basic services for the population. These are fragile settings, or even fragile states, often representing permanent humanitarian crises. In these settings, where (with variation) the government does not function well, civil society is weakened, all poverty indicators are in the red, the fertility rate is very high, urbanisation accelerates and criminality is abundant, development perspectives are difficult to identify. Progress with the Millennium Goals, seen in many parts of the world, bypasses these countries. There is always the risk of relapsing into conflict (Milante forthcoming).

Fragile settings demand a multiplicity of types of aid, varying from emergency aid to development to support for institution building. One will find all kinds of agencies with different types of mandates and programmes in these situations. Single-mandate organisations will usually focus on those areas of the country where violent conflict continues and instances where violence flares up. Multi-mandated organisations switch between direct support of the most vulnerable groups to institution building. They often deal with 'wicked problems': vicious problems which are practically unsolvable and where solutions often evoke new problems. In these situations, aid stands little chance of success in scaling up or bringing about sustainable change. This can feed into the increasing critique on development cooperation. Arguments in favour of maintaining a high level of aid in fragile settings (where 'do no harm and try doing good' is often the leitmotif) include the high level of vulnerability leading into immediate humanitarian needs, and the risks of renewed conflict, which can have all kinds of spill-over effects regionally and internationally.

The vicious nature of the problems does not mean that aid cannot do better than it does. There are some recurring aid 'traps' in these kinds of situations. Aid organisations tend to underestimate, no matter how difficult the situation is, the capacity of local actors to offer appropriate solutions and function in the best possible way within their own ways of coping. Aid organisations also tend to focus on implementation of projects without a holistic view and without investing in coordination mechanisms beyond basic information exchange. Organisations sometimes duplicate work when they simultaneously see the same needs arising. Organisations can be inert, and lack flexibility to switch modes between unconditional relief and other types of support. Aid can often be more effective, and lessons learned in monitoring and evaluations are not always followed-up. Accountability to the local population and local institutions can be vastly improved (Milante forthcoming).

Some of the critiques on aid seem to recur over decades. However, there are progressive developments in aid in fragile settings. Compared to the 1990s, aid is more often focused on existing institutions and resilience of the population (Hilhorst *et al.* 2011) so the likelihood of sustainable change is garnering more strength. Coordination systems have been improved, and governments have more space to take and maintain initiative and define their own development agenda.

Refugees and Displaced Persons

Care for refugees and displaced persons is part of humanitarian budgets and is considered as humanitarian aid. Humanitarian aid in conflict areas – as described above – is highly difficult and, in practice, aid is often provided to people who flee from the open conflict. Internally displaced people (IDP) problems are often more difficult when there are multiple displacements with people fleeing from violence, who arrive in insecure areas and have to flee again.

Humanitarian aid has been criticised for many years, because it did not take into account the resilience of refugees and IDPs and hence did not build on the initiatives of target groups. Even where aid agencies want to break through this situation, they are often constrained by national laws that forbid refugees from undertaking (economic) activities. Currently, however, we see many developments for dealing more effectively with refugees, partly triggered by technical progress. Instead of distributing goods, for example, agencies often provide cash or vouchers so that refugees can decide what they need. Where refugee movements become massive, aid is confronted with huge logistical, organisational and financial problems. Because camps are often the only place where aid can be provided, there can still be an oversupply of aid organisations locally.

Issues of IDPs are complex, because IDPs establish camps in some countries but also often stay in the periphery of cities. Some of them wait to return home at the end of the conflict, while others decide to stay in the city. That is how displacement intertwines with rapid urbanisation in fragile settings. It is not always clear what roles humanitarian action can play in these complex problems and in which ways the government can realise basic rights of these people together with the international community. As IDPs in urban environments usually blend with the urban poor, the issue on how to provide adequate aid is equally intertwined with issues of development, making the concern of IDPs by nature apt for multi-mandate approaches.

Disasters Triggered by Natural Hazards

The world community has vastly improved prevention, preparedness and response to small- and medium-scale recurrent disasters. The Hyogo Framework for Action (HFA) of 2004[1] has played an important role in reinforcing national governments to make disaster prevention and preparedness a policy priority and to improve disaster response. In more and more countries, small- and medium-scale and recurrent disasters are being absorbed by government and non-governmental institutions, sometimes with the cooperation of international development organisations residing in the country.

Extraordinary large-scale disasters are a different story. These disasters cannot be dealt with at national level. They require massive efforts from outside. The international humanitarian system has made enormous progress in the last 20 years on first care and emergency aid in these kinds of disasters. These changes have supported life-saving aid in slow-onset disasters that slowly reach crisis proportion, like the drought in the Horn of Africa in 2011. Despite the momentous logistical challenges of large-scale aid interventions in circumstances where roads are blocked, aid workers are themselves affected and communication lines are broken down, the aid community has managed to significantly bring down mortality figures in these situations.

After the first crisis period, usually lasting several weeks, the situation becomes more complex. The acute needs are not over, but the response falls into a certain routine. Reconstruction also starts. Reconstruction after large-scale disasters is an extraordinarily complex operation which is always politicised. Most efforts occur outside the framework of humanitarian aid like the (corruption sensitive) rebuilding of infrastructure. Humanitarian organisations focus mainly on the local level where communities try to resume daily life together and rebuild their habitats. Reconstruction is often characterised by politicisation and bureaucracy. In this process, aid organisations often make mistakes because their aid supply does not complement activities people undertake themselves and a lack of accountability to affected populations may prevail.

Natural disasters are mainly dealt with by multi-mandate organisations. MSF does not reckon natural disaster its core competency, while the

International Federation of the Red Cross (IFRC) is the more prominent player in the Red Cross family. This is of course different in the large number of cases where disasters take place in conflict areas. Natural hazards do not stop at the border nor wait for peace. The HFA ascribes the primary role in disaster response to the national government. However, disasters occur often in situations where the government does not function well or where more or less intensive conflicts take place. In these situations natural hazards may lead to catastrophes because the response capacity is lacking and people in conflict circumstances become more and more vulnerable and poor.

While natural disaster response is mainly a multi-mandate affair, there continue to be issues concerning the balance between immediate relief and recovery efforts. In the Netherlands, for example, there is a recurrent debate to what extent funds raised from the general public in the aftermath of a big disaster can be diverted to recovery, and what proportion of funding needs to be reserved for acute aid.

Biological, Chemical and Nuclear Disasters

While biological, chemical or nuclear disasters can and will occur in the future and will no doubt raise humanitarian needs, this is not a subject for discussion within humanitarian organisations, and there is no preparation for these types of disasters. This summer brought the spread of the Ebola virus, a disaster caused by a biological vector. While the Ebola virus developed into a crisis, it became clear that the humanitarian world – starting with the UN agencies – had no adequate response. On 2 September 2014, the international Chair of MSF called upon the UN to deploy military troops to deal with this crisis (MSF 2014b). The Ebola crisis raises several questions that are missing in the humanitarian agenda up to now.[2] How can the international community respond to biological, chemical and nuclear disasters? Is this the exclusive domain of military actors? What mandate do humanitarian organisations have to play a role in this scenario? Are they equipped and prepared for it?

Concluding on the Types of Crisis

This overview of different scenarios brings out that single-mandate humanitarian agencies are particularly prominent in open, violent conflict whereas in all other types of crisis, multi-mandate organisations appear to be more dominant and better suited to provide services.

It may be clear that the different types of crisis are not clearly separated in reality. In countries where certain areas or periods are more or less violent, aid is always moving between different objectives and ways of working. It is at the borderlines and overlap between different types of crises that most friction about mandates, finance, support, approach and practice of humanitarian aid occurs.

Multi-mandate Issues around Mandates and Principles

Humanitarian aid is considered different from other forms of international interventions because it is grounded in humanitarian principles, and the nature and importance of these principles is always subject to debate, within and among organisations of different mandates.

Much Ado about Principles

The humanity principle of alleviating life-threatening suffering wherever it may be found is the foundation of the Red Cross/Red Crescent movement and is broadly considered to form the core principle of humanitarian action. Together with the supporting principles of impartiality, neutrality and independence, it is the core principle of humanitarian aid.

There has been a long-term debate about whether humanitarian principles of impartiality, neutrality and independence are compatible with the human-rights approach used by many development organisations. Both approaches have a lot in common, because they are both grounded in international agreements (respectively international humanitarian law, and human rights) and they both have human dignity as their basis. Hence, the approaches are complementary. While humanitarian aid in the short-term aims to guard human dignity by providing direct aid, more rights-based approaches question the structural root causes and solutions to injustice, vulnerability and unrest.

Nevertheless, in practice both approaches can become conflictive. Selecting specific disadvantaged groups can (seem to) be contrary to the impartiality principle. Raising causes of conflict can be contrary to the principle of neutrality. Looking for structural solutions requires working with national and international governments, which can be contrary to the independence principle. The confused practice around principles can lead to problems in communication and images of humanitarian aid. The principles of impartiality, neutrality and independence are in the eye of the beholder. Even if organisations operate according to these principles, they can be seen by the population as partial. Suspected impartiality of humanitarian organisations can be dangerous and be one of the elements explaining increasing violence against aid workers in some crises areas.

The discussion about principles is often only referred to as an identity issue or a choice within the organisations. However, the different crises as described in the section above call for different approaches, in which humanitarian principles are not always equally relevant.

Translating Principles into Standards

In the 1980s, a strong proliferation took place of humanitarian agencies, many of which were in fact development agencies that expanded into humanitarian aid, often as a result of a particular crisis, such as the African famine of 1984. Towards the beginning of the 1990s the need was increasingly felt to develop a standard for humanitarian aid, which resulted in the formulation of the Code of Conduct for the International Red Cross and Red Crescent Movement and Non-Governmental Organisations (NGOs) in Disaster Relief. It contained 10 principles, starting with (amended versions of) the classical principles of humanity, impartiality, neutrality and independence. Six principles were added regarding the quality of implementation, which reflected to a large extent the increasing influence of multi-mandate organisations that brought development notions such as accountability, participation and long-term objectives into the Code.

The Code was quickly signed up by hundreds of humanitarian agencies, and 10 years later a sector-wide survey showed that the principles were widely supported by workers and stakeholders of humanitarian action (Hilhorst 2005). In the meantime, there have also been new standard initiatives, including Sphere Standards, People in Aid and the Humanitarian Accountability Partnership. Several years ago, a process was started to bring about a new, shared standard that would combine the best of existing standards. The resulting Core Humanitarian Standard (CHS) is underpinned by the basic principles. It sets out nine commitments that are based on aid recipients' entitlements to quality and accountable assistance.[3]

The CHS is written from the point of view of crisis-affected communities and people. When the Code is applied, crisis-affected communities and people will receive appropriate and relevant assistance; have access to the assistance they need at the right time; are not negatively affected and are more prepared, resilient and less at-risk as a result of assistance; know their rights and entitlements; have access to safe and responsive complaint mechanisms; can expect improved assistance of learning organisations; receive assistance from competent and well-managed staff and volunteers; and can expect that assisting organisations manage resources effectively, efficiently and ethically. The people-centredness of the CHS empowers communities. It also results in an inclusive standard that can be equally adopted by humanitarian agencies, as well as any other development, peace-building, rights-based or other organisations responding to crises. The Code of Conduct was written from the point of view of organisations and was characterised by language that showed the Code to be an unresolved compromise between single- and multiple-mandate organisations. Because the commitments are written from the point of view of recipient communities, instead of from the point of view of aid agencies, the CHS may overcome some of the divides between single- and multi-mandate organisations.

Issues of Multi-Mandate Organisations in Liaising with National Actors

One distinction between international single and multi-mandate organisations concerns the way they relate to national actors, including the national government and NGOs. It is not a hard distinction, more a gradual scale marked on one extreme by an agency that completely self-implements relief aid and on the other extreme an agency that completely relies on national partners to provide aid. Single-mandate organisations tend to be positioned towards the end of the self-implementing agency, whereas multi-mandate organisations are usually much closer to the end of the partnership organisation.

Collaborating with the National Government

The way in which agencies collaborate with the national government primarily depends on the type of crisis. In the case of open, violent conflict, the government is party to the conflict and sometimes hardly controls its territory. Aid organisations collaborate with the government to get permissions to reach their target groups, but they keep their distance as much as possible. In the case of fragile settings, the international agenda moves to peacebuilding, state-building and institutional development. The importance of collaborating with the government is being emphasised to prevent, as in the past, parallel service delivery by international aid organisations continuing for too long with the risk of undermining institutional recovery. With refugee care, the host government is an important actor, although in refugee camps in developing countries most governmental functions are being delegated to the UN High Commissioner for Refugees (UNHCR). In the case of natural disasters, the national government has the first responsibility to respond and governments in developing countries will be assisted by the UN (Office for the Coordination of Humanitarian Affairs (OCHA) or UNDP). Here we see many developments in the last decade where international NGOs – which usually found their partners in civil society – increasingly work with (decentralised) governments as implementation partners.

The way in which agencies collaborate with the national government further depends on the mandate of the agency. In fragile settings, for example, multi-mandate agencies will be more inclined to work with the government to enable institution building and development, whereas single-mandate agencies will tend to focus on and ask attention for ongoing humanitarian needs. Complications mainly arise when the situation is not clear, or open for multiple interpretations. An example of this was Afghanistan where many actors considered the country in a post-conflict fragile situation, calling for close collaboration with the state, others would consider the country of being at war, calling for a strictly neutral approach (Hilhorst 2008). Another example concerns the peacekeeping force of the United Nations Organization Stabilization Mission in the Democratic Republic of the Congo (MONUSCO), viewed by most agencies as a neutral collaborator, whereas a number of agencies want to keep their distance to this international military actor, because of the low level of trust and legitimacy of MONUSCO among the population at large (see also Chapters 5 and 6).

Collaborating with Local Partners

Practically all humanitarian agencies have local implementing partners. A major difference concerns, however, the objective of these collaborations. A number of these collaborations are strictly instrumental contractual relations, geared to enhance the effectiveness of aid delivery. Especially in the case of multi-mandate organisations, these collaborations take on additional objectives and meaning (van der Haar and Hilhorst 2009). In these cases, aspects of capacity development are part of the partnership relations. It may also include objectives to strengthen civil society or to enhance good governance. On the one hand, these partnerships can draw criticism when these secondary objectives override the humanitarian performance of the organisations. On the other hand, it is also considered crucial to develop local capabilities to respond to crisis, and especially in cases of natural disaster there have been many efforts to forge the local response capacity.

There is a trend to subcontract aid to local implementers, as one of the strategies deployed to access more people in conflict areas. This is also known as 'remote control' or aid managed at a distance. In extremely dangerous situations, partnerships thus tend to be redefined as 'remote control'. Aid in these cases is subcontracted to local implementers without the presence of international staff in the area. There are ethical objections to subcontracting aid in extremely dangerous circumstances when the argument that the situation for local people is less dangerous is not always applicable. There are also doubts about lack of transparency and control on aid in situations where aid can be misused and this might lead to increasing conflict risks (Donini and Maxwell 2014). On the other hand, it was also pointed out during the workshops with multiple mandate organisations geared towards development, that the mistrust that seems to enter with the relabelling of partnership into 'remote control' may not be justified, as these implementers may in fact represent a continuation of longstanding and trusted partnerships, established and built in the period before the (intensification of the) crisis. In the case of Somalia, for example, Oxfamnovib continues to collaborate with local organisations that have been tested and trusted partners for a long time, and would defy the image of remote-controlled aid.

Linking Relief, Rehabilitation and Development

One of the possible strengths of multi-mandate organisations is that they can link humanitarian aid to development. The way humanitarian aid activities are connected with reconstruction and development is referred to in humanitarian jargon with the abbreviation LRRD: linking relief, rehabilitation and development. LRRD is associated with a timeframe in which the three elements are seen as subsequent phases, for example when authorities declare that 'the relief phase has come to an end'. In reality, these phases overlap and coincide, and frequently there is simultaneous movement in the opposite direction. As a result, some scholars refer to two-way LRRD (see Mosel and Levine 2014). Given these realities, it would be more fruitful to approach LRRD as the challenge to make relief as supportive to development as possible. It then becomes a way of working, in which relief is 'smart' and makes as much use as possible of existing capacities, resources and markets so as to disturb local development processes as little as possible. This approach can be labelled developmental relief (Hilhorst 2007).

The 1990s saw much debate about the relative advantages and disadvantages of LRRD. In the case of natural disasters, the question seems largely resolved. There is a broad consensus that the priority should be with enhancing local capacities for disaster preparedness and response, which is among others laid down in the HFA (ISDR 2005). In the case of conflict, the question whether aid must concentrate on saving lives or whether there is a case for more developmental approaches was backgrounded in the years since 2001, when the global war on terror dominated humanitarian debates. We currently see a strong resurgence of interest in developmental relief, in the slipstream of the attention to resilience (Macrae 2012). Advocates of resilience call for a restructuring of how humanitarian relief and development programmes are organised and, in turn, how they interact with one another. It has been proposed that resilience can conceptually transcend the debate beyond LRRD (ibid.; European Commission 2012). Macrae (2012) argues that the starting point here should be an 'empirically grounded analysis of the risks – social, political and environmental facing poor people'.

There are also risks regarding LRRD. Compared to relief, reconstruction and development are often highly politicised and this can rebound on the provision of relief. The different cultures and implementing styles of relief and development can slow down adaptations, both in the transition to reconstruction and in a possible fallback to relief. A Dutch evaluation of LRRD concludes that 'It is a crucial challenge for humanitarian actors to remain committed to humanitarian principles and at the same time to take development and political dimensions in international cooperation into account' (IOB 2013).

The discussion about LRRD seems to assume a high level of control of the humanitarian response, which stands in contrast with the notion of the humanitarian arena where a multitude of actors negotiate the organisation and outcomes of aid. In reality, there are many actors involved in service delivery in crisis who all make their own plans and maintain their own style to a large extent (Hilhorst and Serrano 2010). Humanitarian aid often operates alongside national or private service delivery and with the aid of diaspora populations. Service delivery in crisis is not only the field of humanitarian aid, and inconsistencies in approaches seem inevitable. It is not uncommon, for example, that one organisation in the same village asks for a contribution to health care which is usual in a development context, while another organisation offers the same services for free.

It is important, it seems, to continue and step up the discussion on the parameters, possibilities and perils of linking relief to development. In most situations an explicit preference and space for developmental relief could make a major difference for people struggling to protect their livelihoods and social safety nets in times of emergency. The resilience agenda reminds us that the transition from relief to development is an optimistic slogan that does not apply to most people in emergency situations. Their normality is not one of development but of bare survival, with few services to fall back on. Their return to normality is not a transition from relief to development but a transition from relief to muddling through under adverse conditions. Hence, it could be argued that safeguarding the meagre livelihood, safety net and service options of these people should be a major driving force of humanitarian aid.

Conclusion

As this volume testifies, humanitarian aid is delivered by an increasingly varied array of old and new organisations. Discussions on singe- versus multiple-mandate organisations originate from the early 1990s and have continued throughout this expansion of aid. This chapter reviews these discussions.

The most important finding of a series of workshops in the Netherlands was that for the humanitarian agencies all questions related to mandates are contextual and strongly depend on the type of crisis that is being addressed. Five different crisis scenarios have been identified in this chapter, namely acute and violent crisis, refugees and IDPs, fragile settings, disasters triggered by natural hazards, and biological, chemical and nuclear disasters. The overview of different scenarios brought out that single-mandate humanitarian agencies are particularly prominent in open, violent conflict whereas in all other types of crisis, multi-mandate organisations appear to be more dominant and better suited to provide services. It was also found that general discussions about multi-mandate organisations are often hindered by the fact that proponents have different humanitarian scenarios in mind. Although it would be helpful to differentiate discussions more by type of crisis, it needs to be taken into account as well that the different types of crisis are not clearly separated in reality.

The second half of the chapter zoomed in on three core themes in discussions about multi-mandate organisations. The first concerned the humanitarian principles. While humanitarian principles are often compatible to other sets of principles guiding multi-mandate organisations, such as human rights, these can also be conflictive and show frictions and contradictions in practice. The section discussed the newly adopted core humanitarian standard as a possible contribution to resolve some of the contradictions by systematically making the needs of communities the centre of gravitas of discussions on aid. The second theme elaborated where agencies of different mandate tend to be positioned on a scale running from zero collaboration with national government and agencies to completely relying on partnership, of fully working with the government. One of the pertinent elements found was the need to unpack the notion of remote control, whereby humanitarian aid is contracted out to local actors, and recognise that this label stands for different relations, some of which denote genuine and tested partnerships. Finally, the chapter discussed the theme of linking relief to development. LRRD has recently regained attention and the section brings out the importance of the theme and the continued need to innovate and learn from the good and bad practices on LRRD.

This chapter has thus elaborated three themes that often play a role in the discussion about humanitarian mandates. There are more themes that are relevant yet have not been discussed here. These are, among others, the approach to security and the positioning of agencies in relation to coordination structures. With regards to security, there are differences with regards to 'soft' approaches to security, which principally rely on gaining trust from local communities, and 'hard' approaches, which led Collinson and Duffield (2013) to write about 'fortified aid compounds'. A question for further research is whether multi- and single-mandate organisations differ with regards to these approaches. With regards to coordination, single-mandate organisations may take more distance from the coordination bodies of the United Nations, with the argument that the UN is too politicised. These themes have not been dealt with in this chapter. The chapter has also not discussed the ramifications of mandates among national response organisations and the United Nations family. These issues would merit further discussion in the future.

This chapter has discussed a number of themes regarding humanitarian aid through the lens of mandates of agencies. In doing so, it has actually questioned whether humanitarian mandates are indeed an appropriate entry-point or framework to discuss these themes. Discussions in the humanitarian domain often refer to differences between single- and multi-mandate organisations. In reality, there are only a handful of single-mandate organisations, and much of the discussions related to the mandates are in fact strategic and operational issues that are relevant within multi-mandate organisations, grappling to find the best response to a particular crisis. We may conclude that a focus on the type of mandate is far less important than, and may sometimes even be a hindrance to, ensuring that the right type of aid is delivered at the right time.

This brings back the puzzling question that was raised in the beginning of this chapter: why is such importance attached to a discussion on single versus multi-mandate agencies, with the multi-mandates diverting from the standard, when all but a handful of agencies are in fact multi-mandate? We argued that this is because these organisations challenge the ideal-typical notions associated with humanitarian aid. Refocusing the attention to ensuring that the right type of aid is delivered at the right time for the specific situation thus requires that academic and policy frameworks alter these ideal-typical notions of humanitarian aid and develop a more realistic framework to understand the practices of humanitarian aid.

Notes

1 For further information on HFA 2005–2015, see ISDR (2005).
2 For a discussion of these issues, see Prescott (2003).
3 See www.corehumanitarianstandard.org.

References

Bakewell, O. (2000) 'Uncovering Local Perspectives on Humanitarian Assistance and its Outcomes', *Disasters*, 24(2):103–16.

Collinson, S. and Duffield, M. (2013) *Paradoxes of Presence: Risk Management and Aid Culture in Challenging Environments*, London: ODI.

Donini, A. and Maxwell, D. (2014) 'From Face-To-Face to Face-To-Screen: Remote Management, Effectiveness and Accountability of Humanitarian Action in Insecure Environments', *International Review of the Red Cross*, 95:383–413.

Donini, A., Fast, L., Hansen, G., Harris, S., Minear, L., Mowjee, T. and Wilder, A. (2008) *Humanitarian Agenda 2015. The State of the Humanitarian Enterprise*, Medford: Feinstein International Center, Tufts University.

Dunant, H. (1986) *A Memory of Solferino*, Geneva: International Committee of the Red Cross.

European Commission (2012) The EU Approach to Resilience: Learning from Food Security Crises (http://capacity4dev.ec.europa.eu/article/eu-approach-resilience-learning-food-security-crisis) accessed 1 April 2015.

Hilhorst, D. (2005) 'Dead Letter or Living Document? Ten Years Code of Conduct for Disaster Relief', *Disasters*, 29(4):351–369.

Hilhorst, D. (2007) Saving Lives or Saving Societies? Realities of Relief and Reconstruction, Inaugural lecture, Disaster Studies, Wageningen University.

Hilhorst, D. (2008) 'Understanding and Guiding Reconstruction Processes', in: S.J.H. Rietjens and M.T.I.B. Bollen (eds) *Managing Civil–Military Cooperation A 24/7 Joint Effort for Stability*, Farnham, Ashgate, 111–121.

Hilhorst, D. and Jansen, B. (2010) 'Humanitarian Space as Arena: A Perspective of Everyday Practice', *Development and Change*, 41(6):1117–1139.

Hilhorst D. and Pereboom, E. (2014) Dutch Humanitarian Aid: Now and in the Future. A Sector Consultation in Preparation of the Netherlands Humanitarian Summit 2015 (www.healthnettpo.org/files/1228/20141023-internationale-noodhulp-doorgelicht-definitief-eng.pdf) accessed 1 April 2015.

Hilhorst, D. and Serrano, M. (2010) 'The Humanitarian Arena in Angola 1975–2008', *Disasters*, 34(issue supplement s2):183–201.

Hilhorst, D., Christoplos, I. and Van Der Haar, G. (2011) 'Reconstruction from Below. Magic Bullet or Shooting from the Hip?' *Third World Quarterly*, 31(7):1107–1124.

IOB (2013) Linking Relief and Development: More than Old Solutions for Old Problems? (www.government.nl/documents-and-publications/reports/2013/05/01/iob-study-linking-relief-and-development-more-than-old-solutions-for-old-problems.html) accessed 1 April 2015.

ISDR (2005) Hyogo Framework for Action 2005–2015: Building the Resilience of Nations and Communities (www.unisdr.org/files/1037_hyogoframeworkforactionenglish.pdf) accessed 1 April 2015.

Keen, D. (1994) *The Benefits of Famine: A Political Economy of Famine and Relief in South Western Sudan, 1983–1989*, Princeton: Princeton University Press.

Le Billon, P. (2000) *The Political Economy of War. What Relief Agencies Need to Know*, London: Humanitarian Practice Network.

Long, N. (1992) 'From Paradigm Lost to Paradigm Regained? The Case for an Actor-oriented Sociology of Development', in: N. Long and A. Long (eds) *Battlefields of Knowledge: The Interlocking of Theory and Practice in Social Research and Development*, London: Routledge, 16–43.

Long, N. (2001) *Development Sociology. Actor Perspectives.* London: Routledge.

Macrae, J. (2012) 'The Continuum is Dead, Long Live Resilience', *VOICE Out Loud* (15):8–9.

Milante, G. (forthcoming) 'Security and Development'. In: *SIPRI Yearbook 2015*, Chapter 8.

Mosel, I. and Levine, S. (2014) *Remaking the Case for Linking Relief, Rehabilitation and Development: How LRRD Can Become a Practically Useful Concept for Assistance in Difficult Places*, London: ODI.

MSF (2014a) Where Is Everyone? Responding to Emergencies in the Most Difficult Places (www.msf.org/sites/msf.org/files/msf-whereiseveryone_-def-lr_-_july.pdf) accessed 1 April 2015.

MSF (2014b) Global Bio-Disaster Response Urgently Needed in Ebola Fight (www.msf.org/article/global-bio-disaster-response-urgently-needed-ebola-fight) accessed 1 April 2015.

Prescott, G. (2003) Weapons of Mass Destruction: Hope for the Best, Prepare for the Worst? (www.odihpn.org/humanitarian-exchange-magazine/issue-23/weapons-of-mass-destruction-hope-for-the-best-prepare-for-the-worst) accessed 1 April 2015.

Rieff, D. (2002) *A Bed for the Night: Humanitarianism in Crisis*, London: Vintage.

Slim, H. (2003) Marketing Humanitarian Space. Argument and Method in Humanitarian Persuasion (www.hdcentre.org/files/Marketing.pdf) accessed 23 July 2010.

Spearin, C. (2001) 'Private Security Companies and Humanitarians: A Corporate Solution to Securing Humanitarian Spaces?' *International Peacekeeping*, 8(1):20–43.

Thürer, D. (2007) ''Dunant's Pyramid: Thoughts on the Humanitarian Space', *International Review of the Red Cross*, 89(865):47–63.

van der Haar, G. and Hilhorst, D. (2009) Partners in Crisis, Peer Review of Humanitarian Partnership, The Hague: PSO. https://partos.nl/system/files/Report%20Partners%20in%20Crisis.pdf) accessed 1 April 2015, 92 pages.

Part IV
Armed Humanitarianism

5   Blurred Lines, Shrunken Space?

Offensive Peacekeepers, Networked Humanitarians and the Performance of Principle in the Democratic Republic of the Congo

Ryan O'Neill

Introduction

In recent years three interlinked historical narratives have come to dominate discussion of humanitarian action. One, the question of the appropriate relationship between civilian and military actors. Two, the shrinking of 'humanitarian space' under the political pressure of the war on terror. Three, the increased danger faced by humanitarians now targeted by extremist groups. In fact, the term humanitarian space, generally encapsulates all three narratives, presenting each as evidence of a more general trend towards increased instrumentalisation and insecurity (Collinson and Elhawary 2012).

Importantly, these historical narratives are more than mere academic theories, instead, they are powerful social norms deployed by humanitarians themselves in response to the changing nature of humanitarian practice. Humanitarian space, in this sense, denotes the prominent feeling among aid workers that the neutral space between belligerents has closed, leaving both aid workers and civilians at risk. What is more, by lamenting the 'shrinking' of humanitarian space or the 'blurring' of civilian and military agendas, humanitarians perform or enact the very independence they wish to (re)-establish, asserting an opinion contrary to the now dominant logic of the war on terror. Humanitarian space, in other words, is a countermovement, an attempt to redefine what it means to be humanitarian in the wake of armed humanitarianism in Somalia, Rwanda, Kosovo, Afghanistan and Iraq.

That being said, an increasing number of both historical and ethnographic studies have demonstrated the close relationship between humanitarian and military actors. Fassin (2010), for instance, has argued that humanitarian and military actors inhabit the same 'time-space', their presence in a country signalling the more or less temporary suspension of state sovereignty. Moreover, within this time-space, humanitarian and military actors share a set of norms and institutions separate from those practised by either the local population or the government in question. This may include anything from common social circles to the physical location of team houses in 'green zones' to the sharing of security information and evacuation plans. Indeed, the practice of 'NGOing' (DeMars and Dijkzeul 2015) has always involved forging moral, finance and material connections linking donors in the north to recipients in the south, networks that include both military and political actors.

Viewed in this light, humanitarian space must be viewed as a countervailing movement not only against the *external* manipulation of aid, but, *internal* to humanitarianism itself. It is a reworking and rearticulating of humanitarian principles for the purpose of severing existing networks, delinking humanitarianism from those actors perceived to have tainted humanitarian practice. In fact, while the usual target of humanitarian space advocacy has been the UN, NATO and donors like USAID, as we shall see, NGOs themselves have also become targets.

Along these lines, this chapter makes two interlinked arguments. First, it demonstrates, in the case of Democratic Republic of the Congo (DRC), that humanitarian networking has helped produce and legitimise new forms of hybrid peacekeeping more akin to global counterinsurgency warfare; a further step in the now storied development of humanitarian war. In particular, this chapter describes the intimate relationship between humanitarians and MONUSCO, the United Nations Organization Stabilization Mission in the Democratic Republic of the Congo, especially its new Force Intervention Brigade (FIB). Second, it details the various types of resistance that have taken place in the DRC against this new form of humanitarian war, in particular among international NGOs. Here it specifically argues that humanitarian space advocacy has taken the form of 'Othering', political exclusion meant to shame 'mainstream' NGOs who maintain relations with military and political actors.

More practically, this chapter is divided into four sections that broadly reflect the arguments posed above. First, it reviews the theoretical literature on NGOs as network actors, adding some pertinent insights from the broader field of social theory. Second, it discusses the contribution of humanitarian actors to three top-down UN agendas – integration, stabilisation, and protection of civilians – demonstrating how each has further militarised peacekeeping practice, resulting in the present 'neutralisation' mandate in the DRC. Third, it details the reaction on the part of the NGO community to this latest development. Finally, it concludes by drawing broader observations as to the general challenges faced by NGOs seeking to carve out an independent humanitarian space.

The Ties that Bind: Nodes, Norms and Networks

While it has by now become a commonplace argument among those on the left that NGOs are the 'left-hand' (Agier 2010: 29) or 'mendicant order'

(Hardt and Negri 2000: 36) of empire, such descriptions generally flow from a 'functionalist' theory of political economy which reads off NGO practice broad 'systems needs' which NGOs are then said to fulfil (Ohanyan 2012: 372). While this literature is informative insofar as it embeds humanitarian action within the broader political–economic structures of capitalism, its functionalism severely overlooks the diversity of NGO actions, turning a blind eye to those actions that do not serve predefined systems' needs.

By contrast, some sociological institutionalists have argued that the key function of NGOs is that of 'bridging', creating vertical, horizontal and lateral networks so as to maximise their influence and mitigate their financial dependency (DeMars 2005; DeMars and Dijkzeul 2015). Bridging, it must be understood, can both enhance and constrain NGO behaviour. On the one hand, relationships of financial dependency can ensure that NGOs function as little more than an extension of donor states' foreign policy. Indeed, the internal culture of NGOs has, over the years, become increasingly bureaucratic as humanitarians have bent to the demands of donor 'audit culture' or mimicked the professional values of the UN (Ebrahim 2005, 2008). At the same time, coalitions of NGOs, researchers and activists have managed to use these same connections to influence important policies, for instance, on debt relief and anti-retroviral drugs (Bradol 2012: 214).

Three types of networks can be identified within the field of humanitarianism. First, most people understand by networks time-limited, single-issue, context-specific, advocacy campaigns (Keck and Sikkink 1998). Second, it is possible to speak of humanitarianism itself as a single network internal to global civil society (Leroi *et al.* 2004). Finally, we can speak of humanitarian NGOs as themselves networked forms of association. In fact, given that NGOs exist only insofar as they link First World donors to Third World beneficiaries, more often than not through 'partnerships' with local NGOs, one might argue that the basic *form* of the NGO is that of the network; its legitimacy, and hence power, stemming simultaneously from its ability to move material goods, circulate information and transfer affect (Ohanyan 2012).

Humanitarianism is by no means, however, one big happy family, a proverbial circle of friends. On the contrary, NGOs, as network *nodes*, must also be conceived as interfaces were tensions play out over competing network norms and interests. As DeMars and Dijkzeul describe it, 'every NGO is itself a site for power-laced encounters, a nexus of several other cooperating *and* competing actors', each and every NGO thus 'bridges and institutionalises both cooperation and conflict among its own societal and political partners in several countries, as part of its routine NGOing' (DeMars and Dijkzeul 2015: 19). This makes humanitarianism something akin to what the sociologist Pierre Bourdieu terms a 'social field', a socially constructed professional space, the limits of which are defined by conflicts between the actors themselves (Fassin 2010: 279).

If, then, NGOs are networks, existing within the broader, power-laced, professional field of humanitarianism, then the ultimate form of NGO

agency may be that of 'de-bridging', severing or suspending network affiliations until they can be re-established on better terms. By this logic, all
the aforementioned narratives – 'shrinking humanitarian space', 'blurring
civ-mil lines' or 'humanitarians under fire' – can be usefully construed as
normative 'scripts', the performance of which is meant to assert the very
independence they describe, limiting the size and scope of the humanitarian field (Finnemore 1996; Butler 1997). To be clear, such scripts also
help to build networks among NGOs in opposition to military and political actors and agendas. These networks, however, tend to be small, linking
only those NGOs who identify themselves as single mandate or 'Dunantist',
and/or those multi-mandate NGOs who refuse to do development in the
context of war.

A Strange Case of FIB and DRC: Integration, Stabilisation and Protection of Civilians

On March 28, 2013 the UN Security Council (SC) adopted Resolution 2098
(SCR 2098), which authorised a robust intervention brigade in the DRC.
While MONUSCO has been operating under a Chapter VII 'use of force'
mandate since 2000, SCR 2098 supplements the existing force with a new
Force Intervention Brigade, the mandate of which is to *neutralise* armed
groups and restore state authority (UNSC 2013). What separates the present mission in the DRC from the UN-backed missions in Afghanistan, Iraq,
Libya, etc. is the simple fact that in the DRC, blue helmets are at times
actually doing the fighting. They are actively engaged, alongside a preda-
tory national army (FARDC), in order to save a failing, largely unpopular,
regime, on the assumption that stabilising failed states is the best means
of protecting civilians and hence also preventing further acts of terrorism.

Nonetheless, to argue that the FIB and its neutralisation mandate are
'new' is also to beg the question of its historical emergence, to enquire as to
the historical conditions that gave birth to it. Along these lines, it must be
noted that the present mandate in the DRC is in reality an agglomeration of
at least three past UN initiatives – integration, stabilisation and protection
of civilians – initiatives which, while seemingly top down, actually represent years of networking between NGOs, diplomats, military strategists and
civil-society organisations. I turn now to a discussion of each of the above
initiatives with an eye to how each has influenced the development of the
FIB as a humanitarian armed force.

Integration Fever

In the wake of the Rwandan genocide, the UN undertook a review of its
overall approach to both peacekeeping and humanitarian assistance,
reaching the conclusion that the two had often worked at loggerheads,
humanitarian assistance in particular having served as a substitute for both

military intervention and political action (Annan 1997). It so determined that all UN entities at the country level must operate under a single flag. The Secretary General then released a guidance note which positioned the Special Representative to the Secretary General (SRSG) at the top of the in-country mission, redefining the role of the Humanitarian Coordinator (HC) to include political functions and giving him/her the title of Deputy SRSG (DSRSG). Subsequently, in Sierra Leone, the first so-called 'triple hat' DSRSG position was created, lumping together the political function of the DSRSG, the humanitarian responsibilities of the HC and the long-term development agenda of the Resident Coordinator (RC) (Metcalfe *et al.* 2011: 9). Predictably, this angered many NGOs and UN agencies who felt that humanitarian action had been swallowed up by peacekeeping, thus jeopardising the neutrality, impartiality and independence of humanitarians who would now have to coordinate, if not report, their actions to political and military actors.

In DRC, in particular, the HC, RC and DSRSG positions are combined with this so called 'triple hat' DSRSG/HC/RC also being in charge of the regional Peace Security and Cooperation Framework (PSCF) benchmarks and security sector reform, thus raising fears that principled humanitarian assistance has been pushed further to the backburner (MSF 2013). The Office for the Coordination of Humanitarian Affairs (OCHA), for its part, maintains an identifiable presence outside the mission structure, however, it still reports to the HC/DSRSG and has remained silent, at least publicly, on key issues like humanitarian security and FIB-induced displacement (though it recently took a relatively strong stance against the use of drones by humanitarian actors). Additionally, while not seemingly a problem over the last year, in the recent past humanitarians have complained that the SRSG has used his influence over the DSRSG/HC/RC to enforce de facto 'no contact' policies with various rebel factions, in particular Laurent Nkunda's CNDP (National Congress for the Defence of the People) (Metcalfe *et al.* 2011: 31). As a result, a number of NGO coalitions and advocacy groups, for instance InterAction in Washington, have taken strong positions against integration, arguing that 'No new structurally integrated missions should be established in any situation of armed conflict, political violence, or any context where a UN political or peacekeeping mission implements a partisan mandate' (InterAction 2011).

Nevertheless, on the ground, many NGOs have actually been willing if not enthusiastic participants in integrated planning mechanisms. In particular, humanitarians in the DRC have noted that two initiatives, the Protection Cluster and the Senior Management Group – Protection Policy (SMG-PP), have improved protection outcomes by allowing humanitarians to identify 'must go' areas requiring immediate troop deployment (Metcalfe *et al.* 2011: 35). While disputes have since broken out over a number of key issues – Protection Cluster advocacy, the representation of Cluster interests at SMG-PP meetings (which NGOs cannot attend), information sharing on the part of MONUSCO, as well as inadvertent NGO contributions to MONUSCO intelligence gathering – the Cluster remains an influential planning venue and NGOs and UN agencies continue to use it to influence the direction of troop movements (Kemp 2012: 11).

In fact, rather than boycotting integrated planning venues, most NGOs have sought to use them to their advantage, sometimes even pushing for more integration. To give but a few recent examples, World Vision, following Oxfam's lead, recently sought financing in order to staff the position of Co-Cluster lead for Protection, alongside the UN High Commissioner for Refugees (UNHCR). While the organisation's motivation for doing so were multiple, part of the reason was most certainly to increase World Vision's reputation as a protection actor, while also helping to shape protection policy in the DRC (Interview 2014c). In fact, the individual hired for the job then used this platform to push, in conjunction with Search for Common Ground and Mercy Crops, for a more proactive approach to protection, what they termed the 'Do More Good' network (as opposed to simply 'Do No Harm'). Importantly, their recent report and presentations have called into question some of the priorities of the government and MONUSCO's stabilisation strategy, in particular their unwillingness to tackle urban resettlement and resilience (Rudolf 2014). In another instance, a group of major international NGOs pushed for a MONUSCO–NGO exchange to help better inform humanitarians of upcoming operations. This forum now meets weekly at which NGOs are given updates on the details of MONUSCO deployments, the general security context, and civilian protection related matters. NGOs have used this weekly session as a means of pressuring MONUSCO to proceed with caution during operations against the FDLR rebel group (members of which were part of the Rwandan genocide), given that the group now has deep roots in local communities whose lives will be put in danger by FIB and/or Congolese Army operations (MONUSCO–NGO Exchange 2014). Clearly, then, humanitarians have taken the opportunities afforded them by UN integration in order to expand their reach inside the UN, using the cluster system and other such venues in order to increase their professional and personnel relations with military strategists and stabilisation planners.

Nevertheless, NGOs who partake in integrated forums often end up reproducing, at a structural level, problematic assumptions about how conflicts begin and end. Take, for instance, the Protection Cluster. NGOs who participate in this forum not only share information concerning present threats, but they also help code these threats as either 'must', 'could' or 'should' zones, 'must' zones being those to which MONUSCO is obligated to respond either through active patrolling or the establishment of a temporary operating base (TOB). While these efforts may have deterred attacks in the short run, there is no long-term evidence to suggest that they prevent violence against civilians, and it was in part for this reason that the Force Commander, SRSG, and senior military planners have pushed for the expansion of the 'neutralisation' mandate to cover all MONUSCO battalions (Interview 2014a). NGOs who actively participate in the 'must, should, could protect' system thus lend legitimacy to an approach that simply has provided few long-term results. More importantly, however, the very structure of the 'must, should, could protect' system reinforces the flawed notions that conflicts: (a) begin due to an absence of authority, and (b) come to an end through top-down military intervention (De Waal *et al.* 2012; Mahoney 2013); the same assumptions which underlie the FIB. In fact, most humanitarians are well aware that conflict in the DRC stems from inequitable government policy (e.g. corruption, land tenure and political representation) made worse by FARDC human-rights violations (they are in fact the biggest offenders) (UNHCR 2014: 1). And yet, by continuing to partake in such forums, they lend credence to the now popular idea that conflict in Congo owes to an absence of armed state actors.

To summarise, while NGOs have sought to take advantage of UN integration so as to both increase their own profiles and humanise peacekeeping policy, their actions have nevertheless reproduced problematic assumptions about the origins of violence, the direction of political authority (e.g. top-down), and the necessity of international intervention, assumptions which now guide both the FIB and the broader practice of humanitarian war.

Stabilisation: Mild, Medium and Full Bodied

Owing in large part to the concept of human security *and* the impact of 9/11, international security has come to mean more than simply the enforcement of existing borders and sovereign equality. The threat of terrorism means that the SC must now also take into consideration the internal machinations of every state; monitoring at all times for potential 'black holes', ungoverned spaces where terrorists might set up camp (Collinson *et al.* 2010: 5). Stabilisation is thus best understood as a set of policies and practices aimed at enhancing the gaze of the state, allowing it to see and know its subjects inside out. This includes anything from the use of drones to rapid response police forces and financial controls on aid flows, for instance, those contained in Executive Order 13224 and the US Patriot Act (Minear 2012: 60). Most commonly, however, it has meant the deployment of international military forces operating under the model of 'clear, hold, build', first instituted in Afghanistan and Iraq (US Army 2007).

In Congo, the initial stabilisation plan was drafted in 2007 by a small group at UN headquarters in Kinshasa using the framework of 'clear-hold-build' (Lacaille 2013). This basic model would then become the foundation of the Government's Stabilisation and Reconstruction Plan for War Affected Areas (STAREC) and the UN-led International Security and Stabilization Support Strategy (ISSSS) (usually pronounced I4S) strategy papers, both of which favoured a geopolitical approach to stabilisation focusing on major axis routes and conflict zones but expanding the strategy to include economic development, justice reform, etc. (MONUSCO 2009). In reality, MONUSCO's state consolidation mandate had already begun under MONUC, its predecessor. In 2005, following a number of successful attacks on major cities, MONUC was authorised to use all necessary means, 'to deter any foreign or armed group from attempting to use force to threaten the political process ...' (UNSC 2005). This included backing FARDC cordon-and-search tactics as well as a UN-led offensive against the CNDP rebels outside of Goma (see Chapter 6; Boutellis 2013: 3). While these initial missions were somewhat successful, later joint operations against FDLR[1] (*Kimia II*, *Amani Leo*) led to mass human-rights violations by both rebel and FARDC troops (ibid.: 5). In particular, Kimia II operations against FDLR in Uvira territory in July 2009 led to the displacement of 35,000 people, making the total number displaced during operations against FDLR rebels at the time 536,000 (UNHCR 2009). In North Kivu, similar operations resulted in 1.1 million directly affected or temporarily displaced people (OCHA 2009: 2). As if this was not enough, Operation Amani Leo, while more controlled, still resulted in the displacement of 115,000 people in the first three months of 2010 (Human Rights Watch 2010: 8–9). Stabilisation, in other words, had a destabilising effect.

Due to these past failures, the SC requested that MONUSCO's Stabilization Support Unit (SSU) perform a full review of stabilisation policy commencing in 2011. As part of this process both SSU and certain international NGOs sought out NGO and civil-society opinion on stabilisation strategy. The responses were predictable. For many, the problem was simply that stabilisation had ignored local conflicts, in particular land conflicts. In addition NGOs called for more focus on elections as well as a renewed effort at national reconciliation and decentralisation (World Vision 2012). In other words, NGOs demanded that stabilisation become more akin to 'development'. Following from this process, the SSU released ISSSS 2013–2017 (MONUSCO 2013e) which contained many if not all of the recommendations called for by NGOs, thus making stabilisation arguably the overarching framework within which development was now conceptualised.

Hence, stabilisation in the DRC is not simply a top-down US agenda, as in Afghanistan and Somalia. It is in fact implicitly, if not explicitly, supported by the NGO community. There are four reasons for this.

First, because the FARDC are perceived by the Congolese to be both the biggest threat to security and the only option for the future (Oxfam 2014: 13), many NGOs have embraced the core tenants of counterinsurgency, albeit indirectly, working to make both MONUSCO and FARDC better, meaning more 'liberal' warriors. World Vision, for instance, in conjunction with the Pearson Centre for International Peacekeeping, has conducted education programs with the FARDC concerning child protection. Equally, sexual and gender-based violence programmes have brought organisations like International Rescue Committee into close contact with FARDC. Oxfam, even produced a report, later embargoed, analysing the limitations of FARDC's internal procedures (e.g. troop rotations, vetting criteria, patrol supervision, salary, family support, bases, etc.) (Oxfam 2012).

Second, successive mandates have strung together stabilisation and protection of civilians as if they were one and the same thing. As early as SCR 1649 (2005), MONUC had been charged with both eliminating threats to the electoral process and protecting civilians under imminent threat of bodily harm. Both Kimia II and Amani Leo were framed as protection operations despite the fact that they were part of a deal between Rwanda, Congo and MONUC to eliminate the FDLR rebels (Weir 2010: 12–13). This has made it very difficult for NGOs to take strong positions against stabilisation, for most have active protection programmes.

Third, one of the difficulties stemming from the cyclical nature of war in Eastern DRC is the fact that many communities now fall somewhere in between humanitarian emergencies and regular development contexts, with many donors not wanting to fund longer-term projects out of fears of future conflict (Interview 2014e). At the same time, humanitarian assistance to DRC has ebbed and flowed with broader global trends, higher profile conflicts (e.g. Syria, South Sudan, Haiti) drawing resources away from DRC, a cyclical process aid workers term 'Congo fatigue'. Hence, as of July 2014, allocations for the Common Humanitarian Fund (or 'Pooled Fund') where down 49 per cent when compared to July 2013 (OCHA 2014). NGOs looking to continue humanitarian assistance during these low points or build longer-term community resilience thus face serious financial challenges; challenges which some have 'solved' by accepting funding linked to stabilisation, either through STAREC or the SSU (Interview 2014b).

Finally, owing to the stubborn persistence of war in the East and the growing perception among humanitarians that top-down approaches to peacekeeping alone will not bring an end to war, many mainstream development NGOs have sought to expand their programming into the area of peace building, working alongside a growing number of specialised peace-building NGOs like Search for Common Ground, Life and Peace Institute (LPI) and International Alert. At the same time, owing to a persistent and effective academic critique of top-down peacekeeping, the UN has itself sought to embrace peace building as an inherent part of state reconstruction and global stabilisation. UNDP, for instance, has spoken of 'state-building for peace' (Menocal 2011: 1716), by which is meant building local governance capacity so as to provide peace dividends for war-affected populations. While SSU, for its part, has contracted Search for Common Ground, LPI and Resolve Network to carry out conflict mapping exercises eventually leading to conflict transformation projects in present conflict zones and in areas designated for IDP return. There would appear then to be an emerging consensus among SSU, peace-building organisations, and multi-mandate NGOs that conflict is also a local matter and that peace must begin at the community level.

That said, the SSU's approach remains within the broader MONUSCO and government stabilisation strategy, one that is largely top-down and military. Indeed, on issues like demobilisation and reintegration the government has remained intransigent (Human Rights Watch 2014), while the UN has itself been largely unwilling to touch the question of land reform. Generally, then, the assumption now seems to be that while peace happens from the bottom up, war ends from the top down, in particular by enhancing state visibility and eliminating foreign peace 'spoilers'. There are, of course, any number of problems with this strategy, not the least of which is the fact that conflict transformation, when done well, should generate grassroots demands for justice that cannot easily be met by a state forged out of a complex web of legal and illegal elite business networks. Nonetheless, this most recent amalgamation carves out an important role for NGOs in stabilisation, one much closer to their hearts then that pursued in Afghanistan and Iraq and this has arguably muffled dissent. In fact, I have personally witnessed humanitarians being shamed by fellow NGO staff for their 'unprofessional' attempts to reopen the stabilisation debate.

Again, while humanitarians have largely sought to humanise stabilisation, working with members of the SSU to ensure things like conflict mediation and land reform are part of the overarching military-political strategy for DRC, a mixture of financial and social pressure has stifled their critique.

The Perils of Protection

As indicated above, protection policy is another point of interaction among humanitarian and military actors. Following the Rwandan genocide and the ensuing refugee crisis in the DRC, humanitarians sought to redefine their efforts in line with the principle of 'do no harm'. In the 1990s protection of civilians (PoC) was therefore mainstreamed as a general feature of humanitarian programmes, but, with specific emphasis on the treatment of refugees and IDPs. Along these lines, humanitarians set out to better regulate their own practice, developing a set of guidelines – the Sphere Minimum Standards – regulating humanitarian action. In addition, coalitions of NGOs lobbied diplomats to adopt a UN humanitarian 'right of intervention' to protect populations in danger (Ferris 2011).

The UN, for its part, while at first slow to respond, would eventually make PoC a crucial part of peacekeeping operations. In 1999, SCR 1265 recognised for the first time the implications of civilian atrocities, in particular the Rwandan genocide and the Balkans war, for international peace and security (UNSC 1999b). The same year, the SCR 1270 authorised the UN mission in Sierra Leone (UNSMIL), 'to protect civilians from the imminent threat of physical violence' (UNSC 1999a). One year later SCR 1291 authorised MONUC in the DRC to 'take all necessary action, in the areas of deployment of its infantry battalions and as it deems it within its capabilities, to … protect civilians under imminent threat of physical violence' (UNSC 2000). Subsequently, in 2005, the General Assembly established PoC as a global responsibility to protect (R2P), specifying that, when states fail to protect, they forfeit their right to sovereign equality, opening up the possibility of lawful intervention (UNGA 2005).

In practice, however, there remain significant gaps, if not outright contradictions in PoC policy. On the one hand, the UN-sanctioned NATO airstrikes in Libya sought to remove the existing regime from power according to the emerging doctrine of R2P. On the other hand, in places like DRC support for the re-establishment of state authority is said to be the key to protecting civilians. How the UNSC determines when a state lives and when it fails is by no means clear. Complicating matters further, attempts to save states from failing, especially in the DRC, have made peacekeepers active belligerents in conflict. This, in turn, has made much more controversial the question of peacekeepers own PoC responsibilities (Lilly 2012: 631; UN Secretariat 1999).

The aforementioned controversies have made many humanitarians rethink their earlier advocacy efforts with respect to R2P and the humanitarian right to intervene. Some, like Médecins Sans Frontières (MSF), argue that R2P is more akin to 'just war' than humanitarianism (Weissman 2010: 198). Others have chosen to publicly avoid calling for humanitarian intervention on behalf of PoC, while using code words like 'robust' to indicate their desire to see more aggressive military action taken (Mahoney 2013: 24).

In DRC, most humanitarians remain undecided on the question of the use of force for PoC, if only because, while recognising its potential for abuse, the principle of 'humanity' implores them to take all measures necessary to help civilians under attack. As one aid worker in the DRC put it, 'if you were a peacekeeper and knew where Cheka [a local warlord] was hiding, would you not send in a team to kill him in order to save the lives of future victims?' (Interview 2014d). Similarly, in an earlier discussion of the March 23rd Movement (M23) (see Chapter 6), another humanitarian wondered, 'why the UN hadn't moved to attack Bosco Ntaganda's farm in Masisi or his homes in Goma where everyone knew he was stockpiling weapons, in anticipation of the coming war?' (Interview 2013). After all, another humanitarian asked, was this not the lesson of Rwanda, that Romeo Dallaire could have taken out the Interahamwe's weapons caches prior to the genocide, but didn't owing to the cowardice of the SC (Interview 2014f)?

As former Force Commander Major General Patrick Cammaert argues, however, the more difficult question is determining when a threat becomes real, or rather 'how imminent is imminent?' (Cammaert 2007: 6). Along these lines, a recent DPKO/DFS (UN Department of Peacekeeping Operations/Department of Field Support) training module notes that 'necessary actions' to protect civilians under imminent threat may include: 'preventive, pre-emptive, or responsive actions taken to avert, mitigate or respond to an identified threat'. The module further clarifies that, a threat of violence against a civilian is considered imminent from the time it is identified as a threat, until such a time that mission analysis (a combination of military intelligence, human rights and humanitarian findings, and political analysis) can determine that the threat no longer exists.

While 'the determination of "imminence" is not bound by time or geographic proximity' (DPKO 2011: 25–26). This language, written by a humanitarian who had recently worked in the DRC, is an expansion of MONUC's own principle of 'ongoing imminent threat', which sought to expand the scope of PoC-related peacekeeping activities in the DRC to include offensive engagement with groups with a proven track record of violence (Cammaert 2007: 6).

While imminent threat is very much a military doctrine, it was nevertheless written as a response to humanitarian concerns that MONUC had simultaneously increased popular expectations of protection and failed to deliver on these promises. In particular, in June 2004 MONUC failed to stop Brigadier General Laurent Nkunda from sacking Bukavu and subsequently launching attacks against Rutshuru and Goma. While MONUC would eventually defeat Nkunda during heavy fighting in Saki, for most Congolese citizens stories of peacekeepers hiding in their bases in Bukavu refusing to answer the cries of small children were simply too much to forgive. As a Congolese NGO worker in Goma put it to Oxfam, 'They did nothing to stop women getting raped in Bukavu and Rutshuru. I'm scared they wouldn't protect my daughters either if there is more fighting here' (Oxfam 2007: 10). This in turn placed great pressure on international NGOs to demand more be done with respect to the protection of civilians under imminent threat of attack. Oxfam, for instance, called for 'clearer guidelines' in the Rules of Engagement pertaining to troop responses to threats against civilians, including those of the authorities themselves (ibid.: 11). Refugees International would later call for mandate clarification concerning MONUC's role in PoC versus state enforcement and for the inclusion, within MoUs between Troop Contributing Countries (TCCs) and DPKO, details concerning the use of force for PoC (Weir 2010: 12). Importantly, these statements built upon and extended those of Oxfam, Human Rights Watch (HRW) and Merlin during the 2003 Ituri crisis, during which time, humanitarians denounced the hypocrisy of protection in the DRC, MSF even going as far as to compare it to Rwanda and Srebrenica (Soussan 2008: 131).

PoC language, particularly concerning imminent threat, is thus the product of long-standing interactions between MONUC/MONUSCO, the SC, DPKO, TCCs, NGOs and ultimately Congolese civil society. Within this context, international NGOs have leveraged domestic frustration and outrage as a means of pushing MONUSCO and the SC to live up to its protection mandate.

From Protection to Neutralisation and Back: The FIB in the DRC

Historically speaking, there is nothing new about the operations of the FIB. In both Ituri Province in 2003–2005 and in North and South Kivu during 2005–2008, MONUC carried out offensive cordon and search missions which involved the offensive targeting of armed groups (Cammaert 2007, 2013). In fact, the dominant opinion among senior MONUSCO staff is that there is really nothing new about the FIB, that in reality it was just a kick in the pants to the existing Pakistani, Indian and Uruguayan troops, a means of end-running the politics of their respective governments (Interview 2014a; Cammaert 2013).

Nevertheless, section 12b of SCR 2098 defines a mandate over and above the existing PoC language (reiterated in section 12a). In particular, unlike 12a, which implores peacekeepers to protect civilians under 'imminent threat of physical violence', 12b speaks only of 'robust, highly mobile and versatile' operations carried out by the FIB, in order to neutralise armed groups and restore state authority. In fact, MONUSCO's latest mandate renewal (SCR 2147) does away with the category of imminent threat all together, referring in section 4a only to 'civilians under threat of physical violence' (UNSC 2014), thus providing non-FIB battalions increasingly FIB-like force (though they have challenged this interpretation). Not only does this risk raising the expectations of civilians, expectations which most peacekeepers in the DRC will not fulfil (Cammaert 2013), it also places the entire mission within the broader logic of counterinsurgency, according to which any 'threat' to the state, whether or not it imminently threatens civilians, now becomes a target for international military action.

For our present purposes, it is important to tease out the role played by humanitarian NGOs during both the lead up to SCR 2098 and the recent mandate renewal. Shortly after the announcement of SCR 2098, a group of 14 NGOs sent a confidential letter to the SRSG Roger Meece outlining a number of concerns regarding the FIB. While the authors were cautious to avoid either open criticism or outright approval for the FIB, the letter reads at times as if it were a conditional offer of support. For instance, while noting that the FIB comes with serious risks, they add that, 'A military approach will not succeed unless it is part of an integrated process that includes effective political and nonmilitary components' (Joint NGO 2013b). In other words, robust peacekeeping is a necessary but not sufficient condition for peace in Eastern DRC, for what is also necessary is political dialogue. Indeed, the letter concludes with practical suggestions for the various actors involved, including the development of a realistic plan to 'hold' cleared zones and the coordination of FIB and I4S programmes (ibid.), suggestions which sound as if they were ripped right out of the US Army Counterinsurgency field manual (US Army 2007).

Adding further fuel to the fire, during the lead up to the recent mandate renewal in March, 2014, the advocacy working group drafted a policy paper, which, while later revised, initially pledged support for the renewal of the FIBs mandate. This early draft, unceremoniously leaked by MSF, contained a number of statements which seemed more like military strategy and assessment then humanitarian advocacy. For instance, the paper notes the successful 'deterrent effect' of the FIB, adding that, the presence of the FIB, 'must not dissuade other MONUSCO contingents from undertaking more proactive activity to safeguard civilians from armed groups' (Joint NGO 2014). What is more, at the conceptual level, the draft paper replicated the very structure of MONUSCO's Mission Concept, leading some to believe that the author's had sought MONUSCO approval prior to passing it on to other humanitarians.

Generally, then, the approach of NGOs towards the FIB has been that of cautious 'internal' critique, meaning that humanitarians have sought to evaluate the performance of the FIB against what is contained in the mandate (Interview 2014i). The problem with this approach is that it assumes, for strategic reasons, that UNSC mandates are humanitarian. As one aid worker put it, were they to step out of this limited frame they would lose the ability to influence policy on matters like risk mitigation practices (ibid.). However, by accepting the general framework of neutralisation, as a backdrop against which to pursue their goals, they have invariably sacrificed the pretence of neutrality, to say nothing of independence and impartiality.

Cutting the Umbilical Cord: Counterinsurgency and Humanitarian Space

It would be a mistake to think, however, that humanitarians in Eastern DRC have been enthusiastic supporters of MONUSCO's counterinsurgency agenda. On the contrary, there have been a number of points of tension and NGOs have, on a numerous occasions, asserted their desire for a more independent humanitarian space in the DRC. Yet, the net effect of these assertions has been to further divide the humanitarian community.

In July 2013, MONUSCO circulated a draft concept note entitled, 'Islands of Stability' (IoS). The basic idea behind the concept, in line with the strategy of 'clear, hold, build' (now 'shape, clear, hold, build'), was to, 'stabilise areas freed from armed groups' and 'create the conditions for improved governance and long-term development by addressing the root causes of conflicts at the local level' (MONUSCO 2013d). Initially, IoS was relatively well received, if only because humanitarians had earlier asked for just such a plan and because the initial draft made no reference to humanitarian programmes. However, it did make frequent reference to the integrated role of international NGOs, in particular in the areas of 'social cohesion', 'economic and agricultural recovery', 'mediation in land conflicts' and, most importantly, the 'provision of basic services' (ibid.). A later draft then further confused matters by noting, 'Humanitarian actions will be needs-driven as opposed to politically or military driven'

(MONUSCO 2013c). Not only was this akin to preaching to the choir, but, outlining the role to be played by humanitarian NGOs gave the appearance that humanitarian principles were now subsumed within the broader counterinsurgency strategy.

In response, humanitarians began mobilising against IoS. An NGO commentary on the matter thus notes, '[s]ome humanitarian NGOs do not, on principle, want to be involved in stabilisation plans. While some NGOs do carry out stabilisation projects, others consider that taking part in such a project with MONUSCO would jeopardise their ability to operate' (Joint NGO 2013a). In addition to which, a small group of humanitarians sought the support of members of the SSU who felt IoS had undercut I4S. Coordinating behind the scenes, this group then pushed to have IoS brought back within I4S, which it eventually was, the final draft describing IoS as one 'modality' of I4S. More importantly, it emphasised that interventions under IoS do not include humanitarian action (MONUSCO 2013b). Humanitarians, in other words, had managed to ensure their programmes would remain outside of IoS, at least so long as funding would allow. That said, their success owed much to the fact that the humanitarians in question chose not to question the problematic relationship between development, reconstruction and stabilisation, instead treating I4S as the legitimate framework for action. Not unexpectedly, this did not sit well with the more critically minded NGOs.

The situation then came to a head over the question of mandate renewal. In response to the aforementioned mandate renewal letter, MSF sent out a mass email which called out NGOs in Goma for betraying humanitarian principles:

> In order to ensure that the vast and persistent humanitarian needs in eastern DRC are prioritised in line with impartially-assessed needs, humanitarian organisations must avoid engaging in political positions regarding support to stabilisation initiatives, peacebuilding, and the PSCF. Rather, these organisations should be engaging in the MONUSCO mandate renewal process by highlighting the ways in which the current mandate is contributing to the restriction of humanitarian space required to provide quality assistance to populations in need.
>
> (MSF 2014)

In particular it made the case that multi-mandated NGOs, 'risk contributing to the blurring of lines with politico-military agendas' (ibid.). MSF thus sought to sever what they took to be the main connection linking humanitarian space to counterinsurgency warfare, namely: development NGOs.

While MSF's intervention did incite much needed debate, it also exposed contradictions within its own practice. During interviews and informal conversations, aid workers pointed out that while MSF had accused multimandate NGOs of ignoring need, MSF itself is not entirely needs-based, one individual noting that MSF works mainly in North Kivu when greater needs can arguably be found in South Kivu and Katanga (Interview 2014h). What is more, when asked to respond to such accusations, a senior MSF staff member argued that in North Kivu there will always be emergencies and hence 'we must maintain a presence in the area to ensure we can quickly scale up future operations' (Interview 2014g). North Kivu, in other words, is always on the *verge* of crisis; a logic MSF has long used to justify its presence in non-emergency contexts (Redfield 2010).

Aid workers in Goma also complained that MSF's concerns were not born out in fact. MSF's mass communiqué, for instance, makes reference only to MONUSCO and donor activities, in particular MONUSCO's use of white vehicles for military purposes and supposed cuts to humanitarian funding (MSF 2014), while offering no evidence of NGO involvement in stabilisation activities. In fact, the only real evidence provided in the email was the leaked draft mandate renewal letter itself, which, it must be said, was already being revised prior to MSF's intervention. Clearly, then, MSF's statement was not meant to build solidarity among NGOs. On the contrary, it was intended to shame the authors of the report for betraying humanitarian principles, while driving a wedge between multi-mandated and emergency relief organisations, all within sight of MONUSCO, the ultimate target of MSF's attack.

It is important to recognise, however, that MSF's actions in the DRC are part of a larger pattern. Globally, MSF staff, and French aid workers more generally, often refer to the distinction between 'Dunantist' and 'Wilsonian' NGOs, the former being those who believe, following the founder of the International Committee of the Red Cross (ICRC), Henry Dunant, in a limited project of independent emergency assistance and the latter being those who view emergency assistance as part of a larger trajectory of development (Brauman 2012: 1533). Importantly, however, the line between the two seems always to be shifting, in some instances including just MSF and ICRC and at other moments covering a range of development NGOs, such as Save the Children (ibid.), the only qualification seemingly being that the organisations in question take a position contrary to the norm. The point, in any case, is that the distinction is not really conceptual so much as *performative* (Butler 1997). By making such a distinction MSF has in essence sought to mark the limits of the humanitarian field in order to bring pressure to bear on organisations which it feels have grown too close to the Security Council.

To put it in the language of political theory, humanitarian space advocacy is a kind of *Othering* or *scapegoating* which casts onto others one's own complicity so as to purify the community of which one is a part (Žižek 1989). Simply put, by publicly denouncing the actions of other NGOs as ideological, political or even militant, organisations like MSF position themselves as neutral, non-partisan and independent, disavowing their own complicity (for instance, the fact that they maintain 'observer' status in almost every integrated forum, that they run virtually permanent public health centres in counterinsurgency zones, and, it is rumoured, on one occasion appealed for armed support at one of their own bases). While such 'naming and shaming' may at times effectively goad offending NGOs into shifting their behaviour, it is just as likely to backfire, for the limits of humanitarian space are by no means a given. In fact, many humanitarians in the DRC are now of the opinion that it is essential to mix mandates, that strictly humanitarian NGOs are simply out of touch with the needs of Congolese citizens (Interview 2014e). Defending humanitarian space, in other words, requires more than simply naming and shaming. It requires both inter-NGO debate and civilian-military negotiations over the ever-shifting limits, dangers and possibilities of networked engagement.

Conclusion: Lessons Learned (the Hard Way)

Three lessons follow from the above case study of DRC. First, humanitarian NGOs in the DRC, as networked forms of association, have sought to take advantage of top-down UN reforms like integration, stabilisation and PoC in order to increase their leverage over peacekeeping policy, in part as a means of counterbalancing regional and Security Council demands for more aggressive action. Second, while humanitarian NGOs have sought to expose the most overtly manipulative of MONUSCO's policies, such as IoS, they have also, in their daily interactions with the mission, helped reinforce problematic assumptions about the nature of armed conflict (e.g. the idea that war begins and ends with the absence or presence of soldiers). This, in turn, has both shaped their policy critique (which generally targets MONUSCO's failure to live up to its mandate, without questioning that mandate itself) and lent implicit support to the present 'neutralisation' mandate of the FIB. Finally, NGO engagement with MONUSCO, especially as it concerns the FIB operations, has prompted some humanitarian organisations to reconsider their relationships with both the UN and multi-mandate NGOs, deploying the concept of humanitarian space as a means of shaming 'mainstream' NGOs for their betrayal of humanitarian principles, while presenting themselves as the defenders of tradition. Humanitarian space has thus emerged as a counter-principle, a means of severing civilian-military networks and carving out an independent humanitarian space; though one which, it must be noted, is constantly shifting depending on the protagonists involved. Humanitarian space, in other words, is not simply a question of principle, but politics as well, the limits of the humanitarian community being the product of networking, negotiation and alliance formation.

Note

1 The FDLR is partly made up of Interahamwe génocidaires. They fought the Rally for Congolese Democracy (RCD) and preyed on the local population.

References

Agier, M. (2010) 'Humanity as an Identity and its Political Effects', *Humanity*, 1(1):29–45.

Annan, K. (1997) Renewing the United Nations: A Program for Reform (www.undg. org/docs/1400/Renewing_the_UN_A_Programme_for_Reform_A51_950.pdf) accessed 12 March 2014.

Boutellis, J.A. (2013) 'From Crisis to Reform: Peacekeeping Strategies for the Protection of Civilians in the Democratic Republic of the Congo', *Stability: International Journal of Security and Development*, 2(3):48.

Bradol, J.H. (2012) 'Caring for Health', in: C. Magone, M. Neuman and F. Weissman (eds) *Humanitarian Negotiations Revealed: The MSF Experience*, New York: Columbia University Press.

Brauman, R. (2012) ''Médecins Sans Frontières and the ICRC: Matters of Principle', *International Review of the Red Cross*, 94(888):1523–1535.

Butler, J. (1997) *Excitable Speech: A Politics of the Performative*, New York: Routledge.

Cammaert, P. (2007) Learning to Use Force on the Hoof in Peacekeeping: Reflections on the Experience of MONUC's Eastern Division (http://dspace.africaportal. org/jspui/bitstream/123456789/31169/1/MONUCSITREPAPR07.pdf?1) accessed 1 October 2014.

Cammaert, P. (2013) The UN Intervention Brigade in the Democratic Republic of the Congo (www.ipinst.org/publication/policy-papers/detail/403-the-un-intervention-brigade-in-the-democratic-republic-of-the-congo-.html) accessed 14 March 2014.

Collinson, S. and Elhawary, S. (2012) Humanitarian Space: A Review of Trends and Issues (www.odi.org.uk/sites/odi.org.uk/files/odi-assets/publications-opinion-files/7643.pdf) accessed 10 December 2013.

Collinson, S., Elhawary, S. and Muggah, R. (2010) States of Fragility: Stabilisation and its Implications for Humanitarian Action (www.odi.org.uk/sites/odi.org. uk/files/odi-assets/publications-opinion-files/5978.pdf) accessed 5 March 2014.

DeMars, W.E. (2005) *NGOs and Transnational Networks: Wildcards in World Politics*, London: Pluto Press.

DeMars, W.E. and Dijkzeul, D. (2015) 'Conclusion: NGO Research and International Relations Theory', in: W.E. DeMars and D. Dijkzeul (eds) *The NGO Challenge for International Relations Theory*, London: Routledge, 289–317.

De Waal, A., Meierhenrich, J. and Conley-Zilkic, B (2012) How Mass Atrocities End: An Evidence-Based Counter-Narrative (www.fletcherforum.org/2012/01/31/ dewaal-etal) assessed 5 March 2014.

DPKO (2011) Module 2: International Legal Dimensions of the Protection of Civilians, UN Tactical Level Protection of Civilians Training Modules (http:// peacekeepingresourcehub.unlb.org/PBPS/Pages/Public/viewdocument. aspx?id=2&docid=1368) accessed 17 March 2014.

Ebrahim, A. (2005) 'Accountability Myopia: Losing Sight of Organizational Learning', *Nonprofit and Voluntary Sector Quarterly*, 34(1):56–87.

Ebrahim, A. (2008) *NGOs and Organizational Change: Discourse, Reporting and Learning*, New York: Cambridge University Press.

Fassin, D. (2010) 'Heart of Humaneness: The Moral Economy of Humanitarian Intervention', in: D. Fassin and M. Pandolfi (eds) *Contemporary States of Emergency*, London: Zone Books, 269–295.

Ferris, E.G. (2011) *The Politics of Protection: The Limits of Humanitarian Action*, Washington, DC: Brookings Institution Press.

Finnemore, M. (1996) 'Norms, Culture, and World Politics: Insights from Sociology's Institutionalism', *International Organization*, 50(2):325–347.

Government of DRC (2009) Stabilization and Reconstruction Plan for War Affected Areas (STAREC), Prime Minsters Office.

Hardt, M. and Negri, A. (2000) *Empire*, Cambridge, MA: Harvard University Press.

Human Rights Watch (2010) *Always on the Run: The Vicious Cycle of Displacement in Eastern Congo*, New York: Human Rights Watch.

Human Rights Watch (2014) DR Congo: Surrendered Fighters Die in Camp (www.hrw.org/news/2014/10/01/dr-congo-surrendered-fighters-starve-camp) accessed 5 October 2014.

InterAction (2011) A Humanitarian Exception to the Integration Rule (www.interaction. org/sites/default/files/InterAction%20statement%20on%20integration%20-%20 FINAL%2015%20Dec%202011.pdf) accessed 19 September 2014.

Interview (2013) Anonymous aid worker, Gisenyi, 15 March 2013.

Interview (2014a) MONUSCO military planner, Goma, 1 October.

Interview (2014b) Anonymous aid worker, Gisenyi, 27 September.

Interview (2014c) World Vision manager, Goma, 10 September.

Interview (2014d) Anonymous aid worker, Goma, 19 May 2014.

Interview (2014e) Anonymous aid worker, Goma, 5 May 2014.

Interview (2014f) Anonymous aid worker, email, 14 March 2014.

Interview (2014g) MSF staff member, Goma, 19 February 2014.

Interview (2014h) Anonymous aid worker, Goma, 17 February 2014.

Interview (2014i) Anonymous former aid worker, advocacy, Goma, 17 February 2014.

Joint NGO (2013a) Islands of Stability Concept Note Draft 2: NGO Feedback, confidential, obtained by the author.

Joint NGO (2013b) Confidential Joint INGO Note on the Intervention Brigade, final Draft, 7 May 2013.

Joint NGO (2014) Joint INGO Letter to the United Nations Security Council (www. enoughproject.org/files/JointINGOLetter_MONUSCOMandateRenewal_0. pdf) accessed 30 March 2014.

Keck, M. and Sikkink, K. (1998) *Activists Beyond Borders: Advocacy Networks in International Politics*, Ithaca, NY: Cornell University Press.

Kemp, E. (2012) DRC Protection Cluster Co-Facilitation – Lessons Learned (www. humanitarianresponse.info/system/files/documents/files/lessons_learnt-leadership-protection_cluster-2012.pdf) accessed 1 March 2014.

Lacaille, G. (2013) 'Stabilizing the Kivus – Lessons Learned, the Path Ahead', interview with J. Stearns (http://congosiasa.blogspot.com/2013/03/interview-stabilizing-kivuslessons.html) accessed 1 March 2014.

Leroi, H., Mohan, G. and Yanacopulos, H. (2004) 'Networks as Transnational Agents of Development', *Third World Quarterly*, 25(5):839–855.

Lilly, D. (2012) 'The Changing Nature of the Protection of Civilians in International Peace Operations', *International Peacekeeping* 19(5):628–639.

Mahoney, L. (2013) Non-Military Strategies for Civilian Protection in the DRC (www.rdc-humanitaire.net/attachments/article/3369/Non-military-protection-in-the-DRC.pdf) accessed 12 May 2014.

Menocal, A.R. (2011) 'State Building for Peace: A New Paradigm for International Engagement in Post-Conflict Fragile States?' *Third World Quarterly*, 32(10):1715–1736.

Metcalfe, V., Giffen, A. and Elhawary, S. (2011) UN Integration and Humanitarian Space (www.odi.org/publications/6205-un-integration-humanitarian-space) accessed 10 October 2013.

Minear, L. (2012) "Humanitarian Action and Politicization: A Review of Experience Since World War II', in: A. Donini (ed.) *The Golden Fleece: Manipulation and Independence in Humanitarian Action*, Sterling, VA: Kumarian Press, 43–67.

MONUSCO (2009) 'International Security and Stabilization Support Strategy (ISSSS) 2009–2012', Stabilization Support Unit, Draft Final.

MONUSCO (2013a) 'Peace It: Together on the Journey to Lasting Peace in the Democratic Republic of the Congo', Mission Concept, Draft 4.5.

MONUSCO (2013b) 'Islands of Stability', Stabilization Support Unit, Draft Final.

MONUSCO (2013c) 'Islands of Stability', Stabilization Support Unit, Draft 2.

MONUSCO (2013d) 'Islands of Stability', Stabilization Support Unit, Draft 1.

MONUSCO (2013e) 'International Security and Stabilization Support Strategy (ISSSS) 2013–2017', Stabilization Support Unit, Draft Final.

MONUSCO–NGO Exchange (2014) Meeting Minutes (12 March), confidential, obtained by the author.

MSF (2013) 'Proteger l'independence, neutralite et impartialite de l'aid humanitaire en RDC dans le nouveau contexte de la brigade d'intervention de la MONUSCO', Positioning Paper, October, Draft Final.

MSF (2014) 'Response to NGO MONUSCO Mandate Renewal Letter', email, 17 February.

OCHA (2009) Population Movements in Eastern DR Congo April to June 2009 (http://stopthewarinnorthkivu.files.wordpress.com/2009/08/april-june-2009-ocha-drc_idps-report-july-2009.pdf) accessed 7 March 2014.

OCHA (2014) Monthly Brief #12 DRC – Pooled Fund (https://docs.unocha.org/sites/dms/DRC/PooledFund/Pooled%20fund%20DRC%20Monthly%20brief%20July%202014.pdf) accessed 8 October 2014.

Ohanyan, A. (2012) 'Network Institutionalism and NGO Studies', *International Studies Perspectives*, 13:366–389.

Oxfam (2007) A Fragile Future: Why Scaling Down MONUC Too Soon Could Spell Disaster in DRC (http:file:///C:/Users/roneill/Downloads/bp97-fragile-future-monuc-230207-en.pdf) accessed 14 May 2014.

Oxfam (2012) *In Search of an Army: How the Congolese Army Can Improve Civilians' Safety*, Oxfam Briefing Paper 165, confidential, obtained by author.

Oxfam (2014) In the Balance: Searching for Protection in Eastern DRC (www.oxfam.org/sites/www.oxfam.org/files/bp-in-the-balance-protection-eastern-drc-270114-en.pdf) accessed 7 March 2014.

Redfield, P. (2010) 'The Verge of Crisis: Doctors without Borders in Uganda', in: D. Fassin and M. Pandolfi (eds) *Contemporary States of Emergency*, London: Zone Books, 173–197.

Rudolf, M. (2014) 'Accessing the Humanitarian Response to Chronic Crisis in North Kivu', Report prepared on behalf of the Do More Good Consortium, World Vision, Search for Common Ground, Mercy Corps.

Soussan, J. (2008) MSF and Protection: Pending or Closed? Discourse and Practice Surrounding the 'Protection of Civilians' (www.msf-crash.org/drive/cd8b-cahier-protection-va.pdf) accessed 28 September 2014.

UNGA (2005) Resolution 60/1 2005 World Summit Outcome (www.un.org/womenwatch/ods/A-RES-60-1-E.pdf) accessed 14 October 2013.

UNHCR (2009) DRC: Thousands of Congolese Flee the New Fighting in South Kivu (www.unhcr.org/4a698bf89.html) accessed 5 April 2014.

UNHCR (2014) Protection Monitoring – Nord Kivu, Update No. 20/2014, 12–18 May 2014.

UNSC (1999a) Resolution 1270 (www.refworld.org/pdfid/3b00f22814.pdf) accessed 14 October 2013.

UNSC (1999b) Resolution 1265 (www.securitycouncilreport.org) accessed 14 April 2014.

UNSC (2000) Resolution 1291 (www.securitycouncilreport.org) accessed 14 October 2013.

UNSC (2005) Resolution 1649 (www.securitycouncilreport.org) accessed 14 October 2013.

UNSC (2013) Resolution 2098 (www.un.org/en/sc/documents/resolutions/2013.shtml) accessed 29 March 2013.

UNSC (2014) Resolution 2147 (www.securitycouncilreport.org) accessed 1 October 2014.

UN Secretariat (1999) Observance by United Nations Peacekeepers of International Humanitarian Law (http://www1.umn.edu/humanrts/instree/unobservance1999.pdf) accessed 14 April 2014.

US Army (2007) *Counterinsurgency Field Manuel*, Chicago: University of Chicago Press.

Weir, E. (2010) Last Line of Defense: How Peacekeepers Can Better Protect Civilians (http://refugeesinternational.org/sites/default/files/10_LastLineDefense.pdf) accessed 5 October 2014.

Weissman, F. (2010) '"Not in our Name": Why Médicins Sans Frontières Does Not Support the "Responsibility to Protect"', *Criminal Justice Ethics*, 29(2):194–207.

World Vision (2012) *Stabilization and the New Deal for Aid Effectiveness for Fragile States in the Democratic Republic of Congo*, confidential, obtained by the author.

Žižek, S. (1989) 'Introduction: The Spectre of Ideology', in: S. Žižek (ed.) *Mapping Ideology*, London: Verso, 1–34.

6 Rebels without Borders

Armed Groups as Humanitarian Actors

Ryan O'Neill

Introduction

As the previous chapter argued, humanitarian NGOs are networked forms of association, whose efforts to extend their own influence and reduce direct dependence on any one donor, often bring them into close relations with military actors and principles. In this chapter, I extend this analysis by examining rebel–NGO relations and the adoption of humanitarian ideology by rebel factions. The argument is as follows. During the late Cold War and early post-Cold War period, NGOs made an explicit choice to work with rebels in cases where their national governments had failed to respect the rights of their people(s). While later developments (e.g. the Rwandan genocide and 9/11) forced NGOs to rethink this approach, NGO–rebel relations have now returned to the agenda, this time as a means of counterbalancing the increasingly partisan nature of UN peacekeeping operations. That said, as I demonstrate in the case of the March 23rd Movement (M23) in Democratic Republic of the Congo (DRC), partnering with post-colonial rebels is a dangerous game, for many insurgent groups are now well aware that working with NGOs holds the key to attaining international recognition; some even championing the cause of 'humanitarian independence' as a means of discrediting counterinsurgency operations. Simply put, the space between insurgency and counterinsurgency, the space generally occupied by humanitarians, is now thoroughly saturated, making neutral, impartial, and independent humanitarian action increasingly difficult.

Below, I briefly review the theoretical framework developed in the previous chapter, adding reflections on the ties binding African rebel movements, the UN and humanitarian NGOs. Next, using the case study of Rwandan and Ugandan backed rebel groups in the DRC, I examine the various ways in which rebels have adjusted their actions to fit with changing patterns of humanitarianism, in particular their substitution of 'humanitarian reason' (Fassin 2010, 2012) in the place of political ideology and local popular mobilisation. I conclude by demonstrating the problematic similarity between M23's critique of the UN Organization Stabilization Mission in the Democratic Republic of the Congo (MONUSCO) and that of NGOs like Médecins Sans Frontières (MSF).

Hidden Partners: NGO–Rebel Relations

As argued in the previous chapter, NGOs serve as nodes in broader funding and policy networks, crossing the threshold between civil society, the state and international institutions. This not only makes them agents of global governance, it also means they contribute to the institutional multiplicity of recipient societies, implanting foreign interests, norms and institutions (e.g. audit culture, liberal human rights, etc.) deep within the socio-economic landscape of Third World states. That does not mean, however, that they are mere 'functions' of powerful nation states or even international institutions. On the contrary, their presence within multiple, overlapping funding and policy networks, including informal distribution partnerships with *insurgents* – provides them with their own form of institutional multiplicity, which they draw upon in resisting, or at least putting off, the most intrusive donor demands. It is to these latter connections between NGOs and rebels insurgents that I now turn.

In 1960 the UN adopted Resolution 1514 establishing a 'right of independence' and calling on colonial rulers to transfer, 'all powers to the peoples of those territories, without any conditions or reservations'. Resolution 1514 not only conferred formal recognition upon a number of rebel groups in Southern Africa (i.e. the ANC in South Africa, SWAPO in Namibia, FERLIMO in Mozambique, PAIGC in Cape Verde) (Reno 2011: 16; Schmidt 2013: 82, 113), it also provided NGOs significant room to manoeuvre in terms of support for these organisations. NGOs like Oxfam could thus confidently, if informally, funnel money to the African National Congress in its bid to end Apartheid (Palmer 2008).

UN support for African insurgencies had its limit, however. In particular, while the UN's Decolonization Committee and the Organization of African Unity's (OAU) Coordinating Committee for the Liberation of Africa helped bring an end to Portuguese colonialism and white minority rule, their mandates did not extend to post-colonial Africa. Indeed, both the UN and OAU enshrined the principles of 'territorial integrity' and 'national sovereignty' within their respective charters (Clapham 1998: 4), meaning those post-independence rebels who sought to establish new territories (e.g. in Biafra, Nigeria and Katanga, Zaire) received little international support (Reno 2011: 22). While insurgents who sought to revolutionise the African state and economy (with or without Soviet support) were quickly put down through a mix of violence and cooptation, often at the hands of fellow pan-African leaders (e.g. Tanzania during the Zanzibar revolution) (Wilson 2013).

While the UN and OUA largely stuck by this line throughout the Cold War, working with repressive regimes like the Derg in Ethiopia out of a misplaced respect for African territorial integrity, some NGOs and church groups broke ranks, forging independent relations with major post-colonial rebel groups like the Eritrean People's Liberation Front (EPLF) and the Tigray People's Liberation Front (TPLF) in Ethiopia, and the Sudan People's Liberation Army (SPLA) in southern Sudan. More specifically, in 1975, a group of Scandinavian Lutheran NGOs partnered with the EPLF to set up the Eritrean Relief Association (ERA), eventually convincing the International Committee of the Red Cross (ICRC) to funnel its food aid through the ERA (Reno 2011: 148). Shortly thereafter, the British NGO War on Want would duplicate this process in Tigray, partnering with the TPLF to establish the Relief Society of Tigray or REST (ibid.). While in 1981 a Scandinavian ecumenical NGO consortium set up the Emergency Relief Desk (ERD) in Khartoum to coordinate aid efforts with the ERA and REST (Duffield and Prendergast 1994: 65–74). This strategy was later replicated in South Sudan where the SPLA set up the Sudan Relief and Rehabilitation Association (SSRA) (ibid.: 75).

Together, the efforts of the ERA, REST and ERD are now commonly referred to as the era of 'negotiated access', a reference to the fact that NGOs at the time were willing to negotiate with all sides in order to gain access to populations in need (Duffield 2007: 133). The 1980s are therefore considered by many veteran humanitarians to be the golden age of humanitarian neutrality and independence, a time during which NGOs did not simply 'talk the talk', but also 'walked the walk', forging relations with rebel groups so as to balance the violence of post-independence dictators (ibid.: 39–40).

The classic era of negotiated access did not last long, however. By the mid-1990s, armed humanitarian intervention had redefined the terms of the debate. More specifically, three factors led to the gradual delegitimisation of large-scale, formal, humanitarian–rebel relations. First, unlike ERA and REST, who by most accounts were models of humanitarian impartiality, SRRA in South Sudan was from the start a humanitarian nightmare (Duffield and Prendergast 1994: 167). In particular, the SPLA, through SSRA, 'taxed' food aid to feed soldiers (Maxwell 2012: 212), used these same taxes to finance 'visa' departments dedicated to the seizure and control of aid (Lavergne and Weissman 2004: 155) and, worst of all, directed NGOs to key strategic zones so as to deter government attacks (ibid.: 154). The lesson learned in South Sudan, then, was that aid can help prolong war (LeRiche 2004; Lischer 2003).

Second, in the final days of the Rwanda genocide roughly two million Hutu refugees poured across the border into Zaire and hidden among them were some 70,000 belligerents (Lischer 2003: 80). In response, the international community launched a massive aid campaign to preserve the lives of Hutu refugees, failing, however, to discriminate between civilians and armed combatants and eventually fuelling a resurgence of war. The Rwandan genocide and the subsequent Congo wars thus demanded a major rethink on the part of humanitarians, with a number of NGOs, rights groups and UN organisations undertaking review exercises meant to usher in a new humanitarianism (African Rights 1995; Annan 1997). As part of this process, many NGOs sought greater professionalisation and the community as a whole moved to standardise humanitarian action in particular as it pertains to refugees and internally displaced persons. Gone were the days of heroic adventurism, to be replaced by an increasingly bureaucratic, risk-averse, humanitarian profession increasingly defined by the ethical motto: 'do no harm' (Anderson 1999).

Third, following the Rwandan genocide and corresponding refugee crisis in the DRC, concerns were raised that the humanitarian response in the camps had substituted for a political solution both to the militarisation of the camps and the genocide itself (Annan 1997). To this end, the UN moved to strengthen coordination and integrate its humanitarian and peacekeeping component while also making 'protection of civilians' and the restoration of 'state authority' peacekeeping objectives. As a result, NGOs have developed increasingly close relations with the UN, just as the UN has become increasingly involved in counterinsurgency operations.

Fourth, adding further fuel to the fire, 9/11 and the war on terror have resulted in the gradual shifting of aid flows away from 'negotiated access' agreements with rebel groups like the SPLA to 'post-conflict reconstruction' (Duffield 2007: 133). For many NGOs, this shift in funding has meant greater harmonisation with the government and armed forces and an equivalent marginalisation of rebel groups. While certain organisations, ICRC and MSF first among them, have tried to resist this process, forging new relations with rebel groups as a countervailing force against the war on terror, this is by no means the norm (Crombé and Hofman 2011: 55–6; Donini 2012: 84).

While African rebels were thus once officially recognised members of humanitarian networks, changes to both the political economy of rebellion and humanitarian action have reduced them to minor, often times unacknowledged, or even covert, partners. Indeed, the recent rise in attacks against aid workers in a handful of countries (Pakistan, Syria, South Sudan, Sudan and Somalia), some of which were perpetrated by insurgents, has resulted in the widespread popular belief that humanitarian principles and practices are no longer respected by non-state actors. This, coupled with the indifference, or rather antagonism with which the US and its allies now treat International Humanitarian Law (IHL) has led many to the conclusion that humanitarian space has shrunken to almost nothing and must be rebuilt from the ground up.

Importantly, however, debates over the meaning of humanitarian space and the limits of civilian-military interactions have in many ways been overdetermined by a nostalgic longing for a return to the practice of 'negotiated access'. Champions of humanitarian space like MSF have thus sought to rethink humanitarianism as a pragmatic profession guided not by resolute adherence to any given set of principles, but, careful negotiations with all parties, made possible by a strict process of self-critique and denunciation of all forms of politic manipulation (Allié 2012: 3–5). It is questionable, however, whether such a 'return' is at all viable, if only because the UN's turn towards stabilisation, alongside the war on terror, have largely undercut the spirit of negotiation, which, in any case, had largely become a farce by the mid-1990s, rebel groups forming and splitting in the process of competing over the spoils of peace (Tull and Mehler 2005). At the same time, and this will be the topic of the remainder of this chapter, rebel groups have themselves sought to take advantage of the growing popularity of humanitarian reason, championing the need for neutral, independent assistance and impartial negotiations as part of an ideological strategy to discredit global counterinsurgency warfare.

Acting in Enemy Territory: The Aid-Insurgency Interface in the DRC

Let us turn our attention now to a particular case of rebel–NGO interactions, that between international NGOs operating in Eastern DRC and rebel forces active in that area. While it is beyond the scope of this paper to provide a complete overview of all rebel–NGO relations in Eastern DRC, I focus here on one particular lineage of Rwandan and Ugandan backed rebels. To this end, I begin with an overview of Laurent Kabila's Allied Democratic Forces for the Liberation of the Congo/Zaire (ADFL), moving quickly to a discussion of Ernest Wamba dia Wamba's Rally for Congolese Democracy (RCD) and Laurent Nkunda's National Congress for the Defence of the People (CNDP), before concluding with a more detailed discussion of the present day M23. Throughout, I focus on the manifold ways in which each group has sought to court international opinion by presenting itself as humanitarian, ultimately in order to win diplomatic support for its cause.

ADFL to RDC: The Primacy of the International

On 1 October 1990, 2000 men, mostly exiled Rwandan Tutsis fighting for Yoweri Museveni's National Resistance Army (NRA), crossed the Ugandan border into Rwanda. While initially unpopular, by 1992, with their forces numbering 12,000 and having scored a number of key tactical victories, Rwandans began to join the movement, placing enormous pressure on the moderate Hutu government (Prunier 1998: 131–2). In turn, Hutu extremists reacted by fomenting hatred against all Tutsis and arming youth militias. With terrorising efficiency nearly 1 million Tutsis and moderate Hutus were killed in just over eight weeks by the army, the Interahamwe youth militias and regular Rwandan citizens. By the time the RPF made its way to Kigali on 4 July 1994, nearly two million Hutu refugees, including 20,000 former military and 50,000 militiamen had streamed across the border into Zaire (now the DRC) (Lischer 2003: 80).

Inadvertently deepening the crisis, the UN and international NGOs responded by setting up refugee camps along the border in the DRC, failing both to discern between civilians and combatants and allowing the génocidaires to rearm and reorganise (Reed 1998: 144–5). In response, Rwanda mobilised its own rebel force, the ADFL, led by the 'briefcase guerrilla' Laurent Desiré Kabila. In less than a month the ADFL managed to clear the camps and take control of Zaire's three main Eastern cities, Uvira, Bukavu and Goma (ibid.: 148). The onslaught did not stop there, as the ADFL, aided by the Ugandan and Rwandan armies, moved further North towards the Ugandan border and East to the important diamond producing province of Kasai, before eventually walking their way into the capital Kinshasa and seizing control of the state (ibid.: 150).

By 1997, owing to growing popular discontent, Congo's new President Kabila turned the tables on his Rwandan masters, actively fomenting anti-Tutsi hatred and unceremoniously kicking Rwandan members of his ADFL movement out of the country (Stearns 2011: 183). The Rwandans and Ugandans then set about mobilising yet another rebellion. This second rebellion, known as the RCD, was initially headed by the Marxist professor Earnest Wamba dia Wamba. Wamba had been hand-picked by Museveni to lead an awkward 'coalition of convenience' including former ADFL Lieutenants of Rwandan origin, Mobutu supporters, prominent professionals from within the UN and a mélange of businessmen marginalised by Kabila (Tull and Mehler 2005: 378). From the outset, the RCD, unlike its predecessor, was orchestrated with international opinion in mind, the presence of respected figures like Wamba making up for the movement's dubious affiliation with Rwanda and Uganda (ibid.). In fact, the rebels actually hired a lobbying firm to represent their interests in Washington as a counter to Kabila's close relations with rogue states like Libya and North Korea. And to a certain extent this worked, then US Assistant Secretary of State for African Affairs, Susan Rice, paying a visit to the rebels in Kigali shortly after the start of hostilities in November 1998 (ibid.: 381).

While the RCD never managed to win the support of local populations, owing in no small part to its brutality and factional infighting, Rwandan and Ugandan support allowed the two major factions of the RCD to maintain control of Eastern Congo for the good part of five years (1998–2002). What is more, once it became clear that there would be no repeat of Laurent Kabila's earlier march on the capital (due to the interventions of Zimbabwe and Angola), the rebels benefitted greatly from their prior engagements with the international community, both factions gaining a seat at the table for the Sun City peace talks and later a number of positions in government (Prunier 2009: 244).

In the end, however, it was Joseph Kabila, son of the late Lauren Kabila, who won out, having outmanoeuvred both the RCD and their main rivals, the Ugandan-backed Movement for the Liberation of Congo (MLC). Owing, however, to the US and UN's new-found interest in South African-style *power-sharing* agreements and the skilled attempts on the part of the various rebel factions to exploit this desire, the Sun City accord ended up giving power to a motley crew of rebel leaders, many of whom had commenced their rebellions not long before the Sun City talks began (Tull and Mehler 2005: 277). Rebellion, in other words, had long ceased to be an ideological enterprise. Rather, the end goal of insurgency in Congo was now 'recognition', for in the post-Rwanda, post-Apartheid world, international approval held the key to attaining a piece of the freshly baked power-pie.

CNDP: The Humanitarian Mystique

After his father was killed in 2003, Joseph Kabila emerged as interim President and would eventually use his position to consolidate power over the MLC and RCD(s). As a result, hundreds of 'Banyarwandan' Tutsis and Hutus who had risen to power in the East during the reign of the RCD watched their gains erode, creating conditions ripe for renewed insurgency (Stearns 2008: 246). In September 2003, Laurent Nkunda and two other Tutsi commanders, Colonels Eric Ruohimbere and Elie Gishondo, refused to join the national army citing security concerns and the RCD's poor position within the Peace Agreement (ibid.). Shortly thereafter, they carried out armed action in the eastern DRC. During the 2006 elections, Nkunda, would announce the creation of his own organisation the CNDP, positioning himself as a defender of minorities and calling for national unity (ibid.: 251).

A key part of CNDP's arsenal of propaganda was the manipulation of international opinion. While CNDP did not enjoy the same prestige as the RCD, nor the same level of diplomatic recognition, owing in large part to the electoral victory of President Kabila, they did their best to present themselves as responsible international partners. Along these lines, CNDP developed a sophisticated media strategy which included two websites, print literature, interviews with foreign journalists and a radio station, all of which pushed their humanitarian credentials. Nkunda also invested money in development projects, helping to rebuild local schools and health centres, paying teacher's salaries and buying generators for a health centre (ibid.: 264). Most interestingly, CNDP set up a parallel governance structure including a Social Affairs Commission headed by Dr Alexis Kasanzu (Stearns 2012a: 65). Dr Alexi, as he has come to be known among humanitarians, had formerly been employed at the Community Baptist Hospital of Central Africa (CBCA) in Kitchanga, where he worked alongside health-focused NGOs like MSF and Merlin (Le Bansais 2013: 9). Dr Alexi and his staff thus helped to ensure humanitarian programmes continued to function in CNDP territory, and this created problems for the UN. For instance, in 2007–2008, owing to the growing public profile of Nkunda and CNDP, MONUC attempted to impose an informal 'no contact' policy, interrupting an NGO–CNDP child soldier screening programme so as to erode Nkunda's position at the bargaining table. Humanitarian actors subsequently identified this as a serious violation of humanitarian space (Metcalfe *et al.* 2011: 31).

On 4 January 2009, after a series of failed negotiations, Presidents Kabila and Kagame cut a deal, calling for the integration of CNDP soldiers within FARDC in exchange for the imprisonment of Nkunda. Nkunda had become an increasingly high-profile figure internationally who Kigali feared they could no longer control. Hedging their bets, Rwanda threw their weight behind Bosco Ntaganda, Nkunda's second in command, who unceremoniously removed Nkunda as head of CNDP, handing him over to the Rwandan Government who placed him under house arrest (Stearns 2012a: 34).

M23: Movement Without a Cause

In February 2011, President Kabila then began a *regimentation* process meant to merge army units into blocks of 1200 soldiers, the purpose of which was to break the parallel command structures of CNDP units inside the FARDC (ibid.: 39). Shortly thereafter, Bosco Ntaganda and other former CNDP officers defected, launching a series of attacks in South Kivu (ibid.: 40–43). Their mission, if one can even call it that, was to force Kabila to adhere by the terms of the 23 March 2009 peace agreement (negotiated in conjunction with Nkunda's arrest) (Stearns 2012b). Of course, their official motives were also mixed with clandestine desires for political and financial control of North Kivu, in part in order to appease their Rwandan backers (Stearns 2012a: 55).

Importantly, 'M23', as it came to be known, maintained many of the earlier structures developed by CNDP. For instance, it developed at least two websites (www.soleildugraben.com and congodrcnews.com), a Facebook fan page and numerous twitter feeds, all dedicated to countering the government and UN's line that M23 was just another name for the Government of Rwanda (ibid.: 44). It also set up a formal liaison office for humanitarians working in the area and appointed Dr Alexis as head of their Social and Humanitarian Affairs Department. What is more, like CNDP before it, M23 set up a local tax collection agency through which to finance their military and propaganda operations (UN Group of Experts 2013), including a proposed levy on NGOs operating in the area. In a coordinated response organised by the Office for the Coordination of Humanitarian Affairs (OCHA), however, a consortium of NGOs operating in Rutshuru territory refused to pay taxes to the organisation, a move that, surprisingly, was met with little resistance on M23's part (Interview 2013c). Tellingly, rather than attack NGOs for their non-cooperation, the rebels focused their taxation and predation on local peoples and key transportation arteries, not wanting to jeopardise their international reputation (Kay 2013).

While M23 did its best to facilitate easy access to displaced peoples and their host communities so as to ensure good relations with NGOs, it also deployed humanitarian language and reasoning as part of an ideological war against the UN. Despite mixed local feelings about the November 2012 capture of Goma (ibid.), neighbouring states, in particular those within the Southern African Development Community (SADC), saw this as yet another attempt on the part of Rwanda to destabilise a key SADC trade and investment 'partner' (Shepherd 2013). Accordingly, SADC members revived a decade-old Libyan proposal for a 'neutral' African offensive force in Congo (Prunier 2009: 249). Months later this would result in the passing of UN Security Council Resolution 2098 and the establishment of a new MONUSCO force, the FIB, staffed by Tanzania, South Africa and Malawi, with the mandate to neutralise armed groups (see Chapter 5). In response, M23 launched a media blitz, advancing the argument that offensive MONUSCO operations endangered the lives of civilians living in their territory and threatened to displace thousands (CCTV 2013). The rebel leadership also argued that the new mandate undermined the peace process at Kampala and that the purpose of peacekeeping was to protect peace agreements not destroy one party to the talks (ibid.).

At the same time, M23 used its website and Twitter accounts to discredit Human Rights Watch (HRW) reports, which claimed that the movement had made use of child soldiers. In a press release the rebels argued that they sought to protect children from the violence of organisations like FDLR, the former Rwandan génocidaires. The organisation also made clear that it only accepted adult volunteers and that it had handed over to humanitarian organisations 13 former child soldiers recruited by Bosco Ntaganda, with whom the rebels had by then parted ways (M23 2013a).

It is crucial to place these ideological manoeuvres in the context of M23's overarching military-political strategy. M23's strategy, far from seizing the state or 'balkanising' Eastern Congo – which, despite the musings of certain M23 politicians were never realistic options – was simply to gain control of a 'liberated zone' along the Rwandan and Ugandan borders and to hold fast until the government agreed to a new round of negotiations (Jones 2012; Katabarwa 2013). Once it became clear that the international community would not tolerate rebel control of Goma, the goal of the rebels shrank even further, M23 moving to consolidate its hold on areas north of Goma, implementing a taxation system and minor services (e.g. road repair) while positioning itself as the 'protectorate' of the local population (Kay 2013).

Joint FARDC–MONUSCO offensives had thus to be prevented if this strategy was to work. To this end, M23 sought to paint itself as a reliable humanitarian partner, while publicly demonising the already demonic FARDC so as to dissuade the UN from partnering with the army. For instance, in a letter to the South African parliament during the lead up to the deployment of the Intervention Brigade, M23 wrote:

> The M23, noted the UN resolution 2098, of March 28, 2013, which transforming the UN peace keepers in a belligerent force, entrusted with offensive mission to extend the reign of an army which the crime

rate and rape is the highest of all armies of the world and come to rescue the most corrupt regime in the world. Words of the Secretary General of the United Nations stating in the same resolution that corruption are the main cause of failure of the Congolese Government.

(M23 2013c)

Similarly, M23 also sought to expose connections between the FARDC and the FLDR so as to discredit the army and, as a corollary, MONUSCO (M23 2013b). As indicated below, however, once joint FARDC–MONUSCO operations began, M23's strategy shifted to include MSF-style arguments concerning the blurring of civilian and military actors and the erosion of humanitarian space.

The Humanitarian Response: NGO Perceptions of M23

Before moving on to a more in-depth discussion of M23 and humanitarian space let us consider the response of humanitarians to the aforementioned ideological moves of M23. International NGO workers present in Rutshuru during M23s reign describe the organisation as a relatively good local administrative partner. A French humanitarian, for instance, who had worked with Dr Alexis prior to the UN intervention described him as an experienced and committed humanitarian, a professional who never seemed overtly motivated by ideology (Interview 2013a). Another expatriate humanitarian working in the area of sexual and gender-based violence commented that M23 was generally very responsive to NGO complaints and requests, moving quickly to address problems reported by humanitarians (e.g. road blocks, taxes, intimidation of staff, etc.). In fact, the same humanitarian argued that M23 was actually far more responsive than the FARDC, both during the conflict and afterwards (Interview 2014f). This was a sentiment echoed by many of the individuals interviewed. In particular it was noted that while M23 got all the bad press, the FARDC was a much bigger problem (Interview 2013b). Another humanitarian interviewed lamented the fact that since M23 had been defeated, they had run into problems with a local youth group who had disrupted their programmes and even assaulted a staff member in a bid to win jobs (Interview 2014b).

None of this should suggest, however, that international NGOs and/ or individual humanitarians were sympathetic to M23's cause, far from it. Many told of incidences of sexual violence by the rebels. As one of the above interviewees recounted, during the last days of M23's reign, the NGO in question brought cases of sexual violence to the attention of the rebel leadership, who responded by tracking down and punishing the women who they thought were the source of the accusations (Interview 2014f). For this individual, while M23 was a reasonably reliable administrative partner, its human-rights record negated its many attempts to position itself as a humanitarian actor.

For the vast majority of aid workers who swept in and out of the country between November 2012 and December 2013, the going opinion was therefore similar to that advanced in the mainstream media: M23 was/is a Rwandan rebel group the sole purpose of which was to exploit Congolese mineral deposits both for personal gain and to the benefit of the Rwandan state. Most, in other words, felt that the organisation is little more than a criminal gang run by power-hungry politicians. Indeed, behind the scenes aid workers often echoed the remarks of Che Guevara (2011), arguing that M23 lacked ideology, having set out from the beginning to seize power but not popular opinion.

Most humanitarian organisations thus welcomed MONUSCO's decision to counter-attack and then attack M23 positions north of Goma. This despite the risk that such efforts might interrupt the flow of aid and create further displacement (which, it did, at least one major NGO reported 60 lost programming days during the campaign) (Interview 2014b). Even worse, in direct violation of humanitarian principles, Oxfam publicly condemned M23, calling its actions a violation of international law and the 'territorial integrity' of DRC (Oxfam 2012). Clearly, then, M23's courting of the humanitarian community had failed to produce the expected results.

The one exception to this rule is MSF. Officially MSF does not take a stand for or against M23, or for that matter MONUSCO's intervention brigade. It does believe, however, that the UN's new neutralisation mandate creates confusion between humanitarian and military activities (Interview 2014e, 2013c). The organisation has accordingly pushed MONUSCO to differentiate between its military and humanitarian assets, proposing that it paint any vehicles carrying weapons or troops green, that it cease its Quick Impact Projects carried out by soldiers, and that it reflects upon the fact that offensive operations will likely cause displacement and the disruption of humanitarian assistance (Interview 2014e, 2013c; MSF 2013: 3–4). While these policy proposals are hardly revolutionary and are in fact similar to demands made by NGOs in Afghanistan, its position nevertheless placed MSF at odds with MONUSCO (Interview 2013c, 2014e; Long 2013).

Stuck in the Middle with You: MONUSCO–NGO–M23 Relations

In October 2013, M23 reportedly fired upon a MONUSCO helicopter carrying civilian staff. When questioned about the incident M23 members responded that they had fired upon the helicopter because they had mistaken it to be part of a joint FARDC–MONUSCO operation (Radio Okapi 2013). That said, the explanation given by the rebels was inconsistent at best. Amani Kabashi, an M23 spokesperson, argued that, 'MONUSCO is a belligerent in this conflict now. It is not neutral. If they want to be part of the conflict we'll take them as part of the conflict', strangely adding that, 'We only fired warning shots to show MONUSCO that what they're doing is not fair' (Gander 2013). Such inconsistencies, when coupled with

M23's past record of shooting at unarmed MONUSCO choppers (UN News Centre 2012) and its stated position that it would strike any UN aircraft entering their airspace (Gander 2013), have led many to the conclusion that M23 knew what it was doing; that its reference to 'civilian-military' confusion was but an attempt to take advantage of humanitarian principles in order to discredit MONUSCO's offensive.

In fact, a brief review of M23's website would appear to confirm such a theory. A 26 July 2013 post, for instance, makes explicit reference to MSF's position under the tagline 'Fears Grow over the UN Intervention Brigade in Congo':

> Medical charity Médecins Sans Frontières earlier said it was very concerned about a blurring of the distinction between the UN's humanitarian and military work. Because of the potential confusion between those roles, MSF said it no longer wanted any military – including UN soldiers – deployed near its health facilities. There was a real danger, MSF said, that heightened tension could lead to a targeting of medical activities.
>
> (Congo DRC News 2013)

Shortly thereafter, M23 made the same point in decrying the use of MONUSCO's Munigi base by the FARDC, which it had attacked in 'self-defence':

> The MONUSCO and the Brigade mentioned bases were in truly the positions of the FARDC, which in the normal course of the war, were affected and should not have been therefore mentioned here as simple and innocent victims' targets. This is the case of the MONUSCO base of MUNIGI which had been assigned to the FARDC to shell the M23 positions and was condemned by the M23 Movement through its press release.
>
> (M23 2014: 3)

For M23, in other words, even where MONUSCO was not actively involved in the fighting, use of its resources by FARDC, including bases, intelligence and supply lines, would still constitute a violation of the long-standing principle of distinction (Interview 2013d).

Further complicating matters, MSF then used the above incidences in defence of humanitarian space:

> In October 2013, the M23 fired at a UN helicopter with a UN humanitarian mission inside because they could not distinguish between UN transport bringing aid, and UN transport bringing artillery. It is unacceptable that an attacking force does so from civilian transports, rather than military vehicles clearly recognisable as such. This will have major consequences for the delivery of aid, as the people will no longer know

if a white vehicle driving into their village brings bullets or blankets. The neutrality of humanitarian action must be respected by all parties to the conflict, including MONUSCO, by clearly distinguishing all their military assets from the civilian functions of the UN.

(MSF 2014a)

Not only did MSF take M23 at its word that it had truly confused MONUSCO civilian and military vehicles, but, the above statement seemed to accuse the UN of actively disguising artillery and troop movements in the guise of civilian missions. In fact, during an informal discussion, one senior MSFer argued that confusion over the UN's civilian and military activities was part of the UN's broader counterinsurgency strategy in Congo and elsewhere (Interview 2013c). While it is certainly true that MONUSCO has sought to integrate humanitarian and military action, whether or not it has intentionally sought to disguise combatants as humanitarians for strategic advantage is another matter altogether. Yet, statements of this nature run the risk of blurring the lines between the preservation of humanitarian neutrality and independence and active support for insurgents.

The Fallout: M23, MSF and the Campaign to Protect Humanitarian Space

Sadly, the proximity of MSF's position to that of M23 has contributed to the disdain with which many humanitarians have approached MSF and its policy proposals. While MSF in the DRC has managed to keep the issue of humanitarian space on the agenda – their efforts having helped frame the debate around the use of drones by NGOs – the position of the humanitarian community remains broadly hostile. Consider the following statements. When queried on their opinion of MSF's proposals to paint MONUSCO military vehicles green, international humanitarian workers responded with cynical denunciations of MSF itself. For most, the proposal was simply unnecessary as many NGOs (International Rescue Committee, Norwegian Refugee Council, Oxfam, War Child, etc.) had already moved to distinguish themselves from the UN. For others, the proposal was superfluous because MSF was simply reading off of other situations, namely, Somalia, Afghanistan and Iraq, dangers not present in Congo (e.g. kidnappings and killings of expatriates). Some even pointed to a recent report by the international security NGO, INSO, which indicated that armed groups in the DRC are well informed as to the distinction between humanitarian and military actors (Brabant and Vogel 2014). A few humanitarians took things further, however, one noting that peacekeepers were never meant to be neutral and that in Congo MONUSCO had long been authorised to use offensive force (Interview 2014a). Another argued that MSF was in essence trying to tie the hands of MONUSCO (Interview 2014c); a point made earlier by MONUSCO itself, spokesman Manodge Mounoubai having opined,

'I don't know what MSF wants us to do. Fold our arms and allow armed groups to kill the population? We can't tolerate that' (Long 2013). One NGO worker even pointed out that MSF's position was exactly the same as that of M23 and that this hurt their credibility (Interview 2014d).

While many of the above comments were made in the heat of the moment in response to MSF's accusation that NGOs in the DRC had abandoned humanitarian principles (MSF 2014b), they nevertheless contain a kernel of truth. Although MSF is correct to argue that UN offensive operations politicise humanitarian assistance, the opposite is also the case: in arguing against the blurring of 'civilian–military' lines, NGOs like MSF indirectly advance the political position of insurgents. Al-Shabaab, for instance, has set up an Office for Supervising the Affairs of Foreign Agencies, to help communicate 'conditions and restrictions' of access for humanitarians, principle among them not cooperating with the African Union mission and certain UN agencies (Al-Shabaab 2009). Al-Shabaab, like M23, has thus attempted to split off 'neutral', 'impartial', and 'independent' humanitarians from 'imperialists', precisely by appealing to the logic of humanitarian space (this strategy being essential to the maintenance of aid in the face of immense need). Ironically, then, when MSF speaks out against humanitarian complicity in war, labelling multi-mandate NGOs 'Wilsonian' and denouncing organisations who partake in post-war reconstruction, they make the same point as Al-Shabaab, implicitly accusing these organisations of imperialism.

In part for this reason, some within MSF have sought to rethink humanitarian space advocacy, arguing that humanitarians must keep their distance from *all* armed actors, whether the UN, the national army or insurgents (Interview 2013c; Allié 2012). It remains to be seen, however, whether this is practically viable. Not only would this require NGOs to turn down reconstruction moneys at a time of reduced humanitarian assistance, but, it would also mean refusing to work with rebel groups like M23 who manipulate humanitarian sentiment, potentially sacrificing access to those in need. What is clear, however, is that NGOs need to change the terms of engagement with both rebels and the UN. This could include, for example, working with rebels like M23 in order to better articulate their concerns within the framework of IHL in exchange for significant assurances that they will themselves respect humanitarian law. This might also mean refusing to partake in UN-integrated forums in the context of offensive peacekeeping operations unless the UN clarifies the combat status of peacekeepers and better distinguishes its military vehicles.

Conclusion: A Crowded House!

Extrapolating from the situation in the DRC, we can now conclude that rebel–NGO relations are caught somewhere between all-out war and covert support. On the one hand, the war on terror and certain high-profile kidnappings and killings of aid workers have led many organisations to seek further integration with the UN system. On the other hand, heavy handed US legislation and donor manipulation have led other organisations to pursue renewed connections with insurgents. However, many African insurgents are now 'hip to the game', understanding that international recognition holds the key to accessing state power, some having even created their own humanitarian wings to serve this end. It is fair to conclude, then, that in many cases African rebels have abandoned their old – Marxist, ethnic or other – rhetoric in favour of humanitarian reason, including arguments pertaining to the blurring of civilian–military relations and humanitarian space. Such rhetoric, while often comical, nevertheless places humanitarians in an unenviable position of inadvertently supporting causes with which they would not otherwise agree, if only to help counterbalance the power of the Security Council. The humanitarian arena, in other words, is now an increasingly crowded house.

References

African Rights (1995) *Rwanda: Death, Despair, and Defiance*, London: African Rights.
Allié, M.P. (2012) 'Introduction: Acting at Any Price?' in: C. Magone, M. Neuman and F. Weissman (eds) *Humanitarian Negotiations Revealed: The MSF Experience*, New York: Columbia University Press, 1–15.
Al-Shabaab (2009) Press release on behalf of the Department of Political Affairs and Regional Administrations regarding the status of the various NGOs and foreign agencies operating in Somalia (http://patronusanalytical.com/files/Al_Shabaabs_NGO_liaison_office_announces_closure_of_UN_offices_in_Somalia.php) accessed 1 March 2014.
Anderson, M.B. (1999) *Do No Harm: How Aid Can Support Peace or War*, Boulder, CO: Lynne Rienner Publishers.
Annan, K. (1997) Renewing the United Nations: A Program for Reform (www.undg.org/docs/1400/Renewing_the_UN_A_Programme_for_Reform_A51_950.pdf) accessed 12 March 2014.
Brabant, J. and Vogel, C. (2014) Dans Leurs Yeux (www.ngosafety.com) accessed 17 March 2015.
CCTV (2013) Rebels Oppose UN Intervention Brigade in DRC, CCTV (http://english.cntv.cn/program/africalive/20130412/100598.shtml) accessed 20 April 2014.
Clapham, C. (1998) 'Introduction: Analyzing African Insurgencies', in: C. Clapham (ed.) *African Guerillas*, Oxford: James Currey, 1–19.
Congo DRC News (2013) Fears Grow over the UN Intervention Brigade in Congo (https://m23congordc.wordpress.com/2013/07/26/fears-grow-over-the-un-intervention-brigade-in-congo-drc-m23) accessed 20 April 2014.
Crombé, X. and Hofman, M. (2011) 'Afghanistan: Regaining Leverage', in: C. Magone, M. Neuman and F. Weissman (eds) *Humanitarian Negotiations Revealed: The MSF Experience*, New York: Columbia University Press, 49–69.
Donini, A. (2012) 'Afghanistan: Back to the Future', in: A. Donini (ed.) *The Golden Fleece: Manipulation and Independence in Humanitarian Action*, Sterling, VA: Kumarian Press, 67–89.

Duffield, M. (2007) *Development, Security and Unending War: Governing the World of Peoples*, London: Polity.

Duffield, M. and Prendergast, J. (1994) *Without Troops and Tanks: Humanitarian Intervention in Eritrea and Ethiopia*, Trenton, NJ: Red Sea Press.

Fassin, D. (2010) 'Heart of Humaneness: The Moral Economy of Humanitarian Intervention', in: D. Fassin and M. Pandolfi (eds) *Contemporary States of Emergency*, London: Zone Books, 269–295.

Fassin, D. (2012) *Humanitarian Reason: A Moral History of the Present*, Berkeley: University of California Press.

Gander, K. (2013) Congo Rebels Fire Shots at UN Helicopter (www.independent. co.uk/news/world/africa/congo-rebels-fire-shots-at-un-helicopter-8876263. html) accessed 1 May 2014.

Guevara, C. (2011) *Congo Diary: The Story of Che Guevara's 'Lost' Year in Africa*, Melbourne: Ocean Press.

Interview (2013a) Anonymous aid worker, programmes, Goma, 10 April 2013.

Interview (2013b) Anonymous aid worker, operations/programmes, Goma, 7 November 2013.

Interview (2013c) European-based MSF researcher, Goma, 5 December 2013.

Interview (2013d) Five anonymous aid workers from same NGO, Goma, 5 December 2013.

Interview (2014a) Anonymous former aid worker, advocacy, Goma, 17 February 2014.

Interview (2014b) Anonymous aid worker, operations/programmes, Goma, 18 February 2014.

Interview (2014c) Anonymous aid worker, advocacy, Goma, 18 February 2014.

Interview (2014d) Anonymous aid worker, advocacy, Goma, 18 February 2014.

Interview (2014e) Two MSF aid workers, Goma, 19 February 2014.

Interview (2014f) Anonymous aid worker, sexual/gender-based violence, Goma, 27 June 2014.

Jones, P. (2012) Negotiating with the DRC Rebels: First as Tragedy, Then as Farce? (http://thinkafricapress.com/drc/m23-confused-rebellion-kampala-talks-uganda-rwanda-cndp-goma) accessed 18 November 2014.

Katabarwa, D. (2013) Simplistic Narrative Used to Distort the Truth about the M23 Insurgency (http://ngonewsafrica.org/archives/12441) accessed 20 April 2014.

Kay, J. (2013) Behind Rebel Lines: Living with the M23 in DRC Congo (http:// thinkafricapress.com/author/joseph-kay) accessed 18 November 2014.

Lavergne, M. and Weissman, F. (2004) 'Sudan: Who Benefits from Humanitarian Aid?' in: F. Weissman (ed.) *In the Shadows of 'Just War': Violence, Politics and Humanitarian Action*, Ithaca, NY: Cornell University Press.

Le Bansais, B. (2013) 'Kivu: Les Réfugiés et des Balles', *Là Bas*, 6ème, 1 January 2013:8–11.

LeRiche, M. (2004) 'Unintended Alliance: The Co-option of Humanitarian Aid in Conflicts', *Parameters*, 34:104–120.

Lischer, S.K. (2003) 'Collateral Damage: Humanitarian Assistance as a Cause of Conflict', *International Security*, 28(1):79–109.

Long, N. (2013) Medical Charity Criticizes UN's Congo Mandate (www.voanews. com/content/doctors-without-frontiers-un-congo/1699859.html) accessed 1 March 2014.

M23 (2013a) M23 communiqué denying the recruitment of child soldiers (www. un.org/ga/search/view_doc.asp?symbol=S/2013/433) accessed 1 April 2014).

M23 (2013b) M23 communiqué announcing a ceasefire after their retreat from Mutaho (www.un.org/ga/search/view_doc.asp?symbol=S/2013/433) accessed 1 April 2014.

M23 (2013c) Motion for Cancelling the Sending of South African Soldiers to War in DRC (www.un.org/ga/search/view_doc.asp?symbol=S/2013/433) accessed 1 April 2014.

M23 (2014) The M23 Reaction to the UN Group of Exerpts Report (www. m23-mars.org/wp-content/uploads/2014/01/The-M23-reaction-to-the-UN-Experts-report-1.pdf) accessed 1 April 2014.

Maxwell, D. (2012) 'Those with Guns Never Go Hungry: The Instrumental Use of Humanitarian Food Assistance in Conflict', in: A. Donini (ed.) *The Golden Fleece: Manipulation and Independence in Humanitarian Action*, Sterling, VA: Kumarian Press, 197–219.

Metcalfe, V., Giffen, A. and Elhawary, S. (2011) UN Integration and Humanitarian Space (www.odi.org/publications/6205-un-integration-humanitarian-space) accessed 10 October 2013.

MSF (2013) 'Proteger l'independence, neutralite et impartialite de l'aid humanitaire en RDC dans le nouveau contexte de la brigade d'intervention de la MONUSCO', positioning paper, October, Draft Final.

MSF (2014a) Everyday Emergency: Silent Suffering in Democratic Republic of Congo (www.msf.es/sites/default/files/adjuntos/MSF%20informe%20 RDC%20-%20Everyday%20Emergency%20_0.pdf) accessed 1 May 2014.

MSF (2014b) 'Response to NGO MONUSCO mandate renewal letter', email, 17 February.

Oxfam (2012) We condemn the renewed M23 military campaign, a violation of int'l law & the territorial integrity of DRC, *Twitter*, 21 November 2012 (https:// twitter.com/oxfam/status/271188727307587584) accessed 20 April 2014.

Palmer, R. (2008) *A House in Zambia: Recollections of the ANC and Oxfam at 250 Zambezi Road, Lusaka, 1967–97*, Lusaka: Book World Publishers.

Prunier, G. (1998) 'The Rwandan Patriotic Front', in: C. Clapham (ed.) *African Guerillas*, Oxford: James Currey, 119–134.

Prunier, G. (2009) *Africa's World War: Congo, the Rwandan Genocide, and the Making of a Continental Catastrophe*, Oxford: Oxford University Press.

Radio Okapi (2013) North Kivu: un hélicoptère de la MONUSCO essuie des tirs du M23 à Rumangabo, *Radio Okapi*, 11 October 2013 (http://radiookapi.net/ actualite/2013/10/11/nord-kivu-helicoptere-de-la-monusco-essuie-des-tirs-du-m23-rumangabo/#.U7LVifmSx98) accessed 20 April 2014.

Reed, C. (1998) 'Guerillas in the Midst', in: C. Clapham (ed.) *African Guerillas*, Oxford: James Currey, 134–155.

Reno, W. (2011) *Warfare in Independent Africa*, Cambridge: Cambridge University Press.

Schmidt, E. (2013) *Foreign Intervention in Africa: From the Cold War to the War on Terror*, Cambridge: Cambridge University Press.

Shepherd, B. (2013) The Fall of the M23: African Geopolitics and the DRC (www. chathamhouse.org/media/comment/view/195557) accessed 20 January 2014.

Stearns, J. (2008) 'Laurent Nkunda and the National Congress for the Defense of the People (CNDP)', in: S. Marysse, F. Reyntjens, and S. Vandegiste (eds) *L'Afrique des Grands Lacs: Annuaire 2007–2008*, Paris: L'Hartmattan, 245–267.

Stearns, J. (2011) *Dancing in the Glory of Monsters: The Collapse of the Congo and the Great War of Africa*, New York: Public Affairs.

Stearns, J. (2012a) *From CNDP to M23: The Evolution of an Armed Movement in Eastern Congo*, London: Rift Valley Institute.

Stearns, J. (2012b) Interview with Bertrand Bisimwa, M23 Spokesperson (http://congosiasa.blogspot.com/2012/12/interview-with-bertrand-bisimwa-m23.html) accessed April 20 2014.

Tull, D. and Mehler, A. (2005) 'The Hidden Costs of Power Sharing: Reproducing Insurgent Violence in Africa', *African Affairs*, 104/416:375–398.

UN Group of Experts (2013) Mid Term Report of the Group of Experts on the Democratic Republic of Congo (www.un.org/ga/search/view_doc.asp?symbol=S/2013/433) accessed 1 April 2014.

UN News Centre (2012) UN Peacekeeping Mission in DR Congo Warns M23 Armed Group over Helicopter Attacks (www.un.org/apps/news/story.asp?NewsID=43852&#.U7vpVfmSx98) accessed 1 May 2014.

Weizman, E. (2011) *The Least of all Possible Evils*, London: Verso.

Wilson, A. (2013) *The Threat of Liberation: Imperialism and Revolution in Zanzibar*, London: Pluto Press.

The Military, the Private Sector and Traditional Humanitarian Actors

Interaction, interoperability
and effectiveness

Samuel Carpenter and Randolph Kent

Introduction

In the foreseeable future, the global community will be faced with a major humanitarian capacity challenge. This chapter shows that the old cooperation paradigm, in which non-traditional humanitarian actors simply fit into the tried and tested approaches of traditional humanitarian actors, is not the only way the global humanitarian system may develop. Future modes of interaction will need to reflect the aims and objectives of each actor. Therefore we explore three types of actors, namely humanitarian organisations, the military and the private sector, to better understand their potential interoperability and contribution to humanitarian effectiveness. If the effectiveness of the global humanitarian system as a whole is to increase, there is a need for a greater focus on consistent delivery of humanitarian outcomes for those in need, particularly given the growing array of actors (with their different mandates and values) who serve as inputs into what is an increasingly fragmented system. Meeting the humanitarian capacity challenge will require an understanding of cooperation that is underpinned by an appreciation of each potential partner's core interests and business.

In the second section of this chapter, we set our theoretical framework for understanding the development of the global humanitarian system, drawing on constructivist theory and approaches to transnational flows and action encompassed in global politics. The third section outlines that the intensity, frequency and complexity of humanitarian crises is increasing, in some instances exponentially. Yet, present approaches to humanitarian crises do not reflect the resources, capacities or expertise needed to deal with the crises of the future. Moreover, as we argue in the fourth section, humanitarian crises are moving to the centre of the political fold, placing limitations on access for traditional humanitarian actors and driving a trend towards humanitarian action that reflects local culture, values and language. Greater attention has to be given to ways to address such gaps in capacity and acceptance, including by engaging more effectively with those outside the traditional humanitarian sector, such as the military and private sector. The fifth section explores traditional and emerging perspectives on the roles of the military and private sector in humanitarian action, and how these vary according to context. The sixth section looks at the underexplored capacities of the military and the private sector in relation to humanitarian action, specifically in the areas of strategic planning, innovation and surge capacity. We analyse the private-sector contribution alongside that of the military, as private companies are often essential in the operationalisation of military innovations and can provide an important firewall between the political and strategic objectives of military actors and the principled (specifically, neutral, impartial and independent) provision of assistance and protection by traditional humanitarian actors. The concluding section addresses the challenges and opportunities of increased and new forms of military and private-sector engagement, specifically in terms of their interaction and interoperability with traditional humanitarian agencies. We differentiate between the challenges and opportunities in different regions and operational environments (especially disasters as opposed to armed conflict) in analysing what this means for the future principles, practice and effectiveness of humanitarian action, not least meeting the humanitarian capacity challenge.

The (Re)construction of the Global Humanitarian System

Humanitarian action is no longer solely the preserve of what has become known as the 'international humanitarian system', structured by its three pillars of the International Red Cross and Red Crescent Movement, UN agencies and international non-governmental organisations (INGOs), what we call traditional humanitarian actors. The range of actors involved in humanitarian assistance and protection has increased significantly since the UN General Assembly Resolution 46/182 set out the role of the UN in the coordination of humanitarian assistance in 1991. In recent years, the activities and discourse of a multitude of non-traditional humanitarian actors, including regional organisations, national and local governments, the military, the private sector, the scientific community, non-OECD-DAC (Organisation for Economic Co-operation and Development Development Assistance Committee) donors and diaspora networks, have come to restructure the global humanitarian system.

To explain the (re)construction of the global humanitarian system we draw on constructivist IR theory and global politics. Building on Giddens's (1986) sociological concept of 'structuration', we contend that both the structure of the global humanitarian system and the actors that inhabit it are mutually constitutive. Humanitarian action is not influenced simply either by structure (power and politics, established norms and institutions) or by agency (interaction of actors and associated changes in social constructs), but by the interaction of the two (Wendt 1992). In the same way

that the system within which states interact is a product of those very interactions, the global humanitarian system is a product of the above list of
traditional, non-traditional and emerging actors which constitute it, and
vice versa.

As Sezgin and Dijkzeul (this volume) indicate, institutions and discourses
can constrain the thinking and preferences of (humanitarian) actors, limiting their actions and the resultant structure of the system. Further, the
influence of the actions of different agents within a system on its structure is a consequence of their power, which can lead to social constructs
becoming 'sedimented as structure', resulting in the predominance of a
prevailing structure of practice (Buzan *et al.* 1998: 35). In the humanitarian
sector, this is manifest in the centrality of traditional norms and institutions
including the Geneva Conventions of 1949 and their Additional Protocols,
the Fundamental Principles of the Red Cross ('humanitarian principles'),
the Good Humanitarian Donorship principles and instruments of sectoral professionalisation such as the Sphere Project (Humanitarian Charter
and Minimum Standards) and the Code of Conduct the International Red
Cross and Red Crescent Movement and NGOs in Disaster Relief, as well as
ongoing efforts to develop 'joint standards'.

But these norms can be challenged. New norms are beginning to emerge,
for example from the ongoing discussions on the development of Islamic
humanitarian principles (Ofteringer 2013). Moreover, in a globalised
world, there is arguably not one structure of the humanitarian system but
a number of interconnected systems. Therefore our approach follows the
departure from IR theory to global politics by a number of prominent
social and political scientists. Moving away from the national/international
binary enables us to better understand the interactions between actors at
different levels and in different contexts (Shaw 2003). Using this approach,
we examine the varying challenges and opportunities that face humanitarian actors (both traditional and non-traditional) in different regions and
normative contexts – for example, differing societal and political perspectives on the role of military and the private sector in the Arab Gulf and
Southeast Asia as opposed to Europe, the UK and the US.

The Humanitarian Capacity Challenge

In recent decades, the risk, scale, frequency and complexity of humanitarian
crises has changed rapidly amid wider transformations in politics, economics, technology and culture catalysed by contemporary globalisation. The
risk of disasters is accumulating rapidly, with climate change increasing the
intensity and frequency[1] of extreme weather events and urbanisation expos-
ing greater numbers of people to their impacts (IFRC 2010; IPCC 2012),
as well as the intersection of those impacts with technological hazards. The
chronic, recurring nature of droughts in regions such as the Sahel and
the Horn of Africa and of conflicts in eastern Democratic Republic of the

Congo (DRC), South Sudan and Yemen has entrenched vulnerability and undermined coping capacities.

While various studies show that the number of armed conflicts has decreased in the post-Cold War period (Mack 2014), the number of people forcibly displaced has risen to 51.2 million and the deliberate targeting of civilians shows no sign of abating (UNHCR 2014). One of the main drivers of civilian deaths has been urban violence in Latin America, where deaths from violence linked to drug supply and criminal and territorial gang activity are higher than in many armed conflicts. In Rio de Janeiro State, for example, over 80,000 people were killed and 40,000 disappeared in the decade up to 2011 (ICRC 2011).

Over the last ten years, the combined result of these trends has been a doubling in the estimated number of people directly affected by humanitarian crises, with the figure reaching 144 million in 2012 (OCHA 2013a). The humanitarian system is overheating in its effort to meet the needs arising from simultaneous crises of overwhelming scale. In 2013 alone there were major emergencies or mega-disasters in the Central African Republic, Philippines, South Sudan and Syria. Yet, the humanitarian caseload will continue to increase in coming decades. Therefore, while humanitarian funding still rose in 2013, financing is unlikely to keep pace with growing needs (Swithern 2014).

Unpredictability is also at the centre of shifts in the global risk profile. Indeed, complexity is a defining feature of the systems we inhabit and construct. As Ramalingam (2013: 142) puts it, the contemporary world is characterised by 'interconnectedness, networks, emergence, non-linear change, phase transitions and tipping points, intelligent actors adapting to their circumstances and each other, and systems that evolve together over time'. In light of these dynamics, the humanitarian system will have to respond to a range of interrelated shocks – such as disease outbreaks and pandemics, weather-related hazards, geophysical events, conflicts, economic volatility and technology-related crises such as catastrophic collapse of communications systems and cyber-war – and stresses: natural resource degradation, water scarcity, urbanisation, demographic changes, climate change, migration, political instability and commodity price rises (particularly in food and energy).[2]

The impacts of such shocks and stresses are likely to be increasingly cross-border and cross-regional. While so-called domino effects have been considered plausible in consultations with UN country teams, few people in national authorities or international agencies have given them sufficient credence to date (Kent 2013). For example, the potential for mass migration driven by a range of factors, including the impacts of climate change and environmental degradation, could present major challenges for humanitarian response, as could changes in the distribution of diseases such as malaria driven by climate change (Caminade *et al.* 2014) and antibiotic-resistant superbugs. The 2014 Ebola outbreak in West Africa and the risk posed by our interconnectedness through aviation is but an early signal of an emerging threat.

Drawing on this analysis of trends in disasters, conflict and potential future humanitarian crises, we argue that there is a humanitarian capacity challenge – a gap in the resources, capacities and expertise needed to deal with plausible risks in the foreseeable future.

This is not to suggest that crisis-affected countries in what had been traditionally described as the 'Global South' should be seen as in a state of 'permanent emergency', therefore justifying perpetual international humanitarian engagement (Duffield 2007: 32). Indeed, a number of low- and middle-income crisis-affected states have now developed their own disaster (risk) management policies, authorities and attendant capacities (Harvey 2009; Harkey 2014). Yet, it also does not suggest that the sup- posed 'Resilient North' has or will have what will be required to deal with future crises, its own or others', independent of a more concerted, global approach to crisis-risk management and humanitarian response.

The Political Centrality of Humanitarian Crises

In recent years, a number of political leaders, for example in Italy, Iran, Turkey and the US, have found to their cost that failure to respond to crisis risk or the impact of a disaster can have serious political consequences.[3] While humanitarian crises have in various guises had recognised political ramifications over time, from the obligations of Chinese emperors to deal with floods and Ethiopian emperors to deal with famines, the pressures upon leaders and the institutions of government appear to have increased. In part this is due to the broader economic impacts of crises and the fact that social networking and improved communications, even in tradition- ally remote areas, make their downplaying ever more difficult. Citizens are more connected, better informed and thus have higher expectations of government in preventing and managing crises (OCHA 2013b). It is also due to pressures from neighbouring states to limit crisis contagion and in no small part to fundamental political changes in governance structures – primarily relating to global processes driving democratisation – in many parts of the world (Kaldor 2008).

Increased reputational consequences relating to how disaster risk and humanitarian crises are handled make government authorities increas- ingly cautious as to how they respond to such crises and whom they wish to be involved in that response. In various ways this wariness may result in considerable limitations on traditional humanitarian actors. For these international and non-governmental organisations' interests do not always cohere with government sensitivities. In an increasingly interconnected communications environment, governments are keener than ever to man- age the political risk of humanitarian crises, seeking ever greater control over, and sometimes denying, humanitarian access, and preferring their own forms of humanitarian assistance. Some affected states are also seeking to reassert their sovereignty in light of expanding humanitarian engagement in conflict-related crises (Kahn and Cunningham 2013). Therefore humanitarian agencies are finding it increasingly difficult to ensure safe and timely access to affected populations. Myanmar, Sudan (Darfur) and Syria are just a few well-known examples (Parker 2013).

In 2011, a group of humanitarian officials representing 22 governments in Africa and Latin America were asked what sort of assistance they required from the international community. They responded that they did not need 'boots on the ground', but that they would appreciate expertise and innovation that would strengthen their prevention, preparedness, response and recovery capacities.[4] Hence, the critical consequence of the growing political centrality of crises is that new sorts of expertise and approaches to humanitarian action will be sought to meet rapidly emerging political imperatives.

In the following sections, we address the past and potential contribution of the military and the private sector to humanitarian action. We explore the challenges and opportunities of increased and new forms of military and private-sector engagement in humanitarian action in terms of their interaction and interoperability with traditional agencies in different regions and operational environments, and we ask what their increasing role means for the future principles, practice and effectiveness of humanitarian action.

Traditional and Emerging Perspectives on the Military, the Private Sector and Humanitarian Action

The Military

Military engagement in humanitarian crises is not new. It goes back to the 1935–36 Abyssinian Crisis and the Berlin Airlift in 1948 (Metcalfe *et al.* 2012). Yet, while the military has been an important player in the humanitarian system over the past 50 years, military assistance is poorly reported and often not quantified. Reported funding for humanitarian response channelled through the US military totalled US$685.9 million between 2007 and 2011, with the next largest provider being Germany at US$19.8 million (OCHA 2013b). However, these data are heavily skewed by the large-scale military response to the Haiti earthquake.

In the past decade alone, there has been significant military involvement in humanitarian crises such as the conflicts in eastern DRC, Iraq, Liberia, Libya and Sierra Leone and disasters such as the 2004 Asian Tsunami, the 2005 Pakistan earthquake, the 2010 Haiti earthquake and Pakistan floods and the 2013 typhoon in the Philippines (see Metcalfe 2011; Whiting 2012). Examples abound of the military's contribution to humanitarian action. However, this contribution has focused upon a relatively limited number of response activities, which in turn arguably reflects a limited view of the military's comparative advantages. These contributions have been predominantly limited to provision of logistical support and 'lift capacity' and the protection of civilians in armed conflict, as well as facilitating humanitarian access for civilian relief workers in times of conflict (e.g. the mandate of the UN Mission in the Republic of South Sudan, UNMISS)[5] and, to a lesser extent, offering supplemental humanitarian assistance such as medical relief and drilling boreholes.

After 9/11, the military has increasingly become involved in humanitarian assistance in conflict-affected situations, particularly in the context of the rise of the 'comprehensive approach' (US), 'integrated missions' (UN) and 'stabilisation' operations (US, UK), as well as counterinsurgency/terrorism campaigns (Afghanistan, Somalia) (Metcalfe *et al.* 2011; FCO 2014; MoD 2014). This increasing engagement in humanitarian action has been met by Western-based humanitarian organisations with considerable suspicion over motives and aims, with concerns raised over the politicisation and militarisation of humanitarian assistance. These organisations have highlighted empirical and potential impacts on humanitarian space, in particular safe access to communities in need and staff safety and security (Collinson and Elhawary 2012).

While below we note an alternative approach to this Western-based perspective, these concerns are not without merit. The evidence base, though still to be fully developed, suggests that context is a key factor when it comes to the negative impacts of military engagement. A recent study commissioned by the UN Integration Steering Group highlights that the impact of UN integration on humanitarian space is primarily related to context, including the political and conflict environment (Metcalfe *et al.* 2011; Slim 2011).

However, the hope of winning hearts-and-minds through delivery of humanitarian assistance, or the so-called Quick Impact Projects that are at the heart of the new approaches cited above, has become an important part of Western governments' efforts to bring peace and stability to conflict-affected states. Indeed, this political aim is explicit, with military forces increasingly undertaking a range of humanitarian activities themselves in order to achieve strategic or tactical objectives (Metcalfe *et al.* 2012). Consequently, a structured approach to civil-military dialogue is necessary (ideally, preventatively, at capital level and outside the area of operation), to enable humanitarian agencies to differentiate their activities from those of military and stabilisation actors, either by geography or by activity.

While there is understandable humanitarian concern that military involvement reflects the increasing politicisation of humanitarian assistance, the interface between the military and humanitarian actions can at the same time be viewed from an alternative perspective. Indeed, the military is viewed in different ways in different regions and countries. With the rise of China, India, the ASEAN (Association of Southeast Asian Nations) states and the Arab Gulf, among a host of other emerging powers, non-Western perspectives on the role of the military in society are of increasing prominence, underpinned by a general acceptance of the military as 'first provider' of humanitarian assistance, as opposed to Western assumption of the military as 'provider of last resort'. Further, the civil–military distinction in affected states is often less clear cut, with National Disaster Management Authorities (NDMAs) sometimes led by ex-generals or with the military's chief of staff on their governing councils.

This influences the relationship between the military and traditional humanitarian actors in terms of interaction, interoperability and effectiveness. The Guidelines on the Use of Military and Civil Defence Assets to Support United Nations Humanitarian Activities in Complex Emergencies – the 'MCDA Guidelines' (OCHA 2006) and the Guidelines on the Use of Foreign Military and Civil Defence Assets in Disaster Relief – the 'Oslo Guidelines' (OCHA 2007) state that the use of military assets should be a last resort (and for a limited time only), when there is no comparable civilian alternative for meeting (critical and immediate) needs, and where traditional humanitarian agencies can control and direct the use of the assets. Yet, the guidelines do not address how these agencies should relate to the military forces of affected states when they become engaged. Some states, including India, have rejected the Oslo Guidelines because they were not developed through an intergovernmental process and see them as impinging on their sovereignty (Harvey 2009; Roepstorff, this volume).[6] This is important as, in Pakistan, for example, the military is the first responder in times of disaster (as well as arguably being the country's leading political actor and the leader of a major counterinsurgency campaign) (Madiwale and Virk 2011; Svoboda 2014). A Fritz Institute survey of the response to the 2005 Pakistan earthquake shows that most aid recipients identified the military as the primary provider of food, shelter, livelihoods support and medical services (Harvey 2009).

These norms have also become institutionalised in regional structures. For example, in Southeast Asia, militaries can respond across borders, in line with the legally binding ASEAN 2009 Agreement on Disaster Management and Emergency Response.[7] As the wealth of the BRICS (Brazil, Russia, India, China and South Africa), the MINTs (Mexico, Indonesia, Nigeria and Turkey) and a host of other emerging powers grows, these perspectives on the role of the military in response to disasters become important not only within these countries and regions, but in situations where they themselves may engage in international humanitarian action further afield. With the rise of non-OECD-DAC donors, where such perspectives on the military may hold sway, we are seeing new initiatives to establish so-called 'humanitarian forces', such as the HOPEFOR initiative, where Qatar, Turkey and the Dominican Republic have been spearheading an effort to improve the effectiveness of foreign military and civil-defence assets in (natural hazard-related) disaster response.[8]

At the same time, Western perspectives on the role of the military in humanitarian action are shifting, at least among those outside the traditional humanitarian system. Having withdrawn from Afghanistan at the end of 2014, the British military has been searching for an alternative role in order to protect its budget, particularly in the current climate of austerity. Connected to this, amid challenges to maintaining budgets in an era of public-sector cuts and fiscal tightening, institutional donors are exploring cross-governmental burden-sharing, with militaries increasingly able to access humanitarian and development funding through cross-departmental pooled funds.

The Private Sector

The traditional mode of interaction between the private sector and humanitarian agencies has been based on two foundations: procurement (a source of good and services) and corporate social responsibility (CSR), a source of philanthropic funds and in-kind contributions. Until relatively recently, private business has been seen as self-interested and therefore incompatible with the non-profit and voluntary ethos of humanitarian action. However, there has been a growing acceptance in some quarters of the humanitarian sector of the potential role of the private sector in enhancing the effectiveness of humanitarian action. The sheer volume of platforms, conferences and articles exploring commercial support for humanitarian action is indicative of this perceptual change (Kent and Burke 2011). This wider trend has led to an increase in private funding for humanitarian action. Private funding, including from trusts and foundations, business and corporations, individual supporters and high net-worth individuals, as a share of the total humanitarian response grew from 17 per cent in 2006 to 32 per cent in 2010 (Stoianova 2012).

But it is even more recently that there has been a challenge to the dominant paradigm of CSR. Building on the concept of 'shared value' (MacLeod 2012), where business interests and those of communities are seen to be in sync – creating 'win–wins' – recent engagement has sought to explore how humanitarian needs can be met, while businesses are still able to fulfil their bottom line and satisfy shareholders. This has led to a growing focus on harnessing the core competencies of companies in support of humanitarian action, rather than simply seeing them as a fundraising or resource mobilisation target. Examples include logistical and supply chain companies' involvement in humanitarian responses; the involvement of financial services and credit/debit card firms in facilitating the delivery of cash-transfer programmes (Smith *et al.* 2011); mobile operators support for the communicating with disaster-affected communities agenda; retailers, hotels and architects support in the development of shelter solutions; and the development of partnerships with insurance companies to support improved disaster-risk assessment and insurance, both at the sovereign and micro levels.[9] What is important here is the increasing involvement of core business interests in humanitarian action.

Moreover, the increasing realisation among humanitarian agencies that the private sector is neither a homogeneous entity, nor simply defined in opposition to the principled and voluntary action of humanitarians, has led to greater consideration of the capacities of the private sector, from local entrepreneurs, farmers and other small, community-based businesses to multinational corporations, sovereign-wealth funds[10] and diaspora networks (Carpenter 2012; Zyck and Kent 2014). Other global trends such as the push for the nationalisation and localisation of humanitarian action and urbanisation, which demands greater technical skills in municipal water and sanitation systems and infrastructural rehabilitation, are also adding to the demand for increased private-sector engagement.

However, this trend has not been met with support from all corners of the humanitarian sector, and there is still a level of squeamishness about engaging with business. Major questions remain as to whether international aid agencies should be effectively subsidising the expansion of companies into new markets, as is happening with the Hunger Safety Net Programme in northern Kenya (Drummond and Crawford 2014). Further, in armed conflict, upholding humanitarian and 'do-no-harm' principles and managing reputational risk provide good reason to be cautious, as seen in Somalia (Carpenter 2012). Still, there are continued calls to do more to harness, and not undermine, the skills, capacities and expertise of the private sector, based on missed opportunities and negative impacts in Haiti, Somalia and the Syria regional crises (particularly in Jordan and Lebanon), among others (Bailey 2014; Zyck and Armstrong 2014).

As with the military, this has led to attempts to codify and set rules around private-sector humanitarian interaction, for example, in the Guiding Principles for Public–Private Collaboration for Humanitarian Action, developed by the World Economic Forum (WEF) and the UN Office for the Coordination of Humanitarian Affairs (OCHA) in 2007. However, drawing on the experience of humanitarian civil-military interaction, it is questionable whether greater interoperability could not be more readily achieved through greater dialogue, training and development of trust, for example through the development of 'platforms' for collaboration (Oglesby and Burke 2012), rather than through the codification of norms in new documents.

In view of the humanitarian capacity challenge, the next section looks forward, exploring the added value of the military and the private sector, particularly their underexplored capacities, in addressing increasing risk and meeting growing humanitarian needs globally.

The Added Value of the Military and the Private Sector

A major step towards meeting the humanitarian capacity challenge is to recognise the added value and comparative advantages that those outside the traditional humanitarian sector can provide in strengthening efforts to manage risk and enhance preparedness, response and recovery. However,

the heretofore recognised contributions of the military and the private sector to humanitarian action may not reflect all, or the most appropriate,
capabilities required to prepare for, respond to and recover from (future)
humanitarian crises (Kent and Ratcliffe 2008). Other capabilities that show
significant potential to enhance the effectiveness of humanitarian action
include strategic planning, innovation and surge capacity.

Yet, there are also correlative risks in this process, and therefore analysis of the challenges and opportunities of the direct and indirect use of
military capabilities in support or in place of assistance from traditional
humanitarian agencies should be conducted on an institution-by-insti-
tution and context-by-context basis. Similarly, engagement with private
companies that are often involved in the operationalisation of innovative
technologies and approaches originating in the military sphere should also
be approached in a sensitive manner. This is necessary in ensuring respect
both for humanitarian principles (and the safe access and outcomes they
facilitate) and for the core business interests of private-sector partners.

Strategic Planning

The increasing frequency, intensity and complexity of humanitarian crises
has helped to spur a growing interest in more anticipatory approaches to
preparedness among a number of humanitarian agencies and governments,
both affected states and donors. However, these ventures into longer-term
strategic planning are generally not sufficiently systematic and consistent
or effectively integrated into day-to-day operations on the ground (Kent
2012). Militaries, however, see that it is essential that they devote considerable time to strategic planning and scenario development, for example on
climate change and resource scarcity, and they generally also have greater
resources with which to do this (Morisetti 2012). Similarly, business continuity planning is a core component of corporate strategy and sustainability,
and companies are increasingly focused on natural-hazard risk as their
assets and supply chains are becoming increasingly exposed.

Many military establishments around the world undertake longer-term
anticipatory analyses of future strategic threats and opportunities. One
of the most renowned examples of this sort of analysis is that of the UK
Ministry of Defence through the Development Concepts Doctrine Centre
(DCDC). While humanitarian agencies are now increasingly focused on
global trends and their implications for disaster risk and humanitarian crises, less attention is paid to what the military terms strategic shocks.

Looking out to 2040, DCDC consider issues such as collapse of a pivotal
state, collapse of global communications, discovery of a new energy source
and even a cure for ageing (MoD 2010). In their latest strategic outlook,
they address additional scenarios relating to developments in the security
capabilities of multinational corporations, increasing access to low-cost
drones and satellites among criminal and non-state armed groups and the

potential fallout of developments in environmental warfare (MoD 2014; Norton-Taylor 2014). The example of a cure for ageing may seem somewhat extreme, but it does serve to highlight the gulf in strategic thinking and horizon scanning between the military and traditional humanitarian actors, with the former thinking in time horizons of up to 30 years, while the latter largely restricts itself to a five-year perspective at most.

The fundamental issue here is the extent to which military and private-sector perspectives, strategies and techniques for long-term strategic planning can prove useful to humanitarian agencies. Direct transfer of the strategic analyses of militaries to humanitarian agencies would of course be unacceptable as they would compromise operational independence and could impact on impartiality, particularly in conflict situations. Yet, if handled sensitively, there is potential for military and private-sector strategic planning capacities to help strengthen anticipation, and thus preparedness, on the part of traditional humanitarian agencies.

To take one example, the World Food Programme (WFP) has been working with the US Africa Command (AFRICOM), the Southern African Development Community (SADC), national militaries, government agencies, Red Cross National Societies and private-sector partners such as the freight and supply-chain management company Damco to enhance preparedness to pandemics in Southern Africa. Through their engagement with military and private-sector organisations, participants in this 'whole of society' preparedness and readiness exercise explored cross-sector sharing of disaster management and business-continuity planning methodologies and alignment of preparedness-planning processes which had previously occurred in parallel. Participants noted that significant gaps existed in current plans, highlighting the need for closer cooperation between the private sector, international organisations, governments and NDMAs across southern Africa. They also agreed that engagement needs to occur early, with expectations of the military and private sector's roles clearly defined (WFP 2012).

Such joint anticipatory and strategic planning initiatives are in the immediate future far more likely to be pursued in relation to disaster-affected regions and states, and to involve UN agencies, NGOs and states/ NDMAs, as opposed to agencies such as the International Committee of the Red Cross (ICRC) and Médecins Sans Frontières (MSF) that are strongly focused on principled action in armed conflict. But there is scope for such initiatives to be both successful and sustainable. For that to happen, however, we argue that that they need to tap into the core competencies and core business of all actors involved. For example, it is important that Damco has a real stake in the exercise described above, for it enables the company to mitigate risk (both business and reputational) in emerging markets, scale up market opportunities and achieve sustainable outcomes, while also enhancing organisational reputation. Without such two-way gains, the partnership is unlikely to prove sustainable, and will not harness the real added value of the different actors involved.

Innovation

Translating military capabilities to the humanitarian sector does not necessarily mean direct military engagement in humanitarian action. Instead
the military may be viewed as a learning asset with tangible innovations
that can be utilised by traditional humanitarian actors to meet needs more
effectively. Direct military engagement can be expensive, raising difficult questions about value for money and accountability to crisis-affected
communities. The Spanish army's high-profile vaccination and water-distri-
bution programme in the wake of the Haiti earthquake cost over 18 times
that of comparable civilian efforts (Oxfam International 2011).

Instead, we argue that operationalising innovation that comes from the
military and its deep involvement in science, technology, research and development is an area that merits further exploration. The UK Government's
(2011) Humanitarian Emergency Response Review (HERR) stressed the
importance of far greater involvement of science and technology in the
world of crisis prevention, preparedness and response. As the chief scientist
for the UK MoD put it, speaking to an audience of scientists and humanitarian practitioners, science 'is what the military does'.[11]

From the military's perspective, needs-driven innovation provides an
excellent focus for immediate issues but they are also seized of the need to
explore the longer-term challenges and opportunities posed by science and
technology. Hence, the UK's Defence Science and Technology Laboratory
(Dstl) combines short-term operationally focused research with horizon
scanning and assessment of emerging technologies. Dstl has around 3,500
scientists, technologists, analysts, engineers and systems specialists covering
a very broad spectrum of research interests. Recent examples of short-term
operational innovations that could be transferred from the military include
transportation of fuel to operational areas and reduced consumption, tracking of community needs through Global Positioning Systems (GPS) and social
media and improvements in health protection and disease identification.[12]

There is significant potential for the humanitarian sector to benefit from
this capability. The Humanitarian Response Group in the UK's Department
for International Development, for example, has worked with UK Trade and
Investment on the use of LIFESAVER systems in humanitarian response.
This is a water-purification system using portable nano-filtration technology
which was originally developed by the military and then brought to market
by the private sector. Oxfam deployed 2,500 LIFESAVER jerry cans to the
Philippines following Typhoon Haiyan in November 2013, guaranteeing
50 million litres of clean drinking water.[13]

But the state, and specifically military and defence agencies, are also
leaders in long-term, radical innovations. Contrary to received wisdom, the
state has played a critical role in the high-risk, exploratory research and
development which has led to breakthroughs from all the main technologies found inside smartphones to new and emerging green technologies

(Mazzucato 2014). This includes agencies such as the Defence Advanced Research Projects Agency (DARPA) in the US. To date, however, explorations on the use of technology to enhance humanitarian effectiveness have focused on technologies already in the consumer domain, from the use of open street mapping to plot disaster risk and impacts to mobile and branchless banking to transfer cash to crisis-affected populations (Smith *et al.* 2011).

There is significant potential to explore how emerging technologies such as robotics, 3D-printing, networked sensors, civilian drones, augmented reality, wearable tech and even new materials such as graphene could be used to enhance humanitarian response and manage crisis risk. And the private sector has a vital role to play here in terms of what traditional humanitarian actors may call operationalisation, and which it would term commercialisation. It is not a question of trying to out-strategise the pace of technological change, or give a prognosis on the effects of future technology. Instead, the humanitarian system has a significant opportunity to be more agile in its adaptation of emerging technologies. To date, it has been slow even to adopt technologies already widespread across the developing world – for example, providing support for affected communities to charge their mobile phones via solar charging stations. Such an 'innovation' can be critical in facilitating the humanitarian activity of restoring family links in armed conflict and disasters.

Yet, military innovation in support of humanitarian outcomes is not just an opportunity in the advanced industrialised economies. In emerging economies there are also clear opportunities. In Indonesia, for example, the military has used 'cloud seeding' to speed-up the discharge of rain from clouds before they pass over land, especially in Jakarta, thus preventing further flooding in the capital (Rochmyaningsih 2013). While there is debate as to the evidence for the effectiveness of such geo-engineering, it is an interesting example of the potential role of the military in disaster prevention.

Again, however, in the near term at least, such engagement is more likely to stem from an integrated approach within affected states, donor government or UN system circles, and less from new models of engagement between the military and traditional humanitarian actors. We explore this point further in the concluding section, focusing on the interoperability of diverse actors.

Surge Capacity

There is a need for greater joint effort globally to ensure adequate preparedness and readiness to respond to multiple simultaneous large-scale disasters or armed conflicts, both of which are likely to be of an increasingly complex nature. Take, for example, the situation in 2011, with the political conflict in Libya and across the Middle East and North Africa region, the earthquake in Christchurch, New Zealand and the triple crisis (earthquake, tsunami and nuclear crises) in northern Japan. Further, given the dynamics of relief operations and the uncertainties that shroud such crises, it is vitally important to be able to intensify efforts in unanticipated locales quickly and efficiently. Therefore the need to plan, *per se*, for surge capacities arises as a strategic priority.

Yet, in view of the increasing extent and changing types of needs that are confronting humanitarian agencies, it is evident that the range and scale of human-resource capacity required is rarely adequately anticipated. This situation can, however, be improved with enhanced risk assessment. To take one example from OCHA, it was found that if the agency had used the newly developed Info for Risk Management tool to manage its surge capacity, it would have been able to anticipate 96 per cent of surge deployments in the Asia-Pacific region (OCHA 2014).

Surge capacity is 'the ability of an organisation to rapidly and effectively increase [the sum of] its available resources in a specific geographic location' in order to meet increased demand to alleviate suffering in a given population (Houghton and Emmens 2007). Planning for surge capacities and conducting simulation exercises has been a concern among traditional humanitarian agencies. Though the various rosters of the humanitarian system are an advance in terms of dynamic human-resource mobilisation, military capabilities in the logistics of large-scale rapid deployment, upscaling of alternative support structures and mass distribution measures are potentially of significant utility in humanitarian response.

The military's ability to mobilise and initiate operations quickly and beyond previously anticipated needs has become a particularly well-recognised attribute over the past few years. In response to the 2008 Sichuan earthquake, for example, it was reported that the People's Liberation Army mobilised 113,000 soldiers within 14 minutes of the shock (Hoyer 2009). Within integrated planning approaches to natural hazard-related disasters, there is great scope for transfer of skills and expertise from the military to traditional humanitarian actors. However, it is clear that greater focus on principled interaction and interoperability is needed in order to enhance effectiveness. The response to Typhoon Haiyan in the Philippines provides evidence that this can be done, at least in natural-hazard disasters. In the first weeks after the disaster, 20 countries sent military assets (the largest number ever deployed to a single country), helping to overcome the logistical constraints posed by infrastructural destruction and facilitating the response of traditional humanitarian actors (Bragg 2014).

That there are important capabilities within the military and the private sector is clear. The more challenging question is whether there can be a use of military and private-sector assets, skills and competencies by the International Red Cross and Red Crescent Movement, UN agencies and INGOs in a way that can enhance the effectiveness of humanitarian action, while minimising any negative or unintended consequences for staff, volunteers or affected communities. Or are the risks to the club of traditional humanitarian actors (and by extension outcomes for affected communities) of their entry, particularly in terms of access and staff and volunteer safety and security, too high? By drawing on these capabilities would humanitarian agencies be implicitly legitimising military budgets and private-sector profit motives that may not fit with their humanitarian principles and values? These questions are dealt with in the concluding section.

Conclusion: Interaction, Interoperability and Effectiveness

Interaction between the military, private sector and traditional humanitarian actors has to date been largely piecemeal, reactive or a response to cohabitation in areas of operation. Yet, with the increasing intensity, frequency and complexity of humanitarian crises, a more strategic engagement is required in order to deliver the resources, capacities and expertise necessary to meet emerging and future humanitarian needs. This is likely to require changes to past modes of interaction, with a move from the rather self-referential approach of traditional humanitarian actors to an approach that starts with the needs of the at-risk or affected person – this is the essence of interoperability within an effective humanitarian system.

A starting point is to challenge the assumptions all too often made by the humanitarian sector about collaboration, cooperation and partnerships, namely, that those outside the traditional sector have to fit within a tried and tested humanitarian framework. As recent attempts to convene emerging powers and traditional humanitarian actors have shown, emerging actors do not aim simply to supplement the traditional humanitarian system. Many are looking to develop their own mechanisms and approaches and are reluctant to join the existing multilateral system as it is seen as inadequate, bureaucratic, cumbersome and cost-ineffective (Simonow 2013). Moreover, these non-traditional actors are already starting to influence the structure of the global humanitarian system through their own agency, creating new norms and institutions such as ASEAN's AADMER (Agreement on Disaster Management and Emergency Response).

If greater interoperability and effectiveness are to be achieved, interaction has to increasingly reflect the core business and comparative advantage of the different actors involved – non-traditional as well as traditional. For the military, this means a greater focus on the full range of core competencies that could be utilised to address the humanitarian capacity challenge. For the private sector, this means a greater focus on how the private-sector's core business can function synergistically with that of traditional humanitarian actors, helping to meet needs, as well as exploring its role in the operationalisation of military innovations, providing a firewall from political and strategic objectives.

The starting point for humanitarian agencies' interaction with both the military and the private sector should be the needs of at-risk and affected people and how partnership can be used to harness different actor's comparative advantages in meeting them. Traditional humanitarian actors must make the case that the approach they advocate is in the best interests, not of themselves, as a special interest group, but of the affected people they aim to serve (Svoboda 2014). As Hopgood (2008: 103) provocatively asks, 'Do the dying care, *in extremis*, who feeds or bandages them, or whether that person has a Wal-Mart logo on her vest?'

Yet, in developing new modes of interaction and increasing interoperability, different regions and operational environments (especially armed conflict as opposed to disasters) will present different challenges and opportunities. Context is everything. Indeed, as Labbé (2012: 21) suggests, 'one might legitimately question whether ... an unconditional and systematic claim to abide by humanitarian principles in every situation is not more damaging for the sector as a whole than calling for their respect and abiding by them only in situations where it really matters'. In armed conflict in general, there is a stronger need for the distinction between political and military objectives and humanitarian objectives. Therefore direct interaction between the military and traditional humanitarian actors may be less appropriate than in disaster settings, where both the military and the private sector will likely play an increasingly significant role in humanitarian action. In armed conflict, the potential for interaction to undermine perceptions of principled action, or the so-called NIIHA approach – neutral, impartial, independent humanitarian action – may be too great, with attendant impacts on humanitarian access and the safety and security of staff, volunteers and affected communities.

However, simply because direct interaction is more problematic in conflict situations, this does not mean that increased interoperability between the military, the private sector and traditional humanitarian actors is only viable in natural hazard-related disasters. Rather than being seen as a humanitarian actor, directly involved in assistance and protection, the military may be viewed as a learning asset with expertise, innovations and capacities that can be utilised by traditional humanitarian actors to meet needs more effectively.

If future interaction and interoperability are to be enhanced in order to rise to the capacity challenge, then a new approach to collaboration, cooperation and partnerships is required. The focus on effectiveness and, in turn, partnership must start from the needs of the at-risk or affected person. If the military and the private sector can indeed, in particular areas or contexts, provide resources, capacities and expertise (relating to strategic planning, innovation and surge capacity) that can help meet those needs then they should be carefully considered. This means taking a more fore sighted approach to interaction and interoperability, one focused more on the core competencies and core business of actors.

The alternative is that increased involvement of the military and the private sector in humanitarian action will simply happen anyway – indeed it already is – but it will not be coherent or effectively coordinated, with the goal of increased interoperability missed. The humanitarian capacity challenge cannot be met through an increasingly fragmented global humanitarian system. Instead, humanitarian effectiveness must be increased through a new approach to partnership, helping to reconstruct the global humanitarian system into one which puts those in need at its centre.

Notes

1 Over the last 10 years there was an average of 320 recorded disasters per year, compared to 290 in the 10 years before (Guha-Sapir *et al.* cited in OCHA 2014).

2 This brief review of disaster, conflict and technological risk does not take into account what have been called 'global catastrophic risks', those more extreme risks such as asteroid impacts, nuclear war, biological weapons, advanced nanotechnology, general artificial intelligence and social collapse, that could pose an existential danger to large swathes of the globe in the coming decades (Bostrom and Cirkovic 2011). Nonetheless, these are plausible threats that need to be prepared for.

3 The cases of the 2009 L'aquila earthquake in Italy (Mazzotti 2013), the 1999 earthquake in Turkey, the 2003 Bam earthquake in Iran (Reynolds 2003) and Hurricane Katrina in 2005 and Superstorm Sandy in 2012, both in the US, all show the severity of the political fallout from a failure to effectively communicate or act on disaster risk, or to effectively address the impact of disasters.

4 This point is based on a series of interviews with government disaster-management officials conducted by Kent in 2010 as part of the 2011 UK government's Humanitarian Emergency Response Review.

5 Full details of the mandate of the UNMISS and related UN Security Council resolutions at www.un.org/en/peacekeeping/missions/unmiss/mandate.shtml (accessed 16 August 2014).

6 However, as Harvey (2009) notes, the Inter-Agency Standing Committee (IASC)'s reference paper 'Civil–Military Relationships in Complex Emergencies' covers national militaries, as do guidelines produced by the ICRC on the use of armed protection for humanitarian assistance. But these focus on how traditional humanitarian actors relate to militaries, and not on militaries as providers of humanitarian assistance.

7 The ASEAN Agreement on Disaster Management and Emergency Response (AADMER) has been ratified by all ten member states and entered into force on 24 December 2009. This is a proactive regional framework for cooperation, coordination, technical assistance and resource mobilisation in all aspects of disaster management. See www.asean.org/resources/publications/asean-publications/item/asean-agreement-on-disaster-management-and-emergency-responce-work-programme-for-2010-2015 (accessed 16 August 2014).

8 See http://hopeforinitiativedr.org/?page_id=25&lang=en (accessed 16 August 2014).

9 For example, Willis Re has been investing in the Willis Research Network, the world's largest financial-services research network, with a membership encompassing 50 leading research institutions. The network aims to enhance resilience by integrating first-class science into operational and financial decision-making across public and private institutions.

10 As Zyck and Kent (2014: 1) highlight, 'Private companies are increasingly being considered as an alternative to international aid agencies, particularly in middle-income, "emerging" and state capitalist economies, as well as in states which are sensitive regarding their internal affairs.'

11 Remark at the launch of the UK Government Office for Science (2012) report, *The Use of Science in Humanitarian Emergencies and Disasters*.

12 Focus Group Discussion on Science and Technology, the Military and Humanitarian Agencies, Humanitarian Futures Programme, King's College London, 25 July 2012.
13 LIFESAVER Systems press release (www.lifesaversystems.com/documents/Lifesaver-release-13-11-13.pdf) accessed 18 August 2014.

References

Bailey, S. (2014) *Humanitarian Crises, Emergency Preparedness and Response: The Role of Business and the Private Sector – a Strategy and Options Analysis of Haiti*, London: ODI.

Bostrom, N. and Cirkovic, M. (eds) (2011) *Global Catastrophic Risks*, Oxford: Oxford University Press.

Bragg, C. (2014) Humanitarian Action, Bucking the System, Trends toward New Approach (http://theglobalobservatory.org/component/myblog/humanitarian-action-bucking-the-system-trends-toward-new-approach/blogger/Catherine%20Bragg) accessed 16 August 2014.

Buzan, B., Wæver, O. and de Wilde, J. (1998) *Security: A New Framework for Analysis*, Boulder, CO: Lynne Rienner.

Caminade, C., Kovats, S., Rocklov, J., Tompkins, A.M., Morse, A.P., Colón-González, F.J., Stenlund, H., Martens, P. and Lloyd, S.J. (2014) 'Impact of Climate Change on Global Malaria Distribution', *Proceedings of the National Academy of Sciences*, 111(9):3286–3291.

Carpenter, S. (2012) Somalia's Private Sector Can Help Rather Than Hinder Development (www.theguardian.com/global-development/poverty-matters/2012/may/23/somalia-private-sector-development) accessed 16 August 2014.

Collinson, S. and Elhawary, S. (2012) *Humanitarian Space: A Review of Trends and Issues*, London: ODI.

Drummond, J. and Crawford, N. (2014) *Humanitarian Crises, Emergency Preparedness and Response: The Role of Business and the Private Sector – Kenya Case Study*, London: ODI.

Duffield, M. (2007) *Development, Security and Unending War*, Cambridge: Polity.

FCO (2014) *The UK Government's Approach to Stabilisation*, London: Crown.

Giddens, A. (1986) *The Constitution of Society: Outline of the Theory of Structuration*, Cambridge: Polity.

Harkey, J. (2014) *Experiences of National Governments in Expanding Their Role in Humanitarian Preparedness and Response*, Somerville, MA: Feinstein International Center.

Harvey, P. (2009) *Towards Good Humanitarian Government: The Role of the Affected State in Disaster Response*, London: ODI.

Hopgood, S. (2008) 'Saying "No" to Wal-Mart? Money and Morality in Professional Humanitarianism', in M. Barnett and T. Weiss (eds) *Humanitarianism in Question: Politics, Power and Ethics*, Ithaca, NY: Cornell University Press.

Houghton, R. and Emmens, B. (2007) *Surge Capacity in the Humanitarian Relief and Development Sector: A Review of Surge Capacity and Surge Capacity Mechanisms within International NGOs*, London: People in Aid.

Hoyer, B. (2009) 'Lessons from the Sichuan Earthquake', *Humanitarian Exchange*, 43, June 2009, London: ODI.

ICRC (2011) Brasilia (Regional) Annual Report 2011 (www.icrc.org/eng/assets/files/annual-report/current/icrc-annual-report-brasilia.pdf) accessed 16 August 2014.

IFRC (2010) *World Disasters Report: Focus on Urban Risk*, Geneva: IFRC.

IPCC (2012) 'Summary for Policymakers', in , C.B., Barros, V., Stocker, T.F., Qin, D., Dokken, D.J., Ebi, K.L., Mastrandrea, M.D., Mach, K.J., Plattner, G.K., Allen, S.K., Tignor, M., and Midgley P.M. (eds) *Managing the Risks of Extreme Events and Disasters to Advance Climate Change Adaptation*, Cambridge: Cambridge University Press, 1–19.

Kahn, C. and Cunningham, A. (2013) 'Introduction to the Issue of State Sovereignty and Humanitarian Action', *Disasters*, 37(2):139–150.

Kaldor, M. (2008) 'Democracy and Globalisation', in Albrow, M., Anheier, H., Glasius, M., Price, M., Kaldor, M., and Holland, F. (eds) *Global Civil Society 2007/8: Communicative Power and Democracy*, London: SAGE, 34–45.

Kent (2012) Transition to Transformation: Save the Children in a Futures Context, Humanitarian Futures Programme Stakeholders Forum 2012 Input Paper, March 2012, Unpublished.

Kent, R. (2013) Making Futures Real: The Policy-Maker's Challenge, Geneva: UNISDR.

Kent, R. and Burke, J. (2011) *Commercial and humanitarian engagement in Crisis Contexts: Current Trends, Future Drivers*, London: Humanitarian Futures Programme.

Kent, R. and Ratcliffe, J. (2008) *Responding to Catastrophes: The United States in a Vulnerable World*, Washington, DC: Center for Strategic and International Studies.

Labbé, J. (2012) *Rethinking Humanitarianism: Adapting to 21st Century Challenges*, New York: International Peace Institute.

Mack, A. (ed.) (2014) *Human Security Report 2013 – The Decline in Global Violence: Evidence, Explanation and Contestation*, Vancouver: Human Security Press.

MacLeod, A. (2012) 'Why Go It Alone in Community Development?', *Harvard Business Review Blog*, 13 June 2012.

Madiwale, A. and Virk, K. (2011) 'Civil-Military Relations in Natural Disasters: A Case Study of the 2010 Pakistan Floods', *International Review of the Red Cross*, 93884:1085–1105.

Mazzotti, M. (2013) Lessons from the L'Aquila Earthquake (www.timeshighereducation.co.uk/features/lessons-from-the-laquila-earthquake/2007742.fullarticle) accessed 16 August 2014.

Mazzucato, M. (2014) *The Entrepreneurial State: Debunking Public vs. Private Sector Myths*, London: Anthem Press.

Metcalfe, V. (2011) *Friend or Foe? Military Intervention in Libya*, London: ODI.

Metcalfe, V., Giffen, A. and Elhawary, S. (2011) *UN Integration and Humanitarian Space: An Independent Study Commissioned by the UN Integration Steering Group*, London and Washington, D.C.: ODI and Stimson Center.

Metcalfe, V., Haysom, S. and Gordon, G. (2012) *Trends and Challenges in Humanitarian Civil-Military Coordination: A Review of the Literature*, London: ODI.

MoD (2010) *Strategic Trends Programme: Global Strategic Trends – Out to 2040*, London: Crown.

MoD (2014) *Strategic Trends Programme: Global Strategic Trends – Out to 2045*, London: Crown.

Morisetti, N. (2012) 'Climate Change and Resource Security', *BMJ*, 344:e1352.

Norton-Taylor, R. (2014) 'Warfare by Insects: The World of 2045', *The Guardian*, Saturday 12 July 2014.

OCHA (2006) Guidelines on the Use of Military and Civil Defense Assets to Support United Nations Humanitarian Activities in Complex Emergencies (http://reliefweb.int/report/world/guidelines-use-military-and-civil-defence-assets-disaster-relief-oslo-guidelines) accessed 22 February 2015.

OCHA (2007) Guidelines on the Use of Foreign Military and Civil Defence Assets in Disaster Relief (Oslo Guidelines), Revision 1.1, November, New York: OCHA.

OCHA (2013a) *World Humanitarian Data and Trends 2013*, New York: OCHA.

OCHA (2013b) *Humanitarianism in the Network Age*, New York: OCHA.

OCHA (2014) *Saving Lives Today and Tomorrow: Managing the Risk of Humanitarian Crises*, New York: OCHA.

Ofteringer, R. (2013) The Code of Conduct and Principles of Islamic Charitable Work – Commonalities and Difference, Paper Presented at the Human Security: Humanitarian Perspectives and Responses Conference, Istanbul, 24–27 October 2013.

Oglesby, R. and Burke, J. (2012) *Platforms for Private Sector-Humanitarian Collaboration*, London: Humanitarian Futures Programme.

Oxfam International (2011) *Whose Aid Is It Anyway? Politicizing Aid in Conflicts and Crises*, Oxford: Oxfam International.

Parker, B. (2013) 'Humanitarianism Besieged', *Humanitarian Exchange*, 59, November 2013, London: ODI.

Ramalingam, B. (2013) *Aid on the Edge of Chaos: Rethinking International Cooperation in a Complex World*, Oxford: Oxford University Press.

Reynolds, P. (2003) The Politics of Earthquakes (http://news.bbc.co.uk/2/hi/middle_east/3351121.stm) accessed 16 August 2014.

Rochmyaningsih, D. (2013) Is Cloud Seeding Preventing Further Flooding in Indonesia? (www.scidev.net/global/earth-science/news/is-cloud-seeding-preventing-further-flooding-in-indonesia-.html) accessed 16 August 2014.

Shaw, M. (2003) 'The Global Transformation of the Social Sciences', in M. Kaldor, H. Anheier and M. Glasius (eds) *Global Civil Society 2003*, Oxford: Oxford University Press, 35–44.

Simonow, J. (2013) Conference Report – Advancing Humanitarian Action: Engaging with Rising Global Actors to Develop New Strategic Partnerships, 21–22.October 2013, WP1269, Steyning: Wilton Park.

Slim, H. (2011) NGO–Military Contact Group: Keynote Address, Conference on Civil–Military Relations in Natural Disasters: New Developments from the Field, 12 October 2011, London.

Smith, G., MacAuslan, I., Butters, S. and Trommé, M. (2011) *New Technologies in Cash Transfer Programming and Humanitarian Assistance: A Report for the Cash Learning Partnership* (CaLP), CaLP: Oxford.

Stoianova, V. (2012) *Private Funding: An Emerging Trend in Humanitarian Donorship*, Wells: Development Initiatives.

Svodboda, E. (2014) *The Interaction between Humanitarian and Military Actors: Where Do We Go From Here?*, London: ODI.

Swithern, S. (2014) *Global Humanitarian Assistance Report 2014*, Bristol: Development Initiatives.

UK Government (2011) *Humanitarian Emergency Response Review*, Crown: London.

UK Government Office for Science (2012) *The Use of Science in Humanitarian Emergencies and Disasters*, London: Crown.

UNHCR (2014) *UNHCR Global Report 2013*, Geneva: UNHCR.

Wendt, A. (1992) 'Anarchy Is What States Make of It: The Social Construction of Power Politics', *International Organization*, 391–425.

WFP (2012) Pandemic Readiness and Response Exercise, Muldersdrift, Republic of South Africa 21–24 May 2012: Post Exercise Report, Unpublished.

Whiting, M. (2012) 'Military and Humanitarian Cooperation in Air Operations in Haiti', *Humanitarian Exchange*, 53, London: ODI.

World Economic Forum and OCHA (2007) *Guiding Principles for Public-Private Collaboration for Humanitarian Action*, Geneva: UN.

Zyck, S. and Armstrong, J. (2014) *Humanitarian Crises, Emergency Preparedness and Response: The Role of Business and the Private Sector – Jordan Case Study*, London: ODI.

Zyck, S. and Kent, R. (2014) *Humanitarian Crises, Emergency Preparedness and Response: The Role of Business and the Private Sector – Final Report*, London: ODI.

Part V
For-Profit Humanitarianism

8 Business in Humanitarian Crises

For Better or for Worse?

Gilles Carbonnier and Piedra Lightfoot

Introduction

> I've spent a lot of time in African hospitals. I've seen waiting rooms full
> of people waiting for other people to die in their hospital beds so they
> can be the next people to get in those beds and die ... If you're in a
> position to do something about it, you can't just turn your back on it.
>
> (Forbes 2006)

This quote sounds like a seasoned aid worker's interview, but actually is an
excerpt from an interview of Britain's most popular tycoon, Sir Richard.
Like many other entrepreneurs, Richard Branson has increasingly leveraged his wealth and business acumen with a view to alleviating human
suffering – exemplifying just one of the many ways in which business people
engage in humanitarian crises.

Up to the 1990s, mutual suspicion, if not outright antagonism, characterised the relationship between the business sector and the UN – and
humanitarian organisations in general. By the end of World War II, the
Nuremberg trials saw 23 executives of IG Farben Industries convicted of war
crimes and crimes against humanity, including the deliberate use of slave
labour and production of Zyklon B gas for extermination of concentration camp inmates (*United States of America v. Carl Krauch et al.* 1948). More
recent accounts of trade in 'blood diamonds' lining the coffers of rebels
and warlords in Africa, or accusations of aiding and abetting the commission of torture and extrajudicial killings in Aceh, Indonesia, directed at the
oil giant ExxonMobil, served to compound sentiments among humanitarians that business acts as a driver of armed conflict and human-rights abuses
(Goreux 2001; Amnesty International 2011).

For a long while, this engendered a pointed focus on the negative consequences of business activities in armed conflict, putting the profit motive
and humanitarian objectives at fundamental odds. While such concerns
may not have completely faded away, a new narrative has emerged – one
rooted in an appreciation of mutual interests and of the added value of
constructive engagement. The business–humanitarian interface has come

to be painted with more nuances. Recognising the variety of business actors and potential interactions in humanitarian crises, the humanitarian sector has seized the opportunity to engage business on select fronts. There is a growing consensus among the humanitarian community that the private sector can be a critical stakeholder. On both sides of the fence, there is a greater appetite to clarify the terms of engagement, promote multi-stakeholder initiatives and explore diverse forms of collaboration.

This has happened against the backdrop of a tremendous growth in the humanitarian market, increased funding from non-governmental sources including the private sector and the outsourcing and partial privatisation of a range of services traditionally supplied by state institutions and not-for-profit organisations. The Global Humanitarian Assistance (GHA) Programme estimates that private companies and corporation donated over US$1.1 billion between 2008 and 2012. Non-governmental organisations (NGOs) and the International Movement of the Red Cross and Red Crescent received the bulk of those funds. Yet, the share of UN agencies increased from 1 per cent in 2011 to 15 per cent in 2012 (GHA 2014: 7).

This chapter deals with business enterprises as defined in the 2011 UN Guiding Principles on Business and Human Rights. This definition covers 'all business enterprises, both transnational and others, regardless of their size, sector, location, ownership and structure' (UNHCHR 2011: 6). Here, we use interchangeably business enterprises with companies, firms or businesses. Relaxing the usual unitary actor assumption under which 'business' or the 'private sector' is treated as a homogenous entity, we start by examining the different roles and impacts that businesses can have in humanitarian crises as well as the ensuing entry points, risks and opportunities for business–humanitarian interactions. Looking at the example of the agri-food sector, we conduct a supply-chain analysis and highlight such entry points. We then turn to business as a source of innovations that impact the humanitarian sector. Before concluding, we focus on business–humanitarian partnerships (BHPs), exploring how humanitarian organisations have sought to preserve the integrity and the legitimacy of partnership arrangements.

Business–Humanitarian Endearment in a Changing Landscape

According to the UN Office for the Coordination of Humanitarian Affairs (OCHA), funding requirements in consolidated appeals more than doubled over the past decade, reaching US$12.9 billion in 2014. The people targeted by these appeals increased from 30–40 million to 65 million in 2012 (OCHA 2013). In the face of such growth, humanitarian agencies have worked towards professionalising the sector, borrowing managerial strategies and practices from business (Clarke and Ramalingam 2009: 30). Increased funding from the private sector has led humanitarians to rethink the framework within which they develop relations with corporate actors.

Contributions from businesses to humanitarian operations carried out by the UN, the International Movement of the Red Cross and the Red Crescent and NGOs totalled US$201 million in 2012 (Stirk 2014: 2). This has further translated into a surge in BHPs geared at facilitating innovation, sharing skills and expertise, implementing projects, or raising public awareness on selected humanitarian issues.

Increasingly, governments have outsourced the provision of basic services to private contractors, including those services commonly assumed to be under the remit of the state (Carbonnier 2006). In weak states, such services are often those most relevant to aid practitioners, be it healthcare delivery, water supply, or policing. To perform their work, humanitarians have directly engaged with relevant private actors in the field, which has fostered greater exchanges with private service providers and at times appreciation for the importance of better understanding their objectives, constraints and rationale. Likewise, there has been a rise and consolidation of private firms specialising in the delivery of relief and development projects (Ashurst 2012). Consultancy firms such as Chemonics International, ABT Associates and Development Alternatives often out-compete NGOs for work outsourced by donors. USAID in particular has shelled out massive contracts to development contractors for work in Haiti, Afghanistan and Iraq. A seasoned observer remarked: 'if the for-profit contractor Chemonics were a country, it would have been the third-largest recipient of USAID funding in the world in 2011' (Norris 2012). Humanitarian organisations also rely on private companies for the provision of services such as telecommunications, logistics, transport and financial services. For instance, about 40 per cent of annual spending by the World Food Programme (WFP) accrues directly to private firms, predominantly food and logistics suppliers (Kent and Zyck 2014: 9).

In parallel, the debate on business and human rights has advanced, with greater clarity on the delineation of the responsibility of the business enterprises. The notion of 'negative' responsibilities – that business enterprises should first and foremost do no harm – is now widely recognised by states and the business sector itself. It is the essence of the unanimously endorsed UN Guiding Principles on Business and Human Rights (UNHCHR 2011), which delineate the implementation of the Protect, Respect and Remedy Framework developed by John Ruggie.[1] Together, these cement the idea that business' responsibilities are universal, existing 'over and above compliance with national laws and regulations protecting human rights' (ibid.: 13). However, these principles focus on due diligence and respecting rights by refraining from infringing upon them, as opposed to suggesting that businesses would have a 'positive' responsibility that extends beyond legal requirements. Many now argue that this does not go far enough on the basis that corporations operating in weak states influence local dynamics in ways that can, and should, be capitalised upon to promote human rights and sustainable development. From this vantage point, business engagement with governments, civil-society and international organisations should be pursued not only to mitigate the negative impacts of business operations in fragile states, but also to improve outcomes.

Motives for Business–Humanitarian Engagement

The core objective of business enterprises of course remains profit or share-holder-value maximisation. It is obviously not the same as the objective of humanitarian organisations (i.e. to save lives, alleviate suffering and pro-tect human dignity in an impartial manner). Hence, business enterprises should simply not be labelled as 'humanitarian actors'. This being said, business executives or employees can have genuine humanitarian concerns and provide humanitarian aid, for instance when staff of an extractive industry working on an oil rig on the Mediterranean Sea decide to provide food and water to Syrians and Iraqis who are fleeing from war atrocities and risking their lives in a perilous journey to Europe, as informally reported by oil firm executives.

At the corporate level, there are several good reasons for engaging in humanitarian work. It can prove highly cost-effective in managing repu-tational risks and bolstering public image. For example, the 2005 disaster following the deadly passage of Hurricane Katrina in Louisiana offered Walmart – a company that had been pilloried for unethical sourcing and poor treatment of workers – 'the biggest boost to its reputation in the com-pany's history' after it donated some US$20 million cash together with 1,500 trucks of free goods, 100,000 meals and a promise to reemploy its displaced workers (Mattera 2005).

The business case for engaging with humanitarian organisations does not revolve solely around the benefits of brand association with reputed humanitarian partners. Businesses may also seek to preserve their 'licence to operate' in difficult environments whereby partnering with humanitarian actors stems from a desire to protect investments. Corporations with opera-tions and supply chains that extend into conflict settings and other high-risk environments can be held legally liable for participation in human rights and International Humanitarian Law (IHL) violations. Even as non-state legal entities, private firms active in war zones have a range of obligations under IHL in relation to security management and participation in hostili-ties (ICRC 2006). But they also enjoy rights to the extent that the Geneva Conventions forbid deliberate and indiscriminate attacks on civilians and civilian objects. The latter includes the staff and assets of companies, as long as they do not participate in hostilities and cannot be considered as military objects.[2] Businesses may further be driven by a desire to be among the 'first movers', thereby gaining a competitive edge by (re)entering markets early after a humanitarian crisis or getting the opportunity to establish advan-tageous relations with (new) political leaders (Andonova and Carbonnier 2014: 357). Finally, corporate support for humanitarian causes tends to be an asset in enhancing employee satisfaction as well as attracting and retaining best talents. Surveys generally confirm that employees value working for a company that supports global relief efforts in response to humanitarian crises (Conference Board 2008).

Humanitarian motivations to engage with business are also manifold. On the one hand, the private sector represents a source of financial support and a way to diversify funding sources away from traditional donor states in a world where multiple recipient organisations compete for limited public resources. On the other hand, businesses house technical expertise that can be tapped to enhance operational capacity. Likewise, businesses offer financial clout and political capital that can potentially be mobilised to advance humanitarian causes. Humanitarian organisations also seek to engage the corporate world on two different but complementary tracks: to promote greater respect of IHL and human rights – with an emphasis on the 'negative' responsibility of firms to do no harm – and to establish partnerships with companies with a view to enhancing humanitarian outcomes, which emphasises the 'positive' corporate responsibility to do good.

Different Businesses and Contexts, Different Risks and Opportunities

The specific roles that a company is likely to play in a conflict or disaster-prone environment largely hinges upon the characteristics of the economic sector in which that company operates, its ownership, structure and corporate culture, as well as the context in which the humanitarian crisis unfolds. Slim (2012) identified six main roles that business can typically play in war. These range from perpetrating IHL violations to being victim of such violations, from supplying humanitarian organisations with goods and services to intervening directly in the field as a humanitarian or peace-building actor. In practice, business enterprises often come to play different roles at different times.

It is high time to do away with the unitary actor assumption that considers the private sector a homogeneous group of profit-driven entities. For example, transnational corporations do not resemble domestic small and medium-sized enterprises, nor do state-owned enterprises face the same constraints and incentives as privately owned ones. Some businesses thrive on armed conflicts and disasters that boost demand for their products and services while others, like the tourism industry, tend to lose out. In humanitarian crises, the interests of private military and security companies (PMSCs) differ from those of the telecommunications or food industry. Transnational criminal groups and the insurance industry may both have an interest in dealing with war risks, but for different objectives and following a different approach. Some extractive firms, wilfully or unintentionally, support egregious human-rights abuses while others seek to actively contribute to establishing a more peaceful and stable environment to safeguard their assets – including their reputation – and enhance long-term return on investment.

Being operational on the ground, both for-profit companies and relief agencies influence the political economy of humanitarian crises by affecting the distribution of wealth, income, power and agency in typically fragile institutional environments. Whether they like it or not, business enterprises interacting with war-torn countries influence war economies. Analysing how business enterprises influence war economies requires looking at how their operations interact with legal and illegal economic activities carried out by warring parties and war profiteers. An obvious example is when extractive industries and insurers contribute to feeding the booming kidnap-for-ransom (K&R) market by securing the safe release of kidnapped staff working in risky areas through the payment of ransoms that are eventually reimbursed by a K&R insurance. Business operations may further support or weaken coping mechanisms devised by vulnerable community members who seek to survive and avoid destitution in the midst of war. Finally, business enterprises have an impact through international trade and financial relations that connect domestic war economies to the global marketplace. This includes, for example, trade in arms, ammunitions and security services, or financial intermediation between refugees and their families back home. Humanitarian organisations may work with those business enterprises that proactively seek to minimise the risk of fuelling armed conflict and exercise extensive due diligence through careful, continuous conflict and human rights impact assessments.

A Sectoral Approach to Business–Humanitarian Cooperation

The specific characteristics of individual economic sectors largely determine the potential for humanitarian engagement. For example, BHPs have developed over the past two decades in a few sectors where the core business of companies is the provision of goods and services that are critical to humanitarian action: telecommunications, logistics, pharmaceutical industries, consumer goods typically used for food and non-food assistance, or financial services (Kent and Zyck 2014: 12). As mobile cash and electronic voucher transfers are increasingly used as a means of disbursing direct assistance, telecommunications and financial services providers are playing a more prominent role in relief activities – note, for instance, the collaboration between the WFP and MasterCard to provide e-vouchers to Syrian refugees in Jordan and Lebanon. Even without formal partnership with a humanitarian agency, the establishment of mobile money platforms provides the opportunity to directly assist vulnerable people, as in the case of Tcho Tcho in Haiti, a mobile money platform established by a Canadian Bank and a leading telecommunication company in the Caribbean (Goel and Goss 2012).[3]

The characteristics of different economic sectors also shape how crisis impacts a company. Sectors that are particularly vulnerable to war and disaster include, for example, transport and tourism. The degree to which a business enterprise faces public scrutiny and consumer pressure influences the incentive it may have in mitigating negative humanitarian or human-rights impacts. In addition to sector-specific considerations, firm size matters when it comes to the potential humanitarian impact as well as the ability to invest in careful due diligence throughout the supply chain. Against this background, a sectoral analysis offers a framework for humanitarian actors, policymakers and business people to assess (i) risk areas where a company's operations may result in negative humanitarian and human-rights impacts and (ii) entry points for partnerships and positive humanitarian impacts, drawing on the untapped potential for synergy. A sectoral analysis requires looking not only at the operations in high-risk environments, but also upstream and downstream at the whole supply chain. This helps to identify the critical entry points to mitigate negative humanitarian outcomes and promote positive ones. For humanitarian organisations, carrying out a sectoral analysis is useful to highlight the risks and opportunities of engaging business enterprises. The objective can be advocating for greater respect for IHL and human rights in armed conflict – and thus seeking to prevent negative impacts – or, rather, to tap corporate support in the form of funding, products and services, skills and expertise or outreach.

The agri-food sector provides an interesting case study. It encompasses the aggregate activities, functions and processes of contemporary food production and distribution – 'the collective business activities that are performed from farm to table' (Konig *et al.* 2013). The food sector, including food and beverage companies, traders and grocers, is a business valued at some US$7 trillion and representing roughly one tenth of the global economy (Hoffman 2013). Schematically, on the upstream end of the food supply chain are farms that generate primary products. Then come the commodity traders in charge of the purchase, transfer and bulk sale of these products. Though they are not well known by the public, a few very large trading companies dominate this segment (Archer Daniels Midland, Bunge, Cargill, Louis Dreyfus) and have many linkages to the rest of the food industry (Murphy *et al.* 2012). The traders' equally behemoth clients, food processors, are much better known by the public – visible due to omnipresent marketing and close proximity with consumers. Less than a dozen firms manufacture the vast majority of the food and beverages sold in supermarkets around the world. Finally, on the downstream end of the supply chain, are the grocers and supermarket chains, such as Walmart and Carrefour (Beeler and Lightfoot 2013). Figure 8.1 maps the organisation of the agribusiness sector.

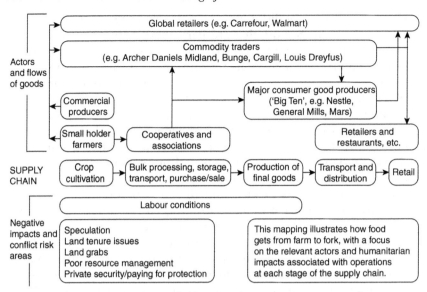

Figure 8.1 Organisation of the agribusiness sector

Identifying Risk Areas: Potential and Limits for Engagement

On the upstream end of the supply chain, agribusiness in war zones may fuel conflicts via various channels, notably by funding armed groups to protect their assets and employees. In March 2007, Chiquita Brands International settled a dispute for US$25 million with the US Department of Justice after acknowledging that it had paid Colombian paramilitary groups listed by Washington as terrorist organisations US$1.7 million to protect its operations (Brodzinsky 2013). Beyond conflict settings, forced and child labour represent major human-rights risks in the agricultural sector. Indeed, 60 per cent of the estimated 129 million children concerned are estimated to work in agriculture, often under risky working conditions and subject to ill treatment (Hurst 2007: 23; ILO 2013).

Large-scale land acquisitions in states with weak institutions – be it by states through sovereign wealth funds and state-owned companies, by large foreign companies, or by domestic investors – have been associated with forced displacement, protest and violence (Deininger *et al.* 2011: 2). In 2011, clashes over contested expansion of cattle ranches and industrial farms in the Brazilian state of Mato Grosso do Sul, where multinational firms like Louis Dreyfus invested, resulted in numerous deadly attacks on indigenous people (Romero 2012). In Indonesia, expansion of palm oil production has long been associated with host communities' protests being countered by violence and human-rights abuses. Over 3,000 conflicts between palm oil companies and local communities have been registered by the Indonesian land agency; protests tend to be harshly repressed by the police (Rainforest Action Network 2013: 16–17).

Shifting focus to the midstream areas of the supply chain, one finds that commodity traders and speculators have been accused of aggravating price fluctuations, thereby fuelling food insecurity. According to the UN Special Rapporteur on the Right to Food's analysis of the 2008 food price crisis that drove 40 million people into hunger: 'the changes in food prices reflected not so much movements in the supply and/or demand of food, but were driven to a significant extent by speculation' (De Schutter 2010: 3). Ensuing food riots contributed to intensifying political instability in several regions, not least in North Africa and the Middle East. Moving further downstream, the main controversies involved with business have more often to do with labour and social issues than with humanitarian crises per se.

Some of these issues are inherent to the agribusiness sector itself. Yet, again, there are great variations between companies with regard to the way they seek to mitigate negative impacts or not. The degree of commitment to, and the quality of, due diligence exerted in conducting peace and conflict impact assessments and human-rights impact assessments differ substantially between individual companies and evolve over time. The largest food processing corporations and global retailers are officially committed to policies that neither tolerate child labour nor forced labour. Yet large gaps remain in the breadth and depth of implementation efforts, reporting, third-party monitoring and the extent of due diligence in sourcing.[4] Among traders, around half of the major players have adopted relevant policies but the extent to which these guide actual practice and shape behaviour remains unclear because of poor public reporting.

Based on a detailed analysis of these various negative impacts and 'risk areas', humanitarian organisations can identify entry points to engage agri-food companies on mitigating negative outcomes. They might do this, for instance, by promoting respect for IHL and human rights in the design and execution of security arrangements between landowners or commercial producers and host states, or by using dialogues with private companies as an entry point for mitigating negative humanitarian impacts of commercial farms, industrial livestock producers, or food-processing firms. These may be of varying interest according to the mandate of different humanitarian organisations – the International Committee of the Red Cross (ICRC) may find these compelling avenues given that it strives to promote awareness of relevant IHL principles, raise awareness on specific humanitarian concerns and share knowledge on 'matters of mutual interest, such as humanitarian, security and health issues, particularly with regard to staff working under difficult conditions' (ICRC 2002). But beyond mitigating negative impacts, detecting potential negative humanitarian outcomes along a sector's supply chain helps to uncover reputation risks and irreconcilable gaps between the identity and core values of a humanitarian organisation and the activities and behaviour of an agribusiness company. This, in turn, can inform humanitarian organisations on the minimal moral acceptability or 'normative fit' when deciding whether to establish a partnership with a specific firm or not (see below).

Identifying Entry Points for Engagement: Seeking Positive Humanitarian Impact

Partnerships between corporations in the agribusiness industry and humanitarian organisations tend to fall under the realm of enhancing positive impacts rather than mitigating negative outcomes (see Table 8.1 on page 182 for a summary). Most are devised to enhance resource mobilisation of humanitarian agencies or revolve around in-kind donations and – to a lesser extent – operational support, capacity building and knowledge sharing.

The partnership between PepsiCo and WFP provides an illustration of collaborative arrangements in this sector that include, but go well beyond, fundraising and joint advocacy. PepsiCo provides WFP with logistical support. It assists the humanitarian agency in developing information and telecommunications capacity to enhance relief delivery systems. The two sides joined forces in a specific initiative in Ethiopia to develop specialised products with high local content (chick-pea-based) with an eye to simultaneously promote economic development and food security (WFP 2011). Care and Cargill have developed a similarly strong partnership: in 2008 they commenced a five-year, US$10 million global initiative on rural development, renewed in 2013 for three years with a further US$7.5 million. Cargill does not only boast to support Care's work in health, education, nutrition and reduction of child labour. The trading company also highlights that it provides rural farmers with inputs, technical advice on crop production and knowledge on market access (Cargill 2014).

By and large, the most obvious area for enhanced collaboration is in the alleviation of hunger and malnutrition. As the examples above highlight, some major food producers already make in-kind donations and, at times, assist in the development of specialised nutritional products and in the logistics of aid delivery. Collaborations also revolve around product innovations, such as ready-to-use therapeutic food developed by the French, family-owned company Nutriset, which has partly revolutionised the way humanitarians respond to food crises. Given the centrality of agriculture in sustaining livelihoods in developing countries, there is a large potential for enhanced technical support with regard to agricultural rehabilitation, livestock production and management, food supply chain management and beyond. Engaging specifically with trading houses remains uncommon and challenging, despite the potential for support and knowledge-sharing around stock management, storage and distribution of food and non-food items – an avenue worth exploring. Yet, it is critical for humanitarian organisations to examine the broader impact of such partnership on agricultural development and food sovereignty issues, including the risks associated with the introduction of genetically modified seeds and to engage in dialogue with the recipient governments and local communities about the potential risks and benefits of such collaborative arrangements with a view to getting their prior informed consent.

Another way for business and humanitarian enterprises to engage is through direct participation in multi-stakeholder initiatives or indirect support to the implementation of such initiatives at field level, in war or disaster-prone areas. Multi-stakeholder initiatives often serve as a means of voluntary self-regulation in response to public pressure. Major initiatives in the agri-food sector include certification schemes related to specific crops (e.g. Roundtable on Sustainable Palm Oil or on Responsible Soy) and those that endeavour to deal with labour issues or concerns over land and water. Here again, it is not so much about businesses becoming new humanitarians, but rather about humanitarians expanding their skills and expertise to meaningfully engage business actors on humanitarian crises and responses.

Beyond the agri-business sector, multi-stakeholder initiatives have focused notably on the oil, gas and mining sector, with the Kimberly Process Certification Scheme applying to so-called conflict diamonds, the Voluntary Principles on Security and Human Rights and the Extractive Industry Transparency Initiative. As with other industry-specific multi-stakeholder initiatives, they largely rely on shaping and institutionalising (new) incentive structures as a pathway to change business behaviour. Simultaneously, they provide institutionalised scripts for further action. Civil-society organisations (CSOs) play a pivotal role in promoting these initiatives, monitoring their implementation and whistleblowing in case of non-compliance, all challenging tasks for which they are often poorly equipped (Carbonnier *et al.* 2011). Humanitarian organisations have at times played a constructive role in supporting the implementation of global initiatives at the field level, where it matters most at the end of the day.

Business as a Driver of Innovation

The business world has also come to influence the corporate culture and management of humanitarian organisations as the latter grow bigger and professionalise. Business enterprises increasingly affect the relief industry itself through innovations that influence how humanitarian action is performed – all the way from how needs are assessed and risks addressed, to what type of response is designed, what kind of assistance is eventually provided in the field, and how it is offered. Likewise, the conscientious pursuit of innovation that has long been a priority for businesses has caught the attention of humanitarians. In recent years humanitarian organisations have increasingly begun to establish innovation units or use third-party strategic platforms to spur innovation through crowd sourcing (Ramalingam *et al.* 2009). As an example, in 2008 the United Nations Children's Fund (UNICEF) created a decentralised, field-based innovation programme and currently runs some 15 'innovation labs' around the world; other actors such as the UN High Commissioner for Refugees (UNHCR), Médecins Sans Frontières (MSF) and ICRC[5] have followed suit, though with great variations in strategic orientations and organising principles across institutions.

'Transformation through innovation' is one of the key priority areas that will be addressed in 2016 at the World Humanitarian Summit, which is being convened by the UN Secretary General to 'discuss the changing humanitarian landscape, share knowledge and best practices, and set a forward-looking humanitarian agenda' (World Humanitarian Summit 2014). We provide snapshots from the ITC and the insurance sectors to illustrate how innovations in products, processes and services can impact humanitarian action.

Rapid technological advances in the ITC sector stand out as one of the greatest opportunities and challenges for humanitarians. The advent of geospatial data and GIS mapping, mobile communication, open-data systems, or satellite imagery has started to affect humanitarian action when it comes to early warning, crisis mapping, needs assessment and coordination. Mobile-phone money transfer systems allowed the emergence of SMS-based mobile giving and the rise of e-vouchers and cash-transfer programmes. In a growing number of cases, the latter replaces traditional and more costly distribution of food and non-food items, with serious implications for humanitarian logistics and accountability. Likewise, these technologies allow web-based leveraging of global volunteer networks and give affected people the opportunity to have a voice in the midst of disaster, seek greater beneficiary participation and hold humanitarian agencies to account.

This is not to say that ITC companies turn into humanitarian actors, or have even developed those technologies for the sole purpose of supporting relief operations. Often actors outside of the humanitarian sector first adopt and adapt those technologies in humanitarian crises. In other words, ITC firms are the engines of technological advances developed for commercial purposes that end up impacting humanitarian work and opening new avenues for interaction. As humanitarians increasingly seek to leverage the transformative potential of new technologies, they will be pulled closer to businesses that research, develop, produce and operate them.

However, the introduction of new technologies is not risk free. It can raise serious challenges and negative externalities. The interface between technology and accountability raises issues related to the digital divide and dual-use products. The emergence of volunteer and technical networks of 'digital humanitarians' unfamiliar with humanitarian principles is another source of concern. The proliferation of open-source information systems and digital data sharing and storage, raises a whole series of challenges relating to data security and privacy breaches that can have major implications for the protection of key informants and beneficiaries. Besides, connectivity can end up increasing the vulnerability of humanitarian workers to attacks by maintaining real-time information on field movements and activities. These issues must be dealt with upfront. A conscientious approach to risk assessment and mitigation deserves high priority in the development and implementation of innovations in products and processes (Vinck 2013).

In addition, not all humanitarian crises weigh the same in the eyes of the private sector. Businesses tend to engage more easily in disaster response following natural hazard than in armed conflict. The latter is politically more controversial and risky. For example, the insurance industry is keener to communicate about disaster risk insurance covering losses from drought, earthquakes and typhoons than to hail the success of kidnap-and-ransom insurance products. Disaster risk insurance, catastrophe bonds ('cat bonds') and other risk-linked securities are set to expand fast in emerging economies exposed to natural hazards, in particular in Southeast Asia. Weather-indexed micro-insurance has been spreading with cheaper premiums and lower transaction costs to service the poor. But as many such schemes are not yet commercially viable, insurance companies have teamed up with development banks, aid agencies and philanthropists in the context of public–private partnerships (PPPs). Major multilateral aid organisations see a great potential for PPPs to strengthen disaster risk governance, increase disaster risk insurance coverage and promote risk-linked securities in developing countries (Carbonnier 2015).

The relationship between the aid sector and the insurance industry is not an easy one. It is certainly characterised by increasing cooperation, but potentially also enhanced competition. A growing, vibrant humanitarian sector seeks to improve the effective and timely delivery of post-disaster relief and recovery assistance. Host governments and local communities often prefer free ex-post assistance and tend to favour foreign aid over the alternative of paying ex-ante disaster risk insurance premiums or interests on cat-bonds. Hence, the humanitarian industry may in some instances end up constraining the development of the disaster insurance market in developing countries. Yet, insurance and derivative products have the advantage of potentially transferring a substantial portion of disaster costs abroad, irrespective of the (lack of) humanitarian response. More importantly perhaps, they contribute to reducing dependency on foreign aid, which is in line with national sovereignty claims in many emerging economies (Carbonnier 2015).

Legitimacy of Business–Humanitarian Partnerships

BHPs appeared in the 1990s as a form of collaboration that typically involve one or more corporate actors together with a (inter)governmental or NGO humanitarian entity. BHPs mainly revolve around resource mobilisation, operational collaboration and more rarely joint advocacy objectives. They often involve a mix of in-kind or cash donations, cause-related marketing, the sharing of expertise, as well as collaboration and exchanges on operational issues. Table 8.1 highlights risks and opportunities typically involved in BHPs.

Recent research highlights that notwithstanding well-publicised efforts of large multinational companies like IKEA, UPS and DHL to get involved in humanitarian action by partnering with major relief agencies, 'the vast

Table 8.1 Risks and opportunities associated with BHPs

	Opportunities	Risks
Humanitarian partner	Benefit from private sector R&D (research and development) enabling product adaptation or innovation; enhanced capacity through business operational support and expertise	Contested moral authority; operational capacity compromised if the partnership negatively affects how the humanitarian partner is perceived in the field
	Improved security management and access generated via knowledge-sharing on local contexts and conflict dynamics	Unwanted association of image as the logo/emblem of the humanitarian partner is used by the business partner, which may erode security
	Enhanced outreach and resource mobilisation via direct contributions from business and/or joint advocacy	Resources perceived as wasted (low comparative benefit)
Business partner	Cost-effective way to improve reputation and public image	Degradation of public image in the event of public termination of partnership by humanitarian partner
		Low return on investment or inability to demonstrate the value added of a BHP to shareholders
	Better risk management (security, due diligence, support in the implementation of multi-stakeholder initiatives in the field, etc.)	
	Enhanced employee satisfaction; retention of best talents	
	First-mover advantage from privileged access to (re)emerging markets	Market share or financial losses due to compliance with more rigorous standards

Source: the authors.

majority of humanitarian work is being undertaken by regional, national and local firms' (Kent and Zyck 2014: 11). Regional financial service providers or mobile communications firms tend to readily establish collaboration in response to an emergency – albeit primarily as commercial suppliers – as is the case in Lebanon: UNHCR and WFP decided to assist vulnerable Syrian refugees through unconditional cash and e-vouchers respectively, in partnership with two Lebanese financial services providers, CSC Bank and the Banque Libano-Française, and with the technical support of MasterCard. Corporate humanitarian engagement is thus not at all limited to well-known Western multinationals. The potential might actually be larger when considering SMEs active at local and regional levels.

The surge in BHPs has accompanied a rebalancing of power between states and non-state actors. Unlike PPPs and many multi-stakeholder initiatives, BHPs rarely involve states. They do not seek to fulfil governance functions, such as establishing standards, regulations, or new norms. Rather, they build synergies between partners to advance humanitarian objectives and support CSR efforts. In this context, the legitimacy of collaborative arrangements between the humanitarian and business sectors is critical for relief organisations. The latter evolve in an arena of internal and external normative scrutiny and deliberation involving multiple audiences, which demands high standards and provides opportunities for contestation. The question of the normative legitimacy of BHPs is particularly relevant in an organisational field constituted by a set of norms, including the essential principle of humanity, simultaneously with the issue of outcome legitimacy related to the comparative benefit of BHPs with regard to their outcomes (see below). The normative framework of global legitimacy elaborated by Buchanan and Keohane (2006) – as we shall elaborate on further below – is well suited to examine the legitimation strategies of BHPs; it relates to three criteria:

1   minimal moral acceptability in order to avoid violations of widely shared moral standards;
2   institutional integrity; and
3   comparative benefit.

More concretely, by allowing an association of image, sometimes lending the use of the UN or Red Cross logos or emblems to corporate partners, humanitarian agencies partly put their reputation and integrity at stake. If a business partner becomes involved in public controversies over human-rights abuses, contributions to humanitarian crises, or unethical behaviour their humanitarian counterpart can be implicated by association. This can undermine perceptions of the humanitarian actor's neutrality, impartiality and independence, compromising operational capacity in the field or lowering moral authority vis-à-vis diverse audiences (donors, staff, advocacy NGOs, etc.). Confronting such legitimacy challenges is a prerequisite for developing BHPs. First, by considering minimal moral fit or acceptability criteria. Second, institutional integrity or input legitimacy requires that the procedural aspects regulating partnerships uphold minimal accountability and transparency standards. Third, since BHPs are meant to enhance the operational capacity of humanitarian organisations, it is critical to look at the comparative benefit or humanitarian outcome of partnerships.[6] One should note that other scholars have questioned whether such standards are *a priori* applicable at the global level, particularly with respect to hybrid institutions that engage different constituencies and audiences (Bernstein 2011).[7]

The third criterion of 'minimal moral acceptability' suggests that the legitimacy of BHPs requires an explicit agreement and articulation of the moral purpose and the principles guarding their moral fit and ethical integrity. This is all the more important for humanitarian organisations such as UNICEF and the ICRC that derive a mandate from international law treaties. An important aspect of the legitimacy of BHPs is the extent to which they contribute to the successful implementation of such norms and, to a lesser degree, to the internalisation of normative standards by corporate actors. This does not discard competing interpretations and contestation of the moral purpose of BHPs. In a contested arena where humanitarian organisations struggle to maintain their legitimacy vis-à-vis diverse audiences, the multiplication of BHPs requires some form of alignment with principles that preserve the integrity and reputation of humanitarian organisations. This fits well with major insights from sociological institutional theory, whereby those parties to a partnership that incorporate societally legitimated rationalised elements in their formal structures and operations maximise the legitimacy of partnerships and increase their resources and survival capacities (Meyer and Rowan 1991).

Legal Frameworks, Voluntary Principles and Ethical Guidelines

The three criteria mentioned above are closely related to the legal frameworks in the international public domain. To put it in more detail, the contemporary global public domain is underpinned by an expanding set of broadly agreed-upon ethical and procedural norms, or ideal-type criteria of moral acceptability that also frame debates on BHP legitimacy.[8] This is particularly relevant in the case of frameworks, principles and guidelines that address the relationship between business operations and human rights in war and weak governance zones. The aforementioned Protect, Respect and Remedy Framework and the Guiding Principles, which were designed after extensive consultations with states, business and civil society across continents, represents the most recent and significant attempt to establish a universal reference on business and human rights. Since their adoption, they have been integrated into a range of voluntary and multilateral initiatives, such as the Organisation for Economic Co-operation and Development (OECD) Guidelines for Multinational Enterprises (Bernard 2012).

In terms of normative fit, these instruments provide a clear reference point to humanitarian organisations seeking to frame BHPs rights. They can refer to established principles and guidelines that can be widely regarded as legitimate. Yet, procedural legitimacy further calls for implementation mechanisms that secure the institutional integrity of partnerships, including vis-à-vis internal audiences and principals (governing boards, donors). As we shall see below, UNICEF and the ICRC have established a set of guidelines and recommendations as normative frameworks that help clarify expectations with regard to the roles and responsibilities of humanitarian and business partners, which provide guidance in the design of stronger and more widely accepted terms of engagement between the for-profit and humanitarian worlds.

The Case of UNICEF and the ICRC

Table 8.2 shows how this concern for normative fit has translated into specific principles and guidelines in the case of the International Movement of the Red Cross and Red Crescent as reflected in the Movement Policy for Corporate Sector Partnerships (2005) and of UNICEF, with its Guidelines and Manual for Working with the Business Community (2001) and its Strategic Framework for Partnerships and Collaborative Relationships (2009). The 2005 Red Cross/Red Crescent Policy seeks to safeguard the integrity and reputation of the Movement while encouraging partnerships with companies that contribute to achieving humanitarian objectives. BHPs are presented as opportunities to influence corporate behaviour on social issues. Both UNICEF and the Red Cross/Red Crescent Movement have adopted clear institutional scripts for action, including no-go sectors and areas with a view to avoiding any partnership with a company whose core business or behaviour would be materially inconsistent with humanitarian objectives and principles. Establishing the normative fit of BHPs thus appears to be an important element of the legitimation strategies in the face of internal and external scrutiny and debate.

The implementing guidelines of both UNICEF and the International Movement of the Red Cross and Red Crescent contain a set of procedures to secure the institutional integrity of partnerships. The UNICEF Guidelines, for example, require a 'due diligence' process for corporate partner selection. The ultimate approval rests with a coordination committee overseen by the Executive Director, and the partnership materialises in a written agreement that specifies the respective roles and responsibilities of the partners. The corporate partnership policy of the Red Cross/ Red Crescent Movement provides detailed advice on how to go about the appropriate screening of companies in order to assess to what extent their behaviour and activities are consistent with the policy. It recommends the Movement's components to 'consult a minimum of three independent, credible sources ... and seek the advice of professional, independent,

Table 8.2 Guiding principles and norms applying to BHPs – The examples of the International Movement of the Red Cross and Red Crescent and UNICEF

	UNICEF	*International Movement of the Red Cross and Red Crescent*
Objectives of BHPs	To assist UNICEF in fulfilling its mission.	To contribute to protecting and improving the lives of vulnerable people. The BHP further represents an opportunity to influence the behaviour of corporate partners.
Principles for identifying business partners	The business partner should display corporate responsibility and a commitment to UNICEF's mandate and values, including responsible labour and environmental practices.	The business partner must in no way be engaged in activities running counter to the Movement's objectives and principles, and should not jeopardise the neutrality and independence of the Movement's components.
Exclusion criteria	Firms materially involved in armaments manufacture (incl. toys), UN sanction busters, pornography, and corrupt practices. Limited possibility for partnerships with firms in the alcohol and tobacco sector.	Firms materially involved in the manufacture and trade of arms and ammunition, or in activities that are deleterious to health, or contributing to humanitarian emergencies. Firms that could compromise the reputation and neutrality and impartiality of the Movement's components.
Restriction on the use of the emblem or logo by the business partner	BHP should be enshrined in a contractual, written agreement, in line with UNICEF Identification Standards Manual. No product endorsement, no exclusivity granted.	Protective; indicative use of the emblems must not be compromised. No product endorsement or exclusivity granted to any corporate partner.

Source: adapted from Andonova and Carbonnier 2014: 359.

specialised rating agencies' (ICRC 2005, 820). The policy further requires that the company formally confirm in the partnership contract that its activities are in line with the selection criteria in Table 8.2. In addition, the contract should include a termination clause allowing any component of the Movement to immediately and publicly withdraw from a partnership if the company does not fulfil the criteria anymore (Andonova and Carbonnier 2014: 361–362).

In practice, the onus of designing broad legitimation strategies has fallen primarily on the humanitarian partners whose own legitimacy depends on normative expectations and is subject to scrutiny by the multiple audiences in their organisational field. Even if UNICEF has a long experience of fundraising with the private sector, collaborative governance arrangements in BHPs required a specific ethical and procedural base, similar to the International Movement of the Red Cross and Red Crescent with the establishment of minimal moral fit and procedural safeguards for BHPs. The Achilles heel of BHPs remains the weak capacity to assess comparative worth or outcome legitimacy: rigorous evaluation of the effectiveness and humanitarian outcome of BHPs remains scarce, not the least because it is methodologically highly challenging.

Conclusion

Business enterprises impact on and intervene in humanitarian crises under a variety of channels and with distinct incentives, constraints, objectives and sensitivities. This depends notably on their size, structure, ownership, sector of activity, history, corporate culture and capacity to adapt to challenging environments. Looking at the agri-food sector in particular, a supply chain analysis allows identifying critical risk areas and opportunities for business–humanitarian engagement.

Business enterprises cannot be labelled new humanitarians. Their core objective of course remains profit or shareholder-value maximisation. Yet, business people display increasing concerns for humanitarian issues out of a multiplicity of motives. This chapter highlights the various ways in which corporations and humanitarians find themselves – purposefully or not – increasingly interacting in crisis situations. The two actors remain 'uneasy bedfellows' in many respects, for example with regard to the risks related to business interactions with war economies. Yet, there is now a growing readiness to redefine relations in a more nuanced manner on the basis that there is no fundamental incompatibility that would require a firewall between the for-profit and humanitarian sectors. More and more companies value the multidimensional benefits of engaging the humanitarian sector. Likewise, relief agencies have sought to tap into business resources and capacities. The business sector is also a source of constant innovations, some of which radically alter the way humanitarian aid can be conceived and delivered. Humanitarian organisations have further adopted some traits of the business culture and models deemed successful to compete on global markets, private and humanitarian ones alike.

This should not come as a surprise. Both businesses and humanitarian agencies are operational organisations driven by a concern for effectiveness. When working in highly sensitive or 'fragile' environments, both engage with the local field reality and political order as it is, rather than as it ought to be, which is a precondition to run complex operations successfully. In practice, there may be more interactions with local domestic businesses than with multinational firms in that humanitarian agencies develop close relations with domestic firms and entrepreneurs in war-torn countries, for example in the transport, logistics and banking sectors.

Except in a few instances where businesses provide direct humanitarian assistance, they increasingly seek to partner with humanitarian organisations. The legitimacy of such BHPs rests on moral fit, procedural integrity and eventual humanitarian outcomes of such collaborative arrangements. Humanitarian organisations are indeed wary of preserving the integrity of their brand and reputation, as exemplified by the case of UNICEF and the International Movement of the Red Cross and Red Crescent. Newly agreed ethical and procedural norms in the field of business and human rights provide a reference for moral fit and overall legitimacy of different forms of BHPs. Evaluating the humanitarian outcomes of such partnerships remains a challenge and requires additional scrutiny.

Notes

1 Prof. Ruggie is the former Special Representative of the UN Secretary-General for Business and Human Rights.
2 See ICRC (2006: 17). This being said, it is common that businesses operating in conflict zones have their facilities attacked or their staff kidnapped for ransom. This has led some of them to resort to illicit securitisation methods such as paying rebels, paramilitary groups or oppressive regimes for protection, which in turn contributes to financing armed groups. But this can also whet business appetite for engagement with humanitarians to strengthen their license to operate and navigate the public-relations landmines that litter the field of relations with unsavoury governments and rebels.
3 The initiative was born from a USAID and Gates Foundation prize challenge.
4 See the special issues of the *Journal of Business Ethics* on Organising CSR (115(4), July 2013) or on the UN Global Compact (122(2), June 2014), the special issue of *Business and Society* on Corporate Responsibility: Initiatives and Mechanisms (53(4), July 2014) and Hoffman (2013).
5 See http://blogs.icrc.org/gphi2.
6 Theoretically, the relevance of normative principles of moral fit, institutional integrity and comparative worth have been advanced by Buchanan and Keohane (2006) with regard to global governance institutions. We adapted their framework criteria to specific BHPs in Andonova and Carbonnier (2014).
7 It is worth noting that hybrid-governance instruments such as BHPs are embedded in the institutionalised global public domain, which entails a set of principled expectations against which legitimation strategies are adopted, but this does not negate the presence of processes, contestation and intersubjective understandings in establishing legitimacy (see below).
8 In other words, this concerns the regulative and normative pillars of sociological institutionalism.

References

Amnesty International (2011) Indonesia: Exxon Mobil Decision a Reminder of Continuing Impunity in Aceh (www.amnesty.org.au/news/comments/26251) accessed 30 June 2014.

Andonova, L. and Carbonnier, G. (2014) 'Business–Humanitarian Partnerships: Process of Normative Legitimation', *Globalizations*, 11(3):349–367.

Ashurst, M. (2012) As the Aid Industry Globalizes, Contractors Race to Keep Up, Devex (www.devex.com/news/as-the-aid-industry-globalizes-contractors-race-to-adapt-78309) accessed 13 October 2014.

Beeler, M. and Lightfoot, P. (2013) Humanitarian Impacts of Business Operations in Areas of High Risk or Conflict, Applied Research Project for International Committee of the Red Cross and Graduate Institute of International and Development Studies, Mimeo unpublished.

Bernard, V. (2012) 'Globalisation Will Only Mean Progress If It Is Responsible', *International Review of the Red Cross*, 94(887):881–890.

Bernstein, S. (2011) 'Legitimacy in Intergovernmental and Non-State Global Governance', *Review of International Political Economy*, 18(1):17–51.

Brodzinsky, S. (2007) Terrorism and Bananas in Colombia (http://content.time. com/time/world/article/0,8599,1616991,00.html) accessed 6 December 2013.

Buchanan, A. and Keohane, R.O. (2006) 'The Legitimacy of Global Governance Institutions', *Ethics and International Affairs*, 20(4):405–437.

Carbonnier, G. (2006) 'Privatization and Outsourcing in Wartime: The Humanitarian Challenges', *Disasters*, 30(4):402–416.

Carbonnier, G. (2015) 'The Rise of Disaster Risk Insurance and Derivatives', in C. Brassard, C. Giles, D. and A. Howitt (eds) *Natural Disaster Management in the Asia Pacific*, Tokyo: Springer Japan, 175–188.

Carbonnier, G., Brugger, F. and Krause, J. (2011) 'Global and Local Responses to the Resource Trap', *Global Governance*, 17:247–264.

Cargill (2014) Care, Corporate Website (www.cargill.com/corporate-responsibility/ partnerships/food-security-and-nutrition-partners/care/index.jsp) accessed 18 September 2014.

Clarke, P. and Ramalingam, B. (2009) 'Organizational Change in the Humanitarian Sector', *8th Review of Humanitarian Action*, London: ALNAP.

Conference Board (2008) *Corporate Responses to Humanitarian Disasters: The Mutual Benefits of Private–Humanitarian Cooperation*, Research Report R-1415-08-WG. New York: The Conference Board.

De Schutter, O. (2010) Food Commodities Speculation and Food Price Crises, Briefing Note, United Nations Special Rapporteur on the Right to Food (www2. ohchr.org/english/issues/food/docs/Briefing_Note_02_September_2010_ EN.pdf) accessed 29 December 2014.

Deininger, K. and Byerlee, D. with Lindsay, J., Norton, A., Selod, H. and Stickler, M. (2011) *Rising Global Interest in Farmland*, Washington DC: The World Bank.

Forbes (2006) 'The $3 Billion Man', interview of Sir Richard Branson by Tara Weiss in *Forbes*, 28 November 2006 (www.forbes.com/2006/11/26/leadership-branson-virgin-lead-citizen-cx_tw_1128branson.html) accessed 14 August 2014.

GHA (2014) *Humanitarian Assistance from Non-State Donors, Global Humanitarian Assistance Programme*, London: Development Initiatives.

Goel, V. and Goss, S. (2012) Case Study: Haiti Mobile Money Initiative, Goel Insights (www.innovationinthecrowd.com/examples/Haiti-mobile-money-initiative.pdf) accessed 7 May 2014.

Goreux, L. (2001) *Conflict Diamonds*, Africa Working Paper Series no. 13, Washington DC: The World Bank.

Hoffman, B. (2013) *Behind the Brands*, Oxfam Briefing Paper, London: Oxfam.

Hurst, P. (2007) Agricultural Workers and Their Contribution to Sustainable Agriculture and Rural Development (www.ilo.org/wcmsp5/groups/public/ —ed_dialogue/—actrav/documents/publication/wcms_113732.pdf) accessed 29 December 2014.

ICRC (2002) Ethical Principles Guiding the ICRC's Partnerships with the Private Sector (www.icrc.org/eng/assets/files/other/guidelines_for_partnerships.pdf) accessed 5 December 2013.

ICRC (2005) 'Resolution 10: Movement Policy for Corporate Sector Partnerships', *International Review of the Red Cross*, 87(860):814–823.

ICRC (2006) Business and International Humanitarian Law (www.icrc.org/eng/assets/files/other/icrc_002_0882.pdf) accessed 13 October 2014.

ILO (2013) International Program for the Elimination of Child Labor (www.ilo.org/ipec/areas/Agriculture/lang–en/index.htm) accessed 25 November 2013.

Kent, R. and Zyck, S. (2014) *Humanitarian Crises, Emergency Preparedness and Response: The Role of Business and the Private Sector*, London: ODI.

Konig, G., da Silva, C.A. and Mhlanga, N. (2013) Enabling Environment for Agribusiness and Agro-Industries Development: Regional and Country Perspectives (www.fao.org/docrep/017/i3121e/i3121e00.pdf) accessed 17 May 2013.

Mattera, P. (2005) Disaster as Relief: How Wal-Mart used Hurricane Katrina to Repair its Image (www.corp-research.org/e-letter/disaster-relief) accessed 13 October 2014.

Meyer, J.W. and Rowan, B. (1991) 'Institutionalized Isomorphism and Collective Rationality', in: W.W. Powell and P.J. DiMaggio (eds) *The New Institutionalism in Organizational Analysis*, Chicago and London: University of Chicago Press, 41–62.

Murphy, S., Burch, D. and Clapp, J. (2012) *Cereal Secrets: The World's Largest Grain Traders and Global Agriculture*, London: Oxfam.

Norris, J. (2012) Hired Gun Fight: Obama's Aid Chief Takes on the Development-Industrial Complex (www.foreignpolicy.com/articles/2012/07/18/hired_gun_fight) accessed 30 August 2014.

OCHA (2013) *World Humanitarian Data and Trends 2013*, Geneva: OCHA Policy Development and Studies Branch.

Rainforest Action Network (2013) Conflict Palm Oil (http://ran.org/sites/default/files/conflict_palm_oil_lowres.pdf) accessed 6 December 2013.

Ramalingam, B., Scriven, K. and Foley, C. (2009) *Innovations in International Humanitarian Action, 8th Review of Humanitarian Action – Performance, Impact and Innovation*, London: ALNAP.

Romero, S. (2012) 'Violence Hits Brazil Tribes in a Scramble for Land', *The New York Times*, 9 June.

Slim, H. (2012) 'Business Actors in Armed Conflict: Towards a New Humanitarian Agenda', *International Review of the Red Cross*, 94(887):903–918.

Stirk, C. (2014) Humanitarian Assistance from Non-State Donors: What Is It Worth? Global Humanitarian Assistance Briefing Paper, London: Development Initiatives.

UNHCHR (2011) *UN Guiding Principles on Business and Human Rights*, New York and Geneva: The Office of the UN High Commissioner for Human Rights.

UNICEF (2001) UNICEF Guidelines and Manual for Working with the Business Community: Identifying the Best Allies – Developing the Best Alliances (www.unicef.org/indonesia/Corporate_Summary_Guidelines.pdf) accessed 29 December 2014.

UNICEF (2009) UNICEF Strategic Framework for Partnerships and Collaborative Relationships (www.unicef.org/about/execboard/files/Expanded_Strategic_Framework_for_Partnerships-27Aug2012.pdf) accessed 29 December 2014.

United States of America v. Carl Krauch et al. (1948) IG Farben Trial, United States Military Tribunal Case No. 57 RG 238 14 August 1947– 29 July 1948 (www.worldcourts.com/ildc/eng/decisions/1948.07.29_United_States_v_Krauch.pdf) accessed 13 October 2014.

Vinck, P. (ed.) (2013) World Disasters Report 2013: Focus on Technology and the Future of Humanitarian Action (www.ifrc.org/PageFiles/134658/WDR%20 2013%20complete.pdf) accessed 7 April 2015.

WFP (United Nations World Food Programme) (2011) WFP, PepsiCo and USAID Fight Child Malnutrition in Ethiopia (www.wfp.org/stories/wfp-pepsico-and-usaid-fight-child-malnutrition-ethiopia) accessed 18 September 2014.

World Humanitarian Summit (2014) Concept Note (https://docs.unocha.org/sites/dms/Documents/WHS%20Concept%20Note.pdf) accessed 2 June 2014.

9 Humanitarian Action for Sale

Private Military and Security Companies in the Humanitarian Space

Jutta Joachim and Andrea Schneiker

Introduction

Over the course of the past decade private military and security companies (PMSCs) have come to play an increasingly important role in post-conflict settings (Rosén 2008). Operating transnationally and offering military, police or security services ranging from logistics, training and consultancy to intelligence and border control to physical protection in armed conflicts, these companies are not only being increasingly contracted by non-governmental organisations (NGOs) and intergovernmental organisations (IGOs), which have traditionally provided assistance; they have also started to specialise in providing humanitarian and development services themselves. PMSCs' involvement in an organisational field that until recently was dominated primarily by NGOs guided by the humanitarian principles raises a number of questions: How do companies with an image of providing (military) protection attempt to establish themselves as legitimate actors in the humanitarian field and what consequences does their involvement have? And how do PMSCs – the 'New Humanitarian Agent[s]', as James Fennell, a representative of ArmorGroup, now part of G4S, referred to them in 2001 (Fennell, cited in Vaux *et al.* 2001: 13) – contribute to the ongoing 'struggle to (re)define the humanitarian identity' (Barnett and Weiss 2008: 5)?

Regarding intervention spaces as social arenas is an instructive analytical perspective to address these questions. We therefore draw on the work of Hilhorst and Jansen, who apply the concept to the humanitarian space, considering it as a space constructed through the practices and discourses of the actors involved, who 'negotiate the outcomes of aid', 'are driven by different motives and decisions' and use the 'language and principles of humanitarian space … strategically or tacitly … to advance or legitimise their respective interests, projects or beliefs' (Hilhorst and Jansen 2010: 1118, 1120). The arena approach implies that the meaning of humanitarianism is not fixed but rather is contingent, 'socially negotiated and acquiring meaning in practice' through a variety of actors who have different understandings of what constitutes humanitarian action (ibid.: 1121). Collinson *et al.* (2013: 2) note that 'humanitarian action, for instance, is unlikely to be based solely on a desire to alleviate suffering, but will also be driven by other motivations'. In addition, the arena approach takes into account the competitive environment in which humanitarians operate and in which they compete for scarce funding and in which a struggle takes place 'over the question of who constitutes a real humanitarian' (Hilhorst and Jansen 2010: 1134).

We conducted a content analysis of the websites of 16 PMSCs[1] and of the publications of their international industry association, the International Stability Operations Association (ISOA). To cross-check our findings and for purposes of triangulation, we reviewed the relevant literature. Based on a comparison of the characteristics generally ascribed to the humanitarian field through the statements, photos and symbols used by PMSCs, and employing the concept of identity, we show how the PMSCs appropriate humanitarian language and images that are strikingly similar to those of humanitarian NGOs: not only do they purport to provide services to those in need, they also claim to have similar altruistic motivations. Moreover, these companies regard themselves as an integral part of the peace-building or, as their industry representatives put it, 'stability operations' industry.

Regardless of the motives that lead PMSCs to adapt to the humanitarian space, the implications of this trend are significant: in practice it becomes difficult for outsiders and those affected by crises to distinguish between PMSCs and traditional humanitarian actors. José Luis Gómez del Prado, a former member of the United Nations Working Group on the Use of Mercenaries, notes that 'these transnational companies do not hesitate to present themselves as peace organisations and utilise the aims of humanitarian non-profit organisations to advertise their activities'; as a result, not only has it 'become difficult for the population to distinguish one from another', but humanitarian assistance 'risks becoming associated with an intervening force as well as with private military and security companies' (Gómez del Prado no date: 5).

In theoretical terms, our findings support the argument that normative institutional settings, such as the humanitarian space, as well as its rules, norms and practices, contribute to isomorphism among the actors who are engaged in them, and also redefine what humanitarianism means. The observed alignment processes prompt us to reconsider assertions about global (security) governance which are premised on the assumption that, depending on their material or non-material resources, different types of actors (state, civil society and business actors) contribute to the resolution of global issues within regulatory schemes such as public–private partnerships or multi-stakeholder processes in different ways.

The chapter begins with a brief characterisation of PMSCs and their identities, and then discusses the characteristics of humanitarianism and the humanitarian space, acknowledging that both are subject to change brought about by the privatisation of aid and security, and the increasing engagement of humanitarian actors in armed conflicts in which they are, or perceive themselves to be, faced with increasing insecurity. The section on our empirical evidence shows that PMSCs not only intrude into and appropriate humanitarian space through the services they perform but also make strategic use of humanitarian discourses, symbols and imagery to assert that they belong to a larger, evolving stability operations industry concerned with peace-building and humanitarian action. The chapter concludes with a discussion of the implications of the 'private–private' encounter and an evaluation of the empirical findings in light of the claims that the boundaries between the different types of actors, tasks and sectors are becoming blurred, and that non-state actors not only contribute to the delivery of humanitarian assistance and other resources but also transform our understanding of these resources with regard to who should deliver them in what ways to which actors.

A Characterisation of PMSCs' Identities

While private security in armed conflict might be considered to be 'as old as war itself' (Singer 2003: 19), PMSCs are a relatively new phenomenon. Over the past 30 years in particular, the security industry has experienced a boom which has seen an increase in the number of companies in this area and the diversification of the services they offer and of the clients for which they work (governments, international organisations such as the UN, other businesses companies and, increasingly, NGOs). Evidence of their growing importance can be found in countries such as Iraq and Afghanistan (Commission on Wartime Contracting in Iraq and Afghanistan 2009) where PMSCs 'operate *alongside* the state-run professional military in theatres of combat' (Dunigan 2011: 53, emphasis in original), assume 'critical jobs' and therefore play 'essential' roles (Singer 2004: 4, 6).

In recent decades international relations (IR) scholars have developed a number of typologies to identify the differences and similarities between PMSCs and other security actors. The one most commonly used is Peter W. Singer's 'tip of the spear' typology, which classifies PMSCs based on their proximity to the battlefield (see Singer 2003). Other authors, such as Abrahamsen and Williams (2007) and Percy (2009), distinguish between private *security* and private *military* companies depending on whether they operate in an *offensive* or *defensive* way. While categories such as these certainly proved useful in the beginning, more recent studies have shed light on their shortcomings. For example, the distinctions on which they rest are far from clear-cut considering that, owing in part to mergers and acquisitions, many companies offer a wide range of services spanning multiple categories (Dunigan 2011: 13). Moreover, these studies fail to consider ideational aspects and the discursive power of PMSCs, which play an increasingly important role in commercial transactions in a competitive market (Joachim and Schneiker 2012: 2). PMSCs 'combine the worlds of the military, the business world, and the humanitarian NGO in unfamiliar ways' (Carmola 2010: 28).

The declared mission of ISOA, for example, is to contribute to 'the enhancement of international peace, development and human security' (ISOA 2013). In response to a critical report by the NGO Global Policy Forum (Pingeot 2012), DynCorp International, a company that, according to its website, offers 'security services' (DynCorp 2013) and whose International Security Services division 'had revenues of [US$]1.8 billion, or approximately 59 percent of [its] total revenues', in Fiscal Year 2009 (DynCorp 2009: 4), states that 'it is not a security company – it provides sophisticated aviation, knowledge-transfer, logistics, humanitarian and operational solutions' (Global Policy Forum 2012). Thus, companies not only provide material humanitarian services but also appropriate the identities of their clients (Carmola 2010; Joachim and Schneiker 2014). Therefore, to understand PMSCs and the boom they are experiencing more fully, we need to look more closely at the images they construct of themselves and at the stories they tell about their products. Analysing their humanitarian identity is instructive in this respect. By discursively drawing on values of the non-profit humanitarian sector and by claiming to have capabilities generally associated with it, PMSCs construct an image to which their potential clients – be they state forces, governmental or non-governmental organisations or other companies – as well as future employees can relate.

That identity is taken seriously by IR scholars can be attributed to what has become known as the 'third debate' between positivists and post-positivists. In the case of PMSCs the concept of identity shifts the focus from the services they offer – and, thus, from a conceptualisation of PMSCs based on typologies – to the ways in which they exert influence and in which they are perceived. Rather than treating identity as an exogenous factor, constructivists and post-structuralists in particular have shown that it has causal and constitutive effects. Social identities are constructed through historically contingent interactions which can be defined as 'sets of meanings that an actor attributes to itself while taking the perspective of others' (Wendt 1994: 385). They are distinguished by '(1) rules of membership that decide who is and is not a member of the category; and (2) content, that is, sets of characteristics ... thought to be typical of members of the category, or behaviours expected or obliged of members in certain situations (roles)' (Fearon and Laitin 2000: 848).

Discourses play an important role in this respect: 'social categories, their membership rules, content, and valuation are the products of human action and speech' (Fearon and Laitin 2000: 848). Being constitutive of various identities, discourses are also essential in that they enable PMSCs to speak to and sell services to different constituencies using language and symbols which resonate with the ideas, needs and self-perception of their clients. We identified two strategies PMSCs use to present themselves as humanitarians: the first is to offer services to traditional humanitarian actors such as NGOs, and the second is to claim to provide humanitarian services themselves. Before we proceed to the analysis of these two strategies, we will briefly sketch the context in which the (re)construction and (re)production of the PMSCs' humanitarian identities take place.

Conceptualising Humanitarian Space

Until recently humanitarian action was the domain of not-for-profit humanitarian organisations within the 'humanitarian space', which was traditionally defined as 'an environment where humanitarians can work without hindrance and follow the humanitarian principles of neutrality, impartiality and humanity' (Spearin 2001: 22). However, this situation is changing as new actors such as state militaries and PMSCs are entering the space. Applying the analytical concept of arena to the rather normative concept of humanitarian space, as Hilhorst and Jansen (2010) do, is useful to understand how this space is (re)constructed through the involvement of non-traditional humanitarians, how these new actors gain access to the space and how they legitimise themselves. The concept of arena is actor-focused and acknowledges 'the messy interaction of social actors struggling, negotiating and at times guessing in order to further their own interests' (Bakewell 2000: 108–9). It thus captures the political dimension of what has mostly been treated as moral space. In this section we will list the characteristics of this space, aware that actors and space are subject to change.

Humanitarianism and its meaning have been defined first and foremost by the International Red Cross and Red Crescent Movement and by NGOs. Humanitarians are expected to be motivated by a sense of moral duty, obligation and responsibility (Barnett and Snyder 2008: 143), and should be at least 'partly non-self-interested' (Fearon 2008: 51). For a long time the principles of humanity, neutrality, impartiality and independence have been regarded as cornerstones of humanitarianism as well (Barnett 2009: 623). Although these attributes are still considered distinctive of humanitarian identity and organisations such as the International Committee of the Red Cross (ICRC) aspire to strictly adhere to them, there have been a variety of different understandings of humanitarianism and security (Barnett and Weiss 2008; Eckroth 2010). These developments must be understood in the context of the changing crises in which humanitarians work and in that of the changes within the humanitarian system.

For example, Cooley and Ron (2002) argue that humanitarian NGOs, faced with new challenges in the field and with an influx of new actors, have started to show signs of commercialisation and to base their decisions as to where to provide humanitarian assistance on financial considerations rather than on considerations of need. This trend in the humanitarian sector is further reinforced by the 'philanthropic capitalism' in which business companies increasingly engage (Hopgood 2008) and by a growing concern with accountability to those funding humanitarian NGOs, which increases the pressure on organisations to be successful. In addition, many humanitarian NGOs have started to change their ways of responding to emergencies by replacing their 'bed for the night' approach (Rieff 2002) with a more ambitious 'comprehensive peace-building' approach (Barnett and Snyder 2008: 150), with the former approach consisting in delivering food, water, shelter and medical supplies, and the aim of the latter being to ensure respect for human rights and to contribute more generally to economic development, democracy and rule of law in a particular state (ibid.). Organisations aspiring to more 'comprehensive peace-building' no longer claim to be apolitical but increasingly regard themselves and are increasingly regarded by others, as political agents (Terry 2002).

These changes within the humanitarian sector are occurring in light of, and in response to, growing insecurity in the field (Stoddard *et al.* 2009b). Between 1997 and 2008 the absolute number of violent incidents affecting aid workers increased about fivefold, and the relative number of aid worker victims doubled (Stoddard *et al.* 2009b: 2–3). In 2011 '308 aid workers were victims of major attacks ... – the highest yearly number yet recorded' (Humanitarian Outcomes 2012).[2]

PMSCs Intruding into the Humanitarian Space

PMSCs are increasingly intruding into the humanitarian space, which used to be reserved to non-commercial actors. Not only do a growing number of them offer services to humanitarian NGOs, provide humanitarian services themselves, or both, they also appropriate discursive elements of humanitarian NGOs such as their language, images and symbols. By referring to themselves as an integral part of peace-building efforts, PMSCs try to legitimise their existence in the field, and to redraw the boundaries between who does and who does not belong to the category of humanitarian actors and to the humanitarian space.

Service Provision for Humanitarians

Hilhorst and Jansen (2010: 1121) note that

the kinds of action or actors considered to be humanitarian are not predetermined, nor are the principles that qualify as humanitarian established in advance; instead we ask ourselves how the conditions of service delivery in crisis situations are shaped in practice.

These conditions are shaped in part by traditional humanitarian actors which establish links to non-traditional ones.

'Over the last five years, humanitarian organisations have increased their contracting of security and security-related services from commercial companies' (Stoddard *et al.* 2009a: 1; Speers Mears 2009: 3). Given that contracting PMSCs is a very sensitive issue for humanitarian organisations, most studies rely on anecdotal evidence (e.g. Vaux *et al.* 2001; Hellinger 2004). The only exceptions are surveys that provide more insights and some comparable data on NGO behaviour with respect to PMSCs (namely Cockayne 2006; Stoddard *et al.* 2008, 2009a). They show that local companies are usually hired by NGOs to provide unarmed guards, while transnational PMSCs are contracted primarily to provide security training for staff, security management consulting, risk assessment/threat analysis and physical security for premises (Cockayne 2006: 8; Stoddard *et al.* 2008: 10). These surveys also show that NGOs attribute the need to hire PMSCs not only to lack of capacities (Stoddard *et al.* 2009a) but also 'to real and perceived growth in insecurity, leading to concern for the safety of staff, sustainability of programs and growing awareness of the legal dimensions of the duty of care' (Glaser 2011: 3; Speers Mears 2009: 6–7). 'Armed security contracting remains the exception ... [but] all major humanitarian actors [i.e. UN humanitarian agencies and the largest international NGOs] report having used armed guards in at least one context' (Stoddard *et al.* 2009a: 1).

When the concept of arena is applied to the humanitarian space, 'humanitarian principles are seen as socially negotiated and acquiring meaning in practice' (Hilhorst and Jansen 2010: 1121). Rather than security or protection, PMSCs present the provision of their services to humanitarian NGOs as helping those in need. For example, according to the company Blue Hackle (2014),

> Non-profits and NGOs need a team of committed security personnel to protect the lives of not only aid workers, but the lives of displaced families and refugees at risk in highly contentious environments. Blue Hackle's attentiveness and flexibility to rapidly changing conditions ensures that aid is distributed and progress continues, day by day.

Similarly, the company Olive Group (2014) states that its aim is 'to provide comprehensive, project enabling protective services that secure the lives and ensure the welfare of NGO personnel while also guaranteeing their on-going access to beneficiaries'.

PMSCs are often less explicit in stating that they provide protective security services to humanitarian NGOs and prefer to describe their services in other ways. Oxberry Risk Strategies (2011), for example, claims to

> provide Non-Governmental Organizations (NGOs) with full support when operating in challenging and hostile environments around the world. We assist humanitarian organizations by providing vital insight into the areas they operate, from initial political and security risk analysis to pre deployment travel security briefings and hostile environment training, to monitoring of NGO workers when in country.

The company CTG Global 'has provided complete Human Resources support packages, recruitment only services as well as turnkey operational support requirements to a plethora of Humanitarian Agencies since 2006' (CTG Global 2014b). Statements such as these lend force to scholars who recognise that humanitarian action is not only inspired by the true desire to alleviate 'life-threatening suffering wherever it may be' (Hilhorst and Jansen 2010: 1122), but can be driven by a range of motives, including profits, corporate interests, or 'organisational politics – the desire to continue operations and retain staff – or as a form of legitimisation politics – showing the public that an agency is doing good work' (ibid.: 1122). Hence, the self-representations of PMSCs are cognisant of the challenges that humanitarian NGOs are faced with nowadays. Nevertheless, they are also indicative of a different understanding of humanitarianism as are the references they make with respect to themselves as humanitarian actors.

Service Provision for Victims

PMSCs construct their role as service providers in different ways, namely by delivering material goods and, discursively, by evoking principles, symbols and imagery associated with the field, thereby presenting themselves as 'the New Humanitarian Agent[s]' (James Fennell, of ArmorGroup, cited in Vaux *et al.* 2001: 14, note 12) and as an integral part of the peace-building – or 'stability operations' – industry.

The PMSC Arkel '[d]elivers food to those who've been hit by disaster and have no means for sustenance [and] provides meals as part of life support in places where food service is remote or non-existent' (Arkel 2014a); Hart 'co-developed "Operation Warm Toes" in Afghanistan that provided more than 3,000 pairs of winter boots and socks to children in need' (Hart 2014); and AECOM

> serves as a global sponsor for WFP [Water For People], having raised more than US$480,000 to provide the developing world access to safe water and sanitation. The company also … provid[es] pro-bono engineering projects to underserved communities to implement sustainable engineering projects such as water systems.
>
> (AECOM 2014)

AECOM (2013) states that it partners with non-profit organisations, such as 'Water For People, WaterAid [and] the International Red Cross and its affiliates':

> As one of the world's largest water engineering firms … AECOM is committed to environmental sustainability and working to ensure that people around the world have access to clean water. Through strategic partnerships with organizations such as Engineers Without Borders

(EWB), Water For People and the United Nations (UN) Global Compact, AECOM and its partners have managed to raise awareness about the growing concern of water disparity around the world.

(AECOM 2014)

This statement is similar in tone to that on the website of the non-profit development organisation Water For People that AECOM is referring to: 'Water For People works to build a world where all people have access to safe drinking water' (Water For People 2014).

Just as their statements remind us of humanitarian NGOs, so do the names PMSCs choose for themselves. For example, International SOS is the name of a private company, but it could also be that of an NGO, one that claims, as International SOS does, to follow the philosophy of 'Worldwide reach. Human touch', and to offer 'emergency assistance during critical illness, accident, or civil unrest' (International SOS 2014a). In the Democratic Republic of the Congo (DRC) the company implemented 'a successful malaria program' which involved 'an anti-malaria chemoprophylaxis program', 'ongoing awareness and education programs', training for 'local [health] staff on early malaria identification' and 'awareness and prevention programs for different community groups' (International SOS 2014b). SOS International (SOSi) is another organisation that could be mistaken for an NGO – in reality it is a large private intelligence company that has multimillion-dollar contracts with the US government, which for its military facilities in Germany alone has provided the company with contracts worth about US$61 million (Brinkmann *et al.* 2013: 9). International SOS and SOSi are no exceptions. In 2010 the international industry association of PMSCs changed its name from International *Peace* Operations Association to International *Stability* Operations Association. According to its former president, the association was established precisely 'because a case needed to be made for the vast humanitarian role of the industry' (Brooks 2011: 6), and because it wanted 'to reflect the broad industry that provides vital services and support to the international community in conflict, post-conflict and disaster relief operations' (Brooks 2010a: 4). According to its proponents, the term 'stability operations' is

> more inclusive and representative of the larger industry and it encompasses disaster relief operations such as Haiti and the 2008 tsunami – catastrophes that our industry has had a very significant hand in addressing with their unique sets of services and expeditionary capabilities.
>
> (Brooks 2010b: 6)

The 'rebranding' of the industry association and the practice of choosing company names that sound similar to those of humanitarian NGOs reveal the strategic dimension of humanitarian discourses through which they signal their belonging to the humanitarian space.

The strategy of identification also extends to assertions related to their actions, which sound almost exactly like those of humanitarian NGOs such as Care International, whose 'member organisations share a common vision to fight against worldwide poverty and to protect and enhance human dignity' (Care International 2012), or World Vision, whose mission is '[b]uilding a better world for children' (World Vision 2013). Compare these with PMSCs such as KBR, which asserts 'to make the world ... a better place' (KBR 2012a); MPRI, which claims to 'help create a safer, healthier and more prosperous world' (MPRI 2009); Arkel, which maintains to 'work ... to make the world a better place to live and work' (Arkel 2014c); Triple Canopy, whose aim is 'to enhance the lives of people in the places where we serve' (Triple Canopy 2012); and AECOM, which contributes to '[b]uilding a better world' (AECOM 2012).

In addition, the imagery PMSCs use on their websites is almost identical to that of humanitarian NGOs. On its website the company Triple Canopy shows a picture of a tent with the logo of the company on it and two sad-looking children sitting inside (Triple Canopy 2014), and the website of DynCorp contains a picture of laughing children (DynCorp 2012a; see also L-3 MPRI 2012). The website of Arkel contains a photo of a white jeep (Arkel 2014b), which evokes associations with the United Nations and NGOs, which typically use white jeeps during field missions. A closer look reveals the logo of the company on the side door of the jeep. The private logistics company RA International (2014) has a logo that looks similar to that of the NGO International Rescue Committee (2014). Less suggestive websites of PMSCs often contain photos that make the links to more traditional humanitarian actors such as the UN explicit. The website of AKE, for example, shows a white airplane with 'United Nations Humanitarian Air Services' written on the side (AKE 2014), and that of AYR Group contains a photo of a helicopter with 'WFP [World Food Programme] Humanitarian Air Services' written on it (AYR Group 2014), which is almost identical to photos on the websites of Hart (see Hart 2014) and CTG Global (CTG Global 2014a), with the website of the latter also containing a picture of an old man sitting behind two bags of grain with the logo of the WFP on them (CTG Global 2014b).

Actors within the humanitarian arena use humanitarian principles and discourses not only 'to gain access' but also 'to discredit competitors' (Hilhorst and Jansen 2010: 1123). This is also true of PMSCs that claim that they are both different from and superior to the more traditional actors, although they are not too proud to appropriate these actors' language. DynCorp (2012b), for example, claims to have 'the capability to respond to all types of natural disasters, including earthquakes, volcanic eruptions, cyclones, floods, droughts, fires, pest infestations and disease outbreaks', and KBR stresses that not only has it been 'first on the scene in the wake of many disasters, providing critical support when it was needed most', but that, more generally, it has 'the ability to react to any challenge anywhere, at any time, providing aid and advice to those dealing with extreme difficulty' (KBR 2012b). In response to criticism of the PMSC industry, former director of ISOA J.J. Messner (2010: 38) asserts that the private sector 'is being called upon to assist in the relief and reconstruction efforts because it possesses critically needed capabilities that do not otherwise exist or are not sufficiently plentiful'. A point made even more explicitly by former association president Brooks (2011: 6) is that 'No matter whether the client is a government or an NGO, only the private sector can effectively address the largest of emergency humanitarian needs quickly and comprehensively.' Claims of superiority are made by most PMSCs, but there is also evidence of their discrediting other humanitarian actors more openly. According to industry representative Whitney Grespin, of Atlantean LLC, the relief efforts of the UN and of the NGOs involved in Haiti were 'uncoordinated multiplicity', 'confusing at best and wasteful at worst', showing a 'lack of both basic logistical coordination and conceptual consensus' (Grespin 2011: 13). The statements of PMSC representatives are also indicative of the inclusion–exclusion dynamics that, according to Hilhorst and Jansen (2010: 1128) are characteristic of spaces defined as arenas. Grespin (2013: 8–9) notes that it is

> U.S. military personnel [who] provide unsurpassed security, but ... the technical experts who follow ... have the skills that are foundational to long term development. [Their] work, and even their presence in itself, in transitional environments has positive implications towards stabilizing communities and incentivizing progress. These stabilization activities transform host community inhabitants into stakeholders in maintaining a secure environment.

While experts in the field regard this division of labour as increasingly typical of civil–military cooperation in stability operations (Franke 2006: 18), in the humanitarian context statements such as Grespin's are reflective of the processes 'by which actors define each other', and which do not 'follow definitions or principles as such' but, rather, 'constitute political struggles in which discourses of humanitarianism and human rights act as major devices' (Hilhorst and Jansen 2010: 1136). Nevertheless, the boundaries that are established between insiders and outsiders are far from clear-cut. PMSCs use their humanitarian identity strategically and selectively depending on the requirements of their clients and on the context (Joachim and Schneiker 2014).

Humanitarianism as we Know it? PMSC–NGO Interactions and Implications

PMSCs increasingly seek and obtain access to humanitarian space. The concept of identity and the actor-based concept of arena help us understand how they legitimise themselves vis-à-vis other actors, if indeed they do at all. In addition to the services they perform for humanitarian NGOs or international organisations and the humanitarian action they carry out themselves, discourses play an important role and are strategically deployed. The findings contribute to the burgeoning literature on the politicisation of humanitarian action and humanitarian actors. While until now scholars have focused primarily on the changes in the surrounding context as a source for this dynamic, this study gives attention to the influx of new actors and to the ways in which they (re)construct humanitarian identity and space. In this section we will discuss likely implications of the presence of PMSCs, which 'has had profound effects on how humanitarian work is conducted' (Carmola 2013). In doing so, we will focus on the blurring lines between humanitarian and military actors, and on the redefinition of humanitarianism (see Barnett and Weiss 2008).

Quite a number of scholars have cautioned against humanitarian assistance becoming indistinguishably linked with either armed actors on the ground, including PMSCs which not only often carry out military services for military actors, but as we have documented work for humanitarians and/or provide humanitarian assistance at the same time and in the same geographical area. The engagement of PMSCs in humanitarian work also has more lasting effects that contribute not only to the legitimisation of private security but also 'to the militarisation of humanitarian services' (Hellinger 2004: 193; see also Stoddard *et al.* 2008: 18). When PMSCs work for humanitarian NGOs on the ground, or when they provide humanitarian services themselves, it becomes very difficult for local populations to distinguish between military and civilian activities and actors 'because commercial providers have multiple associations and affiliations' (Cockayne 2006: 13). The company CTG Global, for example, provides services to humanitarian NGOs and yet at the same time is a private security company with staff that includes 'former serving British and Indian Army Gurkhas, Nepalese, Sri Lankan, Filipino and Thai Army personnel' (CTG Global 2014c). The multiple faces of PMSCs, especially their humanitarian identity, not only make it increasingly difficult for NGOs to find acceptance among locals but also make them likely targets of attack (Cockayne 2006). However, some observers argue that 'the extent to which aid agencies are exposed to violence' (Collinson and Elhawary 2012: 11) cannot only be explained with the changing environment in which they are working, but is also 'a function of the extent and nature of their operational presence' (Collinson and Elhawary 2012: 11). Despite the changes in conflict areas, it is imperative for humanitarian NGOs 'to be present, particularly in high-profile conflict-affected countries' (ibid.: 10), not least because of the rising number of aid agencies and the fierce competition between them (ibid.: 10–11).

PMSCs redefine what humanitarianism means, and their practices and discourses lead to the development of new interpretations. Evidence of a broader understanding of what humanitarianism entails can be found in statements indicative of 'comprehensive peace-building' efforts to 'remove the root causes of conflict' (Barnett and Snyder 2008: 151). For example, DynCorp (2012b) claims that it provides 'shelter and settlement assistance' to 'address both immediate needs and overall recovery and reconstruction'. Signs of an altered conception of humanitarianism may also be found in the fact that PMSCs seem to relate to the military in a much less problematic way than NGOs. KBR (2012c), for example, states that,

> During times of severe emergency, we have successfully delivered humanitarian assistance, base operations support services and disaster response. Honed from our experience with both natural and military contingencies, we are able to generate combat power and logistics sustainment anywhere in the world.

According to the website of SOS International, 'By delivering international law enforcement and security training and advisory services ... SOSi strengthens counterinsurgency, counter-narcotics, institution-building and humanitarian assistance efforts around the globe' (SOSi 2011). Even though Blue Hackle (2014) explains that '[s]ince 2004, Blue Hackle employees helped secure humanitarian organisations in Afghanistan, Iraq, Somalia, Lebanon, Yemen, Syria, and Haiti', the approach they followed is questionable given that the company's 'staff includes experienced UK and US Expats who are knowledgeable and have extensive Special Operations, intelligence, security, anti-terrorism, and counter-terrorism credentials'.

Conclusion

The PMSCs' statements and the humanitarian NGOs' responses are indicative of an ongoing institutionalised process of privatisation, commercialisation and securitisation in the humanitarian organisational field. Although further studies are needed to obtain a more comprehensive picture of the ways in which the humanitarian space is changing, our evidence shows that it is not appropriate to characterise this space as apolitical; rather, who is a humanitarian actor and what actually constitutes humanitarian action is increasingly a matter of (re)negotiation. The strategic use of humanitarian discourses by non-traditional humanitarian actors also draws attention to an aspect of the institutionalisation of the humanitarian organisational field which has largely been ignored, namely the transformation of the humanitarian space into a crowded arena where the actors involved not only are normatively driven but also behave and deploy their resources strategically to realise their interests.

Most scholars studying the regulation of transnational problems assume that non-state actors play an increasingly important role in the regulation of these problems because these actors bring different resources to the table, such as issue-related knowledge and expertise, moral authority and legitimacy. This is also true of PMSCs, which have been assumed to differ from conventional enterprises and from one another in the services they offer. However, the case at hand suggests that more attention must be given to the similarities between the actors involved in governance processes and to the sources related to them. These similarities show simultaneously isomorphism in discourse, symbols and practices, as well as an ongoing redefinition of humanitarianism. Whether the similarities are the result of strategic identification with other actors with the aim of gaining access and entry to a governance field, of the increasing interaction between private and public actors or of structural constraints and existing governance structures can only be determined if we shift the focus from questions of influence, effectiveness and efficiency to questions concerning actual practices and discourses.

Notes

1 The 16 transnational companies include companies which provide humanitarian services: AECOM, AKE, Atlantean LLC, Arkel, AYR Group, Blue Hackle, CTG Global, DynCorp International, Hart, International SOS, KBR, L3-MPRI/MPRI, Olive Group, Oxberry Risk Strategies, SOS International and Triple Canopy.
2 This needs to be seen in context, however. In 2011, the most violent contexts for delivering humanitarian assistance were located in Afghanistan, Somalia, South Sudan, Pakistan and Sudan (Stoddard *et al.* 2012: 3).

References

Abrahamsen, R. and Williams, M.C. (2007) 'Securing the City: Private Security Companies and Non-State Authority in Global Governance', *International Relations*, 21(2):237–253.
AECOM (2012) Building a Better World through Innovation, Experience and Social Awareness (www.aecom.com/deployedfiles/Internet/Brochures/0027-AfricaBrochure-NA-v3-LoRes.pdf) accessed 4 March 2014.
AECOM (2013) Programs and Partnerships (www.aecom.com/News/Social+Responsibility/Programs+and+Partnerships) accessed 28 December 2013.
AECOM (2014) AECOM to Mark World Water Day 2013 as Part of its Commitment to Help Provide Clean Water Globally (www.aecom.com/News/Inside+AECOM+News/World+Water+Day+2013/_carousel/AECOM+to+m ark+World+Water+Day+2013+as+part+of+its+commitment+to+help+provid e+clean+water+globally?languagehoice=es_ES&Go=Go&localeHidden=es_ ES&localeFlash=en_US) accessed 20 January 2014.
AKE (2014) Government and Intergovernmental Organisations. (www.akegroup. com/sectors/government-intergovernmental-organisations) accessed 4 March 2014.
Arkel (2014a) About Us (www.arkel.com/about-us) accessed 4 March 2014.
Arkel (2014b) International Operations (www.arkel.com/about-arkel-services) accessed 4 March 2014.

Arkel (2014c) Our Projects 2 (www.arkel.com/our-projects2) accessed 4 March 2014.

AYR Group (2014) Operating Wing (www.ayrgroup.co.uk/5/operating-wing/14/operating-wing) accessed 4 March 2014.

Bakewell, O. (2000) 'Uncovering Local Perspectives on Humanitarian Assistance and its Outcomes', *Disasters*, 24(2):103–116.

Barnett, M. (2009) 'Evolution without Progress? Humanitarian Organizations in a World of Hurt', *International Organization*, 63(4):621–663.

Barnett, M. and Snyder, J. (2008) 'The Grand Strategies of Humanitarianism', in: M. Barnett and T.G. Weiss (eds) *Humanitarianism in Question: Politics, Power, Ethics*, Ithaca, NY: Cornell University Press, 143–171.

Barnett, M. and Weiss, T.G. (2008) 'Humanitarianism: A Brief History of the Present', in: M. Barnett and T.G. Weiss (eds) *Humanitarianism in Question: Politics, Power, Ethics*, Ithaca, NY: Cornell University Press, 1–48.

Blue Hackle (2014) Non-Profit/NGOs (www.bluehackle.com/?page_id=165) accessed 4 March 2014.

Brinkmann, B., Hollenstein, O. and Kempmann. A. (2013) 'Das Millionengeschäft für die Zulieferer. Sie arbeiten wie Spione: Private Firmen helfen US-Diensten', in: *Süddeutsche Zeitung*, 16 November 2013:9.

Brooks, D. (2010a) 'President's Message: International Stability Operations Association: IPOA's New Name', *Journal of International Peace Operations*, 6(3):4.

Brooks, D. (2010b) 'A New Era', *Journal of International Peace Operations*, 6(3):6–35.

Brooks, D. (2011) 'President's Message', *Journal of International Peace Operations*, 7(3):5–6.

Care International (2012) Who We Are (www.care-international.org/About-Care) accessed 27 August 2012.

Carmola, K. (2010) *Private Security Contractors and New Wars: Risk, Law, and Ethics*, Abingdon: Routledge.

Carmola, K. (2013) Private Security Companies: Regulation Efforts, Professional Identities, and Effects on Humanitarian NGOs (http://phap.org/articles/private-security-companies-regulation-effortsprofessional-identities-effects) accessed 30 June 2013.

Cockayne, J. (2006) Commercial Security in Humanitarian and Post-Conflict Settings: An Exploratory Study (www.ipinst.org/media/pdf/publications/commercial_security_final.pdf) accessed 6 July 2013.

Collinson, S. and Elhawary, S. (2012) *Humanitarian Space: A Review of Trends and Issues*, London: ODI.

Collinson, S. Duffield, M., Berger, C., Felix da Costa, D. and Sandstrom, K. (2013) *Paradoxes of Presence: Risk Management and Aid Culture in Challenging Environment*, London: ODI.

Commission on Wartime Contracting in Iraq and Afghanistan (2009) *At What Cost? Contingency Contracting in Iraq and Afghanistan*, Interim Report to Congress, Arlington, Virginia, US: Commission on Wartime Contracting In Iraq and Afghanistan.

Cooley, A. and Ron, J. (2002) 'The NGO Scramble: Organisational Insecurity and the Political Economy of Transnational Action', *International Security*, 27(1):5–39.

CTG Global (2014a) CTG Global – International Humanitarian Support (http://ctgglobal.com) accessed 4 March 2014.

CTG Global (2014b) Humanitarian Aid Sector (http://ctgglobal.com/ humanitarian_aid_tab.asp) accessed 4 March 2014.

CTG Global (2014c) Security Manpower (http://ctgglobal.com/security_sector. asp) accessed 4 March 2014.

Dunigan, M. (2011) *Victory for Hire*, Stanford, CA: Stanford University Press.

DynCorp (2009) *Annual Report 2009*, Falls Church, VA: DynCorp International.

DynCorp (2012a) Supporting Stability and Human Progress Across the Globe (www. dynintl.com/media/277/development_brochure.pdf) accessed 11 April 2012.

DynCorp (2012b) Development (www.dyn-intl.com/what-we-do/development. aspx) accessed 11 April 2012.

DynCorp (2013) Intelligence and Security (www.dyn-intl.com/what-we-do/security-services.aspx) accessed 2 May 2013.

Eckroth, K.R. (2010) 'Humanitarian Principles and Protection Dilemmas: Addressing the Security Situation of Aid Workers in Darfur', *Journal of International Peacekeeping*, 14(1–2):86–116.

EU (2013) Towards a European Consensus on Humanitarian Aid (http://europa. eu/legislation_summaries/humanitarian_aid/r13008_en.htm) accessed 26 February 2013.

Fearon, J.D. (2008) 'The Rise of Emergency Aid', in M. Barnett and T.G. Weiss (eds) *Humanitarianism in Question: Politics, Power, Ethics*, Ithaca, NY: Cornell University Press, 49–72.

Fearon, J.D. and Laitin, D.D. (2000) 'Violence and the Social Construction of Ethnic Identity', *International Organisation*, 54(4):845–877.

Franke, V. (2006) 'The Peacebuilding Dilemma: Civil-Military Cooperation in Stability Operations', *International Journal of Peace Studies*, 11(2):5–25.

Glaser, M. (2011) Engaging Private Security Providers: A Guideline for Non-governmental Organisations, *EISF Briefing Paper*, London: EISF.

Global Policy Forum (2012) DynCorp Response to Report Raising Human Rights Concerns Over its Operations (www.globalpolicy.org/images/pdfs/DynCorp_ response.pdf) accessed 2 May 2013.

Gómez del Prado, J. L. (no date) *Private Military and Security Companies and Challenges to the UN Working Group on the Use of Mercenaries* (www.havencenter.org) accessed 30 June 2013.

Grespin, W. (2011) 'Aid and Relief in Haiti: Lessons Learned? Assessing International Reconstruction Efforts, One Year after Disaster', *Journal of International Peace Operations*, 6(6):13–14.

Grespin, W. (2013) 'Stability and Development. Getting Strong and Looking Long', *Journal of International Peace Operations*, 8(4):8–9.

Hart (2014) Social Responsibility (www.hartsecurity.com/social-responsibility) accessed 4 March 2014.

Hellinger, D. (2004) 'Humanitarian Action, NGOs, and the Privatization of the Military', *Refugee Survey Quarterly*, 23:192–220.

Hilhorst, D. and Jansen, B. J. (2010) 'Humanitarian Space as Arena: A Perspective on the Everyday Politics of Aid', *Development and Change*, 41(6):1117–39.

Hopgood, S. (2008) 'Saying "No" to Wal-Mart? Money and Morality in Professional Humanitarianism', in: M. Barnett and T.G. Weiss (eds) *Humanitarianism in Question: Politics, Power, Ethics*, Ithaca, NY: Cornell University Press, 98–123.

Humanitarian Outcomes (2012) *Aid Worker Security Report 2012. Preview: Figures at a Glance*, London: Humanitarian Outcomes.

International Rescue Committee (2014) Online (www.rescue.org) accessed 12 May 2014.

International SOS (2014a) About Us (www.internationalsos.com/en/about-us.htm) accessed 4 March 2014.

International SOS (2014b) Case Study: Leading a Successful Malaria Program (www.internationalsos.com/en/case-studies_4909.asp?page=0) accessed 4 March 2014.

ISOA (2013) (www.stability-operations.org/?page=Mission_Statement) accessed 30 June 2013.

Joachim, J. and Schneiker, A. (2012) 'Of "True Professionals" and "Ethical Hero Warriors": A Gender-Discourse Analysis of Private Military and Security Companies', *Security Dialogue*, 43(6):495–512.

Joachim, J. and Schneiker, A. (2014) 'All for One and One in All: PMSCs as Soldiers, Business Managers and Humanitarians', *Cambridge Review of International Affairs*, 27(2):246–267.

KBR (2012a) Social Responsibility (www.kbr.com/Social-Responsibility/Community) accessed 13 April 2012.

KBR (2012b) Rapid Response Delivery (www.kbr.com/Services/Logistics-Support/Rapid-Response-Delivery) accessed 13 April 2012.

KBR (2012c) Contingency Response/Sustainment Support (www.kbr.com/Markets/Government-and-Defense/Contingency-ResponseSustainment-Support) accessed 13 April 2012.

L-3 MPRI (2012) Home (www.mpri.com/web) accessed 15 April 2012.

Messner, J.J. (2010) 'Constructive Reconstruction', *Journal of International Peace Operations*, 6(3):37–38.

MPRI (2009) Index (www.mpri.com/esite) accessed 23 October 2009.

Olive Group (2014) Non-Governmental Organisations (NGOs) (www.olivegroup.com/sectors.php?sectid=15) accessed 4 March 2014.

Oxberry Risk Strategies (2011) Non-Governmental Organisations (www.oxberryrisk.com/non_governmental_organisations.html) accessed 25 November 2011.

Percy, S. (2009) 'Private Security Companies and Civil Wars', *Civil Wars*, 11(1):57–74.

Pingeot, L. (2012) *Dangerous Partnerships: Private Military and Security Companies and the UN*, New York: Global Policy Forum and Rosa-Luxemburg-Stiftung e.V.

RA International (2014) Home (www.rainternationalservices.com) accessed 12 May 2014.

Rieff, D. (2002) *A Bed for the Night: Humanitarianism in Crisis*, London: Vintage.

Rosén, F. (2008) 'Commercial Security: Conditions of Growth', *Security Dialogue*, 39(1):77–97.

Singer, P.W. (2003) *Corporate Warriors. The Rise of the Privatized Military Industry*, Ithaca, NY: Cornell University Press.

Singer, P.W. (2004) *The Private Military Industry and Iraq: What Have We Learned and Where to Next?* Geneva Centre for the Democratic Control of Armed Forces (DCAF) Policy Paper, Geneva: DCAF.

SOSi (2011) Services (www.sosiltd.com/services/sog.htm) accessed 2 June 2011.

Spearin, C. (2001) 'Private Security Companies and Humanitarians: A Corporate Solution to Securing Humanitarian Spaces?' *International Peacekeeping*, 8(1):20–43.

Speers Mears, E. (2009) 'Private Military and Security Companies and Humanitarian Action', *SMI Professional Development Brief* 1, Security Management Initiative.

Stoddard, A., Harmer, A. and DiDomenico, V. (2008) 'The Use of Private Security Providers and Services in Humanitarian Operations', *HPG Report* 27, London: ODI.

Stoddard, A., Harmer, A. and DiDomenico, V. (2009a) *Private Security Contracting in Humanitarian Operations*, HPG Policy Brief 33, London: ODI.

Stoddard, A., Harmer, A. and DiDomenico, V. (2009b) *Providing Aid in Insecure Environments: 2009 Update*, HPG Policy Brief 34, London: ODI.

Stoddard, A., Harmer, A. and Hughes, M. (2012) Aid Worker Security Report 2012 (www.humanitarianoutcomes.org/sites/default/files/resources/AidWorkerSecurityReport20126.pdf) accessed 17 December 2014.

Terry, F. (2002) *Condemned to Repeat: The Paradox of Humanitarian Action*, Ithaca, NY: Cornell University Press.

Triple Canopy (2012) Corporate Social Responsibility (www.triplecanopy.com/philosophy/corporate-social-responsibility) accessed 15 April 2012.

Triple Canopy (2014) Corporate Social Responsibility (www.triplecanopy.com/company/corporate-social-responsibility) accessed 31 October 2014.

Vaux, T., Seiple, C., Nakano, G. and Van Brabant, K. (2001) *Humanitarian Action and Private Security Companies: Opening the Debate*, London: International Alert.

Water For People (2014) Mission (www.waterforpeople.org/about/mission-and-vision) accessed 20 January 2014.

Wendt, A. (1994) 'Collective Identity Formation and the International State', *The American Political Science Review*, 88(2):384–396.

World Vision (2013) Home (www.worldvision.org) accessed 2 May 2013.

Part VI
Diaspora Humanitarianism

10 The Invisibility of a Third Humanitarian Domain

*Cindy Horst, Stephen Lubkemann and
Robtel Neajai Pailey*

Introduction

Humanitarian action is typically thought of as involving two sets of aid-providing actors: international and local. International actors comprise bilateral and multilateral donors, NGOs, and other operational agencies including UN humanitarian agencies and the International Committee of the Red Cross (ICRC). This 'international community' is mostly understood to be primarily located in North America and Europe. Local actors include government agencies of war-torn societies, local NGOs, voluntary associations and other forms of 'civil society'. While there is great diversity *within* these two groups, there are also clear differences between them. One relates to their geographical focus, with 'internationals' largely operating in a range of locations around the world where humanitarian assistance is needed whereas 'locals' are defined as actors that operate within national borders alone.

This representation ignores a third humanitarian domain – transnational humanitarianism during man-made and natural disasters by diaspora individuals and organisations. For instance, Tamil doctors who live in Europe spend their holidays contributing their time and know-how to treat patients and support their colleagues in Sri Lanka. Somali diaspora organisations (DOs) operating from the USA set up emergency shelter and healthcare services in south-central Somalia and in refugee camps in Kenya and Ethiopia. Meanwhile, engaged Liberian, Afghan and Sudanese migrants who regularly contribute remittances to support family members are also among the first to provide donations individually and collectively during humanitarian emergencies.

These transnational engagements, involving flows of people, goods and cash, change the context in which international humanitarian actors operate and have potentially important secondary impacts on other aid-providing actors. We argue that the impact of diaspora humanitarianism has not been fully explored in the academic literature and to a large extent remains 'invisible' in aid policy and practice. While interest in 'diaspora engagement' has grown exponentially in the last decade within the migration-development field (Van Naerssen *et al.* 2007; De Haas 2010), interest is more limited in the field of humanitarianism (Orjuela 2008; Ghorashi and Boersma 2009). Furthermore, interactions among international, local and diaspora actors engaged in humanitarianism are limited and characterised by mutual mistrust and misinformation, with insufficient attention paid to the consequences of these interfaces. In this chapter, we address this gap by focusing on international humanitarians and diaspora actors.

This chapter stems from ten years of empirical research on Liberians and Somalis, who live in the US and Europe but remain closely connected to relatives, friends and communities in their countries or regions of origin. For the Somali case, it draws on research – since 2004 – on diaspora remittances, engagement in peace-building and conflict, returnee contributions to post-war reconstruction, and humanitarian protection efforts. For the Liberian case, the paper builds on research since 2004 on the political and socio-economic influence of diasporas on their country of origin. The chapter is also based on a review of the academic literature on diaspora engagement and humanitarianism. This allows us to draw lessons from a range of examples well beyond the contexts we know best.

We will first describe humanitarian contributions made by DOs, migrant professionals and remittance senders, illustrating the importance of the third humanitarian domain. Then, we will explore the (lack of) interactions among international, local and diaspora humanitarian actors, and the potential implications considering the secondary impacts that diaspora humanitarianism has on the contexts in which international and local humanitarian actors operate. Third, we will discuss what shapes or constrains current collaboration attempts among the three humanitarian domains. Fourth, we will argue that diaspora humanitarianism differs in fundamental ways from 'international' and 'local' humanitarian engagements. Our analysis will draw on a neo-institutional perspective and our conclusion suggests that current attempts by international actors to capitalise on diaspora engagement do not factor in key differences between the two sets of actors or draw on some of the strengths of diaspora engagement. Hence, they risk creating parallel structures that replicate recognised flaws in the current humanitarian system.

A Third Humanitarian Domain

We illustrate the relevance and 'invisibility' of diasporas by focusing specifically on the case of refugee diaspora engagement in (post-)war environments. In our view, refugee diasporas are a particularly interesting group for understanding diaspora humanitarianism because armed conflicts have always produced displaced populations who have been targets of humanitarian assistance. The vast majority of the displaced either move within national borders, as internally displaced persons (IDPs), or cross immediate national borders, as refugees. These populations – who remain within war-torn countries or the immediate region – continue to be the major focus for international humanitarian activity. At the same time, a small minority of those displaced by conflicts finds asylum beyond the region in more distant locations such as the US, Canada, Australia and Europe. These diaspora groups are more significant humanitarian actors than their circumstances might suggest, and are largely seen as receivers of aid, rather than aid providers (Horst 2008a).

Those with the socio-economic means to pursue asylum options in the developed world, despite ever more restrictive immigration regimes, are often the most educated and professionally qualified members of their countries of origin (Van Hear 2004; Horst 2013). Moreover, while in war-torn countries entire generations go without access to education, those who find refuge in the developed world often benefit from new educational and professional opportunities. It is therefore likely that a substantial amount of the human capital of many war-torn countries is embodied in the relatively small population of their diasporas – all the more significant as conflicts become prolonged.

These people are also often extremely motivated to contribute, in light of their personal history of forced displacement and the responsibility they feel towards their countries of origin. As Ali Mohamed, a taxi driver in Oslo who returned to Mogadishu for two years to contribute to the Transitional Federal Government, phrased it: 'My homeland needs my help ... every single citizen has the duty to do something for his/her home country ... I am taking my responsibility as a Somali citizen'.[1] Similarly, Richard Tolbert, who worked on Wall Street in New York before returning to Liberia in 2006 to head the National Investment Commission (NIC), said that he had succeeded in transforming the country's investment climate thereby changing its image internationally: 'We have seen a dramatic increase in the perception of this country [Liberia], and foreign investors are willing to do business with us more than they ever have' (Pailey 2007: 23).

Significant technological, economic and social developments occurring at a global level over the last 30 years have radically transformed the possibilities for diaspora populations to remain involved in shaping the social, political and economic processes in their countries of origin – even when they opt to maintain a permanent foothold in their places of resettlement. Over the last two decades academics and policymakers have increasingly recognised how these features of globalisation render diaspora populations and organisations relevant to their home societies' social and economic development (Basch *et al.* 1994; Glick Schiller 2007). A number of studies have emphasised the growing power of diasporas in shaping the public media within and about their homelands through digital and web-based means (Brinkerhoff 2004, 2006; Bernal 2013). Others have focused on diaspora political contributions, largely in terms of their impact on conflict and peace-building (Smith and Stares 2007; Horst 2008b, 2013).

A gap in this burgeoning scholarship – as well as in policy initiatives that reflect diaspora contributions to their homelands – is that it has focused more on development contributions in stable or stabilising contexts than on humanitarian relief and reconstruction, even in cases when the main object of study has been diasporas from conflict regions. New interest spearheaded by policymakers is focusing on refugee diasporas and development with a particular emphasis on return migration and development (Sinatti and Horst 2015: 145). However, a more systematic discussion of diasporas as central humanitarian actors is missing.

One of the challenges in this respect is the compartmentalisation of activities in development aid, humanitarianism and post-war reconstruction. It is difficult to make sharp distinctions for different types of diaspora activities since compartmentalisation represents a central element of aid bureaucracies but does not reflect realities for diasporas. Since the 1970s, debates on refugee assistance have circled around the importance of bridging the gap between relief and development with very little progress made (Horst 2006). Relief and development bureaucracies are often separate structures with separate funding logics and procedures (Frerks 2005). From a neo-institutionalist perspective, one could argue that each of these organisational environments has developed its own distinctive institutions with normative, regulative and cognitive pillars (Scott 2001). While we mainly focus on 'humanitarian' activities among a range of international actors, we acknowledge that the line between development and humanitarian contributions is very difficult to draw in the case of diasporas.

In the sections that follow, we focus on diasporas as central humanitarian actors by reviewing the contributions of DOs, migrant professionals and remittance senders in conflict and post-war settings. While these categories of differentiation can often be blurred, it is useful to distinguish the many roles diasporas play because they define different types of humanitarian contributions.

Diaspora Organisations

Diaspora organisations have generated increased interest from academics, practitioners and policymakers over the last decade. Within the migration-development nexus discourse, diaspora associations and their development projects have created excitement (Mercer *et al.* 2009), especially after enthusiasm about the potential of remittances was tempered by the realisation that, as private funds, remittances are often sent to families for consumption and their spending cannot be controlled or influenced (Horst *et al.* 2014). Diaspora organisational engagement, however, particularly by home (or home-town) associations, is seen to have the potential to generate resources that can have an impact beyond the micro level and also lends itself to policy intervention. Thus within the last decade major initiatives have been launched by the Inter-American Development Bank

(IADB) to encourage more systematic involvement by DOs in community-level development within their countries of origin.

Studies on DOs, both in Europe and the US, as well as those analysing their impacts in various development contexts, often focus on small-scale initiatives with relatively limited impact. However, there is great variation in these initiatives – from small-scale voluntary collections of goods to fully functioning NGOs set up by diaspora members. For instance, Hirda, a Somali–Dutch NGO, has existed since 1998 and has major programmes in various parts of south-central Somalia. Besides common programme areas like health, gender and education, it also has a diaspora engagement programme. There are many examples of less formalised initiatives that nevertheless have considerable reach and impact, such as FeedSomalia which was started in 2011 by a group of young Somalis in Toronto, and the 'Operation Restore Home' project started by Worldwide Somali Students and Professionals set up by young Somalis in the UK, a number of whom engage very actively with Somalia (Hammond *et al.* 2011). In Norway an informal group of Somalis collected donations of old equipment from hospitals and schools (wheelchairs, crutches, typewriters and the like) and organised a container of these goods to be shipped to Somaliland, while a Somali DO collaborated with a Norwegian organisation to deliver two containers with nutritious porridge to the internally displaced during the drought of 2011–12.

Numerous diaspora humanitarian organisations and initiatives have sprouted up over the last two decades in an effort to provide assistance in Liberia as well. Many have been small, ad-hoc initiatives by Liberian church congregations throughout the US – such as the Bethel World Outreach Ministries in the Washington, DC area – to send containers of food, medicine and clothing to sister congregations in the homeland. When an outbreak of Ebola in 2014 left Liberia in the grip of the infectious disease, the Union of Liberian Organisations in the UK (ULO-UK) established an Ebola Relief Taskforce. ULO-UK swiftly airlifted two consignments of medical supplies and personal protective gear for hospital personnel in Liberia, valued at £9,500. Other efforts have been more ambitious and politically charged, such as the successful efforts by the Coalition of Concerned Liberians (CCL) to lobby for and secure multimillion dollar bilateral aid from the US government for a number of post-war recovery efforts in Liberia.

Migrant Professionals

The potential importance of diaspora human capital to homeland development has increasingly been recognised by major international agencies such as the International Organization for Migration (IOM). Over the last decade IOM and UNDP have developed frameworks for programmes such as QUEST-MIDA and the Transfer of Knowledge Through Expatriate Nationals (TOKTEN) that have sought – with mixed results – to enable diaspora professionals from Africa to contribute to the development of their countries of origin through short-term, circular or permanent return migration. There is also increasing academic interest in the return of migrant professionals who attempt to make political, economic or civil-society contributions to their post-war countries of origin (Oeppen 2013; Sinatti 2014). The real impact of such contributions depends on a range of factors, including the relationship between the diaspora and those who never left the 'homeland' (Abdile and Pirkkalainen 2011; Oeppen 2013).

Nevertheless, we may need to find new ways of understanding professional contributions that do not focus on temporary or permanent 'return'. With increasing numbers of people living mobile lives, operating from various places around the world, 'return' no longer seems the most appropriate frame to adopt. While one suggestion has been to discuss these contributions in different locations from the perspective of 'part-time diasporas' (Hammond 2013), another has been to focus on transnational civic engagement (Horst 2013). Indeed, diaspora contributions to countries of origin often take place from multiple locations. The geographical starting point of diaspora contributions is often less relevant than the motivations for engagement, and an analytical approach that does not compartmentalise such contributions enables a greater focus on the continuity of the engagements of migrant professionals irrespective of the localities from which such contributions are initiated.

In the case of Somalia, diaspora professionals play an important role in governance structures, the state bureaucracy, business enterprises and civil society. The three Somali state entities of Somaliland, Puntland and the Federal Parliament of Somalia are heavily dominated by members from the diaspora, with at least 50 per cent of the top positions held by those with foreign passports. In the 2014 elections in Puntland, Dr Abdiweli Mohamed Ali, who holds both American and Somali passports, was elected as the new president. The Speaker of Parliament of the Federal Parliament of Somalia, Prof Mohamed Osman Jawari, has lived in Norway for over a decade. Diasporas also play an important role in the private sector, particularly in businesses related to migration such as transport, communication and remittances. Several humanitarian organisations operating in Somalia, including the Norwegian Refugee Council (NRC) and Norwegian People's Aid (NPA), hire Somalis who live in Europe or the US because they have the advantage of being qualified with additional language and cultural competencies. In south-central Somalia, such hires are often also understood to be vital for enabling operations.

In Liberia, major efforts have been undertaken by diaspora professionals to contribute to the training of staff at the Monrovia-based John F. Kennedy Medical Center, such as Adama Sirleaf's Health Education and Relief through Teaching (HEARTT) programme, which brings volunteer doctors to Liberia on a rotational basis. Other initiatives have been spearheaded by the Liberian Studies Association (LSA) to build capacity at the University of Liberia and Cuttington University College (CUC), through the provision of lab and library materials as well as volunteer Liberian academics during summer months. The immediate past president and current president of the University of Liberia – Dr Al Hassan Conteh and Dr Emmet Dennis, respectively – were academics based formerly in the US. Largely taking place below the radar of international actors, these diaspora efforts constitute a hitherto unexamined and unaccounted for 'third domain' – structurally different from both the international aid industry and from 'local organisations' recognised as Liberia's civil society.

Remittance Senders

The remittances of individual migrants have long been acknowledged as significant in the development of migrant-sending countries, and are even more consequential in war and post-war contexts (Weiss Fagen and Bump 2006; Young *et al.* 2007). This makes diaspora members highly relevant to relatives and communities in the homeland. Research suggests that conflict in the country of origin exerts an upward pressure on remittance-sending (Carling *et al.* 2012). This is both the effect of migrants' capacity to remit, and the impact of state collapse and absence of human security on migrants' and refugees' desire to remit, as remittances become crucial for survival throughout conflicts.

There has been some work specifically on the impact of remittances in humanitarian situations, based on a range of case studies that involve both man-made and natural disasters (Savage and Harvey 2007; Mohapatra *et al.* 2012). These studies show that remittances increase during and after humanitarian crises, enabling people to survive and recover from disasters. Remittances also have wider positive effects in local economies. Work on remittances in humanitarian contexts furthermore points to a number of differences between conflict/crisis contexts and more stable contexts (Weiss Fagen and Bump 2006; Savage and Harvey 2007). The fact that financial institutions, investment opportunities and functioning government institutions are largely absent or temporarily disrupted in crisis situations prevents the active encouragement and facilitation of remittance sending to guarantee larger societal impact. Also, a lack of (well-functioning) financial institutions means that remittances are often sent through informal channels, such as the *hawala* system in Somalia, which represents the main financial infrastructure that enables remittance transfers.

The impact of remittances in Somalia has been well-documented in recent years (Ahmed 2000; Horst 2008a; Lindley 2010). In the context of a complex emergency that has lasted for well over two decades, these remittances have been crucial not just in enabling survival and recovery in acute disaster but also in allowing for survival in conditions of protracted instability. As Hodan Ali explains in an interview, remittances have played a central role in Somalia:

I think without the diaspora Somalia would have collapsed a long, long time ago. Because we are sending money for the people to survive. They have no jobs, we are taking care of their families, we are giving relatives opportunities to start business, supporting children to go to school in Somalia. Many of the diaspora people are paying for this. I know that my aunt supported many young women to take university degrees. This prevents the people, the young children, who want to flee out of the country. If they have an opportunity to go to school there and somebody is paying for it, then it is safer for them to stay there.

An important, if more general, quantitative measure of diaspora humanitarian importance to Liberia consists of remittances – usually via Western Union transfer – to relatives in Liberia and in refugee camps or informal settlements throughout neighbouring countries in West Africa. Field-based interviews show that on average Liberian households in the US remitted over US$3,000 per year to relatives in West Africa during times of crisis. Many of these households reported that they were the sole source of cash income for relatives in the homeland; in many cases one household in the US supported two or more households in Liberia or within West Africa. Similarly, remittances have become a mainstay since the cessation of Liberia's armed conflict in 2003. While World Bank data shows that transfers to post-war Liberia have ebbed and flowed – from US$58 million in 2004 to US$79 million in 2006 to US$31 million in 2008 – the highest recorded post-war remittance figures stood at US$360 million in 2011 and 2012, respectively (World Bank 2011, 2014). Field-based interviews conducted with Liberians abroad indicate that their remittances have been used for both humanitarian relief and development projects.

Interactions between International and Diaspora Humanitarianism: A Missed Opportunity

So far, we have argued that diaspora humanitarianism, as practised by DOs, migrant professionals and remittance senders, plays an important role in humanitarian contexts such as Somalia and Liberia. The projects of DOs, the work by migrant professionals within government or civil society, and the remittances sent by migrants individually or collectively to people affected by conflict and drought, influence the contexts in which international humanitarian actors operate. And yet, international humanitarian actors have either only recently started exploring the relevance of diaspora humanitarians or remain unaware of humanitarian initiatives undertaken by diasporas. Through mapping household economies, humanitarian organisations have started to explore how to relate to remittances. The NRC, for example, has considered providing displaced beneficiaries with cash-based support through the hawala system in Somalia as this allows them greater freedom of movement. But such ideas are as visionary as they are rare, and the same is true for initiatives targeting DOs and professionals. While international humanitarian organisations like the Danish Refugee Council operate projects to support DOs, this generally happens on a limited and small scale. In projects such as QUEST-MIDA, the human capital of migrant professionals is recognised while their (temporary) return is facilitated. Yet, as Savage and Harvey (2007: 40) point out, 'humanitarian agencies could perhaps do more to tap into the skills and capacities of diaspora populations, for instance through the hiring of staff'.

So while conventional actors engage in some diaspora engagement initiatives, most diaspora efforts, whether through organisations, professionals or remittance senders, take place without support by or cooperation with official diaspora engagement initiatives and outside mainstream humanitarianism. As in the case of development organisations, diaspora engagement by humanitarian organisations – if it happens at all – often takes the form of a purposely designed, small portion of work (Sinatti and Horst 2015). Whereas part of the problem is the invisibility of the third humanitarian domain, another important aspect is that – even if they are aware of diaspora humanitarianism – many organisations and individuals within those organisations do not consider it relevant for their work. As argued by neo-instituationalists, humanitarian actors are embedded in organisational fields, which have their own distinctive logics and governance systems. Part of the logic also relates to established knowledge, in the sense that humanitarian actors (including humanitarian studies scholars) decide what is relevant to include in definitions of humanitarianism. In most cases, diasporas lie outside these definitions and thus, the institutionalised humanitarian system excludes most aid provided by them. In this way, the system governs access to resources, controls inclusion and acknowledgment of certain types of activities at the expense of others, and has the ultimate power to define what is and is not relevant.

There are two main factors at play that prevent an appreciation of diaspora humanitarianism. First, some aspects of diaspora humanitarianism have received more attention than others, and the range of humanitarian contributions by DOs and individuals is often not fully understood. Remittance senders have long been accepted as important contributors to relief in humanitarian crises, but this has been understood as individual and private philanthropic initiatives and thus easily excluded from 'real' humanitarianism – largely organisational and professional. Moreover, migrant professionals and organisations have not received the same level of interest as remittance senders, despite the overlap with international humanitarianism.

Second, the 'added value' of engaging with DOs in humanitarianism – which is understood as fitting the work of DOs within the parameters of humanitarianism by conventional actors – is often not seen. Representatives of international humanitarian organisations often highlight that 'it does not fit their mandate' to engage with diasporas, who are framed as representing small-scale voluntary organisations. International organisations might work with local partners or implement programmes directly, and are unclear how diasporas would fit in. In fact, the initiatives that currently take place in the field of diaspora engagement may perpetuate the invisibility of diaspora humanitarianism and the lack of understanding of its value. These smaller initiatives are largely focused on small-scale financial support and capacity-building for small voluntary organisations and are often understood solely in terms of 'helping the diaspora' rather than in how they benefit traditional donors or reduce humanitarian need (Sinatti and Horst 2015). The 'value added' is then largely understood in terms of how diaspora engagement initiatives benefit the diaspora, and such initiatives have a tendency to 'clone' international humanitarianism (Horst *et al.* 2010).

Yet Western models of civil society do not necessarily match conflict and crisis contexts and requirements for funding are largely based on those models. Most of the 'traditional' Somali systems of assistance and security provision, for example, receive little or no external funding as opposed to 'modern' and far more recent institutional models. Civil-society organisations (CSOs) also fit in this last category, and whereas some transnational Somali CSOs have made these institutional models relevant to the local context, many are just using them as a way of attracting funding without being serious actors in humanitarian assistance. As such, there is a great mismatch between actual Somali diaspora-led assistance on the ground – which operates almost entirely in parallel to international humanitarian aid – and small-scale diaspora initiatives funded by international actors – which often provide limited 'on the ground' humanitarian support.

Recent initiatives in Liberia have been more development focused and aimed at tapping into the skills and willingness to contribute within the diaspora. For instance, the UNDP-funded TOKTEN programme and George Soros-funded Liberian Emergency Capacity Building Support (LECBS) programme – both of which started in 2006 – recruited Liberian diaspora professionals to work in public sector agencies for a number of years after the election of President Ellen Johnson Sirleaf in 2005 (Government of Liberia 2012). Similarly, the International Diaspora Engagement Alliance (IdEA) at the US State Department was set up to support partnerships around entrepreneurship, volunteerism, philanthropy and innovation. Yet, international actors are only starting to explore the third humanitarian domain, with a range of implications.

The fact that diaspora involvement in countries affected by conflict is not recognised as consequential may also mean that international actors are neglecting an opportunity to collaborate and use this important resource. The third humanitarian domain often addresses access gaps in areas where humanitarian access is limited due to security, government repression of a marginal region, hostility/laws against Western donors, etc. Staff-members of international humanitarian NGOs indicate that diasporas operate in areas where international organisations could or would never operate, especially in conflict zones where access to those in need can be a considerable challenge and humanitarians face direct attacks (Collinson and Elhawary 2012). In Somalia, for example, international humanitarian organisations were unable to access many al-Shabaab occupied areas during the 2011–2012 drought. In these instances of limited access, international organisations often explore the option of hiring diaspora staff-members. Yet, the assumption that diaspora and local staff are always immune to security risks is faulty. In the case of Somalia, for example, some diaspora members were deliberately targeted while engaging in humanitarian activities in al-Shabaab-occupied areas during the drought. Still, diaspora individuals and organisations may be in a better position to engage transnationally considering the networks they have in a particular country, thereby enabling international humanitarian actors to reach a greater proportion of people in need.

Simultaneously, providing humanitarian aid in conflict contexts often requires that international organisations are flexible in relating to migration, since one of the most efficient ways in which individuals protect themselves from persecution or violent conflict is to flee (Horst and Sagmo 2015). Diaspora humanitarianism generally accommodates mobility choices more than international humanitarianism. Remittances, for example, are less bound to a specific location as they can be sent to a new destination if the receivers decide to move. This is less the case with conventional humanitarian assistance, which is based primarily on sedentarist understandings of where people should be at particular points in time. Yet remittance sending and receiving practices have implications for the kind of humanitarian aid best provided, and the ways in which it is best delivered. International aid agencies would benefit from recognising that some crisis-affected people are likely to have their own complementary resources during the recovery process. For example, some households maintain livelihoods based on migration and remittances, and humanitarian aid must respect the need for mobility within these contexts (Savage and Harvey 2007: 40).

Diaspora Humanitarianism: How Different?

So far, we have presented an overview of relevant types of diaspora humanitarianism and a discussion of some of the explanatory factors for and consequences of the limited constructive interactions between international and diaspora humanitarian actors. This section explores some of the underlying and assumed differences between the two. Here, we are inspired by the neo-institutionalist view that shared norms and expectations determine common action as people make decisions using a social logic, which is based on social norms and expectations of others within a meaningful community – in this case, a community of humanitarians. If the fundamental structures of the international humanitarian system are social, and these structures shape actors' behaviour, identities and interests (Wendt 1995) while the actors simultaneously shape the structures, what happens when 'new' actors appear within the community? Do these new actors take part in the process of interaction that creates and recreates (changing) normative institutional structures (Introduction, this volume), and if so, how? In order to answer this question we first need to explore the differences between the actors involved, which are presented in an overview in Table 10.1 and further refined below. Only by exploring differences can we begin to understand the potential impact of 'new' actors like diasporas, the challenges they might face in being included in existing structures, and the potential benefits of their inclusion for transforming existing normative institutional structures such that more humanitarian needs are met.

According to Belloni (2007), we need to understand humanitarianism not just as the actions but also as the norms and values of humanitarians. Traditional humanitarian action focuses on the impartial, independent and neutral provision of relief to individuals and groups in crisis situations. Analysing humanitarianism as an ideology, Belloni argues that Western involvement in weak states in order to protect individual and group rights

Table 10.1 Nature of diaspora and international humanitarianism

Parameters of humanitarianism	(Refugee) diaspora humanitarianism	International humanitarianism
Position as helper	Often engaged personally, through ties with affected community	Mostly advocating position of neutrality, impartiality, independence
Relationship helper-helped	Sense of civic responsibility; personal engagement	Professional call, deontological ethic (in case of the core principles)
Relationship to government	(Former) citizens	Foreign agencies
Interactions with government: government side	Governed by diaspora policies	Governed by laws and regulations on operations of INGOs
Interactions with government: humanitarian side	Part of government and/ or opposition	Limited, often creating parallel structures
Access/security restrictions	Generally easier access but may be targeted as diasporas	Higher security restrictions because of vulnerability to attacks
Location	Flexible, remittances/ money transfers are mobile	Largely sedentary approach, less flexible

Source: the authors.

arises from unquestionable altruistic motives that attempt to address human suffering worldwide. However, as an ideology, it originates from and reproduces unequal power relationships by mystifying the 'real' and very complex nature of the relationship between Western states/institutes and the countries/individuals that receive humanitarian assistance (Malkki 1996; Belloni 2007).

While the connection between humanitarian values and realities has been extensively questioned and the politics in and of humanitarianism is now widely accepted in theory (Barnett and Weiss 2008), in practice these ideals are still upheld. The third humanitarian domain, for example, is often not validated because it is perceived as lacking neutrality, impartiality and independence. Many international actors 'express a reluctance to relate to diasporas as political subjects', and are concerned that diasporas from conflict regions have particular positions against current authorities and could possibly exacerbate ongoing conflict (Horst 2013). Yet the relationships that diasporas have with their countries of origin are complex and many governments may even aim to utilise diasporas as agents of change (Turner and Kleist 2013). Some governments have also developed engagement policies intended to encourage financial contributions from diasporas through, for example, high-interest foreign currency accounts, bonds and tax exemptions of various kinds. For instance, the government of Ellen Johnson Sirleaf adopted a duty free waiver on the personal effects of diasporas relocating back to Liberia. These opportunities are crucial for engagement and diasporas are often quite happy to collaborate with their governments, national/local civil society, religious institutions, charities and 'new' donors.

When it comes to remittance senders and DOs, the assumption is that there is a very clear difference between the personally inspired charity that diasporas engage in and the professional humanitarianism of international organisations (Sinatti and Horst 2015). Diaspora humanitarianism is assumed to be driven by motivations related to helping 'one's own', so even though diaspora humanitarian actors operate beyond national borders they are still seen as having a very 'local' focus. However, a review of the initiatives of diaspora associations across various European countries shows that their engagement towards the country of origin may, instead, be rooted in a wide range of affinities that go beyond the geographical links between individuals and their places of origin (ibid.). Diaspora engagement may be stimulated, for instance, by belonging to the same religious community (e.g. *ummah*) (Fiddian-Qasmiyeh 2011; Rosenow-Williams and Sezgin 2014). It can also be stimulated by wanting to contribute as a member of a gender/age cohort, a professional category (e.g. medical personnel), or alumni association – as the proliferation of Liberian high school alumni associations in the diaspora indicates.

As a result of the varying levels of interaction between diasporas and their homelands, the relationship between 'helper' and 'helped' is often less unequal and aid provision in the form or remittances less dehumanising in comparison with international humanitarian actors. Those sending remittances for private causes or as collective donations have different motivations to contribute, which often have to do with a strong sense of (civic) responsibility (Carling *et al.* 2012). Unlike needs-based international humanitarian approaches, remittance senders often relate to humanitarian needs in ways that focus less on vulnerability and weakness, and more on circumstantial factors and uncertainty. Moreover, receiving cash rather than food items, for example, facilitates agency thereby enabling the receiver to decide how to spend the aid. Collective remittances are also different from international efforts to transfer cash to crisis-stricken areas. They are based on community pressure, which makes people more likely to contribute. Furthermore, they are quick, ad hoc responses to various types of emergencies, with often very low administrative costs and high 'accountability' ratings for those who donate. Accountability is guaranteed through videos and other types of material which show results directly. Furthermore, misappropriation is easily checked through trust-based networks. Whereas accountability often means something very different for diaspora humanitarianism, it is by no means less efficient than international humanitarian accounting systems for checks and balances.

In Somalia, the mismatch between international and diaspora humanitarianism is related to a number of factors. First, there is a difference between the focus of international organisations and donors on the status of an organisation/institution and the status of the individuals involved. As Mohamed Shukri, a consultant in Nairobi who used to work for a Somali research institute, explains:

> The culture of having a civil society and institutions is very new. In recent times however, it has really been growing and there is now not just international but also local support. This local support is directed at individuals, not at institutions: if individuals ask for money for a good cause and they are seen to deliver what they said they would, they can get support locally. In Somalia, institutional trust is not there. These local initiatives depend on the person, who will first receive a small amount, to see how they perform, and later receive more, if they do well. Once things start this way, a lot can be achieved, but that is related to the individual and not to his or her institution, if there is even one.

Second, differences can be observed in the level of formality and continuity in operations and procedures required by international and diaspora humanitarian actors. The larger international institutions require fixed, static, long-term structures whereas diaspora humanitarian actors are often governed by more fluid, informal arrangements. A third difference relates to the fact that there is an expectation that international assistance is 'clan-neutral' and preferably national. Yet, the reality is that support and politics in Somalia are taking place within the clan system and are largely regional; reflecting local realities of accountability and security.

Similarly for Liberia, diaspora support to the homeland is often facilitated by hometown associations representing the country's 15 sub-political divisions, called counties. Where the state has failed to provide basic social services such as education, health, sanitation, and clean water in rural Liberia, organisations such as the Bong, Lofa, and Nimba county associations as well as the United Bassa Organizations in the Americas (UNIBOA) and the Marylanders for Progress have responded in kind with scholarships, medical supplies, latrines, and boreholes. These diaspora county associations have thus become channels through which political power and influence can be built in ways not easily accomplished in Bong, Lofa, Nimba, Bassa or Maryland in Liberia. The implications of such immune and at the same time power-privileged spaces for the production of a genuinely 'independent civil society' that calls government to account require further exploration.

Conclusions

In this chapter, we have argued that the third humanitarian domain – diaspora humanitarianism – is substantial and influences the contexts in which local and international humanitarian actors operate. As such, it is important not just to study international and local humanitarian action, but also transnational types of engagements, including DOs, migrant professionals and remittance senders. At the same time, it is important to recognise that there are clear differences between this domain and the local and international ones. Diaspora humanitarianism is based on transfers of cash and skills, financial and human resources, and it is largely driven by a sense of transnational civic responsibility. It is also often characterised by more personally engaged relationships between helper and helped, and a stronger political positioning within local (post)-war contexts.

Many attempts to capitalise on diaspora engagement do not recognise some of these key differences, and risk creating parallel structures based on a model that clones practices of internationally recognised humanitarian actors. This is particularly the case because everything that does not fit within the fundamental structures of the international humanitarian system and its normative, regulative and cognitive pillars is excluded from mainstream understandings of humanitarianism. Furthermore, humanitarian aid can sometimes be provided in ways that make it difficult for people to supplement it with their own resources (Savage and Harvey 2007: 40). Cash-based aid, as indicated in this chapter, provides greater flexibility and choice for recipients – and might be useful in ways that support and sustain remittances, for instance by allowing people to return to their jobs overseas, pay off debts incurred from the migration process, pay travel expenses or just provide the resources to communicate with relatives. In order for such options to be more seriously explored, it is necessary to acknowledge remittance senders, diaspora professionals and DOs as legitimate humanitarian actors. The ways in which aid is institutionalised and thus legitimised also determine which actors and actions are excluded.

Independent diaspora initiatives will continue to impact and be affected by the work of international humanitarians. Even if ignored by international actors, the relevance of diasporas is not lost on Liberian movers and shakers themselves. For instance, in the country's 2005 post-war presidential elections, the three frontrunners had spent considerable amounts of time abroad (Pailey 2007: 12). The eventual winner, President Ellen Johnson Sirleaf, campaigned and raised funds in the diaspora during three successive elections – 1997, 2005, and 2011. Similarly, many of the top political positions in Somalia are contested by Somalis in the diaspora, while those in such positions often lobby for various types of support in London, Minneapolis and Oslo. In Liberia, Somalia and elsewhere, diasporas *are* already involved and *will* be consequential to the future of their homelands – in politics, business and civil society – either positively, negatively or both simultaneously.

International aid industry actors are accustomed to seeing refugees as objects of their activities and by-products of political events and processes – rather than as potentially powerful and effective humanitarian actors and significant shapers of socio-economic and political landscapes (Malkki 1995; Horst 2008a). Diasporas from conflict-contexts challenge us to question conventional wisdom and provide us with a new lens – and possibly a new tool – with which to rethink humanitarian action and post-war reconstruction. In this chapter we have argued, building on neo-institutionalist approaches, that this new lens requires inclusion of diaspora humanitarian actors in arenas where the international humanitarian system is created and recreated in interaction with international and local actors.

Note

1 Names are pseudonyms, with the exception of public figures who have explicitly provided permission to use their names.

References

Abdile, M. and Pirkkalainen, P. (2011) 'Homeland Perception and Recognition of the Diaspora Engagement: The Case of the Somali Diaspora', *Nordic Journal of African Studies*, 20:48–70.

Ahmed, I. (2000) 'Remittances and their Economic Impact in Post-War Somaliland', *Disasters*, 24(4):380–389.

Barnett, M. and Weiss, T. (2008) *Humanitarianism in Question: Politics, Power, Ethics*, Ithaca, NY: Cornell University Press.

Basch, L., Glick Schiller, N. and Szanton Blanc, C. (1994) *Nations Unbound: Transnational Projects, Postcolonial Predicaments, and Deterritorialized Nation-States,* Langhorn: Gordon and Breach.

Belloni, R. (2007) 'The Trouble with Humanitarianism', *Review of International Studies,* 33 (3):451–474.

Bernal, V. (2013) 'Diaspora, Digital Media, and Death Counts: Eritreans and the Politics of Memorialisation', *African Studies,* 72 (2):246–264.

Brinkerhoff, J. (2004) 'Digital Diasporas and International Development: Afghan-Americans and the Reconstruction of Afghanistan', *Public Administration and Development,* 24(5):397–413.

Brinkerhoff, J. (2006) 'Digital Diasporas and Conflict Prevention: The Case of Somalinet.com', *Review of International Studies,* 32(1):25–47.

Carling, J., Erdal, M.B. and Horst, C. (2012) 'How Does Conflict in Migrants' Country of Origin Affect Remittance-Sending? Financial Priorities and Transnational Obligations Among Somalis and Pakistanis in Norway', *International Migration Review,* 46(2):283–309.

Collinson, S. and Elhawary, S. (2012) *Humanitarian Space: A Review of Trends and Issues,* HPG Report 32, London: HPG.

De Haas, H. (2010) 'Migration and Development: A Theoretical Perspective', *International Migration Review,* 44(1):227–264.

Fiddian-Qasmiyeh, E. (ed.) (2011) Special Issue on 'Faith Based Humanitarianism in Contexts of Forced Migration', *Journal of Refugee Studies,* 24(3).

Frerks, G. (2005) 'Refugees between Relief and Development', in: P. Essed, G. Frerks and J. Schrijvers (eds) *Refugees and the Transformation of Societies: Agency, Policies, Ethics, and Politics,* Oxford/New York: Berghahn, 168–178.

Ghorashi, H. and Boersma, K. (2009) 'The "Iranian Diaspora" and the New Media: From Political Action to Humanitarian Help', *Development and Change,* 40(4):667–691.

Glick Schiller, N. (ed.) (2007) *Living Across Worlds: Diaspora, Development and Transnational Engagement,* Geneva: IOM.

Government of Liberia (2012) 'Rebuilding Public Leadership in Post-Conflict Liberia: Case Studies from the Liberia Emergency Capacity Building Support (LECBS)', Monrovia, Liberia: Civil Service Agency.

Hammond, L. (2013) 'Somali Transnational Activism and Integration in the UK: Mutually Supporting Strategies', *Journal of Ethnic and Migration Studies,* 39(6):1001–1017.

Hammond, L., Awad, M., Dagane, A., Hansen, P., Horst, C., Menkhaus, K. and Obare, L. (2011) *Cash and Compassion. The Role of the Somali Diaspora in Relief, Development and Peace-Building,* Nairobi: UNDP.

Horst, C. (2006) 'Refugee Livelihoods: Continuity and Transformations', *Refugee Survey Quarterly,* 25(2):6–22.

Horst, C. (2008a) 'A Monopoly on Assistance: International Aid to Refugee Camps and the Neglected Role of the Somali Diaspora', *Afrika Spectrum,* 43(1):121–131.

Horst, C. (2008b) 'The Transnational Political Engagements of Refugees: Remittance Sending Practices Amongst Somalis in Norway', *Conflict, Security and Development,* 8(3):317–339.

Horst, C. (2013) 'The Depoliticisation of Diasporas from the Horn of Africa: From Refugees to Transnational Aid Workers', *African Studies*, 72(2):228–245.

Horst, C. and Sagmo, T. (2015) *Humanitarianism and Return: Compromising Protection?* PRIO Policy Brief, 3. Oslo: PRIO.

Horst, C., Erdal, M.B., Carling, J. and Afeef, K. (2014) 'Private Money, Public Scrutiny? Contrasting Perspectives on Remittances', *Global Networks*, 14(4):514–532.

Horst, C., Ezzati R., Guglielmo, M., Mezzetti, P., Pirkkalainen, P., Saggiomo, V., Sinatti, G., and Warnecke A. (2010) *Participation of Diasporas in Peacebuilding and Development: A Handbook for Practitioners and Policymakers*, PRIO Report, 2. Oslo: PRIO.

Lindley, A. (2010) *The Early Morning Phone Call: Somali Refugees' Remittances*, Oxford/New York: Berghahn.

Malkki, L. (1995) *Purity and Exile: Violence, Memory, and National Cosmology Among Hutu Refugees in Tanzania*, Chicago, IL: University of Chicago Press.

Malkki, L. (1996) 'Speechless Emissaries: Refugees, Humanitarianism and Dehistoricization', *Cultural Anthropology*, 11(3):377–404.

Mercer, C., Page, B. and Evans, M. (2009) 'Unsettling Connections: Transnational Networks, Development and African Home Associations', *Global Networks*, 9(2):141–161.

Mohapatra, S., Joseph, G. and Ratha, D. (2012) 'Remittances and Natural Disasters: Ex-Post Response and Contribution to Ex-Ante Preparedness', *Environment, Development and Sustainability*, 14(3):365–387.

Oeppen, C. (2013) 'A Stranger at "Home": Interactions between Transnational Return Visits and Integration for Afghan-American Professionals', *Global Networks*, 13(2):261–278.

Orjuela, C. (2008) 'Distant Warriors, Distant Peace Workers? Multiple Diaspora Roles in Sri Lanka's Violent Conflict', *Global Networks*, 8(4):436–452.

Pailey, R.N. (2007) 'A Diaspora Returns: Liberia Then and Now', *Humanitas* 9(1):3–35.

Rosenow-Williams, K. and Sezgin, Z. (2014) 'Islamic Migrant Organizations: Little-Studied Actors in Humanitarian Action', *International Migration Review*, 48(2):324–353.

Savage, K. and Harvey, P. (2007) 'Remittances during Crises: Implications for Humanitarian Response', *Briefing Paper 26*, London: HPG.

Scott, R.W. (2001) *Institutions and Organizations*, Thousand Oaks, CA: SAGE.

Sinatti, G. (2014) 'Return Migration as a Win–Win–Win Scenario? Visions of Return among Senegalese Migrants, the State of Origin and Receiving Countries', *Ethnic and Racial Studies*, 38(2):275–291.

Sinatti, G. and Horst, C. (2015) 'Migrants as Agents of Development: Diaspora Engagement Discourse and Practice in Europe', *Ethnicities*, 14(2): 134–152.

Smith, H. and Stares, P. (2007) *Diasporas in Conflict. Peacemakers or Peace Wreckers?*, Tokyo: UNU Press.

Turner, S. and Kleist, N. (2013) 'Agents of Change? Staging and Governing Diasporas and the African State', *African Studies*, 72(2):192–206.

Van Hear, N. (2004) *'I Went as Far as My Money Would Take Me': Conflict, Forced Migration and Class*, Oxford: COMPAS.

Van Naerssen, T., Spaan, E. and Zoomers, A. (eds) (2007) *Global Migration and Development*, Abingdon: Routledge.

Wendt, A. (1995) 'Constructing International Politics', *International Security* 20(1):71–81.

Weiss Fagen, P. and Bump, M. (2006) *Remittances in Conflict and Crises: How Remittances Sustain Livelihoods in War, Crises and Transitions to Peace*, New York: IPA.

World Bank (2011) *Migration and Remittances Factbook 2011*, Washington, DC: World Bank.

World Bank (2014) *Remittances Data Inflows, as of April 2014*, Washington, DC: World Bank.

Young, H., Osman, A. and Dale, R. (2007) 'Darfurian Livelihoods and Libya: Trade, Migration, and Remittance Flows in Times of Conflict and Crisis', *International Migration Review*, 41(4):826–849.

11 Diaspora Action in Syria and Neighbouring Countries

Zeynep Sezgin

Introduction

The ongoing armed conflicts in Syria have created a gruesome humanitarian crisis. In September 2014, the United Nations Office for the Coordination of Humanitarian Affairs (OCHA) estimated that the crisis left 10.8 million people needing humanitarian assistance (OCHA 2014). The Syrian Center for Policy Research (SCPR) stated that more than half of the population in Syria lives in extreme poverty, which continues to widen across the country due to violence, rising prices for goods and services, job loss, weakened economic activity and growing numbers of internally displaced persons (IDPs) (SCPR 2014). This dramatic economic collapse has been accompanied with the looming breakdown of the education and health systems due to the devastation of educational and medical facilities and infrastructure, flight of teaching staff and health-care professionals, increasing school dropout rates, death and injury of educational and medical staff, and the collapse of the local pharmaceutical industry.

About 6.5 million Syrians, circa one third of the population, are internally displaced (ibid.). IDPs are predominantly women, children and the elderly, some of whom have been displaced multiple times. Many stay in informal shelters, unfinished buildings, makeshift accommodations, or unofficial camps (Margesson and Chesser 2013). Moreover, intensified violence, military operations and blockades lead to human-rights violations and humanitarian access problems (SCPR 2013).

In addition, more than three million Syrians fled their country, with thousands more pouring across the borders every single day (OCHA 2014). Lebanon hosts the highest number of these refugees (roughly 34 per cent), followed by Jordan (roughly 29 per cent) and Turkey (roughly 23 per cent) (SCPR 2013). The refugee camps are often squalid, food is scarce, and hygiene and sanitation facilities are either insufficient or non-existent (CBS 2013; McQue 2013).

Similarly, little humanitarian aid reaches the people in Syria mainly because the government views international NGOs as a 'Trojan horse' for the political objectives of Western powers or considers them as having links with the opposition and thus has restricted their access by imposing bureaucratic and administrative obstacles, such as withholding visas and setting up checkpoints where the passage of aid workers must be negotiated (HPG 2012). Aid workers in rebel-controlled parts of the country have also faced severe threats and dozens have been kidnapped or killed while delivering supplies (ICRC 2013). Especially the brutal kidnappings and killings of aid workers by the Islamic State (IS) militants have made Syria 'a no-go zone for expatriate aid workers' (Behn 2015). The security situation has worsened because of the fighting between the government, IS, al Qaeda-linked groups, other rebels and Kurdish groups. As a result, some of the organisations have reduced their presence, whereas other organisations, such as the UN Children's Fund, have chosen to operate in a more localised manner than they have done in the past, or have tried to work with the Turkish border police and the Turkish Red Crescent to deliver aid through semi-official border crossings, often dirt roads, to get aid in (Holmes and Nebehay 2014).

The international humanitarian response struggles to address the urgent needs. OCHA coordinates the international humanitarian response within Syria and has established relief sectors or 'clusters' where possible (Margesson and Chesser 2013). The United Nations High Commissioner for Refugees (UNHCR) leads efforts to provide assistance to Syrian refugees in the neighbouring countries as well as assistance to host communities supporting refugees.

In the government-controlled areas, aid is managed by the Syrian Arab Red Crescent (SARC) and other local organisations, which are authorised by the government to distribute aid.[1] Moreover, 11 UN agencies, the International Organization for Migration (IOM), the International Committee of the Red Cross (ICRC) and 15 international non-governmental organisations (INGOs)[2] are permitted by the government, but they are obliged to work in partnership with the authorised local organisations (OCHA 2013). A handful of additional INGOs have agreements with relevant Syrian ministries to provide humanitarian assistance (Margesson and Chesser 2013). Some of the well-established INGOs, such as Médecins Sans Frontières (MSF), have continued to petition the government for permission to provide impartial aid. When their entreaties failed, they began working in opposition-held areas and/or in neighbouring countries.

The above-mentioned organisations are not the only actors that provide assistance. MSF reports that especially in areas under the opposition's control, international aid is extremely restricted, and most comes from the Syrian diaspora, countries 'friendly' with the opposition and political-religious networks (MSF 2013). However, the humanitarian assistance provided by these actors remains invisible in humanitarian statistics despite its importance in saving lives and protecting livelihoods. Furthermore, it is not yet clear, how these actors exactly operate, whether and to what extent their engagement is motivated by their political agendas, and how this influences the humanitarian action in Syria.

This chapter analyses how two diaspora organisations (DOs) in Germany – the German–Syrian Association for the Promotion of Freedom and Human Rights (Deutsch–Syrischer Verein zur Förderung der Freiheiten und Menschenrechte, DSV), a human-rights organisation established by Syrian diaspora, and the Islamic Community Millî Görüş (Islamische Gemeinschaft Millî Görüş, IGMG), a faith-based organisation (FBO) established by Turkish diaspora – have responded to the conflict in Syria and the refugee crisis in neighbouring countries. It also examines how these organisations understand the traditional humanitarian principles of humanity, impartiality, neutrality and independence, and why they reject some of them.

In order to learn from existing studies on DOs in humanitarian action and to identify further research needs in this area, the second part of this chapter reviews previous studies on diaspora humanitarianism. Third, the chapter discusses how transnationalism, neo-institutionalism and associational theory provide relevant analytical frameworks for studying diaspora humanitarianism. Fourth, it introduces the case selection and date collection methods used in this chapter. Fifth, it provides information on the history, ideology, transnational ties, members and resources of DSV and IGMG as well as their motivations, aims, activities, roles and cooperation partners in humanitarian action. The sixth part goes beyond the self-portrayal of the organisations based on their websites and official documents. Particularly, it applies the previously mentioned theories to analyse the commitment of IGMG and DSV to the traditional humanitarian principles. The following part critically discusses the implications of diaspora humanitarianism for the humanitarian action in Syria and neighbouring countries. The final part summarises the research results and elaborates on their significance in the broader context of humanitarian studies.

An Underresearched Topic: Diaspora Humanitarianism

Until the 1990s, migration studies was mainly concerned with the roles of DOs in their countries of residence. Over the past two decades, however, interest has grown in DOs' engagement in their countries of origin (Pries and Sezgin 2010, 2012; Halm and Sezgin 2012). On the one hand, there has been a lively debate about the migration-development nexus in general (IOM 2005; Glick Schiller and Faist 2010) and the roles of DOs in attracting and channelling remittances, conflict mitigation, and peace-building in particular (Fahrenhorst *et al.* 2009; Sezgin 2010; Levitt and Lamba-Nieves 2011; Ragab 2013). On the other hand, Diasporas have been described as 'long-distance nationalists', who can exacerbate conflict in their countries of origin (Smith and Stares 2007).

While transnational studies fill a gap in the research on diaspora/DO engagement in their countries of origin, their focus has been often limited to the aforementioned issues. Few studies have considered whether diasporas/DOs are engaged in humanitarian action in their countries of origin or carry out human-rights activities, lobbying in their countries of residence to define or transform humanitarian crises (Sezgin and Dijkzeul 2013; Sezgin 2014). Rosenow-Williams and Sezgin (2014), for example, focus on the diverse motivations of three Islamic DOs to engage in humanitarian action, the scope of their humanitarian activities, and how they respond to the external expectations in their country of residence (Germany) and their country of origin (Bosnia-Herzegovina or Turkey), and what strategies they use to gain and maintain legitimacy in their transnational organisational field. Migration Information Source (MIS 2010) claims that Haitian and Pakistani Diasporas have been significant sources of donations, volunteers and information for crises in their countries of origin, and discusses how Haitian and Pakistani governments have reacted differently to their humanitarian efforts. In a similar vein, HPN (2012) argues that over the past two decades, Somalis from around the world have provided significant humanitarian and development assistance in Somalia. HPN also discusses how traditional rivalries between clans, mistrust and competition for funding have prevented Somalian DOs in the UK from developing long-standing partnerships with one another, despite being involved in similar types of relief and development work.

Additionally, HPG (2012) reports that the efficiency and professionalism of diaspora networks has increased with experience, such that international NGOs have been able to shift some of their focus elsewhere in light of the aid successfully provided through these networks. Similarly, IOM (2013) argues that Haitian, Libyan, Pakistani, Somalian and Syrian diaspora communities in Europe and the US have become influential actors on the international humanitarian stage, often providing assistance in ways that differ from those of the traditional humanitarian actors,[3] such as providing direct cash transfers, sending skilled volunteers with local knowledge, and compiling first-hand crisis information from affected populations.

In spite of these recent studies, the following research questions have not yet been answered:

1   What are the motivations, aims, activities, roles and partners of DOs in humanitarian action?
2   Whether and to what extent do DOs commit to the traditional humanitarian principles?
3   What are the impact and potential of diaspora humanitarianism?
4   How is diaspora engagement in humanitarian action perceived in their transnational organisational environment? and
5   How does diaspora humanitarianism interact and overlap with other humanitarianisms, such as religious humanitarianism?

Theoretical and Methodological Framework

This chapter addresses the first four of the above-mentioned research questions. It also touches on the last research question as one of the selected case studies is a faith-based DO.

This chapter is grounded in a transnational research framework because DOs maintain, build, and reinforce multiple linkages with their members' country of origin and country of residence, and in some cases even with third countries.[4] The assimilative perspective in migration studies argues that there is a negative correlation between transnational orientation of DOs and their social integration in the countries of residence (Esser 1980). Yet the situation is more complex: various situational and structural factors (such as historical context, composition of members, internal and external expectations of legitimacy, and organisational ideology) influence the scope and focus of DOs' transnational activities (Pries and Sezgin 2012). Transnationalism calls for a reconsideration of the traditional research perspectives, like assimilationism, which are based on 'methodological nationalism' (Wimmer and Glick Schiller 2002) and motivates researchers to systematically analyse pluri-local, dense and durable interactions, and networks of organisations (Pries 2010). Yet, it does not explain how the expectations of diverse stakeholders (e.g. members, other organisations in the field, governments in country of origin and country of residence) influence DOs' motivations, aims, activities, roles and partners in humanitarian action, and their degree of commitment to the traditional humanitarian principles. To do so, this chapter combines transnationalism with neo-institutionalism and associational theory.

A central assumption of the neo-institutional approach is that organisations are embedded in an environment, which develops its own distinctive institutional logics and governance systems (Scott 2001). These systems, in turn, influence the structure and activities of individual organisations in the forms of coercion (regulatory orders or government regulations), standards (internalised and shared ideals and ideas) or anticipation (expectations and attitudes of other actors in the environment) (Meyer and Rowan 1991). Organisations try to fulfil the expectations in their environment by employing institutionalised scripts for action, such as the traditional humanitarian principles, because those that 'incorporate societally legitimated rationalised elements in their formal structures maximise their legitimacy and increase their resources and survival capacities' (ibid.: 53).[5] For humanitarian INGOs, access to the people in need and security also increase with higher legitimacy (Sezgin and Dijkzeul 2013).

The strength of the neo-institutional perspective lies in its explanation of the diffusion and reproduction of successfully institutionalised organisational forms and practices, while it can be criticised for not paying attention to 'organisational self-interests' and 'active agency' (Oliver 1991) – which is the strength of the associational theory (Pries and Sezgin 2010, 2012;

Rosenow-Williams and Sezgin 2014). Associational theory indicates that organisations must fulfil the expectations of internal and external stake-holders. On the one hand, they must justify themselves towards public authorities and other organisations in order to obtain resources in the form of recognition, legitimacy, or formal status. On the other, organisational survival depends on the support of its members. Yet, organisations are often confronted with conflicting internal and external expectations, where sat-isfying one group's expectations may come at the expense of another. This situation is treated in the research on associations as the 'logic of members' versus the 'logic of influence' (Child 1976; Schmitter and Streeck 1999; Pries and Sezgin 2012).

The 'logic of members' and the 'logic of influence' are relevant for the analysis of DOs as these organisations are confronted with complex and sometimes contradictory internal and external expectations. Accordingly, this chapter discusses how the motivations and expectations of represent-atives and members influence the aims, activities, roles and cooperation partners of DOs in humanitarian action, and how these organisations react when representative and member expectations contradict with external expectations and institutionalised scripts for action, such as the traditional humanitarian principles.

Methods

IGMG and DSV are selected as case studies to compare their different organisational characteristics (history, ideology, transnational ties, mem-bers and resources), which influence their commitment to the traditional humanitarian principles. An empirical analysis of these organisations pro-vides valuable insights into their diverse motivations, aims, activities, roles and cooperation partners in humanitarian action, and raises questions regarding the way they understand the traditional humanitarian principles.

The information presented on DSV and IGMG is collected both from primary and secondary sources. Their statutes, publications, press releases and websites were analysed between January 2013 and January 2014. This information could be regarded as self-portrayals of the organisations. The accuracy of the information provided by the organisations could hardly be checked, on the one hand, due to the difficulty of conducting field research in the context of continuing civil war, and on the other hand, due to the reluctance of the organisations to disclose information that might jeopardise the safety of aid workers or recipients. In addition, 20 semi-struc-tured expert interviews were conducted with the representatives, members, donors and partners of both organisations, as well as with the representa-tives of traditional humanitarian organisations. These interviews provided a wealth of information about the personal motivations of the representatives, members and donors for engaging in humanitarian action. In addition, they revealed the importance of the expectations of internal and external stakeholders as well as the organisational characteristics, particularly the role of the ideology and resources of organisations, thus broadening our understanding of the factors that influence the humanitarian engagement of DOs and their commitment to the humanitarian principles.

Self-Portrayals of the Selected Diaspora Organisations

The German–Syrian Association for the Promotion of Freedom and Human Rights (DSV)

DSV was established in 2011 in Weiterstadt by Syrian migrants and Germans with Syrian background that no longer wanted to stand idly, while the totalitarian regime in Syria violated human rights and suppressed people (interview with LA). According to its website the organisation promotes a Syria, where all people can: (a) live equally in freedom and dignity, (b) express their views freely without having fear for their lives, and (c) shape a new and secure future (DSV no date a).

For this purpose, it demands the German government to:

1   provide generous humanitarian aid for Syrian refugees in Jordan, Lebanon and Turkey;
2   issue visas in the German embassies as fast as possible to refugees, severely sick or injured Syrians (for medical treatment in Germany) and for family reunification;
3   increase the political pressure on the Assad regime in order to stop the violence against the civilian population and to immediately release all detained demonstrators, opposition activists, journalists and human-rights activists;
4   impose effective sanctions, in particular by stopping the payments to the Assad regime and to the companies supporting the regime; and
5   increase its efforts against the Assad regime in the UN Security Council.

Similarly, DSV demands the UN Security Council: (a) increase the political pressure on Russia, Iran and China to halt arms sales to the Assad regime, (b) establish a no-fly zone to create a humanitarian corridor, and (c) prosecute those responsible for violence against peaceful protesters and civilians in the International Criminal Court (DSV no date a).

DSV does not only promote freedom and democracy in Syria by lobbying against the Assad regime in Germany. It uses its website to inform about the situation in Syria and organises debates with German politicians (such as Uta Zapf, Member of the Bundestag, and Jochen Partsch, Mayor of the City of Darmstadt) (DSV 2013a), institutions (e.g. Pfarrgemeinde St. Elisabeth) (DSV 2013b) and media (e.g. ARD, Mittelbayerische) (DSV 2012a; Mittelbayerische 2013) about the background and solution to the crisis.

Furthermore, DSV collects donations and organises fundraising campaigns. According to its website, 'the daily images from Syria and the humanitarian disaster currently requires DSV to use its whole force to collect donations' (DSV no date a) and 'whether general donations or donations to ongoing fundraising campaigns – any amount helps to improve the living conditions of people in Syria and in the refugee camps in Jordan, Lebanon and Turkey' (DSV no date b). Collected donations (money, clothes, food and medical aids, such as sterilisers, ultrasonic devices, defibrillators, surgical instruments, bandages, prostheses, wheelchairs and canes) are then trucked to the opposition-held areas in Syria (e.g. in or close to Aleppo, Daraa, Damascus, Hama and Homs) and the refugee camps in the neighbouring countries (interview with LA).

DSV has 65 members, a third of them are doctors and physiotherapists (DSV 2013c). In line with the professional knowledge of its members, a major focus of DSV's work lies in the medical care of war-injured people. Since the end of 2012, it regularly organises aid convoys (circa 10 aid convoys each year) (interview with LA).[6] For example, in November 2012 DSV's aid convoy to Syria consisted of a 7.5 ton truck and an ambulance, both loaded with medicines and medical supplies worth €2.4 million. Similarly, an aid convoy in May 2013 included medical supplies worth €160,000, comprising one computer tomography each for Aleppo and Manbidsch. In July 2013, 15 fully equipped ambulances, filled with medical supplies up to their ceilings were convoyed to the contested areas (DSV no date c).

Additionally, since the end of 2012, DSV has supported two rehab facilities in the border regions of Jordan (Irbid) and Turkey (Reyhanli). Weekly, approximately 100 people are treated in the rehab facility in Jordan and 40 people in Turkey (ibid.). In 2013, DSV also helped to establish five infirmaries in the opposition-held areas and continues its financial support. These infirmaries treated 85,000 people within six months (interview with LA). Additionally, DSV equipped four previously decommissioned ambulances with the necessary medical devices and supplies, and provided around 200 people with prostheses (DSV no date c).

In order to provide humanitarian assistance, DSV has been cooperating with various actors in Germany, Syria, and in the neighbouring countries. For example, it cooperates with various NGOs founded by Syrian diaspora in Germany, such as Social Association Lien (Sozialverein Lien e.V.) and the German–Syrian Forum (Deutsch–Syrisches Forum e.V., DSF) to inform the German public about the crisis (DSV 2012b). Moreover, DSV has ensured the work of the only functioning intensive care station in the liberated areas in Aleppo with the support of the German Foreign Ministry and Islamic Relief Germany (interview with SL). This station regularly treats 20–30 dialysis patients and seriously injured people, who would not survive the long-distance transport to the next available intensive care station in Turkey (DSV 2013c). As agreed with the German Foreign Ministry, DSV has also assumed the follow-up treatment for 36 severely injured Syrians in its rehab centre in Irbid.[7] In addition, DSV has cooperated with local professionals, doctors and physiotherapists in Jordan and Turkey.

Self-Portrayal of the Islamic Community Millî Görüş (IGMG)

IGMG was officially founded in 1994 by Turkish migrants in Germany, but its predecessors, the Millî Görüş mosque communities, have existed since 1972 (Seidel *et al.* 2001). It is an umbrella organisation which coordinates 1,800 facilities (including women's, youth, sports and education departments as well as local mosque communities) in 11 European countries: Germany, France, Austria, the Netherlands, Belgium, Switzerland, Italy, the UK, Denmark, Sweden and Norway (IGMG 2009a: 21). Decisions of the central administration in Kerpen, Germany, are binding for all IGMG facilities in Europe.

The German Federal Office for the Protection of the Constitution (Bundesamt für Verfassungsschutz) monitors IGMG and estimates the number of its members in Germany to be around 31,000 (Bundesamt für Verfassungsschutz no date a), which makes IGMG one of the largest Muslim organisations in Germany.[8] According to its own introductory brochure, IGMG has 87,000 members across Europe, and its Friday prayers are regularly attended by approximately 300,000 people (IGMG 2009a: 21).[9] Although IGMG attempts to expand its services to all European Muslims, Turkish migrants and people with Turkish migration background still constitute the majority of its members (interview with AB).

IGMG provides a strong example of a multifunctional organisation offering different types of services to its members. It is

> an Islamic community which comprehensively organises the religious lives of Muslims. However, it does not only aim to maintain the Islamic teachings, proclaim the Islamic creed and to communicate religious duties ... It also addresses all issues regarding Muslims while at the same time representing their interests. Its goal is to improve the living conditions of Muslims as well as to provide for their fundamental rights.
>
> (IGMG 2009a: 4)

The introductory brochure of IGMG states that European Muslims have the privilege of living in wealth and are obligated to provide humanitarian aid to people in need (IGMG 2009a: 27). According to the representatives of IGMG, its members are aware of this obligation and are highly interested in providing humanitarian and development aid in various countries.

> Our members ask us whether we distribute food in Ethiopia or Pakistan. They want us to open wells in various African countries or to help the orphans in Palestine or Bosnia. They want to help the people in need no matter where the help is needed.
>
> (Interview with MG)

IGMG acts in line with these wishes and establishes a bridge between its members and those who are in need (interview with AB). For example, every year, during the Festival of Sacrifice (Eid al-Adha), it collects donations, buys animals, pays for the services required for the slaughter of these animals and distributes their meat to the poor in various countries. The animals are bought in the countries in which their meat is distributed to reduce transport time and costs, to keep the meat fresh and to support the local economy. Money for the needy is also raised during Ramadan[10] and alms are collected and distributed to people in need all year long.

IGMG's roles in humanitarian action go well beyond collecting *sadaqa* (voluntary donations), *zakat* (mandatory alms-giving which is one of the five pillars of Islam) and *fitr* (a payment due on behalf of all Muslims with the termination of the fast of Ramadan). Its humanitarian engagement encompasses natural disasters, armed conflicts and situations of growing vulnerability and displacement resulting from global challenges, such as economic inequalities, fluctuating food prices and environmental degradation. For example, it organised a campaign to help the people in the Gaza strip during the Israeli military invasion in 2009 (IGMG no date). Donations for Gaza were collected in several IGMG mosque communities. Consequently, an IGMG delegation went to Gaza to transfer medical equipment to local hospitals. Similarly, aid packages were delivered to affected people after the 2004 tsunami in Indonesia and Sri Lanka, and various earthquakes in Turkey, Iran and Pakistan, as well as after the 2010 and 2011 floods in Pakistan (interview with BA). Given that the Prophet Muhammad was an orphan, an important part of IGMG's humanitarian activities focuses on orphans. After the flood caused by Cyclone Sidr in Bangladesh, IGMG did not just send humanitarian supplies but set up an orphanage project in four cities in 2008 (IGMG 2009b). Similarly, schools were built in the Kano province of Nigeria in 2011 and the Charsadda district of Pakistan in 2012 (interview with BA).

IGMG has also provided aid to the people affected by the Syrian conflict. IGMG has informed its members about the crisis through its website (www. igmg.org) and internet radio station (igmg.fm).

Additionally, IGMG's yearly Eid al-Adha campaigns have been targeting the people affected by the Syrian crisis. In 2012, Hasene (IGMG's Social Welfare Association) bought 46 tons of meat (18,400 packages, each of them consisting 2.5 kilograms of meat) for the needy in Al-Raqqah, Aleppo, Deir ez- Hama, Homs and Idlib (IGMG 2012). During Ramadan in 2013 and 2014, it distributed evening meals (*iftar*) to thousands of refugees in Kirikhan, Turkey (interview with MG).

IGMG has also organised fundraising campaigns in its mosques. Consequently, 10,000 blankets were bought and distributed to the people in need in January 2013 in Al-Raqqah, Damascus, İdlib, Hama and Homs (ibid.). Since January 2013, 27 tons of food aid has also been provided monthly in the same areas (interview with MG). Likewise, Hasene provided food aid (200 packages consisting of 7 kilograms of food) to the Syrian refugees in the Voenna Rampa Camp in Sofia, Bulgaria (Haber 3 2014). Furthermore, Hasene has been managing a mobile bakery since Ramadan 2013 and has been distributing 7000 buns a day to the Syrian refugees in Kirikhan (interview with MG). In addition, Hasene has financed the rehabilitation centre established by a local humanitarian organisation: Hayad (Hatay Yardimlasma Dernegi) in Kirikhan in 2013 (HatayVatan 2013).

For the distribution of food packages to Syrian refugees in Hassa and Kirikhan (both in Turkey), Hasene cooperates often with local humanitarian organisations, such as KEMEP (Kırıkhan Ensar Muhacir El Ele Platformu), Hayad and the Turkish Red Crescent (interview with MK). Due to the ongoing conflict in Syria, IGMG cannot deliver aid in Syria. Yet, the Turkish Red Crescent is responsible for delivering IGMG's donations (money, food, blankets, etc.) to the organisations in Syria, which are authorised by the Syrian government to distribute aid (interview with MG).

Committed to the Traditional Humanitarian Principles?

Neutrality or Advocacy?

The representatives of DSV argue that they are committed to the traditional humanitarian principles.

> DSV is not a political organisation. Although it is founded just after the revolution in Syria, it is does not oppose the Assad regime in particular but is against each regime, political party and group which limits human rights and freedom ... As a humanitarian organisation, we concentrate on the people in need. We try to help everybody who needs help, regardless of their religion and political views ... We are active in Syria and neighbouring countries, everywhere where it is possible and we try to gain access to all of the areas where help is needed. However, we do not work with the Assad regime and hence we cannot provide help in the government-controlled areas. But this has nothing to do with the lack of humanity, impartiality or neutrality. None of the humanitarian organisations works with the Assad regime because it is already clear that the regime is responsible for the crisis in Syria. We have not been able to gain access to the government-controlled areas due to restrictions imposed by the Assad regime. We work with everybody who facilitates our work, including the opposition groups. We would also be willing to work with the Assad regime, if it would allow us to work in the government-controlled areas.
>
> (Interview with LA)

Although the representatives of DSV claim their organisation to be apolitical, DSV can be defined both as a humanitarian and a political organisation because it is simultaneously engaged in humanitarian action and diaspora politics. It does not only collect resources to support the affected community, provide humanitarian assistance, and support local hospitals, doctors and physiotherapists in Syria, Jordan and Turkey, but also lobbies against the Assad regime.

Hence, DSV ignores the principle of neutrality by openly criticising the governmental policies in Syria and using its political connections in Germany to increase the political pressure on the Assad regime. Furthermore, even if it refuses to be affiliated with any groups, it continues to work with opposition groups to deliver aid.

Additionally, its representatives sometimes have some difficulty with maintaining the independence of DSV's work because some of the projects are publicly financed.

> We cannot always maintain the independence of our work. We prepare projects according to the needs of Syrians but complete independence is only possible when these projects are financed by private donors. When we get public funding for a project, for example from the German Foreign Ministry for our rehabilitation facilities in Turkey and Jordan, complete independence is not possible.

(Interview with LA)

Humanity or Islamic Solidarity and Brotherhood?

Until the late 1990s, IGMG had close ties with the Islamist Millî Görüş movement in Turkey, which aimed to establish an Islamic republic in Turkey (Schiffauer 2010).[11] During the last decade, however, these ties with Turkey have been weakened due to a generational change within the organisation[12] and the weakening of Erbakan's Islamist Millî Görüş movement in Turkey (Pries and Sezgin 2012). IGMG has thus changed from a religious–political DO oriented towards establishing an Islamic state in Turkey into a transnational Muslim organisation aiming to develop a European Islam (Sezgin 2014).

Drawing on the typology suggested by Clarke (2006: 840ff.), IGMG can be defined as a faith-based sociopolitical organisation that unites, organises and mobilises a specific social group (people with a Turkish migration background) on the basis of Islamic identities but in pursuit of broader political objectives. However, a closer look at IGMG's projects and services shows that the organisation also has characteristics of a faith-based charitable or development organisation that mobilises its followers to support the poor and devises activities to address poverty directly or indirectly (Ozkan 2011).

Being under surveillance by the Federal Office for the Protection of the Constitution, IGMG is legally marginalised as an extremist organisation and does not receive any public funding for its activities. Hence its survival depends mainly on the support of its members. The strong dependence on the financial support of members hampers principled independence (Sezgin and Dijkzeul 2013). Although IGMG does not receive any public funding and hence can resist governmental expectations, it has not achieved full autonomy from its members (donors). Its engagement in humanitarian action and the selection of crisis zones in which the organisation conducts its activities are simply based on membership interests (interview with BO). Its representatives argue that IGMG provides aid to the most needy, regardless of their ethnic origin, political opinions or religious affiliations, without getting involved in religious, political or ideological controversies. However, IGMG cannot be said to have committed to the traditional humanitarian principles fully, given that its Islamic character and dependence on members' support continue to prevail.

The Islamic aid culture, which presents all Muslims as parts of the same religious brotherhood, and closely connected, mutually interdependent and obliged to help one another, contrasts sharply with the secular aid culture which is based on the universal notion of humanity, emphasising an obligation to take care not only of members of one's own family or community, but also others (Juul Petersen 2011). Although IGMG provided aid to the people affected by the Syrian crisis, without making any discrimination as to ethnic origin, religious or political beliefs, it framed humanitarian aid as part of a religious obligation and demonstration of solidarity with the worldwide Muslim community (*ummah*). For example, during one of its fundraising campaigns for the people affected by the Syrian crisis, Muslims were represented as

> a part of a religious bond of brotherhood and have particular responsibilities towards their Muslim brothers and sisters. With the consciousness of these responsibilities and the bond of brotherhood, Muslims should become one heart and mind ... It is our duty and task to assist our brothers and sisters in their time of need. Because our Prophet described the Muslims as a body and since a part of this body aches, it is up to us to ease this pain. We can do this both materially and spiritually, by donating for Syrians and speaking prayers for them.
>
> (IGMG 2013)

The same fundraising campaign criticised the Assad regime: 'As you all know, the people of Syria have been oppressed by a dictatorial regime for a long time. In the past two years, more than 700,000 Syrians were forced to live in refugee camps' (IGMG 2013).

IGMG also had difficulty in committing to neutrality in the past, for example during crises in which Muslims faced oppression by non-Muslims, such as in the Israeli–Palestinian conflict. At the time of its previously mentioned Gaza campaigns, for example, IGMG held several controversial demonstrations against the Israeli military operations, during which some anti-Semitic incidents occurred.[13]

Diaspora Humanitarianism: Resource or Hindrance for Humanitarian Action?

The international humanitarian community's role in Syria is limited. As previously mentioned, only a limited number of international actors are permitted to work in Syria. Furthermore, these actors are obliged to work in partnership with the authorised local organisations whose intervention capacity is limited and restricted to certain geographical areas (ECHO 2013).

The international humanitarian community can benefit from engaging with DOs to identify needs and gain insights about crisis situations on the ground. Representatives of DOs have personal ties with their country of origin. These connections have provided them with more than just their motivation. They have also given them a close understanding of the local situation, personal contacts and well-established networks (as in the case of DSV) or in the neighbouring countries (as in the case of IGMG). Because of their personal contacts, the representatives of these organisations claim to know in great detail what is needed and possible on site.

Through well-established networks, DOs are reported to deliver aid where it is needed most, even to the interior of Syria, where only a few or no other aid organisation is represented (MSF 2013). For example, only a handful of INGOs, such as MSF, are operating openly in opposition-held areas. UN agencies and the ICRC believe that their diplomatic status (and the balance of power in the international arena) prevents them from operating in opposition-held areas without the consent of the Syrian government or a binding Security Council resolution. In such cases, cooperating with DOs is essential for gaining access to the people in need (HPN no date).

DO's representatives, staff and members (for example, in the case of DSV, doctors and physical therapists) can also contribute to humanitarian action with their professional knowledge and assist the people affected with the benefit of cultural and language skills. Besides, most DO's representatives and staff are volunteers so that most of the donations can be spent for the needy (contrary to international humanitarian NGOs with overhead operating costs).

These findings are not unique for DSV and IGMG. HPN (no date) claims that Syrian DOs, like the Union of Syrian Medical Relief Organizations (UOSSM),[14] have contributed much more to increasing access to medical services in rebel zones than all of the international NGOs combined and argues that the only realistic way to increase aid in the rebel zones today is to support Syrian diaspora networks, even if this results in some cases in aid diversion and the strengthening of political networks (HPN no date). Similarly, Ahsan (2013) writes on the grassroots humanitarian care provided by Hand in Hand for Syria,[15] despite lack of support from major development agencies. The Syrian American Medical Society (SAMS) reported that Syrian diaspora NGOs in the USA contributed nearly US$43 million to ease the suffering brought on by the conflict and in 2013, this number nearly doubled to US$83 million (SAMS 2013).

Nonetheless, doubts exist about the quality of DOs' humanitarian work among representatives of the well-established international humanitarian organisations (interview with RW and RL). They question the DOs' knowledge of the internationally accepted codes and standards of conduct (such as the Code of Conduct for the International Red Cross and Red Crescent Movement and NGOs in Disaster Relief, and the Sphere Handbook), and DOs' degree of professionalisation (Donini 2010).

Indeed the analysis of DSV and IGMG shows that, depending on their members' interests and backgrounds, many DOs may actually be ethnically, religiously or politically partial (cf. Rosenow-Williams and Sezgin 2014). As a result, traditional humanitarian actors are not sure as to how and to what extent they should interact with DOs (interview with KR).

The Syrian government's suspicion towards DOs is also growing. The government sees many of them as acting at the behest of hostile foreign powers, and as not adhering to humanitarian principles. DOs therefore increasingly face similar challenges in Syria as the international humanitarian actors. In this context, it remains unclear whether DSV's and IGMG's public advocacy is effective or advisable. The Syrian Government pays close attention to the comments and actions of international agents. Advocacy attempts by international NGOs will likely work against their efforts to increase their operations in the country. One can argue that there is enough journalism, so that public advocacy from DOs is neither necessary nor helpful. An alternative can be discreet and person-to-person diplomacy, which facilitates maintaining the humanitarian principles.

It is also not clear, to what extent the tendency of DOs to use opposition channels to deliver assistance affects the way foreign humanitarian actors are perceived by the Syrian authorities. Moreover, DOs attempt to cooperate with local NGOs and loosely arranged citizens' groups in Syria may bring unwanted scrutiny to these NGOs and groups.

In sum, although DOs have access, cultural and language skills, local knowledge and networks that other actors lack, their magnitude and impact on the ground require further scrutiny. The analysis of DSV and IGMG shows that DOs have difficulties in committing to the humanitarian principles. The organisational ideology (political and/or religious) shapes their engagement in humanitarian crises. Furthermore, they are financially dependent on certain actors (governments of the countries in which they are situated and/or members) and hence the type of the activities and the selection of activity locations are mainly based on the interests of these actors.

Conclusion

This chapter shows that humanitarian action in Syria is not the monopoly of traditional humanitarian organisations. In accordance with transnational theory, the DOs studied extend their range of services in the countries of origin (or in third countries) by including new areas of activity such as humanitarian assistance. They use social media networks to create virtual, borderless communities, advocate and raise awareness about crises and collect funds for humanitarian causes.

DSV and IGMG have taken part in humanitarian action in Syria and neighbouring countries, but their motivations, aims, activities, roles, cooperation partners and, most importantly, their level of commitment to the humanitarian principles were different due to different organisational characteristics and member interests (see Table 11.1). IGMG has been motivated by the religious values of its representatives and members, whereas DSV has been motivated by the medical professions and transnational ties of its representatives and members with Syria. Accordingly, IGMG has framed humanitarian aid as solidarity with the *ummah*, whereas DSV has framed humanitarian aid as solidarity with its members' fellow countrymen. IGMG has aimed to fulfil a religious obligation by providing aid to the people in need, and especially to its Muslim brothers and sisters, whereas DSV has both aimed to provide humanitarian aid and to promote freedom and democracy in Syria.

Both of the organisations have played various roles in Syria and neighbouring countries, such as collecting resources to support IDPs and refugees; providing humanitarian assistance; and cooperating with other NGOs in Germany and Turkey and/or with local people in Syria to access people in need. DSV has also helped defining the situation in Syria as a humanitarian crisis by: (a) offering first-hand information to German politicians, institutions and media; (b) debating and/or cooperating with the government agencies, other NGOs and media; and (c) lobbying in Germany for an increase in humanitarian measures and against the Assad regime. Additionally, DSV has taken on advocacy and human-rights activities in the hope of transforming humanitarian crisis in Syria.

Although DOs play important roles in humanitarian action, their transnational ties to a specific country (national orientation), ethnic group (ethnic orientation) or religious community, such as the *ummah* (global religious orientation), and their financial dependence on donors (members) impact negatively on their commitment to the traditional humanitarian principles. This affects the way foreign humanitarian actors are perceived and adds to the Syrian government's suspicions towards DOs.

These findings contradict neo-institutional theory which assumes isomorphism: a growing commitment to institutionalised scripts for action, such as the traditional humanitarian principles. In contrast with neo-institutionalism, DOs do not always incorporate societally legitimated rationalised elements in their formal structures to maximise their legitimacy. Instead, as suggested by associational theory, they try to increase their legitimacy, hence their resources and survival capacities by fulfilling the expectations of their members. Thus they avoid, defy, or manipulate traditional

Table 11.1 Comparative analysis of selected diaspora organisations

Characteristics	DSV	IGMG
Type	Diaspora organisation – political and humanitarian	Diaspora organisation – sociopolitical and faith-based humanitarian
Motivations	Personal ties with the affected community	Islamic traditions of charitable giving (sadaqa), obligatory alms giving (zakat) and notions of Islamic solidarity and brotherhood
Aims	Providing humanitarian aid and promoting freedom and democracy	Fulfilling a religious obligation by providing aid to *Ummah* and people in need
Activities and roles in humanitarian action	Carries out advocacy work for affected communities and human-rights activities; lobbies against Assad regime; informs about Syria and organises debates with German politicians, institutions and media; collects resources to support affected communities; provides humanitarian assistance; supports local hospitals, professionals, doctors and physiotherapists in Syria and neighbouring countries; cooperates with other German humanitarian NGOs and German Foreign Ministry.	Informs about Syria; collects resources to support affected communities; provides humanitarian assistance; supports local Turkish NGOs, which provide aid to refugees in Turkey.
Cooperation partners in Germany	Other Syrian DOs, German Foreign Ministry and Islamic Relief Germany	Local IGMG mosque communities around Germany (and Europe)

Characteristics	DSV	IGMG
Cooperation partners in Syria and neighbouring countries	Local professionals, doctors and physiotherapists in Syria and neighbouring countries, and opposition groups in Syria	Local humanitarian NGOs in Turkey and the cooperation partners of the Turkish Red Crescent, i.e. local organisations in Syria permitted by the Assad government
Commitment to the traditional humanitarian principles	Limited	Limited
Impact	Total number of beneficiaries and exact impact not clear. Yet, beneficiaries exceed hundred thousands of people. Alone within the first six months of a single project, which DSV partially financed five hospitals, 85,000 people could be treated.	Total number of beneficiaries and exact impact not clear.

Source: the author.

humanitarian principles, especially when external expectations conflict with internal expectations. For example, IGMG, while monitored by the Federal Office for the Protection of the Constitution, does not receive any public funding for its activities, became an autonomous humanitarian actor by complying with its members' expectations.

While the deployment of traditional humanitarian actors is urgently needed to help Syrians to cope with the magnitude of the crisis, assistance delivered through DOs and other solidarity, religious and political channels remains the main lifeline for thousands of Syrians in opposition held areas (HPN no date). Hence, rather than ignoring DOs and their role as humanitarian actors, humanitarian studies should explore further which and how many DOs are active, what their actual activities and impact are on the ground, and why these organisations do not operate on the same principles as traditional humanitarian organisations. Further research on the universality, relevance and applicability of humanitarian principles should take DOs into account because ignoring DOs often means ignoring an opportunity to provide desperately needed humanitarian assistance to victims in crisis zones. Last but not least, it should be examined whether DOs' commitment to the traditional humanitarian principles can grow if they become more visible outside of their member base.

Notes

1 The Syrian government authorised 110 local NGOs, later reducing this number to 29, to provide humanitarian assistance in partnership with the UN (Margesson and Chesser 2013).

2 Adventist Development Relief Agency, Action Contre La Faim, Danish Refugee Council, International Catholic Migration Commission, International Medical Corps, Institut Européen de Coopération et de Développement, Help, Oxfam, Première Urgence, Secours Islamique France, SOS International, Terre des Hommes-Italy, Merlin, Mercy Corp and Norwegian Refugee Council are permitted to work in the government-controlled areas (ECHO 2013; OCHA 2013).

3 In this chapter, traditional humanitarian actors refer to the ICRC; UN organisations such as the UNHCR, the United Nations Children's Fund (UNICEF) and the World Food Programme (WFP); well-established international NGOs such as Doctors Without Borders (MSF), CARE, Catholic Relief Services (CRS), Save the Children, and World Vision International; and the OECD-DAC member states.

4 Islamic DOs are often active in their members' country of origin, country of residence and in third countries because their faith motivates them for providing aid to the people in need, especially to the worldwide Muslim community (*ummah*) (Sezgin and Dijkzeul 2013; Rosenow-Williams and Sezgin 2014).

5 Rauh (2010) attributes the donor-driven standardisation (i.e. isomorphism in planning, reporting and accountability) to the power imbalances between Northern donors and NGOs.

6 DSV has organised aid convoys since the middle of 2011. Yet, the number of aid convoys and their content has increased considerably since the end of 2012 with the growing number of members and donors (interview with LA).

7 These patients had been brought to Germany by the Federal Government for medical treatment. After the treatment in the hospitals of the German armed forces, they started their rehab in Irbid.

8 The Federal Office for the Protection of the Constitution is the German domestic intelligence agency. It monitors organisations that hold sharia as an eternally valid system of law for all areas of life and hence try to enforce sharia in Germany or in the countries of origin in order to practice 'true' Islam (Bundesamt für Verfassungsschutz no date b).

9 The accuracy of these numbers is questionable, given the rapidly changing character of IGMG and its member organisations. Also, some mosque communities publicly declare to be IGMG members, while others prefer to keep their ties to IGMG secret. This situation may be due to IGMG's surveillance by the Federal Office for the Protection of the Constitution. IGMG may exaggerate the number of its members and the number of people attending its activities to legitimise itself to its members, the Muslim community in Europe, governmental authorities and other NGOs.

10 Ramadan is the Islamic calendar's ninth month, in which the Quran was revealed. Fasting during Ramadan is one of the Five Pillars of Islam.

11 Erbakan's movement was organised in the form of a political party, which was banned and re-established several times under different names.

12 Today, more young Muslims become members and attain positions within IGMG. Many hold German citizenship and consider themselves an integral part of German society. The change in organisational aims and structures responds to the expectations of this generation, which is not interested in Turkish politics to the same extent as its parents but rather expect organisational activities to institutionalise Islam in Europe and help Muslims throughout the world (Schiffauer 2010: 327ff).

13 When the local IGMG community organised a demonstration in Duisburg, Germany, large numbers of demonstrators attacked a house in which residents had Israeli flags hanging in their windows (Pries and Sezgin 2012).

14 The UOSSM was founded in Paris-France in 2011, from 13 medical and relief organisations and included hundreds of Syrian doctors or doctors with Syrian migration background working in different Arab countries, Canada, Europe, Syria and the USA (UOSSM no date).

15 Hand in Hand for Syria is a humanitarian organisation formed by Syrian migrants in London in 2011.

References

Ahsan, S. (2013) Syrian Diaspora Leads Aid Effort (http://newint.org/features/web-exclusive/2013/02/04/syria-diaspora-aid-humanitarian) accessed 4 February 2013.

Behn, S. (2015) Islamic State, Other Militant Threats Raise Costs for Aid Workers (http://reliefweb.int/report/world/islamic-state-other-militant-threats-raise-costs-aid-workers) accessed 13 March 2015.

Bundesamt für Verfassungsschutz (no date a) Zahlen und Fakten zum Islamismus (www.verfassungsschutz.de/de/arbeitsfelder/af-islamismus-und-islamistischer-terrorismus/zahlen-und-fakten-islamismus/zuf-is-2012-islamistische-organizationen.html) accessed 26 February 2014.

252   *Zeynep Sezgin*

Bundesamt für Verfassungsschutz (no date b) Was genau macht der Verfassungsschutz (www.verfassungsschutz.de/de/das-bfv/aufgaben/was-genau-macht-der-verfassungsschutz) accessed 26 February 2014.

CBS (2013) Syrian Refugee Camps Slammed by Rain, Cold Making Miserable Conditions Unbearable (www.cbsnews.com/news/syrian-refugee-camps-slammed-by-rain-cold-making-miserable-conditions-unbearable) accessed 9 January 2013.

Child, J. (1976) 'Organizational Structure, Environment and Performance', *Sociology*, 6(1):1–22.

Clarke G. (2006) 'Faith Matters: Faith-Based Organisations, Civil Society and International Development', *Journal of International Development*, 18(6):835–848.

Donini, A. (2010) 'The Far Side: the Meta Functions of Humanitarianism in a Globalised World', *Disasters*, 34(2):220–237.

DSV (no date a) Wer wir sind (http://ds-verein.org/ueber-uns) accessed 15 May 2015.

DSV (no date b) Allgemeine Spende (http://ds-verein.org/spenden) accessed 15 May 2015.

DSV (no date c) Medizinische Versorgung (http://ds-verein.org/spenden/medizinische-hilfe) accessed 15 May 2015.

DSV (2012a) ARD berichtet über syrische Flüchtlinge an der türkischen Grenze (http://ds-verein.org/aktuelles/ard-berichtet-ueber-syrische-fluechtlinge-an-der-tuerkischen-grenze) accessed 15 May 2015.

DSV (2012b) Einladung in das Haus der Weltkulturen (http://ds-verein.org/aktuelles/einladung-in-das-haus-der-weltkulturen) accessed 15 May 2015.

DSV (2013a) Prominente Botschafter des DS-Vereins (http://ds-verein.org/aktuelles/prominente-botschafter-des-dsv) accessed 15 May 2015.

DSV (2013b) Syrischer Abend im Gemeindezentrum St. Elisabeth in Darmstadt (http://ds-verein.org/aktuelles/syrischer-abend-im-gemeindezentrum-st-elisabeth-in-darmstadt) accessed 15 May 2015.

DSV (2013c) Deutsch-Syrischer Verein rettet Leben durch Intensivstation in Aleppo (http://ds-verein.org/aktuelles/deutsch-syrischer-verein-rettet-leben-durch-intensivstation-in-aleppo) accessed 15 May 2015.

ECHO (2013) Syria Crisis. Humanitarian Aid and Civil Protection (http://reliefweb.int/sites/reliefweb.int/files/resources/syria_en_13.pdf) accessed 14 February 2014.

Esser, H. (1980) *Aspekte der Wanderungssoziologie: Assimilation und Integration von Wanderern, ethnischen Gruppen und Minderheiten: Eine Handlungstheoretische Analyse*, Darmstadt: Luchterhand.

Fahrenhorst, B., Arndt, C., Jaffer, M., Pfautsch, R. and Zelazny, F. (2009). *Beitrag der Diasporas zu Konfliktminderung und Konfliktlösung in den Herkunftsländern*, Eschborn: GTZ.

Glick Schiller, N. and Faist, T. (Eds) (2010) *Migration, Development and Transnationalization*, New York: Berghan Books.

Haber 3 (2014) Bulgaristan'daki Suriyeli Siginmacilara Yardim (www.haber3.com/bulgaristandaki-suriyeli-siginmacilara-yardim-2614630h.htm) accessed 2 August 2015.

Halm, D. and Sezgin, Z. (Eds) (2012) *Migration and Organized Civil Society: Rethinking National Policy*, London & New York: Routledge.

HatayVatan (2013) Hasene Suriyeli Muhacirler için büyük bir adım daha attı (www.hatayvatan.com/etiket/hasene-dernegi/feed) accessed 7 November 2014.

Holmes, O. and Nebehay, S. (2014) Some Aid Workers Freed in Syria, Risks to Humanitarian Effort Grow (http://uk.reuters.com/article/2013/10/14/uk-syria-crisis-redcross-idUKBRE99D0AU20131014) accessed 13 March 2015.

HPG (2012) Syria Crisis: The Humanitarian Response (www.odi.org.uk/sites/odi.org.uk/files/odi-assets/events-documents/4907.pdf) accessed 14 February 2014.

HPN (no date) Scaling up Aid in Syria: The Role of Diaspora Networks (www.odihpn.org/the-humanitarian-space/news/announcements/blog-articles/scaling-up-aid-in-syria-the-role-of-diaspora-networks) accessed 14 February 2013.

HPN (2012) Working with Somali Diaspora Organizations in the UK (www.odihpn.org/humanitarian-exchange-magazine/issue-54/working-with-somali-diaspora-organizations-in-the-uk) accessed 17 February 2014.

ICRC (2013) The International Red Cross and Red Crescent Movement Deplores the Death of Another Aid Worker in Syria (www.icrc.org/eng/resources/documents/statement/2013/11-18-syria-death-aid-worker.htm) accessed 19 November 2013.

IGMG (no date) IGMG Hilfsteam im Gaza-Streifen (www.igmg.org/gemeinschaft/presseerklaerungen/artikel/2008/02/03/igmg-hilfsteam-im-gaza-streifen-wir-werden-vor-dem-drama-im-gaza-streifen-nicht-schweigen.html?L=.html%20%E2%80%A6//include/lib.inc.php.html.html.html.html) accessed 15 May 2015.

IGMG (2009a) Introductory Brochure, Kerpen: IGMG.

IGMG (2009b) IGMG eröffnet Studentenwohnheim in Pakistan und drei Waisenhäuser in Bangladesch (www.igmg.org/nachrichten/artikel/2009/04/18/igmg-eroeffnet-studentenwohnheim-in-pakistan-und-drei-waisenhaeuser-in-bangladesch.html?L=.html.html.html/phprojekt/lib/include/lib.inc.php.html) accessed 15 May 2015.

IGMG (2012) Camia (www.igmg.org/fileadmin/Publikationen/camia/06-2012/files/camia-sayi-6.pdf) accessed 15 May 2015.

IGMG (2013) Hutba: Unsere Prüfung (www.igmg.org/islam/freitagspredigt/artikel/2013/02/15/hutba-unsere-pruefung.html?%20/phprojekt/lib/config.inc.phppath_pre.html.html=) accessed 15 May 2015.

IOM (2005) *Migration, Development and Poverty Reduction in Asia*, Geneva: IOM.

IOM (2013) Diaspora Communities as Aid Providers (www.iom.int/cms/en/sites/iom/home/what-we-do/migration-policy-and-research/migration-policy-1/migration-policy-practice/issues/augustseptember-2013/diaspora-communities-as-aid-prov.html) accessed 17 February 2014.

Juul Petersen, M. (2011) *For Humanity or for the Umma? Aid and Islam in Transnational Muslim NGOs*, London: Hurst & Co.

Levitt, P. and Lamba-Nieves, D. (2011) 'Social Remittances Revisited', *Journal of Ethnic and Migration Studies*, 37(1):1–22.

Margesson, R. and Chesser, S.G. (2013) Syria: Overview of the Humanitarian Response (www.fas.org/sgp/crs/mideast/R43119.pdf) accessed 14 February 2014.

McQue, K. (2013) Inside Zaatari, the Jordanian Refugee Camp That Makes Syria's Civil War Look Like the Better Option (www.independent.co.uk/news/world/middle-east/inside-zaatari-the-jordanian-refugee-camp-that-makes-syrias-civil-war-look-like-the-better-option-8960804.html) accessed 24 November 2014.

Meyer, J. and Rowan, B. (1991) 'Institutionalized Organizations: Formal Structures as Myth and Ceremony', in: W. Powell and P. DiMaggio (Eds) *The New Institutionalism in Organizational Analysis*, Chicago: The University of Chicago Press.

MIS (2010) Natural Disasters in Haiti and Pakistan Highlight Diaspora Response (www.migrationpolicy.org/article/top-10-2010-issue-10-natural-disasters-haiti-and-pakistan-highlight-diaspora-response) accessed 17 February 2014.

Mittelbayerische (2013) Syrien: Sie schauen hin und helfen (www.mittelbayerische.de/region/neumarkt/artikel/syrien-sie-schauen-hin-und-helfen/923519/syrien-sie-schauen-hin-und-helfen.html) accessed 5 June 2013.

MSF (2013) Syria: Humanitarian Assistance in Deadlock (www.msf.org.uk/article/syria-humanitarian-assistance-deadlock) accessed 6 March 2013.

OCHA (2013) Syrian Arab Republic – Humanitarian Presence: International NGOs (http://reliefweb.int/sites/reliefweb.int/files/resources/05_syr_INGOs_presence_130806.pdf) accessed 3 November 2014.

OCHA (2014) Syria – Key Figures (www.unocha.org/syria) accessed 3 November 2014.

Oliver, C. (1991) 'Strategic Responses to Institutional Processes', in: *The Academy of Management Review*, 16(1):145–179.

Ozkan, M. (2011) 'Transnational Islam, Immigrant NGOs and Poverty Alleviation: The Case of the IGMG', *Journal of International Development*, 24(4):467–484.

Pries, L. (2010) *Transnationalisierung. Theorie und Empirie grenzüberschreitender Vergesellschaftung*, Wiesbaden: VS Verlag.

Pries, L. and Sezgin, Z. (eds) (2010) *Jenseits von 'Identität oder Integration': Grenzen überspannende Migrantenorganisationen*, Wiesbaden: VS Verlag.

Pries, L. and Sezgin, Z. (eds) (2012) *Cross-Border Migrant Organizations in Comparative Perspective*, Basingstoke: Palgrave Macmillan.

Ragab, N. (2013) The Engagement of the Syrian Diaspora in Germany in Peacebuilding (http://mgsog.merit.unu.edu/ISacademie/docs/PB13.pdf) accessed 17 February 2014.

Rauh, K. (2011) 'NGOs, Foreign Donors, and Organizational Processes: Passive NGO Recipients or Strategic Actors?', *McGill Sociological Review*, 1:29–45.

Rosenow-Williams, K. and Sezgin, Z. (2014) 'Islamic Migrant Organizations: Little-Studied Actors in Humanitarian Action', *International Migration Review*, 48(2):324–353.

SAMS (2013) NGO Coordination Meeting for Humanitarian Relief to Syria (http://sams-usa.net/site/ngo-coordination-meeting-for-humanitarian-relief-to-syria) 20 March 2013.

Schiffauer, W. (2010) *Nach dem Islamismus: Die Islamische Gemeinschaft Millî Görüş; eine Ethnographie*, Frankfurt am Main: Suhrkamp.

Schmitter, P. and Streeck, W. (1999) *The Organization of Business Interests*, Cologne: Max Planck Institute for the Study of Societies.

Scott, R.W. (2001) *Institutions and Organizations*, Thousand Oaks, CA: Sage.

SCPR (2013) Syria War on Development: Socioeconomic Monitoring Report of Syria (http://scpr-syria.org/att/1382759391_c6yBX.pdf) accessed 14 February 2014.

SCPR (2014) Squandering Humanity: Socioeconomic Monitoring Report of Syria (http://scpr-syria.org/att/SCPR_Squandering_Humanity_En.pdf) accessed 3 November 2014.

Seidel, E., Dantschke, C. and Yıldırım, A. (2001) Politik im Namen Allahs (http://edoc.bibliothek.uni-halle.de/servlets/MCRFileNodeServlet/HALCoRe_derivate_00001879/politik_im_namen_allahs.pdf) accessed 19 February 2014.

Sezgin, Z. (2010) 'Turkish Migrants' Organizations in Germany and the Flow of Remittances to Turkey', *Journal of International Migration and Integration*, 12(3):231–51.

Sezgin, Z. (2014) 'Turkish Migrant Organizations after the 2011 Van Earthquake: Member Interests versus Humanitarian Principles', *Oxford Development Studies*, 42(1):19–37.

Sezgin, Z. and Dijkzeul, D. (2013) 'Migrant Organizations in Humanitarian Action', *Journal of International Migration and Integration*, 15(2):159–177.

Smith, H. and Stares, P.B. (eds) (2007) *Diasporas in Conflict: Peace-Makers or Peace-Wreckers?*, New York: UN University Press.

UOSSM (no date) About Us (www.uossm.org/index.php/about-us) accessed 26 February 2014.

Wimmer, A. and Glick Schiller, N. (2002) 'Methodological Nationalism and Beyond: Nation-State Building, Migration and the Social Sciences', *Global Networks*, 2(4):301–334.

Part VII

Faith-Based Humanitarianism

12 International Muslim NGOs

'Added Value' or an Echo of Western Principles and Donor Wishes?

Marie Juul Petersen

Introduction

I once participated in this workshop with all these [international] NGOs. This was in 2006, I think. I sat down in a corner, and then, when the people from Islamic Relief came, they sat down next to me. The space next to me on the other side was empty and this lady from ActionAid came, and she didn't want to sit next to me. I think she thought that it was like the Islamic corner or something like that. I felt very bad. We never thought like that. And now, when I go to the coordination meetings, everyone wants to sit next to me.[1]

Recent years have witnessed the increasing popularity of international Muslim NGOs among mainstream humanitarian and development organisations, as the above anecdote neatly illustrates. With the first international Muslim aid NGOs being established in the 1970s, these organisations are hardly new, but their inclusion into the field of mainstream humanitarian and development aid is.[2] For many years most international Muslim NGOs led a largely parallel life to that of mainstream humanitarian and development actors, unnoticed or even deliberately ignored by major Western and international donors.[3] Since the beginning of the 2000s, however, this has changed, and (at least some) international Muslim NGOs have now become part of the mainstream humanitarian and development system, receiving an increasing part of their funding from Western and international donors who have come to consider Muslim – and other faith-based – organisations to bring an 'added value' to the provision of humanitarian and development aid, qua their religious identity.[4] Table 12.1 provides an overview of the main international Muslim NGOs.

There is little research on these 'new' actors in the field of international humanitarian and development aid. Especially since 9/11, much of the existing literature casts on international Muslim NGOs as political actors, analysing them as front organisations for global militant networks such as al-Qaeda or as supporters of national political parties and resistance groups in Palestine, Sudan, Afghanistan and elsewhere (Yaylaci 2007: 2). Few

Table 12.1 Largest international Muslim NGOs

Organisation	Origin	Spending (USD)
Aga Khan Development Network	Switzerland	625 million
Islamic Relief	UK	101 million
Social Reform Society	Kuwait	81 million
Direct Aid/Africa Muslims Agency	Kuwait	66 million
Foundation for Human Rights and Freedoms and Hum. Relief (IHH)	Turkey	63 million
International Islamic Charitable Organisation	Kuwait	59 million
LIFE for Relief and Development	USA	57 million
Muslim Aid	UK	42 million
Dubai Charity Association	UAE	29 million
International Islamic Relief Organisation	Saudi Arabia	19 million
Sheikh Al Nouri Charity Society	Kuwait	17 million
Muslim Hands	UK	15.7 million
Helping Hand for Relief and Development	USA	13.3 million
Comité de Bienfaisance et de Secours aux Palestiniens	France	10.5 million
Human Concern International	Canada	8 million
Interpal	UK	6.4 million
Munazzamat al Da'wa al Islamiya (MDI)	Sudan	6 million
Muslim Charity	UK	4.7 million
Mercy USA for Relief and Development	USA	3.9 million
Human Appeal International	UK	3.8 million
Hidaya Foundation	USA	3.8 million
Kinder USA	USA	0.8 million

Source: Aga Khan Development Network website, www.akdn.org/faq.asp (2010 numbers); Islamic Relief Annual Report 2011; Forbes Middle East, http://english.forbesmiddleeast. com/details.php?row=1553&list=35 (on Social Reform Society and Direct Aid, both 2011 numbers); IHH website, www.ihh.org.tr/en/main/pages/gelir-gider/86 (2011 numbers); IICO Administrative and Financial Report 2010-2011; LIFE for Relief and Development Audited Financial Statements 2011 (www.lifeusa.org/site/DocServer/2011_AUDITED_ FINANCIALS.pdf?docID=1581); Muslim Aid Annual Review 2011; IIROSA Overall Performance Report 2010–2011; Forbes Middle East, http://english.forbesmiddleeast. com/details.php?row=1553&list=35 (on Dubai Charity Association and Sheikh Al Nouri Charity Society, both 2011 numbers); Muslim Hands Ramadan Feed-back 2011 (http:// muslimhands.org.uk/media/46178/feedback-report-2011.pdf); Helping Hand for Relief and Development Consolidated Financial Statements 2011 (www.hhrd.org/auditReport/ FinancialAudit-2011_Final.pdf); Comite de Bienfaisance Rapport Annuel 2010 (www.cbsp. fr/notre-actualite/publications-a-communiques/download-file.html?path=Nos+rapports +annuels%2Frapport_annuel_2010.pdf); Human Concern International Annual Report 2011–2012 (http://3426.bbnc.bbcust.com/document.doc?id=8); Interpal Annual Report and Financial Statements 2010 (http://interpal.org/Files/media/Interpal%20Annual%20

Report%20&%20Financial%20Statements%202010.pdf); Abdel Salam, A.H. and de Waal, A. (2004) 'On the Failure and Persistence of Jihad', in de Waal, A. (ed.) *Islamism and its Enemies in the Horn of Africa*, London: C. Hurst & Co, 21–70; Charity Commission website www.charitycommission.gov.uk/find-charities (on Muslim Charity, 2011 numbers); Mercy USA for Aid and Development 2011 Annual Report (www.mercyusa.org/ezefiles/2011AnnualReport. pdf); Kroessin, M.R. (2009) Mapping UK Muslim Development NGOs (www.birmingham. ac.uk/Documents/college-social-sciences/government-society/rad/working-papers/wp-30. pdf); Hidaya Foundation Financial Statements and Supplementary Information 2012 (www.hidaya.org/about-us/financials); Kinder USA Financial Statements 2010–2011 (www. kinderusa.org/documents/Kinder%202011%20financial%20statements.pdf). All websites last accessed 6 June 2013.

analyses approach international Muslim NGOs as legitimate providers of humanitarian and development aid, exploring their motivations, aims, and activities and discussing their role in the field of mainstream humanitarian and development aid. Why and when do international Muslim NGOs engage in humanitarian and development aid? What are their aims and activities? How do they relate and compare to other actors in the field of mainstream humanitarian and development aid?[5]

Based on qualitative, empirical case studies of two international Muslim NGOs – Islamic Relief and Muslim Aid – that have recently become part of the system of mainstream humanitarian and development aid, the present chapter seeks to answer some of these questions. Loosely inspired by neo-institutionalist approaches to the study of organisations, the analysis explores how these NGOs position themselves within the field of mainstream humanitarian and development aid. As has been described elsewhere in this volume, neo-institutionalism claims that all organisations are embedded in a particular environment (in this case, the system of humanitarian and development aid) which develops its own distinctive institutional logics and governance systems (Scott 2001: 148), and that these, in turn, influence the structure and activities of the organisations in the forms of coercion, standards or expectations of other players in the field (Rosenow-Williams and Sezgin 2014: 7). By employing the system's institutionalised scripts for action, new actors can 'maximize their legitimacy and increase their resources and survival capacities' (Meyer and Rowan 1991: 53). In this perspective, rather than an 'added value' one can expect Islamic Relief and Muslim Aid to present a kind of aid that looks very much like that of Oxfam, ActionAid and all the other organisations in the field of mainstream humanitarian and development aid. The chapter explores this hypothesis, asking whether Islamic Relief and Muslim Aid adopt traditional discourses and practices of aid, responding to external pressures and expectations, and as such presenting a case of what neo-institutionalists term 'institutional isomorphism' (DiMaggio and Powell 1983), or if they are able to act autonomously from these, presenting new discourses and practices of aid and challenging not only the established logics of the environment but also the claims of neo-institutionalist theories?[6]

Introducing Islamic Relief and Muslim Aid

As the introductory anecdote implies, international Muslim NGOs have not always been a part of the mainstream system of humanitarian and development aid, but lived a parallel existence to that of Western NGOs and donor agencies. This is not only true for Middle Eastern organisations such as the International Islamic Charitable Organisation, Direct Aid and International Islamic Relief Organisation, but also for organisations based in the West, such as Islamic Relief and Muslim Aid – the focus of this chapter. Islamic Relief was founded in Britain in 1984 by two medical students from Egypt, prompted by the famine in the Horn of Africa at the time. Like their founders, trustees and staff members were Muslims, many with an Arab or South Asian background. Similarly with Muslim Aid, established the year after by the British convert and prominent folk singer, Yusuf Islam (formerly known as Cat Stevens), together with representatives from 23 British Muslim community organisations. The educational background of founders, trustees and staff members in the two organisations was in engineering, medicine, and accounting, rather than in development studies, and many had professional experience from government or the private business sector, but not from other NGOs. Many people had personal or professional relations to key Muslim organisations in Europe, the Middle East and South Asia, some of them closely related to the Muslim Brotherhood or Jama'at-e Islami movement (Clarke 2010: 517).[7]

Firmly embedded in an Islamic aid culture, neither Islamic Relief nor Muslim Aid had much to do with other British NGOs, with DFID (UK Department for International Development) or other mainstream donor agencies. They had little need for financial support, getting the vast majority of their funds from individual Muslim donors and businesses in Britain and elsewhere. Many people would pay their religious alms, or *zakat*, to Islamic Relief and Muslim Aid; others would give donations in the form of *waqf* or *sadaqa*. In an annual review, Muslim Aid declared: 'We are able to act as a channel for the faithful, who wish to perform their religious duty to the poor and give to charity' (Muslim Aid, Annual Review 2000: 4). In the words of a Muslim Aid staff member, the two organisations perceived themselves as 'the administrator[s] of other people's zakat'. Bound by their donors' wishes, the organisations would focus on traditional Muslim aid activities, including provision of basic relief, orphan sponsorships, and celebration of religious holidays such as Ramadan and Qurbani, concentrating their efforts in Muslim communities and countries.

Western donor agencies and NGOs, for their part, did not seek cooperation either. In fact, many considered the religiosity of Muslim NGOs – and other faith-based – organisations to be an obstacle rather than an asset to the provision of humanitarian and development aid. In their view, these organisations were at best old-fashioned, conservative charities focusing on short-term relief and handouts rather than sustainable development programmes; at worst sectarian and discriminatory, violating mainstream aid principles of non-discrimination and universalism. Underlying this perception of Muslim – and other faith-based – organisations were narratives of modernisation and secularisation, shaping the field of humanitarian and – especially – development aid since the 1950s. In this perspective, religion was seen as a conservative and traditional force, destined to withdraw and eventually disappear from public life as part of societal progress towards an increasingly modern society (Wilson 1992: 49). As such, religion was difficult to reconcile with or relate to development's logic of economic progress and bureaucratic rationalisation (Jones and Juul Petersen 2011: 1292). Adding to the scepticism, Muslim organisations had a reputation as being closely related to political and sometimes even militant Islamic groups, threatening the neutrality of their aid. In 1980s' Afghanistan, several international Muslim NGOs had been accused of supporting the mujahedeen; the same happened in the civil war in Bosnia some years later. And in the 1998 attack on the American embassies in Kenya and Tanzania, five NGOs were banned by the Kenyan government for their involvement in the attacks (Salih 2002: 24).

'In these times, everybody wants to be seen to be involving Islam ...'

This changed in the beginning of the 2000s. In particular two factors paved the way for the inclusion of international Muslim NGOs into the field of mainstream humanitarian and development aid. One was the burgeoning interest in faith-based organisations (FBOs) among Western donor agencies. The increasing visibility of religious actors in the public domain had challenged theories of secularisation, prompting even staunchly secular institutions such as the World Bank to reconsider the role of religion in humanitarian and development aid. Coupled with a disappointment in the effectiveness of 'regular' NGOs, donor agencies started turning to FBOs as the new 'magic bullets' in humanitarian and development aid. Supposedly building on large constituencies and enjoying trust and credibility in local communities, faith-based NGOs were expected by donors to present an 'added value' to development aid. They were seen to have a great potential as promoters of humanitarian and development aid, capable of galvanising moral commitment, translating principles of aid into the idioms of faith and mobilising popular support for donor initiatives (Clarke 2007: 80).[8]

This interest in FBOs was further strengthened by 9/11 and the ensuing war on terror. After it became clear that the attacks on the World Trade Center and Pentagon had been carried out by radical Islamist groups, suspicions quickly rose as to the involvement of certain Muslim NGOs in planning and financing the attacks. A range of measures were introduced by the US and other governments to prevent NGOs from funding militant Islamic groups, including restrictions, control and, ultimately, designations of certain organisations. But the war on terror not only lead to a focus on supposedly 'extremist' Muslim NGOs, involved in financing terrorist activities; it also encouraged an increasing interest in cooperation with so-called 'moderate' Muslim NGOs, seen as potential bridge builders between Islam and the West (Howell and Lind 2009). In this, the system of humanitarian and development aid came to be an important site for dialogue.

In particular the British Charity Commission and the DFID played an active role in the inclusion of international Muslim NGOs into the field. Unlike for example US and Middle Eastern governments which emphasised strict control and sanctions of NGOs, the British authorities put in place a much more supportive NGO regulation regime (Benthall 2008a: 93), opening up for funding and cooperation. In this context, in particular Islamic Relief, but also Muslim Aid, have come to be ideal partners. In contrast with for example Interpal and the Green Crescent, two other UK-based NGOs, neither Muslim Aid nor Islamic Relief were subject to allegations of 'terrorist' connections, but were widely considered to be 'moderate faith-based organisations', suitable for cooperation.[9] At an *iftar* dinner organised by Islamic Relief in August 2010, for instance, Deputy Prime Minister Nick Clegg commented:

> I come here full of admiration for what Islamic Relief does. What you are doing is an example to us all. You are responding with moral and organisational leadership which I think, frankly, has been lacking from the international community as a whole.
>
> (Quoted from Khan 2012: 111)

Likewise, for Muslim Aid's twenty-fifth anniversary, Gordon Brown, then Prime Minister, praised Muslim Aid for its 'valuable work' and 'significant contribution to the Millennium Development Goals'.[10]

To sum up, these developments created an opening for (certain) international Muslim NGOs. As a staff member of Islamic Relief notes with some amusement: 'Because it's Muslim, Islamic Relief enjoys greater access to funding. It's included everywhere, people listen, they have access to the government. In these times, people want to be seen to be involving Islam.' For these organisations, cooperation with Western donors was a chance to ensure new sources of funding, enabling organisational growth at a time when support from individual donors was waning, but it was also a way to protect the organisations against suspicions of terrorist connections, emphasising their identity as 'moderate' Muslim organisations, willing to and capable of cooperation with mainstream Western aid organisations.

Members of the Club

Today, Islamic Relief and Muslim Aid are both well-integrated members of the system of mainstream humanitarian and development aid. This is witnessed first and foremost in their funding sources. Both organisations have experienced a veritable explosion in institutional funding. Islamic Relief's institutional funding has grown from close to zero before 9/11 to almost 25 per cent in 2009 (Khan 2012: 92). And in Muslim Aid, institutional funding today makes up more than one-third the total budget (Muslim Aid, Annual Review 2011). Some of this money comes from Middle Eastern and Islamic donors,[11] but a large portion of funding actually comes from Western donor agencies. One of Islamic Relief's first institutional donors was DFID, offering Islamic Relief a US$42,000 grant for relief work after flooding in Bangladesh in 1998. In 2001, cooperation intensified with funding for projects in Pakistan, Mali and Afghanistan, worth more than US$4 million. In 2006, a three-year Partnership Programme Arrangement was agreed upon, securing Islamic Relief approximately US$4 million funding for the period 2008 to 2011, later extended to 2014 (Islamic Relief, PPA Self-Assessment Review, Reporting Year 2008/2009). Other major donors are the European Union's Humanitarian Aid and Civil Protection department (ECHO), UNDP and the UN High Commissioner for Refugees (UNHCR). Entering the development donor scene a few years later than Islamic Relief, Muslim Aid got its first grant from Oxfam after the tsunami in 2005, financing a US$2 million housing project in Indonesia. The project received a lot of attention, opening up for funding from ECHO, the World Bank, DFID, UNDP, the Asian Development Bank and others. In 2007, Muslim Aid was awarded its first mini-grant of US$50,000 from DFID for a three-year development awareness project in Britain (James 2009: 9), and the organisation is negotiating for a Partnership Programme Arrangement. Other large institutional donors include the World Bank, ECHO, and the Asian Development Bank. See Table 12.2 for an overview of the two organisations' growth in recent years.

Table 12.2 Growth in millions of US$, 2003–2011

Islamic Relief

Year	2003	2004	2005	2006	2007	2008	2009	2010	2011
Income	25.4	35.9	70.3	61.4	66.2	78.8	96.0	86.6	100.8

Source: Annual Reviews 2003–2011.

Muslim Aid

Year	2003	2004	2005	2006	2007	2008	2009	2010	2011
Income	7.4	7.9	16.3	15.3	33.6	40.1	58.1	28.2	42.2

Source: Annual Reviews 2003–2011.

Parallel to this funding from Western donor agencies, the two organisations are increasingly cooperating with other mainstream humanitarian and development aid actors: Both organisations are members of a wide range of networks, including the British NGO network BOND, the Red Cross/Red Crescent Code of Conduct, the Sphere Standards and the Humanitarian Accountability Partnership. Furthermore, Islamic Relief is (the only Muslim) member of Disasters Emergency Committee (Palmer 2011), while Muslim Aid's application is being considered. Both organisations are also active in networks such as the Jubilee Debt Campaign and the Make Poverty History Campaign. In a similar vein, they emphasise their cooperation with mainstream development and humanitarian NGOs such as Christian Aid, Oxfam and others. Interestingly, none of the organisations are members of specifically Muslim networks such as the International Islamic Council for Da'wa and Relief, just like they seem to tone down their partnerships with other Muslim NGOs. In Bangladesh, for instance, neither Islamic Relief nor Muslim Aid has anything to do with other international Muslim NGOs working in the country. Instead, they are part of the so-called international non-governmental organisation (INGO) Forum, together with Action Aid, Oxfam, CARE, Christian Aid, and other mainstream NGOs.

As the above analysis shows, both Islamic Relief and Muslim Aid have become solidly integrated into the field of mainstream humanitarian and development aid in recent years, receiving an increasing share of their funds from Western donor agencies and cooperating with Western, Christian or secular NGOs rather than Muslim ones. But what kinds of organisations are they? Who works there? What kinds of aid do they provide? To whom? And what is the role of religion in this? In the following, I will take a closer look at the ways in which the organisations present themselves, their staff, the activities they provide and the groups that they target, exploring the role of religion in this, and discussing the 'added value' they present to the field of mainstream humanitarian and development aid.

'A Mainstream Development Agency Working towards International Standards'

Having grown immensely since they first started in the mid-1980s, Islamic Relief and Muslim Aid are now two of the world's largest Muslim NGOs, with budgets of respectively US$101 million (2011) and US$42 million (2011). Islamic Relief has fundraising offices, or partners, in 11 countries – including Belgium, Canada, Germany, Italy, Malaysia, the Netherlands, South Africa, Sweden, Switzerland, USA and Australia – and country offices in 28 countries, with Palestine, Pakistan, Somalia, Bangladesh and Kenya as the largest programmes. The organisation employs 160 people in its headquarters in Birmingham, while approximately 2,800 work in one of the organisation's country offices or fundraising offices.[12] Muslim Aid has 11 country offices and two regional coordination offices but works in more

Table 12.3 Overview of Islamic Relief and Muslim Aid

Name	Origin	Year	Budget in US$	Staff	Major countries
Islamic Relief	Britain	1984	101 million	1,650	Palestine Pakistan Somalia Bangladesh Kenya
Muslim Aid	Britain	1985	42 million	2,200	Bangladesh Somalia Pakistan Indonesia Sri Lanka

Source: The table builds on the sources listed by Table 12.1.

than 70 countries, with the largest programmes in Bangladesh, Somalia, Pakistan, Indonesia, and Sri Lanka. The organisation employs around 1,650 employees, of which 60 work in the headquarters in London, while the remaining work in one of the country offices.[13] See Table 12.3 for an overview of the two organisations.

Both Islamic Relief and Muslim Aid present themselves as 'international relief and development agencies'.[14] In this, they emphasise their allegiance to the 'global humanitarian community'[15] rather than the global Muslim community, the *ummah*. In interviews, many people explicitly distance themselves from other Muslim NGOs, claiming that they are not professional development and humanitarian organisations. A staff member bluntly states: 'They are perhaps not the most sophisticated, they don't use LogFrame and all these things'. Another person elaborates a bit more on the distinction:

> The way I see it, there are two different kinds of Islamic organisations – the traditional and the modern. The modern accept the Western system and they give it an Islamic flavour, an Islamic spirit ... The traditional organisations depend only on personal accountability. It's about you as a spiritual person, about whether you are trustworthy or not. It's not about the system; it's about the person.

On websites and in organisational material, cooperation with Western development and humanitarian organisations is emphasised over the many Middle Eastern organisations that also support the two NGOs.[16] For instance, in an article published in the British NGO newsletter ONTRAC, Islamic Relief describes its donor base as follows: 'The organisation receives donations from multilateral and bilateral institutions and individual donors. It has entered into partnerships and cooperation agreements with Christian FBOs, such as CAFOD, as well as secular organisations'. (Abuarqab 2010: 7). Through these partnerships with Western and Christian organisations, the organisations can, in their own words, 'connect ourselves with mainstream agencies' (Muslim Aid, Trustees' Report and Financial Statements 2008: 7) and confirm their status 'as a mainstream development agency working towards international standards' (Muslim Aid, Trustees' Report and Financial Statements 2007: 8).

Cooperation with Christian organisations plays a particularly important role, and Muslim Aid and Islamic Relief actively promote each their inter-faith partnership. The most famous is the partnership between Muslim Aid and the United Methodist Committee on Relief (UMCOR), growing out of cooperation between the two organisations in Sri Lanka in 2006, and in 2007 extended into a formal partnership.[17] Around the same time, Islamic Relief entered into partnership with Christian Aid, following the earthquake in Pakistan in 2005. Such partnerships send strong signals of dialogue and bridge-building, making them very popular with Western donors and governments. At the signing of the partnership agreement between Muslim Aid and UMCOR, then treasury Minister Stephen Timms officiated, and Gordon Brown, then Prime Minister, mentioned the part-nership in a speech to the UN Inter-Faith Conference in November 2008 as an example of 'the potential of faith' (Clarke 2010: n.52), something which, according to Clarke (2010: 11), reflected the British government's support for 'an innovative cross-national and trans-faith partnership'.

'Looking to Employ Professional Individuals'

An important part of being a 'mainstream development agency' is the reliance on 'experienced' and 'professional' staff, presenting 'a wealth of knowledge and expertise', as Islamic Relief puts it (Islamic Relief, Strategy 2007–2009: 2). As the below excerpt from a recent job announcement for a Senior Humanitarian Advisor to Islamic Relief illustrates, this means knowledge and expertise in the field of mainstream humanitarian and development aid:

> The successful candidate will have a Masters in Disaster Management, Development Studies, International Relations or other relevant subject or related field … In addition, a high level of computer literacy, plus expe-rience of using spreadsheets and accounting software is essential. The successful candidate will have a strong experience of policy analysis on humanitarian issues and experience of working in emergency response operations in difficult, challenging environments (at least three years).[18]

While a large part of the first generation of staff in both organisations come from a very different educational and professional background, most of them with no prior experience in humanitarian and development aid, recent years have seen the employment of more and more young professionals, fitting the profile outlined in the above advertisement. 'Most of the older people work here because they want to work in a religious organisation', one of these new staff members explains. 'For me it's different – I work here because I want to work in a development organisation'. 'In my job interview', another young development professional says, 'they told me that they were an organisation driven by faith, but they were looking for professional people'.[19]

An example of this type of staff member is Junaed who worked in Islamic Relief in Bangladesh when I visited the organisation. He was one of the first to take a degree in Development Studies in Bangladesh; later he completed an MPhil in Development and Social Change at an Australian university. Today, he works in Save the Children. Interestingly, there are also examples of older staff members who have undergone a 'development' process. The country director of Islamic Relief in Bangladesh, for instance, is originally a medical doctor, and has previously worked in a Saudi Arabian NGOs, but recently finished an MA in development studies at a university in Bangladesh, thus personifying the move from Islamic aid to a development-oriented professionalism: 'There was a clash between the way I needed to work as a professional and the way they worked', he said, alluding to the dominance of conservative religious staff in the Saudi organisation.

In Islamic Relief and Muslim Aid, religion does not play a formal role among staff, and there are no requirements as to religious affiliation. As noted in Muslim Aid's job advertisements: 'We are an equal opportunities employer and welcome all applications, regardless of age, gender, ethnicity, faith or disability.'[20] This does not mean, however, that religion is entirely relegated to the private sphere. Inspired by traditions of multiculturalism, Muslim Aid and Islamic Relief both present themselves as organisations in which there is room, but not pressure, to cultivate one's religiosity. It is about creating a 'relaxed, Islamic environment', as one top manager formulates it. Among staff, people often engage in religious activities; some send out hadith-of-the-day mails to colleagues, others organise religious discussion groups and many use the organisational prayer rooms regularly. In interviews, many emphasise the role of religion as a source of motivation and community among staff. 'There's a sense of brotherhood, sharing and caring for other people', a staff member from Islamic Relief says, 'and not only caring for the beneficiaries, but for each other as well'.

Aid for Humanity, Not for the Ummah

As professional development and humanitarian organisations, both Muslim Aid and Islamic Relief claim to base their aid on principles of non-discrimination and universalism. When they describe their target groups they use terms such as 'people from across the globe' and 'the whole of humanity' (Muslim Aid, Financial Statement 2008: 11), echoing mainstream aid discourses, and reflecting a rationale predicated on notions of a shared humanity rather than religious solidarity. In the words of a staff member in Bangladesh: 'We care about humanity, we don't care about their faith'. Another staff member, also in Bangladesh, says: 'We tell people that we have come to work for them, whether they are Muslim, Hindu, Christian, it doesn't matter to us. The important thing is that you are a human being'. Aligning this universalist approach with Islamic principles, another person says:

> If you look at it from the side of Islam, most instructions from the Prophet Muhammad and the Holy Qur'an are about motivating people to help others, to support and help especially the poor. And they don't mention what kinds of poor – they don't say what gender, what race, what religion.

A headquarter staff member tells about Muslim Aid's orphan sponsorship programme, aptly termed the Rainbow Family, carrying connotations of diversity and cosmopolitanism: 'The families can be all kinds – that's why we call it the Rainbow Family. They can be black, white, Muslim, Christian, Hindu'. A photo on one of Muslim Aid's brochures hammers home the point, showing a black child wearing a big cross in his necklace and holding a Muslim Aid package (Yaylaci 2007: 31). Likewise, in Muslim Aid's microfinance project in Bangladesh, staff continuously emphasise that 10 per cent of the women are Hindu, reflecting the general composition of the population. Islamic Relief's orphan's sponsorship programme includes Christian children and donors; several recipients of microfinance loans are Hindus; and even Ramadan food packages are distributed to non-Muslims. In recent years, both organisations have also been promoting activities in non-Muslim countries. After the earthquake in Haiti in January 2010, for instance, Islamic Relief set up camps for victims of the earthquake, providing 1,100 families with accommodation, water, food and medicine. Likewise, after the earthquake in Japan in March 2011, both organisations launched emergency appeals for victims of the disaster, urging their donors to contribute.

While this universalist approach is in line with mainstream aid principles, it clashes with expectations of some individual donors who expect their donations to go to fellow Muslims. In his analysis of Islamic Relief's individual donors, Khan (2012: 98) finds that more than one-third, or 37.5 per cent, strongly believed that at least zakat donations should be restricted to Muslims.[21] He quotes one donor, allegedly echoing statements of many others: 'I do not support other charities because I want my donations to go towards helping Muslims' (Khan 2012: 98). In order to satisfy the expectations of such donors, both Muslim Aid and Islamic Relief do maintain a focus on Muslim countries (see Table 12.4 for a list of the top five countries for each organisation). But rather than justifying this with reference to a particular religious solidarity, the two organisations explain it as a logical consequence of the level of poverty in these countries. As Muslim Aid states on its website: '[T]hese are countries that are affected by conflict and natural disasters. We strive to work where the need is greatest.'[22] An Islamic Relief staff member agrees: '[A] lot of the countries in which there is poverty are in fact Muslim.' Others note that Muslim NGOs are better suited to work in Muslim areas because they know the culture and the religion; therefore it makes sense for Islamic Relief and Muslim Aid to work primarily in Muslim countries. An Islamic Relief staff member says: 'We have an understanding of the culture and religion that gives us an advantage'. According to this line of thought, a common religion creates a symbolic sense of community among beneficiaries, NGOs, and other actors in the aid process, which in turn brings about 'added value' through ease of access (Palmer 2011: 97; see also Benedetti 2006; Benthall 2008b). One person from the headquarters tells about the work of Islamic Relief in Pakistan:

> We worked in South Pakistan, which is very very conservative, and we first worked with the male community organisation and it took two years before we were allowed to work with the women. I don't think other organisations would have been allowed.

Table 12.4 Top five countries of operation in terms of allocation of expenditures (2012)

Islamic Relief

Country	Percentage
Palestine	22
Pakistan	14
Somalia	8
Bangladesh	5
Kenya	4

Source: Islamic Relief, Annual Report 2011: 71.

Muslim Aid

Country	Percentage
Bangladesh	28
Somalia	20
Pakistan	10
Indonesia	7
Sri Lanka	2

Source: Muslim Aid staff.

The percentage refers to the percentage of total expenditure. Naturally, the focus varies from year to year, depending on disasters, wars and other emergencies. However, there seems to be some stability as the programmes in these countries have been among the largest for several years.

'Faith-Inspired Action'

Presenting their programmes under headings such as 'Sustainable liveli-hoods', 'Emergency relief and disaster preparedness' and 'Economic empowerment', Islamic Relief and Muslim Aid engage in activities that seem almost indistinguishable from mainstream development and humani-tarian organisations. See Table 12.5 for an overview of the activities of the two organisations. In this, they both claim that they are 'guided by the teachings of Islam'[23] and 'inspired by Islamic faith'[24] – Islamic Relief even uses the phrase 'Faith-inspired action' as the title of its strategy (Islamic Relief, Annual Report 2011: 13). But in concrete terms, religion is almost invisible in most activities. One person, from Islamic Relief's headquarters, says: 'These are all standard programmes, there are no specific Islamic ele-ments in this'. This is particularly emphasised among country office staff, where people rarely mentioned religion: 'We have no intention to use Islam in our work. We feel no need to tell people about Islam', says a man-ager of one of Muslim Aid's projects in Bangladesh, adding with a smile: 'And honestly, how much information do we have about Islam?' There is no mention of mosques, Qur'an schools, or religious doctrines – neither when staff members talk about activities, nor in annual reports or at project sites. At one of Islamic Relief's project sites in Bangladesh, I meet with a group of women, the 'beneficiaries' of the project. In the middle of their weekly meeting with the 'village motivator', all the women are gathered in the village centre – a small square, surrounded by mud huts and palm trees. Here, they learn about topics such as 'group dynamics', 'income gen-eration activities', and 'disaster preparedness', all of them (stereo)typical activities of mainstream aid. 'This way, we try to develop their capacity, so they can join the development mainstream', one staff member explains to me. I ask the women if they talked about Islam at their weekly meetings and they all laugh and shake their heads. 'We talk more about practical things', a woman says. A staff member adds: 'Our main objective is to provide an input to beneficiaries – what they are doing in relation to Allah, to their God, that's their own business'.

In fact, religious activities and development activities are, at least to a certain degree, seen as opposites and the activities of more visibly religious organisations are considered as 'old-fashioned charity' and 'handouts'. 'The classical Muslim way of doing charity is about building a mosque, digging a well, distributing food', one person explains. 'This is fine, it is helpful. But in Islamic Relief, we have decided not to build mosques. We find that funds can be used to something more important such as reducing poverty, building capacity'. 'When we work, we don't go to the Qur'an to see what to do. We work from a development perspective', says a project manager in Muslim Aid, responsible for a health project in Bangladesh. Islam is irrelevant to the installation of water pumps in the villages; to the training of young, unemployed electricians in the slums; and to the running

Table 12.5 Overview of work areas (2011)

Islamic Relief

Activity	Percentage
Protecting life and dignity	47
Providing access to healthcare & water	19
Sustainable livelihoods	14
Caring for orphans and children in need	13
Supporting education	5
Campaigning for change	1
Total	99*

Source: Islamic Relief, Annual Report 2011: 61.

Muslim Aid

Activities	Percentage
Emergency relief	64
Healthcare and nutrition	9
Economic empowerment	7
Education	6
Qurbani/Ramadan	5
Water and sanitation	5
Rainbow family	5
Total	101*

Source: Muslim Aid, Annual Review 2011: np.

* Numbers do not add up to 100 per cent, because they have been rounded up/down.

of health clinics in refugee camps. In fact, it might even be an obstacle to long-term sustainability. As a person from Islamic Relief's office in Jordan says: '[Traditional organisations] spend a lot of money slaughtering sheep for Qurbani and the next day, it's all gone. It doesn't last. They need to think more strategically'.

This does not mean that religion does not play a role at all. 'I would say that our mission is to provide innovative ways of alleviating poverty through Islamic values', says a young development professional at Muslim Aid headquarters. 'We bring something different to the development field'. Other staff members tell me how religion can be a helpful tool in countries such as Bangladesh and Somalia, facilitating communication of development principles to a pious population: 'We tell them, in Islam, education is important', a top manager in Muslim Aid's headquarters says.

'If you don't send your children to school, you are not fulfilling your religious duties'. Another person, also a top manager, but in Islamic Relief's headquarters, says: 'The effect is much stronger if Islamic Relief says the prophet Muhammad encouraged breast feeding than if someone says that professor so and so encourages it'. Likewise, religious structures and leaders can be used to further development projects and ideas. In Muslim Aid, for instance, there are plans to implement a non-formal education programme in Somalia together with the United Nations Children's Fund (UNICEF), and the person responsible for this project tells me that he has suggested that the education be based in local mosques: 'There's no education infrastructure there. So we said, why don't we use the mosques for education? They are only used five times a day for prayer, the rest of the time they are empty. The prophet himself used the mosque as a school.' The current country director of Islamic Relief in Bangladesh is considering a similar idea – training imams in disaster preparedness: 'Because you know, the mosques are the first places people go to when there's a disaster, and the mosque is the first charity to help people', he explains. 'So maybe if we trained the people, we could improve and enhance their capacities to tackle this situation. And working with the mosques, you get access to all locations'.

Conclusions: An Added Value or an Echo of Western Principles and Donor Wishes?

The above analysis has shown that organisations such as Islamic Relief and Muslim Aid are in many ways indistinguishable from mainstream development and humanitarian organisations: they hire the same kinds of staff, target the same kinds of people and implement the same kinds of activities. Thus, the inclusion of these 'new' actors into the field of mainstream humanitarian and development aid does not challenge or renew mainstream aid. Instead, it just leads to more of the same type of aid, carried out by the same types of organisations. This may in part be because Western donors and NGOs choose to include organisations that already look and act like themselves, but it may also be because these organisations, once they are included into the field, start to act and look like Western donors and NGOs, prompted by donor expectations and pressures to conform. In other words, the field of humanitarian and development aid might encourage organisational isomorphism rather than diversity. Reflecting this process of homogenisation, a staff member in Muslim Aid says: '[T] he donor funding is the same, the reporting mechanisms are the same, the places we work are the same, the way we implement projects is the same. So how could there be any differences?' A staff member from Islamic Relief notes: 'In the day-to-day programmes, there is no influence by Islamic principles. There's more of an echo of Western principles and donor wishes'. As such, this analysis hints at the strength and resilience of the institutional logics and governance systems underlying the field mainstream humanitarian and development aid, supporting neo-institutionalist predictions of institutional isomorphism and organisational homogenisation.

A closer look at the aid of Islamic Relief and Muslim Aid, however, reveals cracks in this homogeneous image. Insisting on the relevance of Islam for aid provision, Islamic Relief and Muslim Aid do seem to present an 'added value' to the otherwise secular field of mainstream humanitarian and development aid. Islam influences the work of the two organisations in different ways, whether as source of underlying values and motivation, as a way of gaining access to certain target groups, or as a tool to improve the implementation of aid activities. However, the religiosity they introduce to the field is a kind that does not seriously challenge or alter the field of mainstream aid. The role of religion is first and foremost understood in terms of a sharp distinction between religion and aid, echoing secular principles of mainstream humanitarian and development aid. In this perspective, religion is acceptable as the source of individual values, underlying principles and motivation, but not as public rituals and collective practices influencing the ways in which aid is provided. This conception of religion as almost invisible is reflected in the frequent use of airy terms such as 'Islamic flavour', 'Islamic charitable values' (Islamic Relief, Annual Report and Financial Statements 2008: 5) and 'the humanitarian teachings of Islam' (Muslim Aid, Strategic Framework 2007–2010: 4), denoting an interpretation of Islam as an 'ethical reference' (Benedetti 2006: 855), rather than an orthodox, visible religiosity. Even when religion is part of organisational activities, what is emphasised is not its spiritual value, but structural or institutional aspects, such as access to religious networks and infrastructure, or familiarity with the religious language, based on the argument that these can serve as tools to enhance mainstream aid provision. In other words, the added value of their religious identity lies not in its spiritual contributions but in its contributions to a material humanitarian and development agenda. As such, 'new' actors such as Islamic Relief and Muslim Aid do not substantially change or challenge the institutional logics and governance systems of mainstream humanitarian and development aid, contributing instead to further institutionalising these.

This conception of religious legitimacy resonates well with donor agencies' expectations of FBOs. As noted by James (2009: 5), '[Donors] want to engage with the institutional forms of faith (the religious institution), but remain suspicious about the spiritual dimensions of faith (belief in God)'.[25] But it might be precisely these 'spiritual dimensions' that are important to others, expecting Islamic Relief and Muslim Aid to present a visible, orthodox religiosity that shapes internal organisational practices, defines target groups and profoundly influences activities. As such, the case of Islamic Relief and Muslim Aid directs attention to the fact that organisations are rarely part of just one institutional environment, making processes of institutionalisation less straightforward or unproblematic than some neo-institutionalists may want us to believe. Islamic Relief and Muslim Aid not only have to respond to the expectations of Western donor agencies, but also to those of individual Muslim donors, staff members and recipients of aid, often presenting substantially different expectations to their aid. As was hinted at in the above, many individual donors do not support Islamic Relief and Muslim Aid, because they want to support any development and humanitarian organisation; they want to support a Muslim organisation – and as such, they expect the organisations to focus on what they consider to be 'authentic' Islamic aid, such as the celebration of religious holidays, building of wells and orphan support. Similarly, among the older generations of staff – which still make up a substantial part of the organisations – the increasingly 'secularised' organisational religiosity clashes with many people's more orthodox religiosity. Finally, and perhaps most importantly, a visible, orthodox religiosity might also be what (at least some) recipients expect. Judging from Palmer's (2011) analysis of Islamic Relief's work among Rohingya refugees in Bangladesh, there are indications that the 'secularised' kind of Islam promoted by this organisation, avoiding explicitly religious activities such as mosque building or Qur'an classes, may very well resonate with donor agencies' expectations of a non-confessional, non-discriminatory aid, but not with expectations of Muslims in the refugee camp. According to Palmer (2011: 103), religious leaders in the camp claimed that their religious needs were not being met by Islamic Relief, referring to the lack of key religious facilities, including graveyards, madrasas, and mosques. She quotes a man for saying: 'We want Islamic Relief to establish a mosque inside the camp as we think they are Muslim and they should understand our needs. We can live without food but we can't live without our religion …' (Palmer 2011: 103). Thus, while seeking to adjust their religiosity to Western donor demands in order to present an 'added value' to mainstream humanitarian and development aid, organisations such as Islamic Relief and Muslim Aid might lose the religious legitimacy that is the very foundation for this added value. As such, the analysis of Muslim Aid and Islamic Relief has not only presented a case of organisational homogenisation and institutional isomorphism, but has also shown how such processes of adaptation are not only beneficial for the organisations, but can also prove to be highly risky and problematic, revealing tensions between new and old institutional environments.

Notes

1 Muslim Aid staff member in interview with the author.
2 Naturally, the history of Muslim aid provision to the poor goes much further back than the 1970s, and mechanisms of *zakat* (a religious alms tax) and *waqf* (an endowment for religious or charitable purposes) have historically played an important role in the redistribution of wealth in Muslim societies, just like the concept of *sadaqa* (voluntary charitable giving) has always been central to Islam (see e.g. Singer 2008). Similarly, contemporary Muslim aid is not only provided

by international NGOs but also – and perhaps even more so – by local charities, zakat committees and mosques (e.g. Jawad 2009 or Jung *et al.* 2014).

3 By 'the field of mainstream humanitarian and development aid' I refer to the well-established system of actors, discourses and practices concerned with contemporary international aid provision. This system has grown out of a Western context and is dominated by Western actors (Donini and Minear 2006; Rist 2008). Western states control most money flows, the vast majority of transnational NGOs are from the West and even intergovernmental organisations such as the UN agencies, World Bank and others are arguably dominated by Western actors, with most contributions coming from Western countries. This is not to imply that there are no non-Western actors in the field of development aid, only that Western actors are dominant, numerically as well as economically.

4 Other Muslim NGOs have remained at the periphery of the mainstream humanitarian and development aid system, presenting radically different trajectories than the ones analysed in this chapter. For a case study of two such organisations, see Juul Petersen (2014).

5 Examples of this literature include Burr and Collins (2006) and Levitt (2006). Notable exceptions are Benthall and Bellion-Jourdan (2003), Ghandour (2004), Kaag (2008) and de Cordier (2009). For literature that focuses specifically on Islamic Relief, see Khan (2012), Palmer (2011) and Thaut *et al.* (2012).

6 The analysis of Islamic Relief and Muslim Aid relies on approximately 60 interviews with staff members from the two organisations, in their headquarters in Britain as well as in country offices in Jordan, Lebanon, and Bangladesh; 25 visits to project sites as well collection of organisational material, including annual reports, budgets, website information and PR material. The case studies of the two organisations were part of a larger research project on international Muslim aid organisations. See Juul Petersen (2012a, 2012b, forthcoming).

7 Jama'at-e Islami is a Bangladeshi political party, while the Muslim Brotherhood is a broad, international movement whose members have established political parties in several countries. While consisting in many different fractions, overall these movements are both considered to be relatively conservative in their interpretations of Islam, in particular as regards gender and family values. Both declare themselves to be non-violent but have been accused of connections with violent groups and organisations.

8 For literature on this 'religious turn' in the field of humanitarian and development aid, see e.g. Fountain (2013) or Jones and Juul Petersen (2011).

9 In March 2010, *The Sunday Telegraph* and *The Telegraph* published two articles accusing Muslim Aid of funding organisations that were 'allegedly linked to terrorist groups', one of them (Al Ihsan Charitable Society) an organisation that had been designated by the UK government (Charity Commission 2010:2). These accusations lead to the instigation of a Charitable Commission investigation. The month-long investigation found that Muslim Aid had, prior to the UK government's designation of Al Ihsan Charitable Society in 2005, funded the organisation through its Qurbani programme (approximately US$4,000 in 2002 and US$5,000 in 2003) and had set aside funds for a dentist chair (approximately US$21,500) but had not transferred this money, since Al Ihsan Charitable Society had in the meantime been designated by the government. The Charity Commission concluded that '[w]ithin the scope of this investigation the Commission found no evidence of irregular or improper use of the Charity's funds or any evidence that the Charity had illegally funded any proscribed or designated entities' (Charity Commission 2010: 4).

10 Muslim Aid website, www.muslimaid.org/index.php/media-centre/25th-anniversary/427-messageprime-minister (this and all other websites referenced in the following were accessed 2 March 2014).

11 In 2009, for instance, 10 per cent of Islamic Relief's US$100 million budget came from Middle Eastern donors, with the largest being Sheikh Abdullah Al Nouri Charity, from Kuwait, with a donation of US$4.7 million. More recently, Islamic Relief received a US$5 million donation from the Islamic Development Bank after the Haiti earthquake in 2010. The year before, Muslim Aid was selected as partner in an Islamic Development Bank microfinance project, receiving a US$3 million grant.

12 Information from Islamic Relief, Annual Report 2011, as well as communication with staff.

13 Information from Muslim Aid, Annual Review 2011, as well as communication with staff.

14 Muslim Aid website, www.muslimaid.org/index.php/about-us and Islamic Relief, website, www.islamic-relief.com/Whoweare/Default.aspx?depID=2.

15 Islamic Relief, Annual Report 2006: 2. Likewise, Muslim Aid wants to be 'a key global player' (Muslim Aid, Strategic Framework 2007–2010: 9) and 'achieve international recognition' (ibid.: 13).

16 Interestingly, when the two organisations do engage with other Muslim NGOs, it is often with the explicit goal of professionalising them. For instance, in 2004 Islamic Relief was a founding member of the Humanitarian Forum which, among other things, aims at building capacities among local and international Muslim NGOs. Similarly, the organisation was also a co-founder of Muslim Charities Forum, established in 2007 with the purpose to improve the contributions of UK-based Muslim NGOs to international development. A year before, the Muslim Council of Britain launched its Charitable Foundation Project, funded by Muslim Aid, and aimed at building capacity in Muslim organisations in Britain.

17 For a full account of the partnership, see Clarke (2010).

18 Islamic Relief, website, www.islamic-relief.com/Vacancies/VacanciesDetailsPage. aspx?VacancyID=708.

19 Parallel to the inclusion of more development professionals, both organisations have also started employing more women and more non-Muslims. Today, approximately half of staff is female; with the majority working at either head-quarter level or at project level, and fewer at country office level. In Islamic Relief headquarters, the first non-Muslims were employed in 2005 or 2006, and today, there are approximately 15 non-Muslims, making up a bit more than ten per cent of staff. In country offices, an increasing number of staff members are also non-Muslim. In Islamic Relief Bangladesh, for instance, quite a few staff members are Hindu. However, the organisation has not succeeded in employing any Christians. 'We would like to, but they haven't applied', says a staff member. In Muslim Aid, the pattern is similar.

20 Muslim Aid website, www.muslimaid.org/index.php/about-us/jobs/1174-protection-expert-bangladesh.

21 This number may be higher among donors from the Middle East. In an interview with Khan, a regional fundraiser notes that 'most of the donors I deal with believe that *zakat* donations are restricted to Muslims, in fact if we used *zakat* donations to assist non-Muslims then they would cease giving to the organisation altogether' (Khan 2012: 98, emphasis in the original).

22 Muslim Aid website, www.muslimaid.org/index.php/about-us/faqs.

23 Muslim Aid website, www.muslimaid.org/index.php/about-us.

24 Islamic Relief website, www.islamic-relief.org.uk/about-us.

25 This process of secularisation concurrent with increased funding from development agencies has been noted by other researchers. Both Ebaugh *et al.* (2006: 2269) and Smith and Sosin (2001: 654) find a negative correlation between religiosity and institutional funding, concluding that activities are fundamentally altered in a secular direction when NGOs obtain institutional funding.

References

Abuarqab, M. (2010) 'Islamic Relief: Faith and Identity in Practice', *ONTRAC, The newsletter of INTRAC*, 46:7.

Benedetti, C. (2006) 'Islamic and Christian Inspired Relief NGOs: Between Tactical Collaboration and Strategic Diffidence', *Journal of International Development*, 18(6):849–859.

Benthall, J. (2008a) *The Palestinian Zakat Committees 1993–2007 and Their Contested Interpretations*, PSIO Occasional Paper, Geneva: Graduate Institute of International and Development Studies.

Benthall, J. (2008b) Have Islamic Charities a Privileged Relationship in Majority Muslim Societies? The Case of Post-Tsunami Reconstruction in Aceh (http://jha.ac/2008/06/26/have-islamic-aid-agencies-a-privileged-relationship-in-majority-muslim-areas-the-case-of-post-tsunami-reconstruction-in-aceh) accessed 17 November 2010.

Benthall, J. and Bellion-Jourdan, J. (2003) *The Charitable Crescent. The Politics of Aid in the Muslim World*, London: I.B. Tauris.

Burr, J.M. and Collins, R.O. (2006) *Alms for Jihad: Charity and Terrorism in the Islamic World*, Cambridge: Cambridge University Press.

Charity Commission (2010) *Regulatory Case Report, Muslim Aid*, London: Charity Commission (www.charitycommission.gov.uk/Our_regulatory_activity/Compliance_reports/RC_reports/rcr_muslim_aid.aspx) accessed 25 March 2011.

Clarke, G. (2007) 'Agents of Transformation? Donors, Faith-Based Organisations and International Development', *Third World Quarterly*, 28(1):77–96.

Clarke, G. (2010) 'Trans-Faith Humanitarian Partnerships: The Case of Muslim Aid and the United Methodist Committee on Relief', *European Journal of Development Research*, 22(4):510–528.

de Cordier, B. (2009) 'Faith-Based Aid, Globalisation and the Humanitarian Frontline: An Analysis of Western-Based Muslim Aid Organisations', *Disasters* 33(4):608–628.

DiMaggio, P.J. and Powell, W. (1983) 'The Iron Cage Revisited "Institutional Isomorphism and Collective Rationality in Organizational Fields"', *American Sociological Review*, 48(2):147–160.

Donini, A. and Minear, L. (2006) *The Humanitarian Agenda 2015: Principles, Power and Perceptions*, Medford: Feinstein International Center.

Ebaugh, H.R.F., Chafetz, J.S. and Pipes, P.F. (2006) 'Where's the Faith in Faith-based Organizations? Measures and Correlates of Religiosity in Faith-based Social Service Coalitions', *Social Forces* 84(4):2259–2272.

Fountain, P. (2013) 'The Myth of Religious NGOs: Development Studies and the Return of Religion', *International Development Policy: Religion and Development*, 4:9–30.

Ghandour, A.R. (2004) 'The Modern Missionaries of Islam', in F. Weissman (ed.) *In the Shadow of 'Just Wars': Violence, Politics, and Humanitarian Action*, New York: Cornell University Press.

Howell, J. and Lind, J. (2009) *Counter-Terrorism, Aid and Civil Society: Before and After the War on Terror*, Basingstoke: Palgrave Macmillan.

Islamic Relief, Annual Report 2006 (www.islamic-relief.com/WhoWeAre/Files/ANNUAL%20REPORT%202006%20-%20WEB_2qr034br.wdq.pdf) accessed 2 March 2014.

Islamic Relief, Annual Report 2011 (www.islamic-relief.org.uk/content/uploads/2013/05/Annual_Report_2011.pdf) accessed 2 March 2014.

Islamic Relief, Annual Report and Financial Statements 2008 (www.islamic-relief.com/WhoWeAre/Files/Annual%20Report%20and%20Financial%20Statements%202008.pdf) accessed 2 March 2014.

Islamic Relief, Strategy 2007–2009 (www.islamic-relief.com/WhoWeAre/Files/Islamic%20Relief%20Strategy%202007-2009_2emftn13.ajh.pdf)   accessed 2 March 2014.

Islamic Relief, PPA Self-Assessment Review, Reporting Year 2008/2009 (www.dfid.gov.uk/Documents/ppas/200809selfassessrevs/self-assess-rev-isl-rel-wdwde.pdf) accessed 2 March 2014.

James, R. (2009) *What is Distinctive about FBOs? How European FBOs Define and Operationalise Their Faith*, Praxis Paper, Oxford: INTRAC.

Jawad, R. (2009) *Social Welfare and Religion in the Middle East: A Lebanese Perspective*, Bristol: The Policy Press.

Jones, B. and Juul Petersen, M. (2011) 'Instrumentalist, Narrow, Normative? Reviewing Recent Work on Religion and Development', *Third World Quarterly*, 32(7):1291–1306.

Jung, D., Juul Petersen, M. and Sparre, S.L. (2014) *Politics of Modern Muslim Subjectivities. Islam, Youth and Social Activism in the Middle East*, New York: Palgrave Macmillan.

Juul Petersen, M. (2012a) 'Islamizing Aid: Transnational Muslim NGOs After 9.11.', *Voluntas*, 23(1):126–155.

Juul Petersen, M. (2012b) 'Trajectories of Transnational Muslim NGOs', *Development in Practice*, 22(5–6):763–778.

Juul Petersen, M. (2014) 'Sacralized or Secularized aid? Positioning Gulf-Based Muslim Charities', in J. Benthall and R. Lacey (eds) *Gulf Charities in the 'War on Terror' – and Beyond*, Berlin: Gerlach Press, 25–52.

Juul Petersen, M. (forthcoming) *For Humanity or for the Umma? Aid and Islam in Transnational Muslim NGOs*, London: Hurst.

Kaag, M. (2008) 'Transnational Islamic NGOs in Chad: Islamic Solidarity in the Age of Neoliberalism', *Africa Today*, 54(3):3–18.

Khan, A.A. (2012) 'Religious Obligations or Altruistic Giving? Muslims and Charitable Donations', in M. Barnett and J. Stein (eds) *Sacred Aid. Faith and Humanitarianism*, Oxford and New York: Oxford University Press, 90–114.

Levitt, M. (2006) *Hamas: Politics, Charity and Terrorism in the Service of Jihad*, New Haven: Yale University Press.

Meyer, J.W. and Rowan, B. (1991) 'Institutionalized Organizations: Formal Structures, Myth and Ceremony', in W. Powell and P. DiMaggio (eds) *The New Institutionalism in Organizational Analysis*, London: University of Chicago Press, 337–360.

Muslim Aid, Annual Review 2000 (www.muslimaid.org/images/stories/pdfs/annualreview2000.pdf) accessed 2 March 2014.

Muslim Aid, Annual Review 2011 (www.muslimaid.org/index.php/media-centre/publications) accessed 2 March 2014.

Muslim Aid, Strategic Framework 2007–2010 (www.muslimaid.org/images/stories/pdfs/strategic_framework_2007_2010_final.pdf) accessed 2 March 2014.

Muslim Aid, Trustees' Report and Financial Statements 2007 (no longer available online).

Muslim Aid, Trustees' Report and Financial Statements 2008 (file:///Users/mariejuulpetersen/Downloads/1-05-14_20-16-18_financial_summary_2008%20(1).pdf) accessed 2 March 2014.

Palmer, V. (2011) 'Analysing Cultural Proximity: Islamic Relief Worldwide and Rohingya Refugees in Bangladesh', *Development in Practice*, 21(1):96–108.

Rist, G. (2008) *The History of Development: From Western Origins to Global Faith*, London: Zed.

Rosenow-Williams, K. and Sezgin, Z. (2014) 'Islamic Migrant Organizations: Little-Studied Actors in Humanitarian Action', *International Migration Review*, 48(2):1–30.

Salih, M.M.A. (2002) Islamic NGOs in Africa: The Promise and Peril of Islamic Voluntarism, *Occasional Paper*, Copenhagen: Centre of African Studies, University of Copenhagen.

Scott, R.W. (2001) *Institutions and Organizations*, Thousand Oaks, CA: SAGE.

Singer, A. (2008) *Charity in Islamic Societies*, Cambridge: Cambridge University Press.

Smith, S.R. and Sosin, M. (2001) 'The Varieties of Faith-Related Agencies', *Public Administration Review*, 61(6):651–670.

Thaut, L., Michael B. and Gross Stein, J. (2012) 'In Defense of Virtue, Credibility, Legitimacy Dilemmas, and the Case of Islamic Relief', in P. Gourevitch, D. Lake and J. Gross Stein (eds) *The Credibility of Transnational NGOs: When Virtue is Not Enough*, Cambridge: Cambridge Universiy Press, 137–164.

Wilson, B. (1992) *Religion in Sociological Perspective*, Oxford: Oxford University Press.

Yaylaci, I. (2008) Communitarian Humanitarianism. The Politics of Islamic Humanitarian Organisations (www.hhh.umn.edu/humanitarianisms/presentations/Yaylaci-Communitarian%20Humanitarianism.pdf) accessed 15 May 2011.

13 Writing the Other into Humanitarianism

A Conversation between 'South–South' and 'Faith-Based' Humanitarianisms

Elena Fiddian-Qasmiyeh and Julia Pacitto[1]

Introduction

Since the 2000s, numerous academics have examined the evolution and nature of humanitarianism, typically tracing its origins to the Enlightenment period, to the role of Christian actors throughout Europe's imperial projects (Stamatov 2013: 1–2) and more specifically to the activities of Northern religious groups in the early nineteenth century (Barnett and Weiss 2011; Wilson and Brown 2011). Many such studies note that 'Although the idea of saving lives and relieving suffering is hardly a Western or Christian creation, modern humanitarianism's origins are located in Western history and Christian thought' (Barnett and Weiss 2008: 7). While repeatedly asserting modern humanitarianism's Northern and Christian origins, authors such as Barnett (2011: 15) have at times admitted that despite entitling his book *Empire of Humanity: A History of Humanitarianism* the reader should note that 'Western bias is ahead. This is not a book on the history of all forms of humanitarianism around the world'. Rather than remedying this bias by integrating a nuanced analysis of 'Other' forms of humanitarianism, including a critique of mechanisms through which the history of non-Northern, and indeed non-Christian, humanitarianism(s) has been 'erased' from or 'footnoted' in the hegemonic 'archive of knowledge' (following Derrida and Foucault respectively), the Northern academy as a whole has continued to reproduce this primary focus on Northern-led humanitarianism.

Although religion has long inspired individual and communal responses to the needs and rights of members of their own and other communities, since the late-nineteenth century the humanitarian regime has increasingly been articulated in secular terms (Ager and Ager 2011). In particular, the birth of the professionalised aid industry in the post-Second World War era witnessed the entrenchment of three key assumptions by Northern social scientists, policymakers and practitioners alike:

1   societies would become increasingly secular as socio-economic development took place;

2   secular approaches would invariably offer the strongest means to
     secure peace and stability, democratic political structures, and good
     governance; and
3   religious identity and structures would continue to be foundational
     causes for oppression, conflict and persecution (Fiddian-Qasmiyeh
     2015c).

In spite of secularisation theories being discredited in the 1990s and
2000s and the recognition that we live in a 'post-secular' age in which
religious belief and practice are becoming *more*, rather than *less*, important for individuals and communities around the world, the privileging
of the ostensibly 'secular' principles of Western humanitarianism in both
policy and academia has nonetheless prevailed (Ager and Ager 2011).
Concurrently, contemporary faith-based humanitarianism has often been
constituted as an anomaly and/or potential threat, with the motivations
and aims of such actors viewed with suspicion, and their activities often
denominated as 'political' and 'ideological' rather than motivated by
'humanitarian' principles (Pantuliano *et al.* 2011). In particular, Islamic
faith-based humanitarianism has been subjected to extensive academic,
policy and media scrutiny post-9/11, with state and civil-society responses
inspired by Islam frequently analysed via securitisation frameworks (ibid.;
Guinane 2006).[2] Such work has often either applied, or critiqued, the
securitisation of Islam in these contexts, thereby reproducing *securitisation*
as the primary referent in their analyses.

By exploring faith-based humanitarianism through the lens of emerging
debates surrounding South–South humanitarianism (Pacitto and Fiddian-
Qasmiyeh 2013), we purposefully 'footnote' the securitisation referent
in order to affirm the value of what we refer to as 'writing the "Other"
into humanitarian discourse', and to redress the biases inherent to much
humanitarian studies theory. Although Southern-led development initiatives have enjoyed increasing attention by academics (e.g. Woods 2008;
Mawdsley 2012), and most now recognise the existence of a multitude of
humanitarianisms, including 'humanitarianisms of Europe, of Africa, of
the global, and of the local' (Kennedy 2004: xv), humanitarian action not
borne of the Northern-dominated and highly institutionalised international humanitarian regime has remained largely neglected in academia.

Drawing on examples of Southern[3] faith-based actors' responses to recent
and ongoing processes of displacement, including case studies of Myanmar
and Syria, we address these gaps in knowledge and re-engage with popular debates around religion/secularism, politics and humanitarianism. We
argue, in line with constructivist theory, that ideology and politics pervade
not just humanitarian practice, but the 'humanitarian' epithet itself, and
it is this politics that has for so long footnoted the Other in the study of
humanitarianism. Through these case studies, we demonstrate the significance of current faith-based responses to complex emergencies, arguing

that ignoring or a priori demonising these as a result of the abovementioned bias undermines the ability for policymakers or academics to develop rigorous understandings of, and appropriate responses to, displacement.

Further, we engage with the notions of solidarity that resonate throughout the case studies presented, including those expressed between co-religionists and organisation members of different faiths (or none), to argue in favour of incorporating these multiple and overlapping solidarities in Humanitarian Studies. This incorporation does not reject the existence or legitimacy of notions of global citizenship that inform some humanitarian action. However, by considering how global society is only one of a myriad of potential spheres of solidarity held by individuals and communities, it rejects the contention that this is the *only* legitimate form of humanitarianism, advocating for more academic inquiry into the humanitarianisms of the global South.

Humanitarianism Defined

For many, the International Committee of the Red Cross's (ICRC) definition of humanitarianism is *the* definitive standard (Barnett and Weiss 2011: 9). Ferris, for example, argues that the seven organising principles established by the Red Cross/Red Crescent movement have become fundamental to the humanitarian movement. She asserts that four of these principles have become hallmarks of humanitarian action 'throughout the international community': humanity, impartiality, neutrality and independence (Ferris 2011: 11).

The perspective of humanitarianism borne out of these principles is 'that politics is a moral pollutant' (Barnett and Weiss 2008: 4). This strict dichotomy between morality and politics is robustly posited by the ICRC and other international organisations, and is considered to be central to these organisations' credibility, and thus to their ability to function on the ground in often highly politicised conflict environments. Many observers, however, critique the assertion that humanitarian agencies can be apolitical (ibid.: 4) and suggest that the idea of being able to situate oneself outside of politics is an exercise in self-deception (Rieff 2002: 75).

Egeland (2011: xviii) describes humanitarianism as 'a universal imperative and shared intercultural system of principles' before conceding that the regime has become so deeply influenced by the North in terms of funding, staffing, structure, and political profile that it is under threat of enduring opposition in many Southern contexts. Humanitarian agencies, in these settings, are often viewed as agents of Northern domination, or as proponents of Christian evangelicalism or post-Christian godlessness (Benthall and Bellion-Jourdan 2003: 4; Fiddian-Qasmiyeh and Ager 2013): 'The Red Cross's principle of "universality" is sometimes impugned as a veil for neo-colonial power and a prolongation of religious missionary activity in a new form' (Bitter 1994: 100–101, cited in Benthall and Bellion-Jourdan

2003: 58). Indeed the idea of Northern-dominated humanitarianism as a contemporary manifestation of colonial (including missionary-cum-colonial) imperatives is one of the main critiques put to the international humanitarian regime (Fiddian-Qasmiyeh 2015c). As noted by Chimni (2000: 3), '"humanitarianism" is *the* ideology of hegemonic states in the era of globalisation'.

Despite widely differing in their positions, both a strict adherence to the Northern institutional model and the countervailing post-colonial critique of the Northern system ultimately have the same effect of obscuring other emerging forms of humanitarianism. It is only recently that academics and policymakers in the humanitarian field have paid attention to the rise of 'new' or 'non-traditional' humanitarian actors with roots in the global South (Davey 2012: 1).[4] As a whole, this attention has primarily focused on the financial contributions of *high*-GDP Southern donor *states* which are not members of the Organisation for Economic Co-operation and Development's (OECD) Development Assistance Committee (DAC), while major lacunae remain regarding the plurality of humanitarian responses developed by low- and medium-GDP states, including but not restricted to financial transfers and material donations. Furthermore, although commentators have recognised the increasing contribution of NGOs and civil-society movements from the global South (Egeland 2011: xxi), human-itarian responses initiated by these civil-society networks and displaced populations themselves have largely remained unexplored, including those responses inspired by principles of faith. South–South responses to forced displacement therefore provide an excellent opportunity to substantiate Barnett's contention that: 'We live in a world of humanitarianisms, not humanitarianism' (2011: 10).

Humanitarianism Deconstructed: A Critical Approach to the 'Humanitarian' Label

Although acknowledgement of the significant role of 'new' donors and NGOs in the humanitarian enterprise is widespread, the fear endures that '"non-Western" groups may not subscribe to the principles underpinning the formal system, and may have a misguided understanding of what it is to be "humanitarian"' (Davey 2012: 2; Ferris 2011; Fiddian-Qasmiyeh 2015a). Within this view, there is no attempt to consider the historical basis upon which the humanitarian label is founded or the extent to which formalised understandings of what constitutes 'humanitarian' responses are embedded within Northern practices and systems of knowledge. Slim's analysis of the oligopoly held by NGO humanitarians over the concept of humanitarian action as 'something they want everyone to value and enjoy but which only they are allowed to do' (Slim 2003, cited in Barnett and Weiss 2011: 14), and Haysom's critique of the predominance of what she refers to as the Northern 'relief elite' (cited in Pacitto 2012), are pertinent in this regard.

A prime opportunity thus emerges to problematise Northern appropriations of the humanitarian label, and to enrich and expand popular understandings of the concept. On the one hand, the analytical integrity of an expanded use of the 'humanitarian' label may itself be critiqued; the term was birthed in the European Enlightenment period and is deeply embedded within the philosophical developments of this period, namely with the cosmopolitan principle of a shared 'humanity' irrespective of social, religious and cultural characteristics. As such, trying to incorporate pluralist expressions of compassion into this term may remain open to contention. Indeed, humanitarian action is 'quintessentially cosmopolitan' as it represents an effort to relieve the suffering of strangers (Calhoun 2008: 73). However, multilingual analyses tracing the origins and evolving usages of equivalent constructs used in languages such as Arabic and Chinese demonstrate the heterogeneous historical and etymological roots of the term 'humanitarianism' around the world, thereby critiquing the assumption that 'the term' humanitarian originates from the Enlightenment period (e.g. Davies 2012). A multilingual, cross-cultural approach therefore highlights that although 'the term' may have become part of the 'archive of knowledge' produced and reproduced in a particular hegemonic region and an interconnected set of European languages, alternative labels and concepts have existed and evolved across time and space. Rather than reproducing the assumption that 'humanitarianism' as a term originated in the Enlightenment, it becomes necessary to trace how and why this Northern appropriation of the term 'humanitarianism' has come to be taken for granted and institutionalised in contemporary systems of knowledge and practice.[5]

In addition, the dominant theory on the concept of cosmopolitanism itself, most commonly associated with the Stoics, Pauline Christianity and Enlightenment thinkers like Immanuel Kant (Vaughan-Williams 2007: 107), remains embedded within an explicitly Northern religious and philosophical lineage. In an earlier publication, Calhoun (2002: 871) offers a critique of the way in which the political theory of cosmopolitanism is 'left lacking a strong account of solidarity' which he attributes to the liberal opposition to communitarianism. He concedes that this conception of cosmopolitanism is deeply embedded within a Northern view of the world (ibid.: 873) and advocates rather a cosmopolitan conception of citizenship as multiple and layered, encompassing an array of complex connections. While this argument in no way requires an acceptance of illiberal nationalisms or religious 'fundamentalisms', it finds merit in the idea that both of these forms of community, and indeed many others, are not just foundations upon which xenophobia and persecution are bred, but can also be sources of solidarity and care for strangers (ibid.: 893). This idea is significant when considering responses to displacement emanating from sources that do not necessarily share the Northern liberal tradition, and thus may not conform to the 'humanitarian' principles based upon this tradition.

Critical scholarship from the global South around liberalism and human rights also aids us in advocating for an alternative reading of cosmopolitanism that is sensitive to the different levels at which people experience community. Parekh (1992: 162) offers an important critique of Northern assumptions of the universality of liberal individualism, asserting that liberalism 'abstracts the person from all his or her "contingent" and "external" relations', while simultaneously accepting that certain human rights enjoy a broad cross-cultural consensus. Post-development theorists Esteva and Prakash (1997) engage with Rene Dubos's famous slogan, 'think globally, act locally' to argue that the slogan rejects the illusion of partaking in global action and emphasises the importance of local action. They simultaneously advocate for a transformation of Dubos's slogan, and the substitution of 'global thinking' with 'local thinking'. In challenging the notion of the universality of human rights, a genre closely interlinked with humanitarianism, they highlight that many ordinary people and radical thinkers reject this global vision of rights as an imposition of the specific interests and vision of the West (ibid.: 285). This imposition of an individualistic system of rights, according to Esteva and Prakash, echoing Parekh's argument, threatens to 'dissolv[e] the very foundations of cultures which are organised around the notions of communal obligations, commitment and service' (ibid.: 282).

Writing the 'Other' into Humanitarian Discourse

Recognising the insights emerging from diverse systems of knowledge across both the global North and global South, therefore prompts us to engage with the multiple and overlapping ways in which individuals experience community and communal obligation. We argue that to engage with South–South humanitarian responses in all their diversity is to attempt to move beyond the assumption (see Agier 2010: 29) that the only conceivable form of humanitarian action is that which serves the neo-imperial politics of the 'empire' as part of a global network of control and domination of the South. This has the result of recognising Southern actors' agency and capacity for agency and thus has the potential to challenge and enrich critical interpretations of humanitarian action, which, despite their critical nature, remain focused on the Northern system. This is not to ignore the importance of global processes in shaping the local, but to assert that a more comprehensive engagement with the 'local', including local faith communities, is essential in order to begin to address the Northern biases inherent to academic theorisations of humanitarianism.

In line with the constructivist approach in this volume, as well as advocating for increased focus on local efforts, we must seek to understand the diverse relationships which exist between Southern actors and the broader organisational environment in which they are situated. Indeed, South–South humanitarian initiatives are often situated within a highly complex web of humanitarian action, and many humanitarian actors originating from the global South have strong links with the formalised institutional regime (Davey 2012: 1). Reports identify some 2,800 national NGOs working in collaboration with one or more of the institutions that make up the formal international humanitarian system through partnership agreements (ALNAP 2012, in Davey 2012: 1). This arguably poses methodological and analytical challenges when examining local initiatives without an understanding of how global processes affect local responses. The interconnection of such organisations further problematises the idea of 'South–South' assistance and highlights the often blurred lines between what constitutes 'Southern' and 'Northern' assistance. One such example of this relates to networks of faith-based organisations (FBOs), which as Ferris asserts, 'are unique players in the international humanitarian community in that they are rooted in their local communities and yet have global reach' (Ferris 2005: 325). These interconnections must be considered when assessing the extent to which South–South humanitarian initiatives challenge, or complement, Northern-led humanitarianism. In response to the theoretical arguments outlined above, the remainder of the chapter explores specific faith-based initiatives as modes of South–South humanitarian responses to forced displacement.

Defining Southern (and/or 'Local') Faith-Based Humanitarian Actors

Southern NGO and civil-society efforts have been prominent in the promotion of humanitarian protection for displaced populations, and have included both secular and faith-based initiatives (Fiddian-Qasmiyeh and Ager 2013). The emphasis that such institutions and networks place on providing material assistance *and* spiritual support as part of a holistic service to refugee communities gives pertinence to arguments that local faith communities (LFCs) and FBOs can play an important role as sources of social and spiritual capital for displaced groups (ibid.). Although many actors remain unwilling to use the 'humanitarian' label to describe faith-based initiatives, it is increasingly recognised that LFCs and FBOs are important in this respect (Stawski 2012). Further, faith communities are a significant presence at the front line of many humanitarian situations, and faith-based institutions and organisations, because of their rootedness within local landscapes, often have privileged access to even the most marginalised communities. Unlike more temporary and transient non-local assistance, LFCs and FBOs are also often fixed presences that have intimate connections with the communities they serve, and thus hold the capacity to develop medium- and long-term programmes to implement durable solutions (Fiddian-Qasmiyeh and Ager 2013; Pacitto 2012). Indeed, the potential for communities of faith and FBOs to support displaced persons is increasingly being recognised; for instance, the 2012 United Nations High Commissioner's Dialogue examined the role of faith in protecting forced migrants, and in 2013 the UN High Commissioner for Refugees (UNHCR) launched a 'Welcoming the Stranger' initiative (UNHCR 2014).[6]

Stawski (2012) concedes that there are contexts in which the 'truth claims' of religions are presented in a discriminatory manner towards vulnerable groups and 'other' faith communities, and the potential negative impact of this should not be taken lightly. The fear of proselytisation and the possible relationship between religion and faith on the one hand, and power and control on the other, remain significant issues that must be addressed in engaging with faith-based and faith-inspired organisations, be they (as explored below) regional and international organisations such as the Organisation of the Islamic Conference, local community groups like those found in Amman, or evangelical humanitarian-relief providers like Karen refugees on the Thailand–Myanmar border. Hence, 'alternative' humanitarian perspectives should not be idealised. Rather, they must themselves be critically assessed and their power dynamics must be examined.

Faith-Based Humanitarianisms: Regional and International Mechanisms

The Organisation of Islamic Cooperation (OIC), an intergovernmental organisation with 57 member states across four continents, has a specialised institution, the Islamic Committee for the International Crescent, which was established in 1977 and is mandated to '[help] alleviate the sufferings causes by natural disaster and war' in particular through the provision of medical assistance. Since 2008, the OIC has had its own humanitarian-affairs department, which both implements humanitarian aid on behalf of the OIC in different countries and engages in policymaking and dialogue facilitation, for instance among humanitarian NGOs in OIC member states (Binder *et al.* 2010).

At the end of 2011, the OIC contributed to the humanitarian efforts following Tropical Storm Washi in the Philippines (OIC 2011), a disaster that resulted in the displacement of 285,000 people (NRC/IDMC 2011). The OIC has also been approved access by the government of Myanmar to provide 'necessary assistance' to the displaced and persecuted Rohingya Muslim minority (OIC 2012), in a country where Northern NGOs and UN agencies have often been denied access, largely as a result of the tense relationship between Myanmar and many Northern states for almost 20 years (Pacitto and Fiddian-Qasmiyeh 2013). In the aftermath of cyclone Nargis in 2008, international humanitarian actors were prevented from accessing Myanmar, while local faith communities, monasteries and churches delivered emergency supplies, and aid organisations already operating in the affected regions collected information on the damage and the needs of those affected. The task fell to the regional organisation, the Association of Southeast Asian Nations (ASEAN), to convince Myanmar, one of its member states, to provide access for humanitarian relief efforts. Despite initial resistance to foreign involvement, Myanmar agreed on an ASEAN-led mechanism upon assurances that assistance provided through ASEAN would not be 'politicised' (Marr 2010; Fan, this volume).

These events are a clear example of an instance in which Northern humanitarian organisations, despite their purportedly 'apolitical' and 'neutral' character, are not perceived as such by other actors. The OIC's and the ASEAN's success in negotiating and reaching an agreement with the government of Myanmar demonstrates the privileged position that Southern actors may hold in certain geopolitical contexts. These examples resonate with Six's research (2009) on Southern development actors and their capacity to hold a distinct place in the global landscape. In an era where rhetoric around 'shrinking humanitarian space' is ever-present, the 'privileged access' afforded to certain Southern organisations demands further inquiry.

The OIC also coordinates with, rather than explicitly competes against, the UN. However, the OIC has simultaneously presented itself in a way that rejects principles that have been enshrined within the Northern regime. One example is the Cairo Declaration on Human Rights – originally drafted in 1990 – which attempted to establish a set of human rights compatible with the teachings of Islam, and specifically with Shari'ah Law (Kayaoğlu 2012). Although references to the Cairo Declaration were removed from the 2008 revised Charter of the Organisation of Islamic Cooperation, elements within the Charter continue to demonstrate the distinct character and values of the community that it purports to represent. For example, the Charter calls for member states to reaffirm support for the rights of *peoples*, as stipulated in the UN Charter, thereby clearly placing an emphasis on communal, rather than individual rights. The idea that human rights represent a specific, Northern vision of the world that does not necessarily reflect the prevailing values of Southern cultural communities, as noted by Esteva and Prakash (1997: 278), gains pertinence when we see it manifest itself in the principles that underpin Southern institutions such as the OIC.

Another stipulation of the Charter is 'to enhance and strengthen the bond of unity and solidarity among the Muslim peoples and Member States.' As Davey (2012: 4) argues, 'for some Islamic organisations, humanitarian action is an expression of solidarity with other Muslims and is part of a broader effort to defend the Islamic community (*ummah*) from outside threats'. Benthall and Bellion-Jourdan (2003) discuss the Islamic charitable tradition of *zakat*, stating that it is often understood that the recipients of *zakat* must be Muslims. Although this proposition is frequently rebutted and other interpretations extend the concept to encompass non-Muslim poor, the stated foundations for partialist assistance in the Islamic tradition exposes the non-universal nature of what is seen to be one of the core principles of humanitarianism. Here, notions of 'solidarity' and 'community' correspond with a particular religious identity (in this case, Islam), although these concepts can be manifested in different forms and on a variety of scales across different faiths.

Southern State and Civil-Society Responses to Syrian Refugees' Displacement

The popular uprisings that swept across North Africa and the Middle East from the end of 2010 were characterised by significant upheavals, including major episodes of displacement. In particular, the ongoing conflict in Syria has been described by the High Commissioner for Refugees, Antonio Guterres, as 'the most dramatic humanitarian crisis that we have ever faced' (Chulov 2013), with over 4 million refugees having fled Syria to neighbouring countries and North Africa by May 2015.[7] The significant role played by Southern actors at a multitude of levels has been one of the key features of the response to this forced migration. Some of these initiatives have adopted the 'apolitical' and secular identity of formal international humanitarian organisations, while others, including groups affiliated with the opposition Muslim Brotherhood in Syria, retain a highly politicised character, and/or identify themselves as being motivated by faith. Indeed, notions of solidarity and brotherhood have been a distinctive feature to some aspects of the relief efforts in the region.[8]

In 2012 alone, the Arab League pledged US$100m in aid to Syrian refugees (Gulf Times 2012), and Arab states' responses have ranged from reports of the Moroccan government sending aid convoys comprising the resources for a field hospital in Jordan (Aujourd'hui Le Maroc 2012) to the Qatar Charity providing food and non-food aid and medical assistance both in Lebanese border areas and in Jordan, as well as assisting with rent and health services in Jordan (Gulf Times 2012). On a national level, the Jordan Hashemite Charity Organization (JHCO) was charged by the Jordanian government to coordinate the aid response to Syrian refugees (IRIN 2012); the JHCO established Za'atari refugee camp, delivering aid and overseeing partnerships with major UN agencies including the United Nations Children's Fund (UNICEF), the Office for the Coordination of Humanitarian Affairs (OCHA), UNHCR and the World Food Programme (WFP), and with a range of Islamic and Christian FBOs including Islamic Relief, Latter Day Saints, and the Lutheran World Federation.[9]

Importantly, although the English version[10] of the JHCO's website makes no reference to Islam, the Arabic version[11] notes that the organisation was established in 'The Arab and *Islamic* world' in 1990 and that the JHCO supports projects which 'deepen the concepts of justice and equality at the national, Arab, *Islamic* and international levels' (Fiddian-Qasmiyeh's translation, emphasis added). The erasure of the Islamic referent in the English language version of the official JHCO website[12] is particularly relevant in light of the above-mentioned securitisation frameworks that have typically been applied in analyses of Islamic faith-based humanitarianism. Publicly distancing itself from the Islamic referent, in addition to stressing its roles in providing assistance and establishing partnerships 'regardless of their religion, origin or creed'[13] are all means of asserting the JHCO's official commitment to internationally recognised humanitarian principles, and can be seen as supporting the organisation's broader declarations that it is 'making great strides to becoming an *international* humanitarian organisation' (emphasis added).[14]

In spite of the central role officially played by JHCO, the Integrated Regional Information Networks (IRIN) have reported that it is arguably civil-society groups that have played the largest role in responding to the refugee influx. In addition to the pre-existing Syrian community in Jordan providing significant support, some Jordanian landlords have also allowed Syrian refugees to stay free of charge (IRIN 2012). Furthermore, faith-based Muslim organisations are playing a key role in Jordan; these include the Syrian Women's Organization – established in 2006 by the children of Syrians who had fled the repression of the Muslim Brotherhood's revolt in 1982 – which has registered and provided essential supplies to new arrivals in Amman, and the Islamic Charity Centre Society – also reported to be linked with the Muslim Brotherhood – which has registered refugees and distributed aid in the border regions (ibid.). According to RFI, reporting from the Jordanian town of Mafraq, aid has been coordinated via the JHCO civil-society umbrella group, and distributed to refugees in Mafraq via three organisations; Latine, Al Kitab wal Sunnah and Merkez Islami, the latter of which is connected to the opposition Muslim Brotherhood (Michaelson 2012).[15]

These examples of regional, state, NGO and civil-society responses to the mass displacements across the Middle East and North Africa highlight the need to critically assess the historical and cultural context of humanitarian responses by state and non-state actors alike. This includes recognition of the influence of Islamic traditions of asylum, protection and charity, which are by now well documented (Türk 2008; Fiddian-Qasmiyeh 2011a; Guterres 2012). For instance, a number of relevant concepts and mechanisms of protection (including *jiwār* – offering protection – and *amān* – the provision of safe conduct) are central to Islam and oblige Muslims to offer assistance and safety to Muslim and non-Muslim displaced persons alike. While not part of the international institutionalised humanitarian system, Muslim state and non-state actors have historically responded to forced migration in a multiplicity of ways, highlighting the partiality of the above-mentioned classification of 'traditional' and 'non-traditional' humanitarian donors.

Indeed, an extensive body of literature explores faith-based *state* responses to displacement, including in particular a plethora of studies of Gulf state-led Islamic Faith Based Humanitarianism post-9/11 (Benthall and Bellion-Jourdan 2003; Barakat and Zyck 2010), increasingly being complemented by the recognition that 'the protection of both migrants and refugees have been universally and unequivocally regarded as moral and legal obligations, *not only by states and governments, but also by individuals and civil society*' (Abd al-Rahim 2008: 15, emphasis added). As reflected in the role played by the Syrian Women's Organization and as discussed further in the case study from the Thai-Myanmar border, the individuals who are inspired by their faith to provide protection and assistance to displaced populations are often themselves refugees.

Humanitarian Refugees: Views from the Thailand–Myanmar Border and Beyond

In the protracted Myanmar refugee situation, with over 100,000 refugees living in refugee camps and settlements along the Thailand–Myanmar border since the 1980s, an extensive range of services, welfare and relief is provided by Karen Christian refugees on both sides of the border. In addition to providing assistance to refugees in the camps, Karen refugees frequently re-enter Myanmar's border zone as 'soldiers–medics–missionaries' (Horstmann 2011), accessing an area known to be largely inaccessible to international humanitarian NGOs. This multifaceted project of evangelisation, assistance and reconstruction is 'fuelled by global alliances with American Christian churches (Wuthnow 2009), South Korean Pentecostals, and international advocacy networks' (Horstmann 2011: 515). Many Christian Karen refugees use their institutional resources in Thailand to actively support IDPs in Myanmar's Karen state. Examples include the Karen Baptist Convention, which assists both refugees at the border and IDPs in Myanmar, and the Karenni Social and Welfare Centre which, in coordination with the Thailand Burma Border Consortium and the Burma Relief Centre, provides emergency relief and training, and documents human-rights abuses. Since its inception in 1998, the Back Pack Health Worker Team has recruited and trained health workers from displaced communities, working from Mae Sot, a Thai border town that serves as a base for Myanmarese refugee groups. Those recruited are trained by technical experts from Johns Hopkins School of Public Health and the American NGO Global Access Health Program, and subsequently travel into Myanmar by foot to provide medical assistance to displaced communities (Tang 2011).

The notion of refugees acting as the providers of humanitarian assistance for members of their own community and other displaced populations in some respects represents the ultimate paradox with regards to Northern assumptions of the roles of different stakeholders in the humanitarian arena. The ascription of 'victimhood' and 'passivity' onto refugees in humanitarian circles has been extensively critiqued in the refugee studies literature, with Harrell-Bond (1986) arguing that refugees are rendered docile and dependent because of the practices of the humanitarian system, whose main agenda is one of control, and Hyndman (2000: 121) analysing the ways in which refugees are represented in the humanitarian arena as vulnerable and in need of care from outsiders. The example of Karen refugees coordinating and implementing humanitarian action for their own community and other displaced persons, thus directly challenges these presumptions, situating refugees as the providers and coordinators of aid and protection services, while simultaneously raising concerns regarding the power imbalances which may characterise the work of those we may refer to as 'refugee-evangelists' in contexts of displacement, and the extent to which Karen refugees implement a faith-centred – or ethnic – rather than a universalist approach to humanitarian action (Ferris 2011).

The high level of interconnectivity between Northern and Southern actors in the Karen case also confirms Ferris's contention that FBOs are 'rooted in their local communities and yet have global reach' (Ferris 2005: 325), while concurrently raising questions relating to the dynamics of North-South relations in these contexts and the extent to which these initiatives can be conceptualised as 'Southern' in nature. The 'evangelical' and mission-ary-inspired approach to humanitarian action adopted by these Christian refugee groups and their international networks undoubtedly comes into conflict with the ICRC's stated principles, and yet to take these principles as ahistorical and thus to disregard these forms of humanitarian response is to ignore the contingent nature of the term and the temporal specificity of the ICRC's definition. As Rieff argues with regards to the origins of Northern humanitarianism, 'Historically ... the treatment of the sick, the insane, and wounded soldiers on the battlefield has largely been the work of religious orders' (2002: 57). The missionaries, who by the middle of the nineteenth century were committed to eradicating slavery, simultaneously promoted the 'civilising' practices thought to run parallel to conquest and imperial domination (ibid.). The persistence of global evangelical networks work-ing in the humanitarian arena (Fiddian-Qasmiyeh 2015b) and the historical connections between humanitarianism and missionaries is itself therefore a valuable point of study (Horstmann and Jung 2015), especially in order to better understand the roles, continuity, and implications of refugee-evangel-ical humanitarian providers in the global South.

Karen refugees' explicit engagement with proselytisation and the stated aim of bringing the Good News to other displaced (and indeed non-dis-placed) populations living on the Thailand–Myanmar border is different in degree and method from the activities of Syrians who became refugees in Jordan in 1982 and who are active in the Syrian Women's Organization, and of Jordanian citizens offering assistance via the Islamic Charity Centre Society or the Merkez Islami. Indeed, while these and other FBOs are often intimately related to political struggles – for national as well as religious self-determination in the Karen case, and in support of the Muslim Brotherhood in the Jordanian case – the (official) religious identity of the majority of Syrian refugees as Sunni Muslims means that *da'wa* (conversion) activities are largely unnecessary on the 'external' level (i.e. activities encouraging the conversion of non-Muslim recipients to Islam). Nonetheless, further research remains to be conducted into the extent to which these organisations may engage in processes of 'internal' *da'wa*, to encourage Sunni Muslim benefi-ciaries in Jordan to meet certain religious or political conditionalities, for instance with regards to adhering to a particular interpretation of the Islamic dress code, or attending Friday prayers, in order to secure the continuation of assistance in this protracted displacement situation. An additional major difference is that Karen refugee-evangelists on the Thailand–Myanmar border are actively supported by an extensive church and advocacy network which extends across the global North and global South alike, and yet Muslim FBOs responding to displacement from Syria (especially those which are – or are believed to be – affiliated with the Muslim Brotherhood) have continued to be scrutinised by the media, politicians and policymakers across the global North, with the 'humanitarian' motivations, nature and implications of these organisations and their many supporters (also across the global North and global South) continually questioned. Given this chapter's aim to footnote rather than centralise the securitisation framework, we will leave this dimension aside at this point; nonetheless, it is a poignant reminder that not all religions, and not all transnational networks of support, are equally positioned in the international arena.

Conclusions

This chapter has not aimed to identify or classify the similarities and differences which may exist either between Muslim or Christian modes of humanitarian action, or between Southern and Northern humanitarianisms. Rather, it has aimed to demonstrate the need for an expansion of the field of inquiry in humanitarian studies, and to illustrate the ways in which writing the 'Other' into humanitarian studies has the potential to both challenge and enrich our understandings of the multiple and overlapping modes through which different actors respond to those affected by contexts of forced displacement. While the enduring influence of the Northern-dominated international regime in the humanitarian arena should not be trivialised, nor should the capacity of Southern stakeholders, including refugees and forcibly displaced persons themselves, to exert agency as actors in the humanitarian sphere. The networks and relationships between Northern and Southern humanitarianisms are deeply rooted and complex. In many instances, exploration into Southern humanitarian initiatives, including those designed and implemented by local faith communities, must be coupled with an investigation into these intricate networks in order for these different North–South dynamics to be better understood.

If humanitarianism is said to be birthed from cosmopolitanism, and if we can conceive, as Calhoun (2002) does, of a cosmopolitanism which balances a liberal idea of rights with a stronger conception of the realities of solidarity and community, then academic legitimacy demands a reconceptualisation of the term. Within the cosmopolitan ideal is respect for cultural diversity and the idea of multiple and overlapping solidarities, including, but not restricted to the idea of a global solidarity (ibid.: 893). The concepts of solidarity and community that resonate throughout the case studies above echo the ideas of critical scholars who seek to reaffirm the importance of local communal obligations in opposition to a Northern-conceived universality. Promoting an understanding of Other forms of humanitarianism, including those which are 'local' and 'faith-based', is not to reject the existence or legitimacy of humanitarianism based upon the notion of global citizenship. However it is to reject the contention that this is the *only* legitimate form of humanitarianism.

Rather than offering a critique of the Northern humanitarian regime, this chapter has critiqued the assumption that a limited and historically specific institutional definition of what constitutes humanitarian should be mirrored at the theoretical level. To restrict the area of research in humanitarian studies to organisations purporting to be working under the strict principles laid out by the ICRC is not just fraught with Northern bias, but it also fails to recognise that claims of impartial, apolitical universality can equally be interpreted and understood to be partial, politicised neo-imperialism. The example of Myanmar, given above, clearly demonstrates this. Politics pervades humanitarianism, and not just humanitarianism in the sense of the practices carried out by 'humanitarian' organisations; it is interwoven within the fibres of the epithet itself. It is this lexical politics that has for so long footnoted Other actors and Other modes of action in the study of humanitarianism. A holistic understanding of the complex heterogeneity of humanitarianisms, in the plural, as they are conceptualised across the South, as well as the North, may help us to transcend the monopoly held by the Northern institutional regime on the humanitarian label. In keeping with the critical tradition, however, these humanitarianisms must simultaneously themselves be rigorously assessed, and the complex power dynamics intrinsic to them must be exposed. Through expanding the use of the humanitarian label we promote a lexical counter-politics that unravels the very fibres of the epithet and what it represents. Broadening the field in this way opens the possibility for new and exciting research trajectories in humanitarian studies, forced migration studies and beyond.[16]

Notes

1 This chapter is based on research conducted as part of Elena Fiddian-Qasmiyeh's investigation into South–South Humanitarian Responses to Forced Migration funded by the OUP John Fell Research Fund (Award 113_363).
2 Media reports of the Syrian conflict have also reflected this suspicion of Muslim civil-society networks providing assistance to refugees from Syria (e.g. Ghader 2013).
3 Oppositional categorisations, such as North/South, West/East, developed/developing, fail to reflect the complexity and diversity of global realities, and yet the terms 'global North' and 'global South' are used here in line with McEwan's (2009: 13) suggestion that 'it is most useful to think of North/South as a *metaphorical* rather than a *geographical* distinction'. Furthermore, these terms transcend the connotations of typologies such as 'First' and 'Third World', 'developed' or 'developing' which 'suggest both a hierarchy and a value judgment' (ibid.: 12), in addition to transcending the inherently *negative* framework implicit in the usage of the term '*non*-West' as counterpoint to 'West'. Where used, the term 'North' or 'Northern' refers to Europe and North America (see Pacitto and Fiddian-Qasmiyeh 2013).

4 These states' denomination as 'new' donors is often historically inaccurate. Reeves and Aneja have respectively documented the long history of financial, material and social support offered by Chinese and Indian state and non-state actors as a response to conflict and disasters on local, national and international levels (verbatim conference proceedings, *Between the Global and the Local in Humanitarian Action*, Save the Children, April 2014).

5 Palestinian and Sahrawi refugees' own conceptualisations of 'humanitarianism', 'politics' and 'ideology', as *participant* observers of South–South assistance programmes, are explored in Fiddian-Qasmiyeh (2015a).

6 See (www.unhcr.org/51b6de419.html) accessed 10 August 2014.

7 Syria Regional Refugee Response: Inter-agency Information Sharing Portal (http://data.unhcr.org/syrianrefugees/regional.php) accessed 15 May 2015.

8 Also see Pacitto and Fiddian-Qasmiyeh (2013) on Southern-led responses to displacement from and in Libya, Egypt and Tunisia.

9 The Jordan Hashemite Charity Organisation for Development: Syria Response (www.jordankorea.gov.jo/content/jordan-hashemite-charity-organization-relief-development) accessed 1 July 2014. This erasure can be understood as a decoupling strategy consistent with neo-institutional theory.

10 English version (www.jhco.org.jo/?q=content/about-us) accessed 4 February 2013.

11 Arabic version (www.jhco.org.jo/?q=ar/content/%D8%B9%D9%86-%D8%A7%D9%84%D9%87%D9%8A%D8%A6%D8%A9) accessed 4 February 2013.

12 Equally interestingly, an English language summary of JHCO's aims on the web-based *Comprehensive Guide to Civil Society Organizations in Jordan* reads: 'Conveying the message of the Hashemite Kingdom of Jordan in Arab communities and showing it, fostering the relations between the people of Jordan and Arab and *Islamic* communities, deepening solidarity and cooperation at Arab and *Islamic* levels, through combating poverty, sickness and ignorance, in addition to contributing to the dissemination of Arab and *Islamic* culture in the international arena' (emphasis added). See (www.civilsociety-jo.net/en/index.php/special-commissions/201-jordan-hashemite-charity-organisation-jhco) accessed 4 February 2014.

13 The Jordan Hashemite Charity Organisation for Development: Syria Response (www.jordankorea.gov.jo/content/jordan-hashemite-charity-organization-relief-development) accessed 1 July 2014.

14 Such a strategic representation of Self is common in refugee (and non-refugee) situations, in which certain characteristics – such a religious identity – are variously magnified or minimised during interactions with diverse audiences to ensure a continuation of support and assistance. See Fiddian-Qasmiyeh (2011b and 2014).

15 Further research into the motivations and implications of these and other faith-based actors' responses to displacement in Jordan has been completed in 2015 under the auspices of a Henry Luce Foundation funded project led by Columbia University. One of the authors of this chapter (EFQ) is leading a parallel research project, also funded by the Henry Luce Foundation, which examines faith-based actors' responses to Syrian displacement to Lebanon.

16 The above-mentioned research projects into the nature and impacts of responses motivated or inspired by political or religious solidarity examine the relationship between the provision of assistance and exclusionary practices.

References

Abd al-Rahim, M. (2008) 'Asylum: A Moral and Legal Right in Islam', *Refugee Survey Quarterly*, 27(2):15–23.

Ager, A. and Ager, J. (2011) 'Faith and the Discourse of Secular Humanitarianism', *Journal of Refugee Studies*, 24(3):456–472.

Agier, M. (2010) 'Humanity as an Identity and its Political Effects: A Note of Camps and Humanitarian Government', *Humanity*, 1(1):29–45.

ALNAP (2012) *The State of the Humanitarian System 2012*, London: ALNAP.

Aujourd'hui Le Maroc (2012) Réfugiés Syriens en Jordanie: Le Maroc dépêche plusieurs convois d'aide humanitaire et logistique (www.aujourdhui.ma/maroc-actualite/24-heures/refugies-syriens-en-jordanie-le-maroc-depeche-plusieurs-convois-d-aide-humanitaire-et-logistique-97149.html) accessed 14 August 2012.

Barakat, S. and Zyck, S.A. (2010) 'Gulf State Assistance to Conflict-Affected Environments', *The Kuwait Programme on Development, Governance and Globalisation in the Gulf States*, London: The Centre for the Study of Global Governance.

Barnett, M. (2011) *Empire of Humanity: A History of Humanitarianism*, New York: Cornell University Press.

Barnett, M. and Weiss, T. (2008) 'Humanitarianism: A Brief History of the Present', in: M. Barnett and T.G. Weiss (eds) *Humanitarianism in Question: Politics, Power, Ethics*, New York: Cornell University Press, 1–48.

Barnett, M. and Weiss, T. (2011) *Humanitarianism Contested: Where Angels Fear to Tread*, Oxford: Routledge.

Benthall, J. and Bellion-Jourdan, J. (2003) *The Charitable Crescent: Politics of Aid in the Muslim World*, London: I.B. Tauris.

Binder, A., Meier, C. and Steets, J. (2010) 'Humanitarian Assistance: Truly Universal? A Mapping Study of Non-Western Donors', *GPPi Research Paper Series*, Global Public Policy Institute, 12:1–41.

Bitter, J. (1994) Un Outil de Travail pour Les Organisations Humanitaires Face au Radicalisme Islamiste: Typologie et Images Réciproques. *Volume 4 of Mémoire pour l'obtention du Diplôme de spécialisation en théologie pratique*, Lausanne: Institut romand de pastorale.

Calhoun, C. (2002) 'The Class Consciousness of Frequent Travelers: Toward a Critique of Actually Existing Cosmopolitanism', *The South Atlantic Quarterly*, 101(4):869–897.

Calhoun, C. (2008) 'The Imperative to Reduce Suffering: Charity, Progress, and Emergencies in the Field of Humanitarian Action', in: M. Barnett and T.G. Weiss (eds) *Humanitarianism in Question: Politics, Power, Ethics*, New York: Cornell University Press, 73–97.

Chimni, B.S. (2000) 'Globalisation, Humanitarianism and the Erosion of Refugee Protection', *Refugee Studies Centre Working Paper*, 3, Oxford: Refugee Studies Centre.

Chulov, M. (2013) 'Half of Syrian Population Will Need Aid by End of Year', (www.theguardian.com/world/2013/apr/19/half-syrian-population-aid-year) accessed 1 August 2014.

Davey, E. (2012) 'New Players through Old Lenses: Why History Matters in Engaging Southern Actors', *HPG Policy Brief*, 48: July 2012.

Davies, K. (2012) 'Continuity, Change and Contest: Meanings of "Humanitarian" from the "Religion of Humanity" to the Kosovo War', *HPG Working Paper*, August 2012.

Egeland, J. (2011) 'Foreword: Humanitarianism in the Crossfire', in: M. Barnett and T.G. Weiss (eds) *Humanitarianism Contested: Where Angels Fear to Tread*, Oxford: Routledge.

Esteva, G. and Prakash, M.S. (1997) 'From Global Thinking to Local Thinking', in: M. Rahnema and V. Bawtree (eds) *The Post-Development Reader*, New York: Zed, 277–289.

Writing the Other into Humanitarianism 299

Ferris, E. (2005) 'Faith-Based and Secular Humanitarian Organizations', *International Review of the Red Cross*, 87(878):311–325.

Ferris, E. (2011) *The Politics of Protection: The Limits of Humanitarian Action*, Washington, DC: Brookings Institution Press.

Fiddian-Qasmiyeh, E. (ed.) (2011a) 'Faith Based Humanitarianism in Contexts of Forced Displacement', *Journal of Refugee Studies*, 24(3).

Fiddian-Qasmiyeh, E. (2011b) 'The Pragmatics of Performance: Putting "Faith" in Aid in the Sahrawi Refugee Camps', *Journal of Refugee Studies*, 24(3):533–547.

Fiddian-Qasmiyeh, E. (2014) *The Ideal Refugees: Gender, Islam and the Sahrawi Politics of Survival*, Syracuse: Syracuse University Press.

Fiddian-Qasmiyeh, E. (2015a) *South-South Educational Migration, Humanitarianism and Development: Views from the Caribbean, North Africa and the Middle East*, Oxford: Routledge.

Fiddian-Qasmiyeh, E. (2015b) 'Conflicting Missions? The Politics of Evangelical Humanitarianism in the Sahrawi and Palestinian Protracted Refugee Situations', in: A. Horstmann and J-H. Jung (eds) *Building Noah's Ark: Refugees, Migrants and Religious Communities*, London: Palgrave Macmillan, 157–179.

Fiddian-Qasmiyeh, E. (2015c) 'Engendering Faith-Based Organizations: Intersections between Religion and Gender in Development and Humanitarian Interventions', in: A. Coles, L. Grey and J. Momsen (eds) *The Routledge Handbook of Gender and Development*, Oxford: Routledge, 560–570.

Fiddian-Qasmiyeh, E. and Ager, A. (eds) (2013) *Local Faith Communities and the Promotion of Resilience in Humanitarian Situations*, RSC/JLI Working Paper 90, Oxford: Refugee Studies Centre.

Ghader, D. (2013) British Aid Charity in 'Terror' Inquiry, (www.thesundaytimes.co.uk/sto/news/uk_news/National/article1296135.ece) accessed 10 June 2014.

Guinane, K. (2006) *Muslim Charities and the War on Terror*, Washington, DC: OMB Watch.

Gulf Times (2012) $100mn Aid to Syrian Refugees (www.gulf-times.com/site/topics/article.asp?cu_no=2&item_no=520873&version=1&template_id=36&parent_id=16) accessed 22 August 2012.

Guterres, A. (2012) Opening Remarks by Mr. António Guterres, OIC Ministerial Conference on Refugees in the Muslim World, 11 May 2012, Ashgabat.

Harrell-Bond, B.E. (1986) *Imposing Aid: Emergency Assistance to Refugees*, Oxford: Oxford University Press.

Horstmann, A. (2011) 'Ethical Dilemmas and Identifications of Faith-Based Humanitarian Organizations in the Karen Refugee Crisis', *Journal of Refugee Studies*, 24(3):513–532.

Horstmann, A. and Jung, J-H. (eds) (2015) *Building Noah's Ark: Refugees, Migrants and Religious Communities*, London: Palgrave Macmillan.

Hyndman, J. (2000) *Managing Displacement: Refugees and the Politics of Humanitarianism*, Minneapolis: University of Minnesota Press.

IRIN (2012) Jordan: Civil Society at Heart of Syrian Refugee Response (www.irinnews.org/printreport.aspx?reportid=95273) accessed 27 August 2012.

Kayaoğlu, T. (2012) It's Time to Revise the Cairo Declaration of Human Rights in Islam, (www.brookings.edu/research/opinions/2012/04/23-cairo-kayaoglu) accessed 4 April 2013.

Kennedy, D. (2004) *The Dark Sides of Virtue: Reassessing International Humanitarianism*, Princeton: Princeton University Press.

Marr, S. (2010) Compassion in Action: The Story of the ASEAN-Led Coordination in Myanmar, Jakarta: ASEAN.

Mawdsley, E. (2012) *From Recipients to Donors: The Emerging Powers and the Changing Development Landscape*, London: Zed.

McEwan, C. (2009) *Postcolonialism and Development*, Abingdon: Routledge.

Michaelson, R. (2012) 'Where's The Aid? Syrian Refugees in Jordan Ask', (www.english.rfi.fr/middle-east/20120425-wheres-aid%20syrian-refugees-jordan-ask) accessed 28 August 2012.

NRC/IDMC (2011) Philippines: Over 285,000 People Displaced by Tropical Storm (www.refworld.org/docid/4f0ede362.html) accessed 21 August 2012.

OIC (2011) OIC Participates in the Humanitarian Efforts Made by the Philippines (www.oicun.org/73/20120103053151996.html) accessed 21 August 2012.

OIC (2012) Myanmar Approves Access for OIC Assistance in Arakan (www.oic-oci.org/topic_detail.asp?t_id=7080) accessed 28 August 2012.

Pacitto, J. (2012) Workshop Report: South-South Humanitarianism in Contexts of Forced Displacement, (www.rsc.ox.ac.uk/publications/rsc-reports/wr-south-south-humanitarianism-261012.pdf) accessed 10 April 2014.

Pacitto, J. and Fiddian-Qasmiyeh, E. (2013) Writing the 'Other' into Humanitarian Discourse: Framing Theory and Practice in South-South Humanitarian Responses to Forced Displacement, *RSC Working Paper* 93, Oxford: Refugee Studies Centre.

Pantuliano, S., Mackintosh, K. and Elhawary, S. with Metcalfe, V. (2011) *Counter-Terrorism and Humanitarian Action: Tensions, Impact and Ways Forward*, London: ODI.

Parekh, B. (1992) 'The Cultural Particularity of Liberal Democracy', *Political Studies*, 40(1):160–175.

Rieff, D. (2002) *A Bed for The Night: Humanitarianism in Crisis*, London: Vintage.

Six, C. (2009) 'The Rise of Postcolonial States as Donors: A Challenge to the Development Paradigm?', *Third World Quarterly*, 30(6):1103–1121.

Stamatov, P. (2013) *The Origins of Global Humanitarianism: Religion, Empires, and Advocacy*, Cambridge: CUP.

Stawski, H. (2012) South to South Humanitarianism: Understanding the Social and Spiritual Capital of Local Faith Communities, Unpublished conference presentation, *South-South Humanitarianism in Contexts of Forced Displacement*, Refugee Studies Centre, University of Oxford, 6 October 2012.

Tang, A. (2011) 'In Eastern Burma Conflict, Medics Faced the Same Dangers as Those they Treat,' (www.guardian.co.uk/world/2011/jan/25/thailand-burma-conflict-medic-tang) accessed 14 August 2012.

Türk, V. (ed.) (2008) 'Special Issue: Asylum and Islam', *Refugee Survey Quarterly*, 27(2).

UNHCR (2014) *Partnership Note on Faith-Based Organizations, Local Faith Communities and Faith Leaders*, Geneva: UNHCR.

Vaughan-Williams, N. (2007) 'Beyond a Cosmopolitan Ideal: The Politics of Singularity', *International Politics*, 44:107–124.

Wilson, R. and Brown, R. (2011) 'Introduction', in: R. Wilson and R. Brown (eds) *Humanitarianism and Suffering: The Mobilization of Empathy*, Cambridge: CUP.

Woods, N. (2008) 'Whose Aid? Whose Influence? China, Emerging Donors and the Silent Revolution in Development Assistance', *International Affairs*, 84(6):1205–1221.

Wuthnow, R. (2009) *Boundless Faith: The Global Outreach of American Churches*. Berkeley: University of California Press.

Part VIII

Regional and Local Humanitarianism

14 Regional Organisations and the Humanitarian System

History, Trends and Implications

Lilianne Fan

Introduction

Overview

The end of the colonial era gave rise not only to new states, but also new groupings of states into regional intergovernmental organisations. Born in the context of decolonisation and Cold War, the principal mandate of many regional organisations (ROs) was to promote economic development and regional stability. Since the end of the Cold War, however, many ROs have become increasingly engaged in responding to, preparing for and preventing humanitarian crises. Forms of engagement have included: disaster preparedness and response; conflict management; the facilitation of humanitarian aid to refugees, internally displaced people and crisis-affected populations; and the development of policies, institutional frameworks and procedures on humanitarian assistance, response preparedness and addressing vulnerability.

What are the implications of this trend for the ability to meet humanitarian needs? Does the increase in regional humanitarian structures and action by ROs signal a shift in the governance of the humanitarian system, or the emergence of parallel systems? Or do the approaches of ROs simply supplement the work on more traditional actors?

This chapter will trace the historic evolution of ROs as humanitarian actors in the context of their relationship to the multilateral system, first in relation to peace and security and secondly in relation to the humanitarian system. It will then examine some of the areas in which humanitarian action is currently being undertaken by regional intergovernmental organisations. Next, the chapter will take a closer look at two organisations that have been involved in humanitarian engagement – the Association of Southeast Asian Nations (ASEAN) and the Organisation of Islamic Cooperation (OIC) – and examine more closely the particular approach to humanitarian engagement that each organisation has institutionalised, both conceptually and operationally. Finally, it will consider the broader implications of these developments, both for humanitarian crises and for the future of the humanitarian sector as a whole.

The chapter adopts a 'discursive institutionalist' approach, theorised by Schmidt (2010) as being concerned with both 'the substantive content of ideas and the interactive processes of discourse in institutional context' in order to enable an analysis of regional organisations that considers the dynamics of institutional exchange through contextually, historically, conceptually and politically informed analysis.

Definitions

The definition of 'regional organisation' used in this chapter is from the Humanitarian Policy Group's 2013 report 'Regional Organisations and Humanitarian Action' as an institution which meets the following criteria:

1   substantial geographic proximity or contiguity;
2   an official intergovernmental status enshrined in a treaty or comparable legal instrument;
3   a cooperative or collaborative mandate rather than a primarily defensive mission; and
4   a multi-sectoral focus (Zyck 2013).

This definition includes organisations such as ASEAN, the South Asian Association for Regional Cooperation (SAARC), the Pacific Island Forum (PIF), the African Union (AU), Economic Community of West African States (ECOWAS), Southern African Development Community (SADC), OIC, the Arab League and CARICOM (Caribbean Community).

Regional Organisations and the Multilateral System

The Peace and Security Agenda

The role of ROs as an important element of the multilateral system on issues of peace and security is recognised in the 1945 United Nations Charter, under Chapter VIII on 'Regional Arrangements'. Article 52(1) of Chapter VIII stipulates that 'nothing in the Charter is to preclude the existence of regional arrangements or agencies for dealing with such matters relating to the maintenance of international peace and security as are appropriate for regional action.' It goes on to invite member states entering into such arrangements or disputes through such regional arrangements or constituting such agencies to 'make every effort to achieve pacific settlement of local disputes through such regional arrangements or by such regional agencies before referring them to the Security Council' (UN Charter 1945, Chapter VIII, Article 52 (1)).

After the fall of the Berlin Wall in 1989, there was an increased push by member states of the UN to further elaborate the specific role that ROs could play in the maintenance of international peace and security. In 'An

Agenda for Peace', published in 1992, then UN Secretary-General Boutros
Boutros-Ghali recommended a greater role for ROs, as part of the international peace and security architecture. In the report, the Secretary-General
made the case that ROs should be mobilised for preventive diplomacy,
peacekeeping and peace-building. The report noted that while the Security
Council should continue to hold primary responsibility for maintaining
international peace and security, the role of ROs should be strengthened:

> ... in this new era of opportunity, regional arrangements or agencies
> can render great service if their activities are undertaken in a man-
> ner consistent with the purposes and principles of the Charter, and
> if their relationship with the United Nations, and particularly the
> Security Council, is governed by Chapter VIII. ... Under the Charter,
> the Security Council has and will continue to have primary responsi-
> bility for maintaining international peace and security, but regional
> action as a matter of decentralization, delegation and cooperation with
> the United Nations efforts could not only lighten the burden of the
> Council but also contribute to a deeper sense of participation, con-
> sensus and democratization in international affairs. ... and should the
> Security Council choose specifically to authorize a regional arrange-
> ment or organization to take the lead in addressing a crisis within its
> region, it could serve to lend the weight of the United Nations to the
> validity of the regional effort.
>
> (A/47/277-S/24111, paras 63–65)

The report of the Secretary-General made several recommendations,
including consultations between UN and regional agencies on particular
situations and appropriate measures that could be taken at regional levels;
ROs undertaking collaborative action with or complementary to those of
the UN; and further exploration of mechanisms to authorise ROs to take
the lead in addressing crises within its region.

In response to the Secretary-General's report, the Security Council issued
presidential statements on 29 October and 30 November 1992 express-
ing its recognition of the role of ROs and welcomed the strengthening of
regional involvement in UN efforts to support peace.

In the following decade, the UN faced a dramatic increase in peacekeeping responsibilities, including in Somalia, Bosnia and Rwanda, while
also facing enormous resource constraints. This period also saw the increasing involvement of ROs in peace-making and peacekeeping activities in
many parts of the world. Conflicts and complex emergencies that attracted
regional involvement included Liberia, Sierra Leone, Croatia, Tajikistan,
Bosnia and Herzegovina, Cambodia and Papua New Guinea. According to
a report by the UN Department of Peacekeeping Operations (DPKO), by
March 1999 there were 16 ROs and arrangements engaged in collaboration
or interested in cooperating with the UN in peace-related activities (DPKO

1999). It also found that in the 49 UN peacekeeping operations launched between 1949 and 1999, 15 had involved cooperation with ROs or arrangements in one form or another. The report concluded by recommending a set of principles and mechanisms to enhance cooperation between the UN and regional bodies.

Regional Organisations and the Humanitarian System

While recognition and discussions on the role of ROs in the context of peace and security were taking place at this time, discussions on the humanitarian role of ROs were not equally prominent. In the DPKO report, humanitarian assistance was only mentioned several times in the annex as a potential area for cooperation for a small number of regional bodies. Notwithstanding the humanitarian nature of some peace-related activities such as protection of civilians, further explanation of this apparent imbalance is warranted. One explanation might be that threats to peace were more prevalent at the time and ROs were seen to have a more critical role to play in supporting peace processes rather than facilitating the delivery of humanitarian aid. This explanation, however, overlooks the fact that millions were affected by the conflicts in question and that UN and humanitarian agencies were working to deliver assistance even as peace-making and peacekeeping processes were also under way. An alternative explanation is that the late recognition of regional bodies in humanitarian action might be due the nature of the evolution of the international humanitarian system itself and the fact the official system still has an uneasy relationship with Southern structures and non-traditional humanitarian actors, including ROs, local organisations, the private sector, faith-based organisations (FBOs) and diaspora networks.

The institutional architecture governing humanitarian assistance emerged much more recently than that of the peace and security agenda, which was the *raison d'être* of the UN and is enshrined in the UN Charter. With the exception of the International Committee of the Red Cross (ICRC), the primary guardian of international humanitarian law, the agencies that were to become central to the humanitarian sector were established or originated in the years during or immediately following the end of the Second World War and the establishment of the UN. During the Second World War, the UN Relief and Rehabilitation Administration (UNRRA) was the main agency responsible for delivering humanitarian assistance to refugees. Established in November 1943 and wound down in June 1947, in just over three and a half years UNRRA distributed over 9 million tonnes of food and other supplies. UNRRA's remaining assets and personnel were distributed between the specialised agencies of the newly formed UN — the UN International Children's Emergency Fund (UNICEF) in 1946,[1] the Food and Agriculture Organization (FAO) in 1945, the World Health Organization (WHO) in 1948, the International Refugee Organization – which evolved into the Office of the UN High Commissioner for Refugees

(UNHCR) in 1951, and the World Food Programme (WFP) in 1961. It was not until December 1991 that the Department of Humanitarian Affairs (DHA) and the role of the Emergency Relief Coordinator were established through the adoption of General Assembly Resolution 46/182, to coordinate the UN's response to complex emergencies and disasters. In 1998, the DHA was reorganised into the Office for the Coordination of Humanitarian Affairs (OCHA) and its mandate refocused to include the coordination of humanitarian response, policy development and humanitarian advocacy.

Unlike the UN Charter which explicitly deals with ROs and arrangements in Chapter VIII, the GA Resolution 46/182 mentions regional arrangements only once under coordination, subsumed into a section on country-level coordination of humanitarian assistance, where it is simply recommended that the Resident Coordinator 'promote the use of all locally or regionally available relief capacities' (GA Resolution 46/182).

One important obstacle to the development of equal partnerships between traditional humanitarian actors and ROs lies in the fact that the humanitarian system continues to be a highly imbalanced and closed structure which is still largely dominated by a small number of Western-based organisations. The Humanitarian Policy Group's 2012 report on humanitarian space revealed that:

> (in) 2008, the largest six organisations/federations had a combined humanitarian spending of US$ 1.7 billion, compared to the US$ 193 million of the next 11 largest organisations/federations. The dominance of the largest UN and NGO agencies in financing and governance means that the humanitarian system resembles an oligopoly with power concentrated in a few organisations. Despite differences in specific missions and mandates, these major organisations operate as a closed group or 'cartel' with interrelated histories and limited scope for new entrants.
>
> (Collinson and Elhawary 2012: 19)

This does not mean, however, that ROs were not engaged in humanitarian action or that collaboration with the formal system did not happen. But it might go some way in explaining why ROs' engagement with the formal humanitarian system has been neither clear cut nor without problems.

The Emergence of Regional Humanitarian Engagement

Institutional Context

The establishment of distinct humanitarian capacities within ROs themselves increased in the late 1990s and 2000s. While in 1995 there were only seven regional organisations with dedicated humanitarian capacity, this number had grown to 27 in 2012 (Figure 14.1; Zyck 2013).

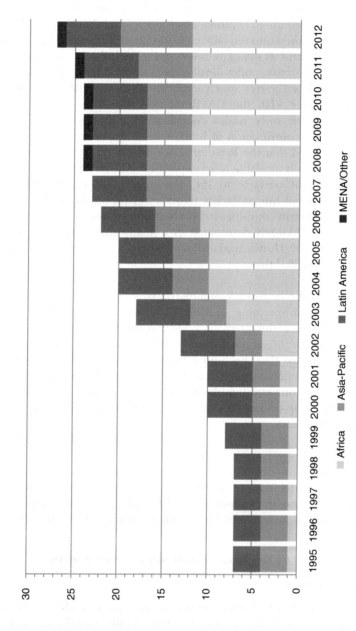

Figure 14.1 Trends of cumulative number of humanitarian departments/centres, 1995–2012

This trend was driven by a number of factors. Some organisations built on initiatives that had been implemented in preceding decades, such as the OAS Inter-American Emergency Aid Fund of 1965, the SAARC Food Reserve of 1987 and the East African Inter-Governmental Authority on Drought and Development (IGADD) founded in 1986 (Zyck 2013). At the same time, the member states of ROs were also engaged in international processes, goals and frameworks such as the Millennium Development Goals (MDGs) in 2000 and the Hyogo Framework for Action (HFA) on disaster risk reduction (DRR) in 2005, both of which explicitly engaged regional capacities and mechanisms. In addition, ROs were also keen to demonstrate both their increased capacity as well as their ability to take the lead on humanitarian issues within their own regions.[2]

Perhaps most significant to the emergence of regional humanitarian action was the occurrence of a number of crises, including genocide, ethnic cleansing, drought and mega-disasters, that took on regional dimensions. These included the war in Bosnia and Herzegovina in 1992, Somalia in 1992, the Rwandan genocide in 1994, the Kosovo war in 1998, the Indian Ocean tsunami of 2004, Cyclone Nargis in Myanmar in 2008, and, more recently, Typhoon Haiyan in the Philippines in 2013. Reflecting their response to such crises, from the late 1990s to mid-2000s ROs were more involved in peace and conflict, while from the mid-2000s onwards these organisations were increasingly involved in disaster response and disaster management. For example, the development of the ASEAN Agreement on Disaster Management and Emergency Response (AADMER) was influenced both by preparation for the Kobe conference and the HFA as well as the aftermath of the 2004 Indian Ocean Tsunami (Kamal 2009). The OIC's establishment of their Islamic Conference Humanitarian Affairs Department (ICHAD) in 2008 was driven primarily by member states interest to better structure the OIC's delivery of humanitarian assistance to people in need across the Muslim world, including Bosnia, Aceh, Palestine, Afghanistan, Somalia and Niger.

Areas of Humanitarian Action

ROs are involved in wide and diverse range of humanitarian action. These include the provision of humanitarian assistance to refugees and displaced populations, disaster response and preparedness, conflict management and early warning.

While the frameworks, modalities and approaches, levels of assistance and types of activities, differ across ROs, some trends can be observed. The Humanitarian Policy Group found that several ROs were involved in direct aid delivery to refugees, including the AU, the ECOWAS and the League of Arab States, and that many more had established agreements on refugees with UNHCR and other refugee institutions (Zyck 2013).

Another area in which ROs have been very active is disaster management and risk reduction. The Brookings Institution found that many

ROs, including ASEAN, the Pacific Island Forum, SAARC, ECOWAS and CARICOM, are interested in DRR even where they do not have the mandate, capacity or resources to deliver aid directly (Ferris and Petz 2013). This interest was strengthened by the recognition by the HFA of the particular role that ROs could play in DRR, including developing common policy frameworks and indicators, strengthening capacity of national disaster management agencies and establishing early warning mechanisms (ISDR 2005).

ROs have also been involved in conflict management, including preventive diplomacy, peacekeeping and the protection of civilians, conflict monitoring, and sharing lessons on peace-building and conflict management at the regional level. Examples include the AU's Standby Force (ASF) and Peace and Security Council (PSC), ECOWAS' Monitoring Group (ECOMOG), IGADD's Conflict Early Warning and Response Mechanism (CEWARN), OAS's Fund for Peace and the ASEAN Regional Forum (ARF) (Zyck 2013: 22–3).

These are only some examples of areas in which ROs undertake humanitarian action. In all areas, however, effectiveness remains uneven and each regional organisation's approach to humanitarian action is determined by its specific mandate, the interests of its member states, capacity and resources. For a deeper understanding of how ROs are actually engaging in humanitarianism, we will now examine two organisations: ASEAN and the OIC.

Regional Humanitarianism in Practice

ASEAN

By mandate of its member states, ASEAN's humanitarian engagement focuses on natural disasters. Disaster management is approached comprehensively, from risk reduction and preparedness to response, reflecting ASEAN's view that disasters are not only a humanitarian issue but also a development concern and non-traditional security threat. ASEAN, which remains strongly bound by the principle of non-interference, does not have a mandate to engage in humanitarian action in conflict-related situations.

ASEAN's efforts to institutionalise its disaster management framework began in the early 2000s. In early 2003, ASEAN established the ASEAN Committee on Disaster Management (ACDM), consisting of heads of national agencies responsible for disaster management in its member states. The ACDM assumes overall responsibility for coordinating and implementing regional activities on disaster management and is governed by the ASEAN Ministerial Meeting on Disaster Management. Through the ACDM and the ASEAN Secretariat, ASEAN has also established working relations with external partners, such as OCHA, UNICEF, the International

Federation of the Red Cross (IFRC), Oxfam, the US Department of Agriculture Forest Service, the Pacific Disaster Centre and the Asian Disaster Preparedness Center (ADPC) (Labbe *et al.* 2013: 11).

ASEAN's disaster management framework is the legally binding ASEAN Agreement on Disaster Management and Emergency Response (AADMER). The AADMER was signed by ASEAN Foreign Ministers in July 2005. It was ratified by all 10 member states and entered into force on 24 December 2009. The AADMER contains provisions on disaster risk identification, monitoring and early warning, prevention and mitigation, preparedness and response, rehabilitation, technical cooperation and research, mechanisms for coordination, and simplified customs and immigration procedures. The AADMER seeks to provide an effective mechanism for substantial reduction of losses due to disasters and a joint response to disaster emergencies through concerted national efforts and intensified regional cooperation. Under the AADMER, policies are established at the regional level, while programmes are carried out at the national level by member states (ibid.).

ASEAN has also developed Standard Operating Procedures for Regional Standby Arrangements and Coordination of Joint Disaster Relief and Emergency Response Operations (SASOP) for establishing joint operations in providing relief aid to disaster affected areas of member states in line with the AADMER. Annex D of the SASOP is a draft concept paper on 'The Use of ASEAN Military Assets and Capacities in Humanitarian Assistance and Disaster Relief', which aims to accelerate the effective cooperation of the ASEAN military in HADR (humanitarian assistance in disaster relief) operations regionally and internationally (ASEAN 2009).

Under the SASOP, militaries are recognised as being among the first responders to natural disasters, so the principle of 'last resort' as outlined in the Oslo Guidelines (Guidelines on the Use of Foreign Military and Civil Defence Assets in Disaster Relief) does not always apply. The challenge in the Asia-Pacific region is to harmonise existing agreements and guidelines, be they ASEAN documents such as the AADMER, Asia-Pacific-wide guidelines such as the Asia-Pacific Conference on Military Assistance to Disaster Relief Operations (APC-MADRO), or bilateral agreements. In addition, the fact that national armies in the Asia-Pacific region often respond first to natural disasters makes them less accustomed to the Oslo Guidelines, but may also make them cautious in agreeing to a binding document. Another issue that can potentially hamper the rapid deployment of foreign military assets is the lack of Status of Forces Agreements (SOFA). The presence of foreign military forces is governed by a SOFA, which, if not already in place prior to a disaster, can take time to conclude and thus delay the arrival of assistance.

The AADMER also provides for the establishment of an ASEAN Coordinating Centre for Humanitarian Assistance on disaster management (AHA Centre) to undertake operational coordination of activities under the Agreement. ASEAN foreign ministers signed an agreement to do so at the 19th ASEAN Summit in Bali, Indonesia on 17 November 2011. The role of the AHA Centre includes facilitating cooperation and coordination among the parties, and with relevant UN and other international organisations, in promoting regional collaboration. The AHA Centre works on the basis that the party will act first to manage and respond to disasters. In the event that the party requires assistance to cope with such situation, in addition to direct request to any assisting entity, it may seek assistance from the AHA Centre to facilitate such request. ASEAN countries have committed to annual and equal contributions for the AHA Centre Fund to provide sustainable resources for the operationalisation of the centre. A number of ASEAN dialogue partners have supported the AHA Centre since its establishment, including the United States of America, Australia, Japan and New Zealand. The AHA Centre is now fully operational and is actively supporting governments in the region. Recent examples include support following Typhoon Bopha in the Philippines in 2012, the earthquake in Central Aceh in July 2013 and Typhoon Haiyan in November 2013.

While ASEAN's legal and institutional framework is one of the most advanced among ROs, its actual activities have been discreet and largely policy-oriented rather than operational. Further, ASEAN's humanitarian engagement has remained largely state-centric and efforts to build partnerships with civil-society and private-sector actors within the ASEAN region have been limited. These characteristics stand in sharp contrast with the OIC, the organisation we shall examine next, which has a weaker institutional framework, but yet has been far more active in humanitarian affairs and does not differentiate between disaster-related and conflict-related humanitarian crises, thus adhering more closely to the core humanitarian principle of impartiality.

OIC

The OIC's commitment to humanitarian action is enshrined in the OIC Charter, which was adopted in 1972, and revised in 2008. Chapter 1, Article 1 (19) of the OIC Charter states that one of the OIC's objectives is 'to cooperate and coordinate in humanitarian emergencies such as natural disasters' (OIC Charter, Chapter 1, Article 1 (19)). The Charter also states its commitment 'to promote inter-state relations based on justice, mutual respect and good neighbourliness to ensure global peace, security and harmony' (OIC Charter, Chapter 1, Article 1(6)) and 'to reaffirm its support for the rights of peoples as stipulated in the UN Charter and international law' (OIC Charter, Chapter 1, Article 1 (7)).

The OIC's engagement in humanitarian activities is also driven by the number and scale of humanitarian crises affecting its 57 member states and its constituency (the *ummah*), including the crises in Bosnia and Herzegovina, Palestine, Somalia, Afghanistan, Yemen, the Central African

Republic and Myanmar. In addition, OIC countries host a large number of refugees, reaching 18 million in 2010, according to UNHCR, which has increased rapidly further in particular due to the Syrian refugee crisis.

While the OIC has been engaged in various forms humanitarian action for many years, the institutionalisation of these activities has only occurred over the past decade. In 2005, at an Extraordinary Summit, OIC heads of states adopted the OIC 10 Year Programme of Action which set the guiding principles for the organisation's engagement and activities in the humanitarian domain. In June 2008, the OIC's Council of Foreign Ministers adopted Resolution No. 11/35-C establishing ICHAD (Bakhit 2008).

Prior to the establishment of ICHAD, the OIC had already been involved in numerous humanitarian initiatives in the Muslim world, including the funding of hospitals and schools and the provision of emergency relief to people affected by conflict and disasters. After the Bosnian war, for example, the OIC established a Fund for the Return of Bosnia Refugees in Sarajevo through resources from its member states and benefactors, which has helped to deliver humanitarian assistance to refugees, rebuild schools, hospitals and houses for returning refugees. In response to the Indian Ocean tsunami, the OIC launched an appeal and established an OIC fund for the orphan victims of the tsunami with a scheme that enabled philanthropists, benefactors, and member states to sponsor orphans below the age of 18 through donations of US$30 a month. The OIC has also long been involved in Gaza, sending humanitarian convoys in cooperation with the Hashemite Red Crescent, an engagement that has continued since the establishment of ICHAD. The OIC has also responded to natural disasters in Yemen, Mozambique, Algeria, Bangladesh and Pakistan, and to food insecurity and drought in the Sahel region. ICHAD has also worked to address the root causes of conflict, including convening a donors conference for Darfur aimed to address economic inequities and contestation over resources.

The best known humanitarian role played by the OIC, however, is their role in coordinating, facilitating and delivering assistance in Somalia following the 2010–2011 famine, at a time when few organisations could secure access. The Humanitarian Coordination Office–Somalia was established in 2001, and worked closely with a coalition of 47 members of humanitarian Islamic organisations and other humanitarian key actors in Somalia. The OIC also raised US$350 million in famine relief from its member states at an international conference in August 2011. ICHAD partnered with both Muslim and non-Muslim agencies in its operational response in Somalia, including working with the Federation of Arab Doctors on emergency medical services and with the WFP to deliver emergency food aid to 40,000 people in the Afgooye corridor near Mogadishu (OIC 2011).

ICHAD has also convened annual conferences of OIC humanitarian NGOs, the first taking place in 2008 in Senegal with the participation of over 60 NGOs (Bakhit 2008). Hence, in contrast to ASEAN's state-centric approach, the OIC has been proactive and effective in engaging non-governmental actors, including philanthropists and NGOs in the Muslim world.

Broader Implications for the Humanitarian Sector

The past few decades have seen a rise in the humanitarian activities of ROs. We have considered here the historical evolution of this phenomenon in relation to the humanitarian system, looked at which areas they are active in, and examined more closely what humanitarian engagement means concretely for two ROs. We can conclude from the analysis here than ROs are indeed becoming more visible and important players in the humanitarian landscape.

As asked in the introduction: what are the implications of this trend for the ability to meet humanitarian needs? What are the implications for the humanitarian system itself? Does the increase in regional humanitarian structures and action by ROs signal a shift in the governance of the humanitarian system, or the emergence of parallel systems? Or do the approaches of ROs simply supplement the work of more traditional humanitarian agencies?

On the first question, while ROs have indeed become more involved in humanitarian affairs, the impact of their interventions have remained highly uneven. This is true between organisations as well as with the same organisation in different contexts. For example, while the OIC was able to secure humanitarian access in Somalia when many Western agencies were not, they have been unable to secure access to operate in Rakhine State in Myanmar, where mass protests have been held over the OIC's perceived support of the stateless Rohingya. Even ASEAN, of which Myanmar is a member state, has been unsuccessful in convincing its 10 member states that the regional body had a potential role to play to address the humanitarian crises in Rakhine State, as well as the resulting regional refugee crisis. Hence, general conclusions cannot be made about the humanitarian impact that ROs have had in spite of their best efforts. At the same time, ROs continue to be constrained by their own mandates and principles, such as non-interference, respect for sovereignty and consensus, which can, at times, cripple organisations from mobilising effectively in the face of humanitarian crises, such as the case of ASEAN whose humanitarian mandate is limited to 'natural' disasters and lacks a mechanism to address man-made humanitarian crises. Unlike the African Union, whose constitution allows it to intervene in countries where atrocities are being committed, ASEAN lacks effective human-rights, peacekeeping and conflict-resolution mechanisms (Fan and Krebs 2014: 13). Indeed, some ROs, such as ASEAN, have a tendency to view humanitarian assistance more as continuum of wider development cooperation, with an emphasis on stability, socio-economic development and capacity development, rather than as an end in itself.

Institutional weakness and a lack of resources also hinder the ability of ROs to be effective humanitarian actors. With many regional organisations already faced with budgetary and human-resource limitations, humanitarian operations often depend on a high level of external funding as well as expertise. For example, during Cyclone Nargis, funding for ASEAN's engagement primarily came not from its member states but, rather, international donors, with some contributions from private foundations. Human resource constraints are also common, constraining regional organisations ability to become effective humanitarian actors. A 2014 report by the Humanitarian Policy Group on ASEAN observed: 'staffing limitations also need to be borne in mind when considering the scope of ASEAN's humanitarian capacity. With a staff one-tenth the size of the European Commission's, the ASEAN Secretariat in Jakarta does not have sufficient manpower to address critical regional issues or conduct detailed research' (Fan and Krebs 2014: 13).

These findings underline the reality that ROs are not monolithic but rather consist of a diverse set of institutions, each with its distinct mandate, interests, capabilities, ambitions and evolution. As such, hopes that rise of regional humanitarian action would lead inevitably to a general regionalisation of a standard form of humanitarian action, with each RO taking the lead for its own region, seem to bear little grounding in reality. Equally, fears that regional organisations' humanitarian engagement would lead to a fragmentation of the humanitarian system also appear to misread and exaggerate the nature of change. Given the limited financial and human resources of many ROs, and, indeed, their divergent mandates and capacities, international humanitarian organisations will likely continue to provide the core functions of humanitarian aid delivery and traditional donors will continue to provide the bulk of global humanitarian financing for some time to come, even as other actors, including ROs, play increasingly active humanitarian roles. It is more likely that each RO will develop particular areas of expertise, in accordance with its mandate, priorities, capacities and interests, and that these will complement the broader international humanitarian system rather than replace it. In terms of discursive institutionalism, the regional organisations espouse different ideas about their humanitarian roles and therewith institutionalise their humanitarian activities and discourses, as well as their identities, in different ways, but they have not (yet) left a huge impact on the humanitarian system.

Nonetheless, the rise of regional humanitarian action and other types of actors active in humanitarian crises, combined with the assertion of sovereignty by many countries in managing humanitarian affairs, is at least challenging the traditional UN-centric humanitarian system to become more inclusive, not only on the principle of diversity but as the only way to remain relevant and effective. ROs are comprised of member states in the developing world, many of whom are middle-income countries, high-income countries and emerging humanitarian donors. In the changing landscape of development cooperation and humanitarian action, the humanitarian system cannot afford to remain a closed exclusive 'club'. The challenge will be to find ways of building partnerships in a way that retains the best of the traditional system while embracing the potential of regional actors and the opportunities that such collaboration could create.

Notes

1 UNICEF retained its acronym, but changed its name into the United Nations Children's Fund to highlight its growing developmental role.
2 More generally, the growing role of the EU provided an institutional example for the possibilities of regional cooperation. Interestingly, most regional organisations focus on disasters in their own region, in contrast with the European Union's Humanitarian Aid and Civil Protection department (ECHO) which works outside the EU.

References

ASEAN (2010) *ASEAN Agreement on Disaster Management and Emergency Response (AADMER)*, Jakarta: ASEAN Secretariat.

ASEAN (2009) *Standard Operating Procedures for Regional Standby Arrangements and Coordination of Joint Disaster Relief and Emergency Response Operations* (SASOP), Jakarta: ASEAN Secretariat.

Bakhit, A.M. (2008) 'The OIC Humanitarian Activities', Panel on inter-institutional dialogue on development issues and humanitarian assistance, OIC Inter-institutional Forum on the Occasion of the Celebration of the 60th Anniversary of the Universal Declaration of Human Rights, Geneva.

Collinson, S. and Elhawary, S. (2012) *Humanitarian Space: A Review of Trends and Issues*, London: HPG.

DPKO (1999) *Cooperation between the United Nations and Regional Organizations/ Arrangements in a Peacekeeping Environment: Suggested Principles and Mechanisms*, New York: UN.

Fan, L. and H. Krebs (2014) *Regional Organisations and Humanitarian Action: The Case of ASEAN*, Humanitarian Policy Group Working Paper, London, September.

Ferris, E. and D. Petz (2013) *In the Neighborhood: The Growing Role of Regional Organizations in Disaster Risk Management*, Washington DC and London: The Brookings Institution-London School of Economics Project on Internal Displacement.

ISDR (2005) Hyogo Framework for Action 2005-2015: Building the Resilience of Nations and Communities (www.unisdr.org/files/1037_hyogoframework foractionenglish.pdf) accessed 1 April 2015.

Kamal, A. (2009) 'Progress of the HFA Implementation in the ASEAN Region', Presentation at the Global Platform for Disaster Risk Reduction, Geneva, 16–19 June 2009.

Labbé, J., Fan, L., Kemp, W. (2013) *Cooperation from Crisis? Regional Responses to Humanitarian Emergencies*, New York: IPI.

OIC (2008) *Charter of the Organisation of Islamic Cooperation* (www.oic-oci.org/oicv2/ page/?p_id=53&p_ref=27&lan=en) accessed 7 July 2014.

OIC (2011) 'OIC Member States pledge $350 million for Somalia', *OIC Journal*, June-August 2011, Issue 18, Jeddah: OIC.

Schmidt, V.A. (2010) 'Taking Ideas and Discourse Seriously: Explaining Change through Discursive Institutionalisms the Fourth "New Institutionalism"', *European Political Science Review* 2(1):1–25.

UN Charter (1945) Chapter VIII (www.un.org/en/documents/charter/chapter8.shtml) accessed 5 June 2014.

UN General Assembly (1991) GA Resolution 46/182 (www.un.org/depts/dha) accessed 5 June 2014.

Zyck, S. (2013) *Regional Organisations and Humanitarian Action*, London: ODI.

15 Traditional and Non-Traditional Humanitarian Actors in Disaster Response in India

Tony Vaux

Introduction

The term 'traditional' has come to refer to the established Western humanitarian system, but this is largely a reflection of the dominance of Western perspectives.[1] The first line of response to many disasters, especially smaller ones, is through local organisations (LOs) that have existed in one form or another for a long time. The need for funding and media attention makes Western humanitarianism more prominent and this creates a pressure to diminish or ignore the role of other more genuinely 'traditional' responders such as national governments, civil-society and local communities. This leads to a paradigm of aid based on 'what the West can offer' rather than what may be needed locally. The differences in approach between Western and 'traditional' systems may be exacerbated by the charitable aspect of Western humanitarianism and its need to respond to the preferences and interests of givers. In particular, public appeals in the West can lead to pressure for rapid spending, excessive supply of Western materials and staff, and competition for profile among agencies. This tendency can put LOs either into contractor roles or leave them out of Western support, as was generally the case in the examples described below.

Western humanitarianism has institutionalised an approach largely governed by principles and standards but traditional local organisations may be more pragmatic because they need to be highly responsive to the needs of their constituents and may be subject to local political pressure. While the strength of traditional LOs lies in rapid response and long-term commitment, this may be a limitation in case of highly political issues that entail risk to local people, especially violent conflict. Traditional LOs must be cautious in speaking out about injustice and human-rights issues because of possible repercussions against themselves and the people they work with. Western humanitarianism is also selective in 'speaking out' but may be able to take greater risk.

The separation of the two systems, with their different strengths and weaknesses, can lead to an aggregation of benefits. The Western system may generate resources and open possibilities for advocacy while LOs mobilise local voluntary effort and knowledge. But there are disadvantages. The dominance of the Western system can undermine LOs and weaken their ability to respond in future crises without further support from the West. As the Western system becomes more rigidly attached to principles and standards, and more frequently linked to Western political interests, the opportunity for fruitful communication and cooperation between the two systems is diminishing.

This chapter consists of six parts and focuses on three disasters in Gujarat State, Western India, comparing the responses of the Western system with local responses, focusing particularly on the Self-Employed Women's Association (SEWA). This organisation provides a particularly useful comparison because it keeps to its own approach rather than compromising with the Western system. The second section studies the Morvi flood, a small disaster in which local responses dominated and Western organisations were barely active. The third section focuses on the 2001 Gujarat earthquake – a large-scale disaster that attracted international attention. The fourth section focuses on SEWA's approach to disasters and specifically considers its response to the Gujarat earthquake. The fifth section looks at the Communal Violence in 2002 and compares the SEWA response with the actions of Western humanitarian organisations, focusing on the issue of 'speaking out'. The chapter ends with a comparative analysis of the relationship of the Western system to LOs and makes some observations about how they could cooperate better.

The Morvi Flood: A Small-Scale Local Disaster

In 1979, I reached the town of Morvi in Gujarat within hours of a devastating flood and, almost for the only time in my 28 years with Oxfam, saw dead bodies still being cleared away after a disaster. In this case the task was being performed mainly by members of a Hindu nationalist organisation, the Rashtriya Swayamsevak Sangh (RSS), recognisable by the huge rubber gloves they used to handle corpses. They were trained and equipped for this work. Normally, by the time Western aid agencies reach the site of a disaster the people who clear away the bodies have disappeared. The only sign of their existence is that the bodies have gone. Generally the humanitarian literature and guidance has little to say about this necessary and significant task. Equally it has little to say about first aid. These tasks are performed by local people, community organisations and governments, usually before the 'traditional' Western agencies have arrived. This vital part of humanitarian action is largely neglected – contributing to a general underestimation of the role of local agencies.

The Morvi Flood was typical of the many thousands of local disasters that are too small to register on the radar of the international aid agencies. As the Oxfam representative my job was focused on development programmes but because a local church organisation offered to take me to the site, I

was able to mobilise a modest amount of funding (around £2,000) as a
token gesture. Oxfam maintained a 'Catastrophe Fund' out of its general
income and could release such small amounts to help in local disasters.
From Oxfam's point of view there was no point trying to hit the headlines
or try to recover money spent from the public or donor institutions. In
such cases the local representative was generally given a free hand – but
very limited resources. In these recurrent, small-scale local crises, the main
response would come from local sources, sometimes including government. Often they relied more on voluntary effort than funding. The level
and professionalism of such responses varied widely and was usually much
less than was needed. In general, the Western system does little to support
such organisations and help them prepare for future disasters. Instead it
focuses on larger-scale disasters such as the earthquake that struck Western
Gujarat in 2001.

The 2001 Gujarat Earthquake

The Gujarat earthquake of 26 January 2001 quickly became international
headline news. As many as 20,000 people died, most of them crushed to
death when buildings collapsed. Approximately 167,000 people were
injured and 339,000 homes destroyed (USGS no date). Within a few days,
Western emergency teams had arrived and were trying to locate people
trapped in the rubble. This became the focus of the international media:
cries for help were recorded and rescue teams took credit for the dozen
or so lives they were able to save. Conspicuous by their absence from the
international media, and uncounted, were the tens of thousands of people
pulled from the rubble by family, friends and neighbours, as well as by local
and national organisations. Before any international teams had arrived,
the Government of India mobilised 15,000 soldiers to rescue people, clear
the bodies and remove the debris. But it was the foreign 'rescue' teams
that captured the news. From the perspective of the international agencies,
this was necessary to generate the funding that would provide relief and
reconstruction.

   It was not only the army and LOs that were absent from the media record.
An evaluation for the Disasters Emergency Committee (DEC) found that
'respectively the contributions of British Government, DEC and Indian
Government are £10m, £24m and £1 billion' (DMI 2001: 4)[2] but the contribution of the Government of India was not a matter of interest to the global
media. Indeed, Western agencies had an interest in minimising the scale of
the national response in order to boost their claims for public donations.
The image that had to be projected for successful fundraising was that people were helpless until the Western agencies arrived. The earthquake left
many people injured but affected only a small part of the country and so the
Government of India arranged to fly injured people to hospitals in other
areas. Nevertheless an emergency hospital was set up in the earthquake area

by a Western agency and attracted far greater attention than the huge airlift organised to take people to government hospitals elsewhere.

The media focus on Western action reinforced a notion of helplessness among the local people and even the government. It also led to a serious distortion of priorities. The Western media gave credit to agencies that filled planes with Western materials and sent them off within hours of the disaster. But in the first hours after the earthquake, although aid agencies did not know what was needed, they dispatched large quantities of bottled water by airfreight, even though bottled water was readily available in Gujarat. They sent large numbers of international staff despite the availability of competent staff and organisations in Gujarat. These newly arrived expatriate staff were under pressure to show results quickly and this created a tendency to ignore LOs or treat them as contractors to perform tasks that had been decided by the Western agency. The DEC Report concluded that agencies would have done much better if they had deployed fewer international staff and instead developed more effective partnerships with organisations that were already present in Gujarat.

Viewed from the logic of a Western charitable system, images of rescue teams, field hospitals, airfreighted relief items and expatriate supervisors were the essential fuel for a successful public appeal. There was no way of aligning the amount raised to the needs and so the availability of public appeal funds became a significant factor in determining the nature of the response. The preference for high-profile Western activity, contrasted with local helplessness, perpetuated the distribution of clothes, utensils, food, water, etc. In fact many people had been able to recover their clothes and utensils from the rubble of their houses and were quickly in a position to resume normal life. But in order to qualify for relief goods, they had to stay in tented camps or at home to be registered by different organisations. Those who went to the fields or migrated with their animals might miss out on such offers. Tensions arose when assessments forced people to relive painful experiences or debate different priorities. People distrusted leaders who negotiated deals with the agencies and disputed whether to trust the promises of one organisation or to turn to another which might offer more.

The relief phase continued for at least three months and some Western agencies withdrew at that point without addressing the issue of recovery. At the end of the three-month period agencies began to conduct lengthy surveys as the basis for livelihoods support but by that time many of the affected people had lost their trade connections and markets. The issue of house reconstruction was delayed by discussions about selecting beneficiaries, designs and compensation for partial repairs. There was a long debate about the importance of 'earthquake-proofing' the houses. All this prevented people from resuming a normal life and meanwhile the linkages and relationships that underscored livelihoods were eroded. The government's process for assessing damage was deeply flawed and had to be redone.[3] It was more than a year after the earthquake before houses were rebuilt on any scale. Meanwhile many people lost their livelihoods because markets and contacts disappeared. Thus the overall effect of the Western humanitarian system was to undermine self-reliance.

SEWA and Disasters

SEWA is an organisation in which the voice of vulnerable local people is particularly well represented. It is a union of working women[4] founded in Gujarat in the 1960s and has now spread to many other areas of India. At the time of the earthquake in 2001 it had 200,000 members[5] but partly because of its successful response now has more than a million members nationally. It has linkages with international movements of working women. A key feature of SEWA is that it is not a charity or conventional NGO but a union. Its income derives mainly from the dues collected from its members and their voluntary savings. Its activities are directed by the decisions of the members. It draws some of its leaders from sections of society other than poor working women but the members ultimately dictate the policy.

The reason for this unusual degree of democratisation (many unions in India are dominated by a single leader or ruling clique) lies in the unusual qualities of its founder, Ela Bhatt, and her strong adherence to Gandhian principles of self-reliance coupled with a (perhaps less Gandhian) belief in working women as leaders. Throughout her 50 years' association with working women, Ela Bhatt has developed SEWA's leaders from among the members and insisted that the small cadre of senior workers drawn from outside always give way to the collective decisions of the members (Bhatt 2006; Crowell 2003).

After a decade in which SEWA's membership and savings hugely increased, the idea of a bank controlled by the members began to emerge and the SEWA Bank was created in the 1970s. Even at this early stage the underlying concept of SEWA was a focus on women's livelihood as the essential basis for all other forms of well-being.

By the 1980s SEWA was responding to epidemics and floods affecting hundreds of members at a time. SEWA conducted surveys and passed information to the government agencies responsible. By studying the cause of each crisis, SEWA identified services that would provide members with crucial support through difficult times. SEWA members say that its evolution was based on crises and disasters. Whenever something happened that caused distress to a member or group of members, the larger organisation came together to analyse the problem and find a solution. This approach was applied to domestic crises as well as epidemics, fires, floods and droughts. 'A disaster is an opportunity to learn' became a guiding principle. By overcoming these challenges, without recourse to international or government support, SEWA members developed confidence and leaders emerged. In reviewing their actions, SEWA members often referred to this development of individual and collective strength as a key outcome in itself.

A series of severe floods in Ahmedabad in the 1970s turned SEWA's attention towards disasters on a larger scale. Debates among the members, especially at the annual plenary meeting, led to the development of an optional insurance scheme. As well as their savings, SEWA members could choose to set aside additional amounts to cover against the loss of productive items. Because many members worked from home, this included their house. The aim of the insurance was to provide enough compensation (for damage to dwelling, tools etc.) to enable the workers to continue their livelihood despite a significant disaster.

Although SEWA tried to link its members into government schemes this did not always yield the desired results and SEWA has reverted to self-reliance. In the case of insurance, the Government of India put pressure on banks and insurance companies (which were mostly government-owned) to provide insurance for poor people. SEWA struck a deal with one such company and in order to reduce transaction costs, SEWA agreed to do all the paperwork although the insurance company reserved the ultimate right to inspect the damage and decide on claims. This arrangement was tested in floods in Ahmedabad in the 1980s. SEWA conducted assessments of damage but the company failed to respond until it could send its own inspectors to cross-check the assessments. SEWA members realised that if the payment came even a few weeks after the disaster the members would not be able to survive. They would be forced into debt and might lose their markets. This experience led to a decision by SEWA members to revert to self-insurance by SEWA underwritten by the SEWA Bank.

SEWA's Response to the 2001 Earthquake

By contrast with the focus on relief by the Western humanitarian system, SEWA focused on livelihoods from the start. The insurance scheme was put into immediate effect and by paying out claims rapidly from the SEWA Bank, it allowed women to continue working. This made SEWA hugely popular and led to an immediate increase in members both of SEWA and of the insurance scheme.

But SEWA's main focus was on the majority of members (and other working women) who could not recover their livelihood on the basis of insurance payouts alone. Most of SEWA's members in Kutch were engaged in embroidery as a cottage industry.[6] This was a traditional craft which had been adapted from the 1970s onwards to provide 'ethnic' goods to shops in the cities and abroad. Typically, women would embroider while engaged in other tasks such as care of children. After the earthquake many men were out of work or injured and the women saw an opportunity to expand the embroidery work. SEWA accepted that this would not only recover livelihoods but also restore self-reliance and boost women's status and leadership.

SEWA did not put out an appeal for funds or send requests to specific aid agencies. Instead it set out the plans developed by the members on its website and invited international agencies to offer support but there was no significant response. These agencies preferred to make their own assessments, set their own priorities and then look for local NGOs to implement them. For SEWA this was an unacceptable relationship. Unable to secure Western support for its own plans, SEWA supported its disaster response by drawing on the resources of the union. Embroidery did not require expensive tools and the women were already skilled (to varying degrees); the problem was working capital. This was solved, although at considerable risk, by drawing on the SEWA Bank.[7] The Bank put forward the working capital necessary for the livelihood programme but it was clear from the start that the outlay would have to be recovered.

The weekly collection of savings, often accompanied by talk and exchange of news, had already formed close links between SEWA members and the 'activists' (*aagewans*) who went from house to house. The first act of many of these activists after the disaster was to take the bus and find out about other SEWA members and activists.[8] The activists returned to their village and shared the news. Many of the male village leaders had succumbed to shock after the earthquake but the activists had kept busy and their knowledge put them in a leadership position despite traditions of male domination. With the skills developed in the SEWA groups, several SEWA members became de facto village leaders and in a few cases continued in this role long after the earthquake. As SEWA members later recalled, their confidence and links with other members enabled them to turn the disaster into an opportunity. The dynamism of the SEWA members was in stark contrast with the passivity of those waiting for relief from the Western agencies.

Meanwhile, SEWA's leaders in Ahmedabad, over 200 miles from the main earthquake area in Kutch, despatched a team to meet with the SEWA workers. They arrived on the borders of Kutch on the evening of the day of the earthquake.[9] SEWA activists had already made their analysis and reached the town where the SEWA team was staying. The first question asked was 'Have you brought us work?' The discussion then focused on how to recover their livelihoods.

SEWA recognised that this did not mean that other issues were unimportant. But with their philosophy was that self-reliance, livelihoods and savings were the key to meeting other needs such as health, child care, education and house reconstruction. The challenge for SEWA was to support livelihoods on the necessary scale. There were 5,000 existing members in the region but many other women wanted to join SEWA and this created a unique opportunity to expand SEWA's presence and make SEWA stronger.

In the days after the earthquake, SEWA developed a plan to support the employment of 20,000 women. Finding the materials was not a problem nor was it necessary to offer basic training because embroidery was a traditional skill that all girls learnt before they were married. The main challenge was to market such a huge amount of 'ethnic' goods through the outlets already available – and SEWA could not afford to make a loss on the operation. Another challenge was to start work immediately so that the members would not be forced to migrate, sell their property or move into the relief camps run by Western agencies. A week after the disaster, SEWA began accepting a wide range of embroidered goods made according to traditional styles and patterns. But it soon became obvious that because so many women were now working, the range of products was too diverse. Without adequate guidance and supervision the quality was inconsistent. After much discussion among the members it was decided that the basis of production had to be changed. The designs had to be standardised and the products must be consistent.

The proposed solution was to break down production into different stages, giving women small specialised tasks rather than leaving them responsible for an entire product such as a cushion-cover or dress. This enabled SEWA to offer goods of a specific quality and design to shops in different parts of the country, many of which were keen to take the goods as a gesture of support for people affected by the earthquake but would not accept goods that were below standard. The shop-owners also wanted to select certain items rather than others and to influence the colours and designs.

Within two months of the earthquake, membership had increased and SEWA now needed to support 40,000 women embroiderers. SEWA's expert advisers in its cooperatives and other institutions concluded that new markets had to be found. They contacted designers in Mumbai who came up with a plan to create fashion clothes using traditional embroidery skills but adapting the colours and designs to the market among wealthy people in Mumbai. The message went out to the villages to use different colours and designs. While the products never became totally divorced from the traditional craft, the skills had to be developed in new ways. Training was needed to ensure that the new approach could be standardised.

SEWA members had no objection to this. Their focus was on recovering through their livelihood. Some were proud to know that their production was being shown off in fashion shows in Mumbai and other glittering cities. Activists from the earthquake region attended these fashion shows and gave talks about traditional embroidery. The success of the women earned respect from men in the villages. Because women were earning money and men (in many cases) were still negotiating relief from Western aid agencies, the status of women increased and they were given further chances to improve their skills by speaking at village meetings and taking a wider interest in village issues.

Six months after the earthquake, nearly 80,000 women were receiving enough income from embroidery to maintain their families, and the goods were being sold all over India and abroad. In their annual review at the start of 2002,[10] members from across the state noted that the members as well as SEWA as an organisation were much stronger. All this was achieved without any significant input from the government or from aid agencies.

Although financial support would have been welcome, reliance on any such institutions could have undermined the principle of self-reliance and the development of responsibility and leadership among SEWA members. As it was, working women in Gujarat had greatly increased their ability to cope with future disasters.

Communal Violence in Gujarat in 2002

Not all agencies in the Western system accept a responsibility for 'speaking out' about the political factors affecting disasters but most of the larger established agencies now regard this as part of their work to a greater or lesser degree. Although 'speaking out' can help to raise profile at home, the problem is that it can lead to countermeasures by those being criticised, especially national governments (Weissman 2004). It might be expected that the Western system would be more active in 'speaking out' than LOs because the latter may lack the resources and detachment to do this. The following example indicates that while this may be broadly true, Western agencies also face serious inhibitions.

The events that were often described in the media as the 'Gujarat riots' were really a series of pogroms against the State's Muslim minority with some counter-attacks against Hindus. According to official figures, the riots resulted in the deaths of 790 Muslims and 254 Hindus; 2,500 people were injured non-fatally, and 223 more were reported missing. Other sources estimate that up to 2,000 Muslims died. There were instances of children being burned alive, and widespread looting and destruction of property (BBC 2005). The State Government, which had links with Hindu nationalism, took little action to protect Muslims especially in the early days of violence.

With its pragmatic approach, SEWA is open to any course of action that might benefit its members. As previously mentioned, it puts considerable emphasis on researching issues and often uses this research to influence other stakeholders, especially the government. Drawing on support from specialised analysts willing to give their time at little cost, the SEWA Academy has developed within SEWA as the centre for such research. As part of its response to the communal violence SEWA published reports on the underlying causes of these events (see SEWA 2002). The SEWA Academy estimated that over the 20-year period before the violence of 2002, more than 80,000 regular mill workers and 50,000 casual workers had been laid off. Including families, as many as 700,000 people in the city had been affected. Communal violence was closely associated with these events. Violence occurred in 1969 at the end of a severe period of factory closure and retrenchment of workers. In the next major outbreak in 1985, 19,000 people (mostly Muslim) fled from their homes in Ahmedabad to makeshift camps. There were further 'riots' in 1986 preceded by the closure of 17 textile mills. Over this two-year period 40,000 workers had been made redundant.[11] The Textile Labour Association (TLA) which had helped restrain violence in 1969 had become ineffective because it had lost its impartiality, mainly because of increasing political involvement.

When the violence erupted, the challenge for SEWA was the inactivity of the State Government. SEWA had access to politicians and officials at the highest levels both in the State and in the central Government in Delhi. As soon as the 'riots' began, Ela Bhatt contacted senior politicians and officials in the State but it quickly became clear that they were not committed to restraining the violence. Ela Bhatt tried to persuade senior officials in the police and other services to intervene and stop the violence even if it meant a confrontation with the State leadership but without effect.

In the first few days Ela Bhatt and other SEWA organisers were not allowed to visit the affected areas ('for their own safety') but eventually made a visit to one of the most badly affected areas, Aman Chowk, and listened to SEWA members. It quickly became clear that the primary concern of the members (both Muslim and Hindu) was for security (hers as well as theirs) and they begged Ela Bhatt to do nothing that might inflame the situation. SEWA's report describes the frustration of those first few days: 'It was becoming clear that the police and other state machinery were not only incapable of controlling the murderous mobs, but also did not want to. With a few exceptions, they either turned a blind eye or actively aided the attackers' (SEWA 2002: 6).

Pressed to 'speak out', SEWA found itself in an extremely difficult position. About a third of SEWA's members at the time were Muslims and SEWA itself was being targeted because of its connections with Muslims. SEWA received threats and a small bomb was planted outside its main office in Ahmedabad. There was also a serious prospect of division within SEWA. In some areas Hindu and Muslim members had been provoked to attack each other. The cadre of professional staff, including Ela Bhatt, were mainly Hindu. Muslim husbands were putting pressure on their wives not to support SEWA. Hindu husbands accused SEWA of being pro-Muslim and told their wives to abandon SEWA. Some members became deeply cynical about SEWA's ideals and good intentions, including its Gandhian commitment to religious unity. One of SEWA's Muslim activists, Rahimaben, said: 'Now so many women were bitter and accusing. They would see me and say "where is your unity now?"' (SEWA 2002: 5)

As in the case of the earthquake, the desire to find out about and contact other SEWA members was a driving force. One of SEWA's longest-standing organisers, Manaliben, recalled:

> Many of the local leaders … were on the road, defying the mob and curfew, inquiring about their colleagues and other SEWA members. They would call me and often give me account of the areas. I was very worried about them. I sometimes shouted at them 'What are you doing so far away from home? Go home, it is too dangerous to venture out'.
> (SEWA 2002: 7)

After a few days in which observers were deliberately kept out of the main areas of violence, passes were obtained for SEWA workers to make a full assessment across the city. Teams were formed from among the grassroots workers, mainly from the trade committees, health programme and the SEWA Bank. They arranged for savings to be withdrawn from members' accounts so that they had the means for survival. They surveyed the loss of life, health problems and damage to property. Preliminary assessments for insurance claims were also made – it was estimated that 30,000 urban members would be eligible for compensation. More than 10,000 members' houses had been burnt down or otherwise destroyed. A further 2,000 members' houses had been completely looted. Just four members had died – fewer than initially feared.

Having assessed what it could do by supporting the members, SEWA decided not to 'speak out' about the government's inaction. The decision was taken by the elected representatives after consultation with the members. These representatives came together in an Executive Committee meeting on 4 March, a week after the violence. In the account published on SEWA's website the question was addressed in the following way:

> Should we make a public appeal for peace? Will anyone listen in this charged atmosphere? What is the first priority of our sisters? Survival. We decided to concentrate on reaching out to our members and other affected people ... On the one hand there was no denying that the government had failed in its primary duty to protect Gujarat's citizens. At the same time we had to urge our government to provide security and to develop programmes to help people to rebuild their lives.
>
> (SEWA 2002: 11, 25)

After much debate SEWA representatives took a pragmatic view. The violence was now over and any criticism of government was likely to deter it from playing a full role in rehabilitation. A public statement might also increase tension between the communities and lead to repercussions against SEWA and SEWA members.

In order to conduct its activities SEWA needed the collaboration of the police and it would have been very easy for the State Government to halt all the activities if it wished to do so. Very few organisations were working in the areas affected by violence and this put further pressure on SEWA as the organisation with the best understanding of what had happened. Western aid agencies arrived too late to witness the delayed action of government that was the key grievance of the Muslims. Moreover, the 'Gujarat riots' received very little attention in the global media and the coverage was not conducive to fundraising. The term 'riots' implied that both sides were equally to blame and this undermined any charitable feeling on the part of the Western public.

Hence, despite the scale of the disaster, the Western humanitarian response was limited and most of the responsibility fell on LOs such as SEWA. This increased the pressure on them both to address the immediate needs and also to 'speak out'. But the two actions were not compatible, especially as, in the long run, it would be government aid that people must rely on for recovery and reconstruction.

SEWA put out requests for aid on its website but received no significant international support. It had to concentrate on what could be done without financial resources. If members had lost the papers on which their loans were recorded the SEWA Bank provided new records, negotiated extended periods for repayment and supported members in their claims for compensation from government and from SEWA's insurance scheme. The SEWA Bank made new loans to members to replace their losses. This proactive banking process not only enabled members to recover their livelihoods but also became one of the first ways of re-establishing contact between the communities. The local organisers for the bank, who collected savings, resumed their practice of moving around the city, visiting all religious groups.

SEWA's position was to avoid confrontation and focus on influencing government actions behind the scenes in order to benefit its members. Ela Bhatt told the Chief Minister that the government's support for relief camps was inadequate and that it should budget for at least three months instead of just 15 days. This initiative opened up a dialogue and three hours later, the Revenue Department phoned to ask her for budgets to support this extension. In addition, the Indian Prime Minister, who remained in New Delhi during the immediate aftermath of the violence, asked Ela Bhatt to brief him on the situation. She told him that the compensation given to the victims was 'haphazard and ridiculous'. A Director from the Prime Minister's Office was sent to investigate and as a result, a full reassessment was carried out, in which SEWA participated. Ela Bhatt was later appointed as a member of the State committee on relief and rehabilitation.

The government promised compensation for each person killed in the riots but in many cases the body could not be found and police officers sometimes refused to cooperate in issuing papers. SEWA worked to facilitate this process and pressed the government to increase the level of compensation. It took up a number of legal cases on behalf of the members, finding documents and pressuring the police to provide the necessary endorsements.

When the Prime Minister of India finally visited Gujarat on 4 April, over a month after the violence,[12] Ela Bhatt said in his presence at a public meeting:

> We are ashamed that the Prime Minister of our country has to visit Gujarat at this time. What has happened in Gujarat is terrible. The country was divided in 1947. Today it is as if our hearts were divided … There can never be peace by making Muslims insecure. That is not nationalism. Why don't our political parties understand this?
>
> (SEWA 2002: 25)

The Prime Minister visited some of the affected areas and spoke with the people, including some of the Muslim SEWA members. He requested SEWA to take over from government the responsibility of looking after widows and orphans and promised financial support from the Prime Minister's Relief Fund.

In a major study of ethnic violence in India, Varshney (2002: 293) concludes that 'without SEWA, the loss of lives would undoubtedly have been greater, not smaller. It not only provided a better livelihood to the poor; it also saved lives during the riots.' SEWA's pragmatic position of engagement was formally endorsed by the members at the annual review of its work in 2002, which noted that SEWA had been successful in relation to its primary goal of achieving strength through numbers. Membership rose from 284,000 at the end of 2001 to 530,000 in 2002 – by far the fastest increase in its history. The majority of new members were Muslims and today around half of SEWA's members are Muslim.

The 'Gujarat riots' received little media attention in the West and there was little public sympathy for what appeared to be an entirely 'political' event in which there were no clearly 'innocent' victims. Western agencies played little role in relief or recovery, perhaps considering that if the State Government was responsible for the event then it was the State Government that should respond. But they did not say this openly. Without staff on the ground during the main period of violence, the agencies felt unable to substantiate the common view that the State Government had been seriously at fault. Only one major Western agency (ActionAid) focused on the task of holding the State Government to account and this was done largely through its Chief Executive in India acting in a personal capacity. Having 'spoken out' ActionAid was not then in a position to take part in the relief and recovery efforts. It also faced repercussions from the State Government and virulent criticism from Hindu nationalists. Nevertheless it is arguable that this effort to expose the State Government's role may have had some positive impact in preventing any recurrence of the 2002 violence and perhaps making the Chief Minister more cautious about his links with Hindu nationalism. The issue became the focus of public enquiries, which largely cleared the Chief Minister but left many doubts and put him under pressure to sever his direct links with Hindu nationalism. The UK, EU and USA imposed travel bans on the Chief Minister. These bans were lifted after he became Prime Minister in 2014 – apparently on the understanding that he had moved away from the stance he took in Gujarat in 2002.

The case illustrates some fundamental points: although 'speaking out' is difficult for LOs they may be able to achieve considerable results behind the scenes while still maintaining their essential role of supporting local people. The open public statements and press conferences of Western agencies may be appropriate for addressing the 'big picture' but less effective in finding practical ways forward. Second, the security of local people is a paramount concern for an LO. Third, different approaches may lead towards a more comprehensive response to the overall problem: SEWA focused on practical results for its members while a less vulnerable Western agency was able to tackle the more sensitive issue of openly influencing the State Government.

Institutionalised Principles and Contextualised Approaches

One of the themes of this book is the contrast between the institutionalisation of principles in the Western system with the more contextualised approach of LOs. These examples provide some evidence for examining this contrast.

The most fundamental principle of Western humanitarianism is that 'needs come first'. This is the first principle of the Code of Conduct for The International Red Cross and Red Crescent Movement and NGOs in Disaster Relief. SEWA was not a signatory to the Code and was unaware of it at the time of the disasters described above. The evidence above indicates that SEWA recognised a wider range of needs than is commonly assumed in the Western system. Its aim was the self-reliance of members through secure livelihoods and it measured success in relation to targets, such as increased membership. It saw relief as a means towards that wider aim rather than as an aim in itself.

Secondly, SEWA was concerned with its members rather than with the whole population. SEWA did not make an overall assessment of needs. It focused on its members but also accepted a responsibility towards any working women who might wish to join SEWA. This selectivity may seem to be a fundamental difference in relation to the Western system but despite the principles of the Code, many Western agencies also preselect the groups on which they focus. Save the Children, for example, focuses on children. Other agencies may channel aid through partners, such as church organisations, that have a tendency to work with particular groups and in particular areas of the world.

The most important difference may be that between SEWA's 'demand-driven' approach and the generally 'supply-driven' approach of the Western system. For the latter, much depends on what an agency can do, what resources happen to be available and how the system as a whole happens to fit together in each specific case. The Western response to the Morvi Floods was insignificant; in response to the Gujarat earthquake it was characterised by over-supply and competition, and the humanitarian response to the 'riots' was so cautious that it was ineffective. Similarly, the limited Western advocacy following the 'riots' may be attributed to a similar 'supply' bias. Western agencies have great capacity to address their own governments and the UN but are poorly equipped to put pressure on other governments, especially very powerful ones such as Gujarat State or the Government of India. Western advocacy is only effective in certain situations that play to its strength.

The Western charity-based model of humanitarianism leads towards a comprehensive view of disasters in the sense that each area of need is considered specifically and separately. This leads to the well-known problems of coordination and sequencing that are often cited as limitations of the Western system.[13] By contrast, SEWA cannot rely on 'more money' to solve problems; it can only think of 'more work'. Forced into a 'self-reliance' mode, it has to make choices and consider how the different needs fit together: what is the most important and fundamental? This has led SEWA to a focus on livelihoods as the basic generator of all other possibilities. This gives SEWA a strong strategic focus that still does not exclude any other type of activity, including advocacy, which might support livelihoods.

The Western institutionalised approach sets out minimum standards (notably those of the Sphere Project) for all the different sectors of support. Initially, the Sphere Standards did not include livelihoods and many agencies still consider livelihoods as an optional extra to be considered only after the all-important relief phase is well under way. As in the case of the earthquake, the Western system can often prolong and expand the relief phase because it becomes 'supply-driven'. From the outset, SEWA focuses on livelihoods as the source of other benefits, leaving the members to decide how to allocate their resources. It views health, childcare, education, etc. not as absolutes in themselves but as contributory factors to livelihoods which then provided the resources to support those services. Thus, for example, SEWA's approach to housing is not so much focused on technical issues as on the ability of housing to support livelihoods.

Similarly, SEWA's focus on working women is fundamentally different from the focus on children by many Western agencies. The Western focus reflects the concerns of the givers, whereas SEWA's focus on working women reflects an understanding of women's livelihoods as the chief source of child welfare. SEWA works on the basis of relevance to the actual social system rather than the compassion of outsiders. In doing so SEWA also avoids the trap that many Western agencies fall into of channelling aid through the existing power structures (village leaders for instance) which may themselves be sources of inequality and poverty.

Another key difference is that for many Western agencies a disaster is considered as a special event. It triggers an engagement that is short-term and separate from development. The aim is simply to reach the minimum humanitarian standards and then withdraw. Western practice is varied, with organisations such as Oxfam usually accepting a long-term responsibility for recovery and (more recently) reduction of future disaster risk. But the system itself, with its short-term funding and pressure to spend money quickly, does not favour long-term engagement. For SEWA, disasters are always the basis for long-term engagement and provide an opportunity not only to increase the self-reliance of individual members but also the strength of the union as a whole. This means that disaster risk reduction is built into the response to disasters, not added on as an afterthought as may be the case with the Western system.

For SEWA, cooperation with Western agencies presents considerable risks. Generally they do not perceive the self-reliance of SEWA members and of SEWA itself as key aims. SEWA is unwilling to compromise with Western agencies but many other LOs are tempted to take on what are in effect contractor roles. This may provide a temporary boost but often leaves them weakened in the long term. Voluntary effort may be replaced by hired staff and payment of allowances. When salaries can no longer be paid from Western funds such agencies may face crises or collapse. Although sensitive Western agencies can make adjustments to minimise this risk there is a fundamental difference between their supply-driven model and the demand-driven model of LOs. Their interaction is likely to have negative effects for the LO while the Western agencies may, in effect, capitalise on the goodwill, voluntary traditions and local understanding of their 'partners'.

Instead of SEWA's emphasis on self-reliance, the Western system to a greater or lesser extent supports a rights-based approach putting consider-able emphasis on the duties of governments and the benefits arising from claiming support from the state. In this model the need for charity from the Western system is to be replaced by functioning and democratic states. SEWA would not dispute this as a long-term vision and itself engages in advocacy around 'rights' (although focused on the duties of the state rather than citizen rights). It has taken cases of abuse to the Supreme Court but ultimately decided that this type of action rarely provides final solutions. Even the decisions of the Supreme Court may not be implemented with-out active support from other bodies and they can be bypassed by abusers within the system who find new ways to exploit poor people. Thus, SEWA decided to get on with restoring houses immediately after the earthquake so that members could work. At the same time it assisted the government to provide longer-term solutions but did not wait for these solutions to come about. As in practically all its activity, SEWA's approach is pragmatic rather than based on international policies and principles.

The area in which the Western agencies should have a clear advantage is in 'speaking out' about the political issues and abuses that underlie dis-asters. Generally their greater resources and remoteness allow them to research such issues and they may also have better contacts with power-ful bodies that can make a difference. However, the case of the Gujarat Violence shows that there are cases in which the Western system lacks the information or is itself unwilling to take risks. SEWA has shown that even an organisation that raises its resources from poor people can conduct sig-nificant research and can work behind the scenes to make a significant difference even in the most sensitive situation.

Finally, in comparison with LOs such as SEWA, Western agencies are much more willing to recognise a responsibility for the system as a whole. They have supported the development of principles and standards and increasingly converge around notions of 'best practice' reaching into practically every aspect of humanitarian action. By contrast, SEWA has focused on extending itself into other parts of India and globally but has shown little interest in the development or protection of a system for different types of LO. Like all the points above this essentially reflects a difference between a supply-driven system and a demand-driven LO.

Conclusion

Leaving aside the hybridisation caused by contractor relations between them, the contrast between the Western humanitarian system and LOs focuses around the dominance of 'supply' in one case and 'demand' in the other. At worst, Western humanitarianism focuses on profile and undermines the self-reliance both of people affected by disasters and of LOs. It has no real focus on developing local leadership. By contrast, LOs may suffer from lack of resources unless they are willing to submit to external influences and pressures. This is summarised in Table 15.1.

For the two systems to work well together representatives of Western agencies need to have time and scope to understand the perspectives and mandates of LOs. They need the space and capacity to respond to plans that have already been developed by LOs rather than rely solely on their own assessments and analysis or on supply-led preferences.

Table 15.1 Comparison of local organisations with typical Western agencies

	SEWA/Local organisations	*Western Agencies*
Political economy	Demand-led	Supply-led
Norms	Duties of both citizens and states	Rights-based entitlement to external support
	Cooperation, voluntarism, self-reliance, local leadership	Principles and standards
Operating style	Pragmatic	Consistent, mandate-driven
	Dominance of local views	Sensitive to Western donors
	Democratic control by members (SEWA)	Favours contractor relationships with LOs
Humanitarian focus	Livelihoods and recovery from the start	Full range of relief (minimum standards) before moving to recovery
Disaster Risk Reduction	Built into a long-term engagement	Add on after humanitarian action (at best)
Public policy	Limited by resource constraints; sensitive to local repercussions	Focused on Western system; not much real influence on national governments

Source: the author.

Similarly, in the case of 'speaking out' about the causes of humanitarian problems, LOs could benefit from partnerships with Western agencies that have the capacity and relative freedom to challenge local power. But again it will be necessary for Western agencies to listen very carefully to the concerns and sensitivities of LOs that must focus on practical results rather than principled stands.

Change in this direction necessitates greater willingness on the part of Western agencies to challenge current practices relating to 'accountability'. Despite the Red Cross Code principle that agencies should be accountable both to the givers of aid and the 'beneficiaries', there has been a tendency to strengthen accountability to givers through increasingly elaborate systems. The process of preparing plans is now often delegated to specialists who know how to present proposals rather than listen to and understand complicated analysis. The increasing dependence of aid agencies on government donors has led to government systems of public accountability (accountability to taxpayers) to be incorporated into agency systems. This makes it increasingly difficult to accommodate organisations such as SEWA that refuse to take on contractor roles.

Agencies need to tackle other distortions that arise from a supply-driven approach. Public perception has a considerable effect on initial responses, usually giving preference to materials, speed and expatriate presence. Agreements to limit the negative effects of competition among agencies could be beneficial especially if they create space for proper consultation with local people and agencies.

Although this chapter has focused mainly on higher-profile disasters in which Western agencies were active, small-scale disasters such as the Morvi Flood are far more common than the high-profile disasters that tend to dominate the Western system (World Bank 2014). These smaller disasters seriously undermine development and can increase vulnerability to yet more disasters in the future. It is important to provide ongoing support to local and national organisations and if possible make funds available in advance to national organisations or underwrite drawdown arrangements.[14]

For their part, LOs may do well to build relationships with Western agencies on a long-term basis without waiting for a disaster. This would make it possible for contentious points to be debated outside the context of an emergency. The practice of LOs putting their assessments and plans on websites and sending them to Western agencies could lead towards a more demand-driven approach to humanitarian aid, if it received proper attention and support from these agencies. The underlying issue is the need for a better balance between top-down supply-driven approaches and bottom-up demand-driven ones.

Notes

1 This chapter is based on my experience as a Field Director for Oxfam in Gujarat, India from 1976–80 and in Kutch in 2001. I made several further visits over the following years to write reports and papers about disaster-related issues for SEWA and the All India Disaster Mitigation Institute. See DMI (2001); Vaux and Lund (2003); Vaux (2002; 2009).
2 The DEC is the coordinating body for public appeals by major international charities in the UK. I was the team leader for the evaluation.
3 In fact the government turned to SEWA to help with this process.
4 In the context, 'working' generally means 'poor': women in wealthier households traditionally do not work, although this is changing to some extent. The term 'self-employed' distinguishes them from the more privileged workers in regular employment.
5 205,985 in December 2000. This rose to 284,317 by the end of 2001 largely because of SEWA's successful response to the earthquake (see SEWA Annual Reports at www.sewa.org as well as Vaux and Lund 2003).
6 This was by no means the only occupation. Agriculture, keeping animals and gathering gum Arabica were also important but SEWA focused mainly on embroidery.
7 SEWA commissioned me to study this issue (see Vaux 2002).
8 It may seem strange that the buses continued to run even on the day of the earthquake but the drivers, immured in their rickety vehicles in the semi-desert of Kutch, did not necessarily realise that there had been an earthquake or how serious it was until they were told by passengers or reached a destroyed village. Many of them continued on their journey according to schedule, providing transport for SEWA members carrying news. Fortunately, the mortality among SEWA members was relatively low.
9 They reached Sabarkantha and went on to Bhuj, capital of Kutch, the next day. The earthquake took place soon after 9 am on Republic Day when many schoolchildren were out on parades and so escaped being crushed in falling houses. Women with very young children were generally inside the house and suffered the highest mortality.
10 Delegates elected from each work group attend this annual event and scrutinise presentations made by the officers in charge of each main branch.
11 For more analysis of the violence, see Varshney (2002: 252).
12 The Prime Minister represented a different political party from the Chief Minister and the whole response, both in humanitarian action and advocacy, became caught up in this political division.
13 For example in the DEC Evaluation after the Gujarat earthquake, see DMI (2001).
14 The Disaster Response Emergency Fund of the Red Cross movement, for example, provides such support.

References

BBC (2005) Gujarat Riot Death Toll Revealed (http://news.bbc.co.uk/2/hi/south_asia/4536199.stm) accessed 2 October 2014.
Bhatt, E.R. (2006) *We Are Poor but So Many: The Story of Self Employed Women in India*, New York: Oxford University Press.
Crowell, D (2003) *The SEWA Movement and Rural Development*, New Delhi: Sage Publications.

DMI (2001) *Independent Evaluation: The DEC Response to the Earthquake in Gujarat*, London: DEC.

Harvey, P. and Bailey, S. (2011) *Cash Transfer Programming in Emergencies*, London: ODI.

SEWA (2002) Shantipath – Our Road to Restoring Peace (www.sewa.org) accessed 29 December 2014.

USGS (no date) Historic Earthquakes (http://earthquake.usgs.gov/earthquakes/eqarchives/year/2001/2001_01_26.php) accessed 2 October 2014.

Varshney, A. (2002) *Ethnic Conflict and Civic Life – Hindus and Muslims in India*, New Haven/London: Yale University Press.

Vaux, T. (2001) *The Selfish Altruist – Relief Work in Famine and War*, London: Earthscan.

Vaux, T. (2002) *Disaster and Vulnerability*, Ahmedabad: Disaster Mitigation Institute/Self Employed Women's Association.

Vaux, T. (2009) 'Work-Focused Responses to Disasters: India's Self Employed Women's Association', in: E. Enarson and P. Chakarabarti (eds) *Women, Gender and Disaster*, India: SAGE, 212–223.

Vaux, T. and Lund, F. (2003) 'Working Women and Security: Self-Employed Women's Association's Response to Crisis', *Journal of Human Development*, 4(2):265–287.

Weissman, F. (ed.) (2004) *In the Shadow of Just Wars*, London: Hurst and Company.

World Bank (2014) *World Development Report – Risk and Opportunity, Managing Risk for Development*, Washington DC: World Bank.

Conclusions

Convergence or Divergence?

Dennis Dijkzeul, Ryan O'Neill and Zeynep Sezgin

Introduction

In their chapter, Kent and Carpenter remark that the old cooperation paradigm, 'in which non-traditional actors simply fit into the tried and tested approaches of traditional actors, is not the only way the global humanitarian system may develop'. The authors of this volume have accepted this paradigm as an *ideal type*, against which to assess each actor's convergence with, or deviation from, the well-established humanitarian principles. Here, we adopt the same approach. Rather than focusing on any individual actor, however, we juxtapose the normative vision of *humanitarian space* against the reality of institutional multiplicity, that is, a wide array of actors with different norms and principles, often leading to collective action dilemmas. In each case discussed below, we highlight particular divergences from the ideal humanitarian norm, suggesting a cumulatively fragmenting system. At the same time, we also draw out lines of continuity that link non-traditional and traditional actors. Although the old cooperation paradigm based on the well-established humanitarian principles is not the only game in town, the humanity principle remains the common link suturing together an increasingly divergent array of actors. The actors reviewed in this volume interpret this principle differently (e.g. deontologically or consequentially) and implement it through the use of divergent supporting principles (not just neutrality, independence and impartiality, but also sovereignty, self-help, profit-motive, etc.). As the basic motivation of helping those in need humanity continues to unite, albeit often in a minimalist fashion.

We first review the ideal-typical notion of humanitarian space before contrasting it with the concept of the humanitarian arena. Next, we analyse to what extent the new actors remain faithful to the principle of humanity, while pushing the boundaries of humanitarian action. We draw out some conclusions as to the present state of humanitarianism, noting in particular that diversity tends to beget more diversity, leading, in the end, to diverging understandings of what effective humanitarian action might look like. In the following section, we allow the case evidence to reflect back upon the theoretical framework(s). In the final section, we discuss what this all means for the legitimacy and effectiveness of humanitarian action and whether new, parallel, competitive or complementary humanitarian systems are in the making.

Humanitarian Space?

According to Brauman, humanitarian space is,

> primarily a way of measuring the humanitarian conditions ... How freely you can talk to patients, how freely you can move around or go to other places to see the problems, how freely you can monitor the delivery and distribution of goods.

In practice, however, none of these 'freedoms' are ever 'absolute'. As Brauman, notes, humanitarianism always takes place 'within power relations', meaning humanitarian space is primarily 'a tool for measuring our distance from powers' (cited in Weizman 2011: 57). To translate this into the language of sociology, we might say that humanitarian space is an 'ideal type' against which to measure the reality of humanitarian action. Just as Max Weber used an ideal type as a methodological tool to show how empirical reality deviated from an absolute standard – for example, on bureaucracy – humanitarians can use humanitarian space as a tool to see how actual humanitarian action deviates from the norm, formulated through the traditional humanitarian principles.

The International Committee of the Red Cross (ICRC) and Médicins Sans Frontières (MSF) are the strongest proponents of humanitarian space. For ICRC, humanity, independence, impartiality and neutrality are part of its mandate under international law. These two Dunantist organisations consciously focus on emergency services, and do not advocate or participate in conflict-resolution, human-rights or development activities, in order to remain above the political fray. They see humanitarian aid as an independent and duty-based activity. Put differently, they follow a deontological ethic. For these organisations, the ideal-typical humanitarian space includes (see von Pillar 2002: 167):

- free access and communication with people who receive or need aid;
- independent assessment and evaluation of their needs;
- independent control and distribution of relief goods and services;
- independent monitoring and evaluation of humanitarian action; and
- proper safeguards for the protection of victims, including refugees, displaced persons and those that remain behind.

This checklist is in fact an inverted form of the classic humanitarian principles, in particular impartiality and independence. While the principles describe how humanitarians ought to behave, the checklist details what a specific humanitarian activity should look like. Together these serve as powerful normative tools that help to 'sell' or 'market' a particular image of humanitarian action, one which should be acceptable to all actors and which therefore helps to ensure access to those in need. As Slim (2012) puts it, humanitarian space is an effect of humanitarian persuasion and persuasion is itself an effect of perception. When other parties view humanitarians as impartial, neutral and independent then they are more likely to provide them the opportunity necessary to do their job. In sum, through principled acts of persuasion humanitarians seek to create a situation of exception – for example a neutralised zone inside of war or a time-limited agreement on access to people in need – that applies only to their activities.

Humanitarian space, in other words, is not only an ideal-type concept used to evaluate humanitarian action, but also a strategic 'norm' or script which guides humanitarian advocacy and negotiations with combatants and other parties. This ideal type can even serve as a rallying point around which humanitarians may converge in order to oppose being instrumentalised. Yet, the normative claim (how things should be) does not present a causal claim (how to get there), meaning the concept provides no guidance on how to achieve this ideal. What is more, the structural repetition of this ideal in, for example, advocacy and reporting hides the particularity of imperfect humanitarian relationships, including those with military and political actors, and thus 'inadvertently help[s] *conceal the full spectrum of real politics* in which' humanitarians are immersed (DeMars and Dijkzeul 2015: 25–7, original emphasis). Ideal types, in other words, can become ideology.

The above concerns have led some researchers to move away from the ideal-typical approach. Those who study humanitarian action ethnographically prefer to speak of a humanitarian arena, that is, a diverse array of actors united as much by competition and conflict, as normative convergence. Ethnographic or actor-centred approaches start from the assumption that the ideal-typical approach to humanitarian space masks the real politics, which take place on the ground between an assortment of political, military, private and humanitarian actors. They ask what organisations actually do and with whom they interact, and build upwards from there, eventually arriving at the humanitarian system as an arena of struggle, linking NGOs, donors, international organisations, private-sector firms, the military, recipients and other actors. The upside of this approach is that it captures maximum variability and emphasises divergence and conflict over and above an imagined consensus. Its downside, however, is that to date research of this nature has failed to capture how humanitarian space, as an advocacy strategy pursued by certain organisations, can function normatively to enforce some degree of coherence at the system-wide level or expose actions which should not be considered humanitarian.

While there is a tendency to juxtapose humanitarian space against the humanitarian arena or to argue that humanitarian space is becoming an

arena of struggle, this is in reality a false dichotomy. The term 'humanitarian arena', like institutional multiplicity captures empirical variability in
humanitarian action, while humanitarian space offers a normative, ideal-
typical vision of what humanitarian action should look like – one that is
performed by individual organisations seeking to enforce normative convergence. Simply put, the ideal type can have both an enabling effect (on
mainly traditional Western actors) and a constraining effect on other
(mainly non-traditional) actors.

In the following section, in line with the concept of the humanitarian
arena, we focus on the diversity of humanitarian actors and divergence
among them. We do this empirically by drawing upon the case evidence
presented in this volume to identify the variability of principles and action
that takes place under the common normative framework of humanity.
We weigh the diversity of case evidence against the normative, ideal-typical
notion of humanitarian space. By measuring real diversity against this ideal
type, we reveal exactly those conflicts that are presently driving a wedge
between humanitarians themselves.

Contested Principles, Continuous Inspiration

Throughout this volume we have used the terms 'traditional', 'well-established', 'old' and even 'old guard' to differentiate some of the better
known humanitarian actors from the emergent ones. However, the 'old'
humanitarians do not form a stable bloc or network of actors. Most chapters suggest significant historical divergence both within and among them.
For instance, Eberwein and Reinalda identify broad and narrow interpretations of 'humanitarian'. In a similar vein, Hilhorst and Pereboom point
out differences between single-mandate and multi-mandate humanitarian
organisations. Furthermore, O'Neill demonstrates the types of conflicts
that occur between traditional multi-mandate and Dunantist organisations
in the context of armed humanitarianism.

In line with these findings, humanitarian history shows many cases of
normative divergence. After the Second World War, the ICRC came under
fire when it became known that the organisation had knowledge of the
concentration camps and decided not to speak out. Thus began the debate
over the ethics of neutrality and protection. After Biafra, MSF was founded
in reaction to the perceived passivity of ICRC, sometimes partially aban-
doning neutrality in favour of an ethics of 'bearing witness' to genocide.
NGO calls for armed intervention in order to stop the killing in Kosovo and
Rwanda then contributed to the integration of peacekeeping and humanitarian action. Similarly, in Somalia, Colombia and Democratic Republic of
the Congo (DRC), chronic complex emergencies have meant long-term
engagement resulting in the blurring of humanitarian, peace-building and
reconstruction agendas. While in Afghanistan and Iraq, the direct provision of humanitarian assistance by coalition forces and military influence

on coordination led to demands on the part of NGOs for independent humanitarian space. In short, the old humanitarians were never as unified on the principles as they sometimes now appear.

While the history of humanitarianism can thus be read as a series of diversions from the norm, beginning with the debate over the meaning of protection and ending in military humanitarianism, it is crucial to bear in mind the principle of humanity. The meaning of humanity has varied over the course of history. From the feudal understanding of humanity as the 'great chain of being', to the liberal concept of humanity as 'the law of nations', to the utopian socialist 'new man' and finally the more neoliberal *droit d'ingérence* and 'responsibility to protect' (Heller-Roazen 2009). Indeed, 'humanitarianism' is itself one possible meaning of humanity, with liberals like Ignatieff (2001) arguing that the alleviation of bodily suffering is the essence of what it means to be human.

Humanitarians, for their part, have drawn from this multiplicity of meaning inspiration for their actions. Dunant's Geneva Conventions, for instance, were clearly framed within the liberal tradition of the law of nations, though infused with a good dose of Christianity. Equally, during the independence era, many development NGOs were influenced by a more socialist concept of humanity which also motivated the Non-Aligned Movement. In fact, the International Red Cross and Red Crescent Movement's definition of humanity includes aspects of all of the above definitions, denoting a duty 'to prevent and alleviate human suffering, and to protect the life, health, dignity of all human beings' (Pictet 1979; Carbonnier 2015: 196).[1]

Defining humanity in this manner, however, has both costs and benefits. On the one hand, it is a broad norm, which brings traditional humanitarian actors in contact with a diverse array of other actors motivated by the desire to help those in need (as well as those who mask their own self-interest in the guise of humanitarian concern, for instance the private companies Bechtel (civil engineering) and Blackwater (security/training) who supplied coalition forces in the Iraq War, or rebel 'humanitarians'). This not only allows for the widest possible funding networks, but also implementing partnerships and even political coalitions in cases like the campaign for free anti-retroviral drugs. On the other hand, wide networks of this nature tend to internalise those political differences captured by the various interpretations of humanity outlined above. In the definition of the International Red Cross and Red Crescent Movement, for instance, the deontological injunction to 'alleviate human suffering' is conjoined with the consequentialist approach of *preventing* suffering and *protecting* the 'life, health and dignity' of all human beings. None of these combinations rest easily together, however, with protection (through force if necessary), potentially jeopardising opportunities to alleviate suffering (while potentially also eroding the sovereign rights of Third World countries).

Nonetheless, was it not for the broad principle of humanity, there would be no humanitarianism(s). The other principles – neutrality, impartiality and independence – tell us only how to act in context, they do not provide the motivation for action. Yet, they are not just supporting principles. Rather, they also narrow the norm of humanity in a deontological direction.

With the above point in mind, we treat humanity as a 'first order' principle within which the remaining humanitarian principles (both old and new) must be embedded.[2] As it unites the various actors, it fosters some isomorphism and thus a limited degree of convergence. However, as we demonstrate below, it can be realised through various supporting principles, meaning simultaneous convergence and divergence

Persistence, Convergence or Divergence among Humanitarian Actors

This section compares the principles of different actors both with each other and with the ideal-typical norm discussed above. Overall, this section seeks to draw out general trends of persistence, divergence and convergence among emerging actors.

Table C.1 provides a general overview of the particular vision of humanity professed or at least practised by the different actors described in this volume. It also details supporting principles used by differing actors in the implementation of their version of humanity. These include not only impartiality, neutrality and independence, but, broader and more political principles like sovereignty, Third World or religious solidarity, and self-help. Along similar lines the table also tracks 'other concerns' or interests which might shape either the actor's particular understanding of humanity or the way, in which it implements this most basic of principles through operational norms. The final two columns evaluate whether the humanitarian ethic, operational principles and interests of each actor fall in line with the normative ideal-typical understanding of humanitarian space and/or to what extent they may be 'instrumentalised' to military, political or profit-seeking ends.

Persistence

Although many of the actors reviewed above are frequently called 'new', several chapters have shown, on the one hand, their long historical roots, and on the other hand, their recently emerging nature. For example, faith-based aid is as old as religion itself, but Muslim humanitarian organisations have grown in number and size in the last two decades (Juul Petersen in this volume). Similarly, several diaspora organisations (DOs) were already active during the 1970s but their efficiency and professionalism has increased with experience and they have become increasingly influential actors on the international humanitarian stage (Sezgin, this volume; Horst et al., this volume). Furthermore, according to international humanitarian law, the military must protect and address the needs of the population in

Table C.1 Summary of the chapters

Type of Humanitarianism	Specific Actor	Interpretation of Humanity	Supporting Principles/Aims	Other Concerns	In Line with Humanitarian Principles	Instrumentalisation
Dunantist	ICRC, MSF	Narrow, traditional deontological	Impartiality, Neutrality, Independence	'Old cooperation paradigm'	Yes. Deontological ethic provides a push for action that can be implemented in consequentialist manner.	Organisations occasionally fail to respect the principles due to a narrow interpretation, staff incompetence, organisational self-interest (e.g. survival, growth, status) or the influence of other actors (e.g. negotiating with warlords).
Donor Government	India	Broad, consequentialist	Sovereignty	Interpretation of national interests: colonial history, non-aligned movement, focus on near abroad	Due to their sovereign status and funding position, donors can in principle support all forms of humanitarianism, traditional or emergent. It is therefore a conscious choice to support the traditional principles (or not), as well as (when) to instrumentalise them.	
	Turkey	Broad, consequentialist	Sovereignty	National geopolitical interests, political and religious motivations of the Islamic party AKP		

Continued

Table C.1 Summary of the chapters, *continued*

Type of Humanitarianism	Specific Actor	Interpretation of Humanity	Supporting Principles/Aims	Other Concerns	In Line with Humanitarian Principles	Instrumentalisation
Developmental	Multi-mandate Organisations	Broad consequentialist	Political goals (e.g. development, conflict-resolution)	They often profess to follow the core principles.	Partly	Possible with human rights, conflict-resolution and development
Military and other armed actors	Military as learning opportunity	Depends on specific partnership	Humanitarian control	Support for traditional principles possible	Partly	Unlikely and organisation can sanction this
	Peacekeeping/Enforcement	Broad, consequentialist	Military control	Security/Protection	In name only	Yes, such as hearts-and-minds operations
	Rebels	Broad, consequentialist	Territorial control/political goals	Security/Protection	In name only, as PR	Yes

Type of Humanitarianism	Specific Actor	Interpretation of Humanity	Supporting Principles/Aims	Other Concerns	In Line with Humanitarian Principles	Instrumentalisation
For-Profit	Humanitarian Business Partnership	Depends on specific partnership	Humanitarian control	Profit-principle less important	Yes	Possible, but humanitarian organisations can sanction this
	PMSC	Consequentialist	Profit-principle	Claims of superior performance	No	Yes, isomorphism in language and symbols with the aim of making profit
	Private enterprise for procurement and strategic learning	Depends on the specific activities of the relationship	Humanitarian control	Profit-principle less important	Yes	Possible, but humanitarian organisations can sanction this and/or go to other vendor/partner

Continued

Table C.1 Summary of the chapters, *continued*

Type of Humanitarianism	Specific Actor	Interpretation of Humanity	Supporting Principles/Aims	Other Concerns	In Line with Humanitarian Principles	Instrumentalisation
Diaspora	Somali and Liberian Diaspora	Ethnic/clan solidarity	Self-help, self-reliance	Legitimacy towards members	Partly	Yes
	Syrian and Turkish Diaspora	Solidarity based on their members national or religious affiliations	Political aims and/or religious principles	IGMG: legitimacy towards members, DSV: public and private legitimacy	Partly	IGMG: possible to promote Islam but German government can sanction this DSV: carries out human-rights activities and lobbies against the Assad regime
Faith-based	South-South	Faith-based solidarity (in this volume)	Religious solidarity	Learning opportunity	Partly	Possible, e.g. to help (only) fellow believers
	Muslim NGOs	Traditional humanitarian (in this volume)	Solidarity with the worldwide Muslim community[4]	Legitimacy towards traditional organisations	Partly	Like traditional organisations (in this volume)

Type of Humanitarianism	Specific Actor	Interpretation of Humanity	Supporting Principles/Aims	Other Concerns	In Line with Humanitarian Principles	Instrumentalisation
Regional and local	Regional Organisations (OIC, ASEAN)	Broad, consequentialist	Sovereignty	Great differences among regional organisations	Due to their sovereign status and funding position, donors can in principle support all forms of humanitarianism, traditional or emergent, consciously choosing to support the traditional principles (or not), as well as (when) to instrumentalise them.	
	Local Organisations (SEWA)	Broad, consequentialist	Ghandian self-reliance of members, women empowerment, democratic principles	Local political pressures	Partly	No

Source: the authors.

the territory under its control. In this sense, military forces have always had to carry out or enable humanitarian work. Yet, as discussed by Carpenter and Kent as well as by Joachim and Schneiker (this volume), recently, the level of civil–military cooperation has been increasing and new institutional structures have been established between political, armed and humanitarian actors.

Not unexpectedly, the 'new' humanitarians express an eclectic mix of old and new principles, both ethical and operational. Table C.1 identifies at least five additional principles: territorial control, sovereignty, the profit principle, Ghandian self-help and religious solidarity. All five have venerable roots in political and economic philosophy and each can be more or less grafted on to one of the various historical definitions of humanity discussed above. Moreover, these principles have played a key role in past generations of humanitarian action. For instance, both sovereignty and self-help were key norms guiding humanitarian action between multi-mandate NGOs, certain UN bodies and Third World states during the independence era.

The principles identified above and their affiliated organisations might therefore be usefully construed as 'silent partners'. That is, the principles and actors in question have long existed side-by-side mainstream NGOs and donors, running along similar but somewhat separate normative 'paths' with little official recognition. Yet, as Juul Petersen (this volume) argues, more recent convergence with the humanitarian mainstream has brought their history to light. Particularly, in her analysis of Islamic Relief and Muslim Aid, Juul Petersen demonstrates that Muslim humanitarian NGOs long lived a parallel existence to their Christian and secular counterparts, only breaking into the mainstream after 9/11. For these NGOs, however, access to mainstream funding has been a double-edged sword: 'mainstreaming' has meant recognition of their efforts and opportunities for expansion as well as institutional 'isomorphism' and/or political 'conformism'.

Juul Petersen's study shows that Muslim organisations particularly, and faith-based organisations (FBOs) generally, are now recognised partners in humanitarian assistance. Recognition, in turn, has opened up humanitarian history to critical re-evaluation, such that Barnett (2011) can speak of a dual origin of humanitarianism, not only a secular legal origin on the battlefields of Europe, but, a faith-based origin among missionaries in Africa and anti-slavery campaigners in England and America. This diversity is itself important insofar as it allows present day humanitarians to go 'norm shopping' to draw from multiple sources of inspiration. It also breaks down the barriers of entry for other FBOs looking to forge partnerships with traditional humanitarian actors. Though, as Juul Petersen notes, normative scripts tend to regulate and constrain who gains entry to the field and what they will have to change in order to maintain these partnerships.

In short, while this book demonstrates a significant amount of persistence with respect to both principles and motives for humanitarian action, what we are in fact talking about are multiple, path-dependent norms, some more dominant then others. Only now, with the convergence and acceptance of formerly silent partners by traditional donors has this diversity come to the fore.

Convergence

The above section has already demonstrated convergence between several Muslim humanitarian NGOs and mainstream Western donors. In a similar vein, Roepstorff (in this volume) describes India's slow convergence with DAC donors. India's donor credentials trace back to the post-colonial era and its leadership in the Non-Aligned Movement. More recently, however, India's desire to support Third World sovereignty has been tempered by both the Organisation for Economic Co-operation and Development's (OECD) demands for standardisation and its own interest in opening up opportunities for Indian business abroad. India, in other words, has begun to 'professionalise' its aid policy, moving away from almost exclusively funding projects in neighbouring states and politically allied nations, to, for example, disaster risk reduction in Africa and Asia.

These, however, are not the only types of partial convergence within this volume. Interestingly, one of the most obvious cases of convergence noted is mainly discussed as a negative development. Here, we refer to the fact that since 9/11 military and humanitarian actors have come into ever closer contact. As Eberwein and Reinalda, as well as Carpenter and Kent, show, military and humanitarian actors have long shared the crisis zone, operating in close proximity to each other though without a great deal of coordination. Since 9/11, however, donor demands to link humanitarianism and development to military stabilisation have meant the blurring of civilian and military lines, as soldiers and peacekeepers have taken on Quick Impact Projects (or more generally 'hearts-and-minds' work) and humanitarian organisations have weighed into the murky waters of human-rights training for the military, to name but a few examples.

As in the case of Muslim humanitarian and development NGOs, the convergence or isomorphism between military and humanitarian actors has been at the hands of donor demands. Yet, it has forced the complex history of civilian military relations to the surface, that is, their different and yet overlapping normative paths. It has also led to interesting attempts to negotiate, regulate and limit these interactions so as to avoid endangering aid workers and recipients (e.g. the Oslo Guidelines). In fact, the ideal-typical norm of humanitarian space reviewed above has been in part a response to the increased frequency and formalisation of civilian-military relations. Meaning that donor-enforced isomorphism has actually produced the opposite of what it has intended to produce: a degree of institutional multiplicity. Indeed, Dunantist organisations specifically sought to craft this ideal-typical norm in part in order to track military and political instrumentalisation.

While we might wish to measure organisational as well as systemic change against the ideal type of humanitarian space, in fact, this norm has itself entered the game. That is, both emergent and old humanitarian actors now deploy this norm as a means of insulating both themselves and the humanitarian field as a whole from politicisation or militarisation. In other words, there has been a strategically calculated convergence around the norm of humanitarian space, which aims at counterbalancing the power of mainstream donors. Further complicating matters, however, as O'Neill has shown, the ideal of humanitarian space has also been used by single-mandate NGOs to alienate and discredit multi-mandate NGOs and local actors so as to increase their own strategic position in terms of both funding and influence (see also Hilhorst and Jansen 2010). Paradoxically, normative convergence has thus created a series of subdivisions internal to the humanitarian community itself.

Divergence

Table C.1 indicates that the actors studied in this volume have different understandings of what it means to serve humanity, and how to implement humanity in practice. The principal difference is whether or not the actors in question conceptualise humanity deontologically or in a consequentialist fashion. Most emerging actors, such as non-DAC donors and private military and security companies (PMSCs), apply a consequentialist ethic insofar as their interpretation of humanity is defined in line with their own interests. In their view, humanity is consistent with any number of ethical or operational principles, whether the profit motive or sovereign equality and self-determination. Importantly, consequentialist actors follow a humanitarian *impulse*, assisting those with whom they share an affinity, identity or interest, instead of a deontological humanitarian *imperative* to help, in principle, all people in need. Hence, consequentialists treat some victims as more deserving than others and are not fully impartial.

The extent to which self-interest can support the humanitarian ideal outlined above, however, will always depend on the other actors involved. As O'Neill argues, all humanitarian actors exist within networks which link donors to implementers and recipients. When assessing whether a given actor's consequentialist ethics converge or diverge from the humanitarian norm, we must then bear in mind the types of partnerships in which they are engaged. In some cases, for instance, offensive PMSCs, the profit motive drives actions, which not only diverge from the ideal type, but, actually negate the deontological ethic of other humanitarian actors. The key distinction is that PMSCs do not just provide security for humanitarians or civilians, they also carry out counterinsurgency operations on behalf of politicians and private-sector leaders who are themselves seeking profit through exploitation. Offensive PMSCs thus fuse their own profit motive with the profit motive and (sovereign) self-interest of either belligerents or governments themselves. In such cases, the self-interest of self-professed 'humanitarian actors' may actually create the very suffering humanitarians seek to limit.

This need not always be the case, however. When, in the context of private-sector-humanitarian partnerships, traditional humanitarians remain in control, the profit motive may play a supporting role. If, for instance, the role of the private-sector actor is simply financial support, training, procurement or logistics, and their humanitarian partners set clear standards to control these partnerships (see Carbonnier and Lightfoot, this volume), making clear that they cannot come at the expense of impartial selection of recipients, political neutrality and independence from donors, then consequentialism may in fact assist in the implementation of a deontological ethic. After all, the more limited an organisation's finances become, the more it will have to put in place 'triage' criteria meant to choose between victims.

Interestingly, divergence also takes place *within* multi-mandate organisations (see Hilhorst and Pereboom, this volume), who often sit at the intersection of multiple, competing consequentialist, as well as deontological, interests. Owing to their desire to remain in place and tackle the long-term causes of poverty and inequality, multi-mandate NGOs come under heavy financial pressure, always having to 'grow the office' or at least 'keep the office open'. This need for funding brings them into contact with both state and private donors many of whom explicitly make use of foreign aid for political or ideological agendas. Moreover, many multi-mandate organisations are also faith-based (World Vision, CRS, etc.) and are confronted with tough choices about when and how to make use of private donations from religious groups who may be associated with missionary work. The offices of multi-mandate NGOs thus become the sites of intense debates over whether or not a particular donor's interests will impede their ability to implement projects in an independent, impartial and neutral manner. Hence, divergence and conflict between deontological and consequentialist approaches does not just happen at the inter-organisational level, but, within organisations themselves, often between department heads where ethics meet operational and financial realities.

At the same time, divergence does not just flow from the top down as new donors with competing consequentialist ethics enter the field. Divergence can also be tracked from the ground up, as changing emergency scenarios give birth to new actors who compete with traditional actors. Vaux, for instance, indicates that many crises never trigger international humanitarian responses either because they are too small or because they are perceived to be linked with unpopular ethnic or religious cleavages. In such cases, local communities respond, often deploying very different principles and norms, such as the Ghandian principles of self-help and self-sufficiency. Not only then does the size of the crisis matter with respect to what types of actors will respond, but, whether or not the crisis in question is 'internationalised' will affect what types of norms and principles are exercised and defended by the organisations in question. For SEWA, for instance, there is little point quibbling over whether or not to work within the framework of state sovereignty since its members are all citizens of the state in question. Indeed, for SEWA, independence is not so much a question of distance from the Indian state, though this is a factor, as whether or not to partner with international NGOs, whether Dunantist or Wilsonian multi-mandate ones.

As Vaux explains, SEWA's roots are to be found in the Ghandian inspired Indian labour movement not the NGO sector. Hence, while SEWA members do not object to the core principles, these principles are placed within the framework of organisational democracy, meaning members choose how they will interpret and implement the humanitarian ideal based on its own members' needs. Similarly, Sezgin describes how DOs often choose to provide aid on the basis of nationality, ethnicity, religious belief or the political opinions of their members. Put differently, the 'logic of membership' trumps the deontological humanitarian duty, for the survival of these organisations depends mainly on the support of their members. While local NGOs and DOs are interested in seeking partnerships with international NGOs and donors, their membership-driven approach often makes partnership difficult. Indeed, these organisations serve as a constant reminder of the inherently undemocratic, often top-down nature of many traditional humanitarian actors.

Explanations of Persistence, Convergence or Divergence in Theory

Having drawn out general trends of persistence, divergence and convergence among emerging actors, this section places these trends within the theoretical frameworks identified in the introduction (see Table I.1 on page 15) as a means of drawing conclusions as to the humanitarian system as a whole.

Rational Choice Institutionalism

Rational-choice institutionalism assumes that humanitarian and other actors strategically pursue their interests. Accordingly, Eberwein and Reinalda (this volume) argue that neither the states nor the parties to armed conflicts take the obligations imposed by international humanitarian law seriously if they regard them as contrary to their objectives. Likewise, Carbonnier and Lightfoot (this volume) show that business enterprises continue to follow their core objective of profit or shareholder-value maximisation independent of their increasing interaction with traditional humanitarians in crisis situations.

Rational-choice institutionalism says nothing, however, about the origins and content of actors' interests. It thus leaves open the question whether specific actors perceive and pursue their interests in line with those of others. It suggests, however, that states and other actors are not interested in establishing efficient institutions when such institutions limit their autonomy. As we have seen above, most new actors believe – or pretend to believe that – their particular strategic interests align in some way with the interests of those in need, this being the basis of their humanitarian claim. Whereas some traditional actors may disagree with this characterisation, this need not block collective action. If agreeable standards and procedures can be developed which shape self-interest in a particular case then cooperation may ensue (see Carbonnier and Lightfoot, this volume).

However, even when agreements have been reached between new and old humanitarian actors, this does not necessarily mean successful cooperation and consensus at the field level. When individual organisations lack an overview of other relevant actors and their activities, they are unable to establish efficient institutions, for they cannot see when maximising their own interest will have suboptimal effects for the whole sector. In other words, limited information can lead to a collective action dilemma. For example, DOs' tendency to use opposition channels in armed conflicts may affect the way foreign humanitarian actors are perceived by local authorities and may bring unwanted scrutiny to local NGOs and groups cooperating with DOs (see Sezgin, this volume).

In addition, some actors may manipulate humanitarian action to their own benefit at the expense of others, such as when donor governments fund humanitarian action as a fig-leaf for their inaction to address the root-causes of crises. In a similar vein, they may allow humanitarian action to continue even if its results disappoint, because the other political alternatives (e.g. peacekeeping, long-term social investment and setting up an interim administration) may be more expensive. Hence, they provide (or withdraw) funding on political grounds rather than on the basis of need.

Moreover, low barriers of entry for new actors, lack of voice for people in need and relatively weak coordination institutions, such as the Office for the Coordination of Humanitarian Affairs (OCHA) or international humanitarian law, that cannot institute sanctions for ineffectiveness, as well as a wide diversity of additional standards (see below) reinforce the collective action dilemmas. Indeed, as new actors have entered the field there has been no corresponding 'cull' of ineffective organisations as a result of increased competition.

Sociological Institutionalism

Unlike rational choice theorists, sociological institutionalists, emphasise that formal and informal norms help shape and define behaviour. Hence, actors or organisations working closely together tend towards isomorphism. Along these lines, Juul Petersen (this volume) argues that the inclusion of Muslim NGOs into the field of mainstream humanitarian action do not challenge or renew mainstream aid. Instead, it just leads to more of the same type of aid, carried out by similar organisations. Juul Petersen concludes that

> this may in part be because Western donors and NGOs choose to include organisations that already look and act like themselves, but it may also be because these organisations, once they are included into the field, start to act and look like Western donors and NGOs, prompted by donor expectations and pressures to conform.

Interestingly, Joachim and Schneiker (this volume) demonstrate that PMSCs, despite their military focus, make use of language and images strikingly similar to those of traditional humanitarian NGOs. While the more offensive minded of these organisations may still have a hard time justifying their humanitarian credentials, it is nevertheless the case that mercenary organisations have converged around humanitarian jargon and images, just as some traditional humanitarian actors have come to accept the need for military protection. Isomorphism, in other words, is clearly a factor even in the most extreme cases of armed humanitarianism.

Alternatively, Hilhorst and Pereboom (this volume) remind us that traditional actors remain faithful to the core principles of impartiality, neutrality and independence, while emergent actors, including diversifying multi-mandate NGOs, have tended to mix these principles with new priorities (e.g. development, human rights, conflict-mitigation, etc.). Along similar lines, Sezgin (this volume) details how and why DOs do not always incorporate societally legitimated rationalised elements in their formal structures, and how they avoid or defy traditional humanitarian principles, especially when these principles conflict with the expectations of their members.

One way to address the diversity of actors is to establish codes, standards, and norms of professionalisation, as well as to establish coordinating bodies and unified funding structures. Similarly in all crises zones, there are also informal networks, temporary and opportunistic arrangements that have their own ad-hoc norms and rules, (e.g. agreements on access between NGOs and militia). These all enhance predictability and transparency in the expectations of the different actors (and ideally bring down transaction costs). The humanitarian community has worked hard on establishing such codes and bodies.[3] Yet, as Eberwein and Reinalda point out (this volume), such codes and bodies do not necessarily guarantee better practices. A study for the preparation of the Core Humanitarian Standard estimated that '70 local, regional and global standards ,... are applied in humanitarian response, leaving time-pressured aid workers struggling to meet sometimes contradictory demands' (Core Humanitarian Standard 2015). In a related vein, respect for humanitarian law has declined over the years and legal enforcement mechanisms to ensure compliance are weak. Even the coming World Humanitarian Summit focuses more on technocratic solutions than the underlying normative differences and political issues. Consequently, emergent actors and their wide variety of norms increasingly disrupt isomorphic processes, so that different norms coexist, which hampers establishing legitimacy and effectiveness of the humanitarian system.

Historical Institutionalism

Historical institutionalism highlights path dependency. As demonstrated above, humanitarianism is defined by a growing number of path-dependent actors and initiatives with trajectories that overlap, duplicate and complicate the humanitarian system (Vijge 2013: 172). Yet, suggestions to centralise the system have fallen on deaf ears (Weiss 2013). As Eberwein and Reinalda indicate, there is no convincing new set of overarching norms. Even major disasters, such as the Rwandan genocide, the Indian Ocean Tsunami and the Haitian earthquake, which laid bare systemic weaknesses, have mainly led to incremental change, rather than systemic overhaul. Moreover, not all forms of path dependency are virtuous; the sum of many incremental changes in the humanitarian system is greater incoherence, contributing to fragmentation.

Most of the debates about humanitarian action are inward focused; they centre more on what *ought* to be done then what *is* done or *can* be accomplished in any given context given the external limits imposed upon the system as a whole (de Waal 2010: 297). Yet, addressing crises also relates to the general global North–South problematic, which can only be reversed through forms of political mobilisation which go well beyond the normative ideal-typical understanding of what humanitarian action and humanitarian actors ought to be (Qasmiyeh and Pacitto, this volume). In this respect, most periods of institution building in the international system have occurred after critical junctures, for instance the birth of the League of Nations after the First World War and the UN following the second World War. We simply do not know when the next such juncture will take place and what its consequences will be for the humanitarian system.

Institutional Multiplicity

Institutional multiplicity has become a strong feature of the international/transnational humanitarian system as the number of humanitarian-isms, interventions and actors has grown. At the most basic level, every humanitarian crisis brings together four separate, though interlinked, institutionalised systems: the international state system, the multilateral system of international organisations (UN, World Bank, IMF, OECD, WTO, etc.), transnational civil societies (NGOs, human-rights groups, unions, environmentalists, etc.) and what are oftentimes 'weak states' composed of competing legal, political and economic (if not insurgent) institutions. Each and every organisation that enters a crisis zone is thus confronted with a complex network of other actors with overlapping and competing norms, which will invariably pull the organisation in different directions. The humanitarian arena is now filled with a multitude of organisations that fulfil related, but not identical, mandates, according to overlapping and potentially contradictory principles. In general, and as described in the chapters on India, Turkey, regional, diaspora and FBOs,

> rising global actors do not aim simply to supplement the traditional humanitarian aid system. Many are looking instead to develop their own mechanisms and approaches when responding to humanitarian crises. There is a reluctance to join existing multilateral networks as the current system is seen as inadequate, bureaucratic, cumbersome and cost-ineffective – issues that this [humanitarian] sector has grappled with for decades.
>
> (Pantuliano 2014)

Hence, there is no longer one organisational humanitarian field as traditional sociological institutionalism expected, but several, partly overlapping transnational/international organisational fields that apply different institutional logics, the core principles being but one of them, often applied inconsistently by different networks of actors. For example, ASEAN's direct influence on humanitarian activities, which support sovereignty and government control, logically only holds in Southeast Asia (Fan, this volume).

Hence, the term institutional multiplicity is not only an important descriptive tool but also a useful counterpart to the sociological institutionalist concept of organisational field. Both are descriptive terms that do not prejudge which actors or activities belong to the humanitarian sector, but whereas the concept of organisational field is often used in conjunction with isomorphism leading to convergence, institutional multiplicity is more strongly associated with divergence and the continuation of collective action problems. In addition, the term 'institutional multiplicity' also overlaps with the more specific term 'humanitarian arena', suggesting diverse professional fields that may very well be formed through conflict. Hence, in the study of humanitarian action, institutional multiplicity and arena describe the types of empirical variability increasingly detailed in aid ethnographies. That is, they work against the ideal-typical notion of a smooth and homogenous humanitarian space.

Constructivism

Just like sociological institutionalists, constructivists take cultural norms seriously, however, constructivists focus more on identity and worldviews, and how these shape interests and conflicts. This volume shows the limits of socialisation, professionalisation, persuasion and even learning. These social processes are not absent in the humanitarian system, but they are too weak to prevent conflicting identities or worldviews. For instance, Özerdem describes how Turkey went its own humanitarian way in Somalia. While Joachim and Schneiker describe how PMSCs use humanitarian language and symbols, as well as claims of greater effectiveness, to create for themselves a humanitarian identity that many traditional and emergent actors abhor. Humanitarian action can sometimes be instrumentalised as a symbolic or sham institution by politicians, PMSCs, the military and other actors either to hide a lack of political action to address a crisis and/or pursue their own interests. What we are left with then is a bricolage of converging and contrasting humanitarian identities each drawing, more or less intentionally, from the other. When, for instance, offensive PMSCs redeploy traditional humanitarian idioms to describe their for-profit activities, they also shift the meaning of related identities, breaking down the symbolic barriers between 'the peacekeeper', 'the peace activist', 'the police', 'the humanitarian' and 'the mercenary', to give but one example. Traditional actors, then, are often forced to defend their identities by downplaying their connections with political and military actors, for instance, through humanitarian space advocacy.

Joint Analysis

Together the five theories provide more complementary than exclusive explanations (Vijge 2013). They show that the traditional cooperation paradigm is not dead; there still is limited convergence around the humanity principle. This minimal convergence, however, cannot overcome all the collective action problems associated with institutional multiplicity and bricolage. The five theories all show that many initiatives at the micro- and meso-level, such as new organisations, new standards or funding mechanisms, do not add up to meaningful change at the macro level of the whole system. And without political consensus, financial resources and technical tools to change this, the system will muddle through.

What then does the future hold? Most likely we will see the continuation of meso-level, ad hoc networks which bring together coalitions of divergent actors for short periods before dissipating, though not without a degree of norm perfusion (each actor taking with them common experiences). Take, for example, the Ebola epidemic. Originally, no humanitarian or other organisation was well prepared for the outbreak. The initial response was slow. However, over time, the World Health Organization, MSF and the US Center for Disease Control took on leading roles. In terms of theory, actors will thus occasionally take the initiative to build temporary institutionalised cooperation across sectoral divides, but this is not necessarily pre-planned. Sometimes this will be slow, but it will always be flexible. After the crisis, these weakly institutionalised forms of cooperation may quickly wind down. In fact, as MSF has noted, the Ebola crisis exposed all the, 'age-old

Table C.2 Processes of change and persistence

Theory	Rational Choice Institutionalism	Sociological Institutionalism	Historical Institutionalism	Institutional Multiplicity	Constructivism	Comparison
Convergence	Few institutions, e.g. IHL or OCHA, help *reduce transaction costs* and improve coordination but lack authority and resources to impose sanctions or create stronger incentives for cooperation.	The principles (in particular humanity), established practices, standards, coordination bodies and IHL foster some *isomorphism*, but there are (too) many different standards and respect for IHL has decreased.	*Path dependency* after critical junctures, such as the end of Cold War and 9/11, has led to incremental change and older *lock-in effects* lead well-established organisations to follow their own mandate and interests.	Convergence not likely due to the low degree of institutionalization in the international humanitarian system and in crisis countries. No *central authority* for the whole system.	*Discursive action*, such as *socialization*, *professionalization*, *learning* and *persuasion* to influence actors' world views, identities and acceptance of (existing) norms and principles is weak.	Mechanisms towards convergence are weak.
Persistence	Actors purposely maintain institutions to reduce uncertainty, but insufficient information leads to *collective action dilemmas*. donor governments do not necessarily sanction ineffectiveness and recipients lack voice.	'Business as usual' reduces uncertainty and preserves taken-for-granted ideas, institutionalised scripts for well-established organisations most of the time.	Reduced uncertainty due to *lock-in effects*: the system is not optimally organised, but can continue as it is presently operating.	Traditional and emergent actors lack *power* to effect change with other actors, while economic benefits from the current situation accrue to the individual organisations.	Socialization, professionalization, learning and persuasion have led to stable identities and taken-for-granted ideas of well-established actors, but only a few new actors are likely to conform, and if they do, only slowly.	The well-established humanitarian actors continue, but they do not sufficiently influence the emergent actors towards convergence: system does not become more coherent.

Theory	Rational Choice Institutionalism	Sociological Institutionalism	Historical Institutionalism	Institutional Multiplicity	Constructivism	Comparison
Divergence	Low barriers to entry allow new organisations to enter, but do not help address the inefficiencies that cause a *collective action dilemma*: donor governments do not necessarily sanction ineffectiveness and recipients lack voice.	Without legal sanctions/enforcement, new actors, ideas and values increasingly disrupt isomorphic processes. Criticism of effectiveness or legitimacy after failures (Rwanda, Indian Ocean Tsunami) does not lead to wholesale change of the system.	Gradual feedback, inefficiencies and incrementalism continue, but without *critical junctures* no efforts to ensure coherence succeed.	Diversity of actors leads to co-existence of different institutions and *institution/norm shopping* in crisis zones, no 'cull' of inefficient organisations.	*Discursive action*, in particular *bricolage* leads to co-existing or conflicting world views, norms and identities.	Absent critical junctures, institutional multiplicity and bricolage continue.

Source: the authors.

failures of the humanitarian aid system', including, most importantly, the unwillingness of the international community to properly support African national health-care systems. Whereas MSF generally limits its advocacy to emergency matters, in this case it has specifically called for health-care development, making clear that World Health Organization's (WHO) calls for faster epidemic response are insufficient (MSF 2015: 21). Nevertheless, each organisation will take with them lessons learned, both in terms of treating Ebola and working with competing organisations. This, in turn, may make future cooperation easier, even if it may not alter either organisations' norms or interests. Indeed, the same actors may simultaneously compete and cooperate with each other. We can therefore expect intermittent, overlapping periods of bricolage and collective action dilemmas in a system of institutional multiplicity.

In this respect, it is important to remember that humanitarian action focuses on saving lives and alleviating suffering. Despite efforts to broaden humanitarian action by multi-mandate organisations and several emerging actors, there are many aspects of humanitarian crises humanitarians simply cannot address. Within states, a crisis is often associated with a (partial) breakdown of state and society institutions and forms of authority. At the global level, it involves structural inequality between the global North and South. Humanitarian action is deeply influenced by these aspects of crises, but it is not intended to solve them. In this sense, humanitarian action is the lowest common denominator for political elites who do not really want to address the systemic roots of humanitarian crises, and/ or who simply do not know how to fight global inequities, and rebuild states successfully. Hence, humanitarian action is as much an expression of global political and societal problems, as an indicator of the desire to help people in need. As a result, its legitimacy and effectiveness will always be disputed.

It is no wonder then that the humanitarian field remains split from within, for the very practice of carrying out humanitarian activities means that they are pulled in multiple directions by various actors at once, thus militating against consensus or synthesis. Although the old cooperation paradigm refuses to die, at times it appears that the only thing now linking old and new humanitarians is their common commitment to the principle of humanity, as well as their disagreements over how this might be practised.

Conclusions

In the introduction, we asked whether there is a place for 'new' humanitarians within the existing humanitarian system. In many ways there is, however, only because the system is fragmenting, even bursting at its seams. Although the old cooperation paradigm plays a central role in debates and definitions of humanitarian legitimacy and effectiveness, its role is diminishing.

Is there a place left for both the core principles and the deontological approach to humanitarian action? Briefly, while humanitarian action has always been hampered by competing political agendas and associated funding priorities, which make completely impartial, independent and neutral humanitarian action a virtual impossibility, the deontological commitment to all those in need remains the heart and soul of the humanitarian tradition. As we have argued above, humanitarian actors cannot do without an ideal type, normative yardstick, if only because such an ideal helps to convince other actors to allow or support humanitarian action. Moreover, the normative ideal, as embedded in the concept of humanitarian space and the principle of humanity, serves as a bridge linking humanitarians together, even those who fervently disagree on what exactly this 'space' might look like. At the same time, however, this ideal type can also serve as an ideology masking real politics. Hence, the ideal type of deontological, principle-based action will only remain relevant insofar as humanitarians acknowledge that this ideal type is just that, a methodological and rhetorical tool used to collectively evaluate, negotiate and defend humanitarian action.

The present tensions internal to the humanitarian system are apparent in the conflicting attitudes of 'old' actors towards the new 'upstarts'. On the one hand, they often accept that new actors are necessary to meet unaddressed needs, for instance, in the case of Muslim NGOs or local organisations who can sometimes work where Western organisations cannot. On the other hand, the 'old guard' fears that new actors with different interests and values undermine the effectiveness of principled humanitarian action. Nevertheless, the same criticisms made about new or alternative humanitarians have long been made of multi-mandate NGOs, suggesting that tensions and debates between new and old actors are actually a constant in humanitarian action. As needs are increasingly outstripping resources, the whole system, including both traditional and emergent actors, is found wanting.

The argument posed here is that institutional multiplicity is dominant, and normative diversity and path dependence reinforce it. Humanity is a broad ideal that can be interpreted in both deontological and consequentialist ways, and is prone to instrumentalisation. It needs supporting principles, which may in turn also vary in their interpretation and implementation. As a result, the principle of humanity alone provides an incentive for greater coherence and convergence, but is simply too weak to overcome the general trend towards divergence. In the final analysis, then, what we are witnessing is not completely new or parallel humanitarian systems but shifting networks of diverse actors driven together by the need to respond, but hampered by inter- and intra-organisational competition and conflicts over resources, norms, principles and identities.

The relative absence of large-scale public discordance among the various actors owes to the fact that competing norms, principles and identities can often be combined in every-day practice, at least in the short run. The overarching norms are so broad that they usually can be merged or mixed with some creativity or simply as ad-hoc bricolage. Only when crises occur at a large scale and humanitarian failures are internationally visible, as happened after the Rwandan genocide, the Indian Ocean Tsunami, and the Haitian earthquake, do the tensions among the different actors boil over. As a result, more incremental changes in funding, coordination and service delivery are afoot, but they will not necessarily lead to greater coherence and effectiveness. In fact, humanitarians seem to be guided by the unspoken acknowledgement that no single approach has ever worked all the time; that the classic principles of the ICRC have failed at times just as assuredly as, for instance, developmental humanitarianism or armed humanitarianism. Ultimately, this means that the humanitarian field will always be open to new actors and initiatives, but this is as much a liability as a strength.

Notes

1 The ICRC definition reads 'The Red Cross, born of a desire to bring assistance without discrimination to the wounded on the battlefield, endeavours – in its international and national capacity – to prevent and alleviate human suffering wherever it may be found. Its purpose is to protect life and health and to ensure respect for the human being. It promotes mutual understanding, friendship, co-operation and lasting peace amongst all peoples.' Commenting on the above, Pictet (1979: 16) argues that 'what counts is to be effective, that it be beneficial to those who suffer ... It does not matter ... in what spirit the act is performed.' Put differently, even for the ICRC humanity can be interpreted in a consequentialist manner (Carbonnier 2015: 197).

2 We differ from Pictet (1979: 8), who sees humanity, non-discrimination and proportionality (merged under the heading of impartiality) as the essential principles, because humanity is also crucial for all other humanitarianisms, whereas this is not always the case with impartiality.

3 A recent review by Action Contre le Faim (ACF) of the Transformative Agenda (TA), concludes 'while setting the right direction, the TA has not addressed some of the major structural problems of humanitarian coordination and has left untouched two pillars of the HR, namely Humanitarian Financing and the Principles of Partnership. The TA roll-out in the field has been taken up slowly and has influenced unevenly across different geographic areas' (Dyukova and Chetcuti 2014: 5). The Principles of Partnership address cooperation with non-traditional actors. The slow progress implies that the emergent actors, such as national NGOs, are too slowly or incompletely integrated into the coordination bodies.

References

Barnett, M. (2011) *Empire of Humanity: A History of Humanitarianism*, Ithaca, NY: Cornell University Press.

Carbonnier, G. (2015) 'Reason, Emotion, Compassion: Can Altruism Survive Professionalisation in the Humanitarian Sector', *Disasters*, 2:189–207.

Core Humanitarian Standard (2015) Frequently Asked Questions (www.corehumanitarianstandard.org/resources/faqs) accessed 21 April 2015.

DeMars, W.E. and Dijkzeul, D. (2015) 'Introduction: NGOing: Practice, Bridging and Power', in: W.E. DeMars D. Dijkzeul (ed.) *The NGO Challenge for International Relations Theory*, Oxon: Routledge, 3–38.

de Waal, A. (2010) 'An Emancipatory Imperium?: Power and Principle in the Humanitarian International', in: D. Fassin and M. Pandolfi (eds) *Contemporary States of Emergency*, London: Zone Books, 295–317.

Dyukova, Y. and Chetcuti, P. (2014) *ACF International and the Transformative Agenda*, Paris: Action Contre La Faim.

Heller-Roazen, D. (2009) *The Enemy of All: Piracy and the Law of Nations*, New York: Zone Books.

Hilhorst, B. and B.J. Jansen (2010) 'Humanitarian Space as Arena: A Perspectives on the Everyday Politics of Aid', *Development and Change*, 41(6):1117–1139.

Ignatieff, M. (2001) *Human Rights as Politics and Idolatry*, Princeton: Princeton University Press.

Juul Petersen, M. (2011) 'Islamizing Aid: Transnational Muslim NGOs after 9/11', *Voluntas*, 23(1):126–55.

MSF (2015) Pushed to the Limit and Beyond: A Year into the Largest Ever Ebola Outbreak (www.doctorswithoutborders.org/article/msf-welcomes-news-liberia-ebola-free-while-urging-continued-vigilance) accessed 14 May 2015.

Pantuliano S. (2014) Sara Pantuliano on the Changing Humanitarian Landscape (www.una.org.uk/magazine/spring-2014/sara-pantuliano-changing-humanitarian-landscape) accessed 28 April 2015.

Pictet, J. (1979) *The Fundamental Principles of the Red Cross: Commentary*, Geneva: International Federation of Red Cross and Red Crescent Societies.

Slim, H. (2012) Marketing Humanitarian Space: Argument and Method in Humanitarian Persuasion (www.alnap.org/resource/6392.aspx) accessed 19 May 2015.

Vijge, M.J. (2013) 'The Promise of New Institutionalism: Explaining the Absence of a World or United Nations Environment Organisation', *International Environmental Agreements*, 13:153–176.

von Pillar, U. (2002) 'Die Instrumentalisierung der humanitären Hilfe', in: W-D. Eberwein and P. Runge (eds) *Humanitäre Hilfe statt Politik: Neue Herausforderungen für ein altes Politikfeld*, Münster: Lit Verlag, 163–188.

Weiss, T.G. (2013) *Humanitarian Business*, Cambridge: Polity Press.

Weizman, E. (2011) *The Least of All Possible Evils*, London: Verso.

Index

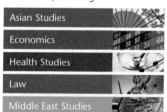